The Unfavored

Siphrut
Literature and Theology of the Hebrew Scriptures

The Unfavored

Judah and Saul in the Narratives of Genesis and 1 Samuel

by
Josef Sykora

EISENBRAUNS
University Park, Pennsylvania

Library of Congress Cataloging-in-Publication Data

Names: Sykora, Josef, author.
Title: The unfavored : Judah and Saul in the narratives of Genesis and 1 Samuel /
    by Josef Sykora.
Other titles: Siphrut.
Description: University Park, Pennsylvania : Eisenbrauns, 2018. |
    Series: Siphrut: literature and theology of the Hebrew scriptures |
    Includes bibliographical references and index.
Summary: "Examines the concept of chosenness in the Hebrew Bible, centering on the
    role of the unfavored characters within Israel, specifically Judah and Saul"—
    Provided by publisher.
Identifiers: LCCN 2018031295 | ISBN 9781575069586 (cloth : alk. paper)
Subjects: LSCH: Jews—Election, Doctrine of. | Judah (Biblical figure) | Saul, King of Israel.
    | Bible. Genesis—Criticism, interpretation, etc. | Bible. Samuel, 1st—Criticism,
    interpretation, etc.
Classification: LCC BM613.S95 2018 | DCC 221.6—dc23
LC record available at https://lccn.loc.gov/2018031295

Published by The Pennsylvania State University Press,
University Park, PA 16802-1003

Eisenbrauns is an imprint of The Pennsylvania State University Press.

The Pennsylvania State University Press is a member of the Association of University
Presses.

It is the policy of The Pennsylvania State University Press to use acid-free paper.
Publications on uncoated stock satisfy the minimum requirements of American National
Standard for Information Sciences—Permanence of Paper for Printed Library Material,
ANSI Z39.48–1992.

For Janek

Table of Contents

Abbreviations

Bible Texts, Versions, and Ancient Sources

4QSam^a	Dead Sea Scroll containing 1–2 Samuel (also known as 4Q51)
Aq.	Aquila
Ant.	Josephus: *Jewish Antiquities*
BHS	*Biblia Hebraica Stuttgartensia*
ESV	English Standard Version
Gen. Rab.	Genesis Rabbah
LXX	Septuagint
LXX^B	Codex Vaticanus
LXX^L	Lucianic Recension
MT	Masoretic Text
NAB	New American Bible
NASB	New American Standard Bible
NETS	*A New English Translation of the Septuagint.* Edited by Albert Pietersma and Benjamin G. Wright. New York: Oxford University Press, 2007
NIV	New International Version
NJPS	*Tanakh: The Holy Scriptures: The New JPS Translation according to the Traditional Hebrew Text*
NRSV	New Revised Standard Version
NT	New Testament
OT	Old Testament
SP	Samaritan Pentateuch
Sym.	Symmachus
Syr.	Syriac
Tg.Jon.	Targum Jonathan
Vulg.	Vulgate

Secondary Sources

AASOR	Annual of the American Schools of Oriental Research
AB	Anchor Bible
ABD	*Anchor Bible Dictionary.* Edited by David N. Freedman. 6 vols. New York: Doubleday, 1992
AJSRev	*AJS Review*
ALGHJ	Arbeiten zur Literatur und Geschichte des hellenistischen Judentums

ANEM	Ancient Near Eastern Monographs
Anton	*Antonianum*
ApOTC	Appolos Old Testament Commentary
ASOR	American Schools of Oriental Research
ATANT	Abhandlungen zur Theologie des Alten und Neuen Testaments
BAR	*Biblical Archeology Review*
BdA	La Bible d'Alexandrie
BDB	Brown, Francis, S. R. Driver, and Charles A. Briggs. *A Hebrew and English Lexicon of the Old Testament*
BETL	Bibliotheca Ephemeridum Theologicarum Lovaniensium
BG	Biblische Gestalten
Bib	*Biblica*
BibInt	*Biblical Interpretation*
BKAT	Biblischer Kommentar, Altes Testament
BLS	Bible and Literature Series
BN	*Biblische Notizen*
BRev	*Bible Review*
BTC	Brazos Theological Commentary
BThSt	Biblisch-theologische Studien
BWA(N)T	Beiträge zur Wissenschaft vom Alten (und Neuen) Testament
BZ	*Biblische Zeitschrift*
BZAW	Beihefte zur Zeitschrift für die alttestamentliche Wissenschaft
CBET	Contributions to Biblical Exegesis and Theology
CBQ	*Catholic Biblical Quarterly*
CBQMS	Catholic Biblical Quarterly Monograph Series
CC	Continental Commentaries
CurBR	*Currents in Biblical Research*
CTR	*Canadian Theological Review*
DCH	*Dictionary of Classical Hebrew.* Edited by David J. A. Clines. 9 vols. Sheffield: Sheffield Phoenix Press, 1993–2004
EstEcl	*Estudios eclesiásticos*
ETR	*Etudes théologiques et religieuses*
ExpTim	*Expository Times*
EZ	Exegese in unserer Zeit
FAT	Forschungen zum Alten Testament
FAT II	Forschungen zum Alten Testament 2 Reihe
FB	Forschung zur Bibel
FRLANT	Forschungen zur Religion und Literatur des Alten und Neuen Testaments
GKC	*Gesenius' Hebrew Grammar.* Edited by Emil Kautzsch. Translated by Arther E. Cowley. 2nd ed. Oxford: Clarendon, 1910

HALOT	*The Hebrew and Aramaic Lexicon of the Old Testament: Study Edition.* Ludwig Koehler, Walter Baumgartner, and Johann J. Stamm. Translated and edited under the supervision of Mervyn E. J. Richardson. 2 vols. Leiden: Brill, 2001
HBM	Hebrew Bible Monographs
HThKAT	Herders Theologischer Kommentar zum Alten Testament
HTR	*Harvard Theological Review*
HUCA	*Hebrew Union College Annual*
IBC	Interpretation: A Bible Commentary for Teaching and Preaching
IBHS	*An Introduction to Biblical Hebrew Syntax.* Bruce K. Waltke and Michael O'Connor. Winona Lake, IN: Eisenbrauns, 1990
ICC	International Critical Commentary
IEJ	*Israel Exploration Journal*
Int	*Interpretation*
ITQ	*Irish Theological Quarterly*
JANESCU	Journal of the Ancient Near Eastern Society of Columbia University
JBL	*Journal of Biblical Literature*
JBQ	*Jewish Bible Quarterly*
JES	*Journal of Ecumenical Studies*
JHebS	*Journal of Hebrew Scriptures*
Joüon	*A Grammar of Biblical Hebrew.* Paul, Joüon. Translated and revised by T. Muraoka. 2 vols. Rome: Pontifical Biblical Institute, 1991
JPSTC	JPS Torah Commentary
JSJSup	Journal for the Study of Judaism Supplement Series
JSOT	*Journal for the Study of the Old Testament*
JSOTSup	Journal for the Study of the Old Testament Supplement Series
JTI	*Journal of Theological Interpretation*
JTISup	Journal of Theological Interpretation, Supplements
JTS	*Journal of Theological Studies*
KAT	Kommentar zum Alten Testament
KHC	Kurzer Hand-Commentar zum Alten Testament
LD	Lectio Divina
LHBOTS	The Library of the Hebrew Bible/Old Testament Studies
MLBS	Mercer Library of Biblical Studies
NAC	New American Commentary
NCBC	New Cambridge Bible Commentary
NICOT	New International Commentary on the Old Testament
NTS	*New Testament Studies*
OBO	Orbis Biblicus et Orientalis
OBT	Overtures to Biblical Theology

OTL	Old Testament Library
OtSt	*Oudtestamentische Studiën*
PBM	Paternoster Biblical Monographs
PEQ	*Palestine Exploration Quarterly*
Presb	*Presbyterion*
Proof	*Prooftexts: A Journal of Jewish Literary History*
RB	*Revue biblique*
ResQ	*Restoration Quarterly*
RRJ	*Review of Rabbinic Judaism*
SAIS	Studies in the Aramaic Interpretation of Scripture
SANT	Studien zum Alten und Neuen Testaments
SBET	*Scottish Bulletin of Evangelical Theology*
SBLDS	Society of Biblical Literature Dissertation Series
SBLSCS	Society and Biblical Literature Septuagint and Cognate Studies
SBLSP	Society of Biblical Literature Seminar Papers
SEÅ	*Svensk exegetisk årsbok*
Sem	*Semitica*
SemeiaSt	Semeia Studies
SHAW	Sitzungen der heidelberger Akademie der Wissenschaften
SHBC	Smyth & Helwys Bible Commentary
Siphrut	Siphrut: Literature and Theology of the Hebrew Bible
ST	*Studia Theologica*
TDOT	*Theological Dictionary of the Old Testament.* Edited by G. Johannes Botterweck and Helmer Ringgren. Translated by John T. Willis et al. 8 vols. Grand Rapids: Eerdmans, 1974–2006
THOTC	Two Horizons Old Testament Commentary
Tradition	*Tradition: A Journal of Orthodox Jewish Thought*
TWOT	*Theological Wordbook of the Old Testament.* Edited by R. Laird Harris, Gleason L. Archer Jr., and Bruce K. Waltke. 2 vols. Chicago: Moody Press, 1980
TZ	*Theologische Zeitschrift*
UBL	Ugaritisch-biblische Literatur
UF	*Ugarit-Forschungen*
VT	*Vetus Testamentum*
VTSup	Supplements to Vetus Testamentum
WBC	Word Biblical Commentary
WMANT	Wissenschaftliche Monographien um Alten und Neuen Testament
WTJ	*Westminster Theological Journal*
ZAW	*Zeitschrift für die alttestamentliche Wissenschaft*
ZDMGSup	Zeitschrift der deutschen morgenländischen Gesellschaft Supplementbände

Acknowledgements

This manuscript represents a slightly revised version of my dissertation submitted to the Department of Theology and Religion at the University of Durham. I am thankful to Jim Eisenbraun and the editors of the Siphrut series for accepting my thesis for publication and to Duncan Burns for preparing it with such care and attention to detail.

My doctoral study took almost seven years. To me it seemed like a few days because I loved it. But since not everybody shares this perspective, and many people have been instrumental in this undertaking, a few words of appreciation are in order.

First and foremost, I would like to thank Professor Walter Moberly, who was willing to take me on as a part-time student and whose insightful and probing comments have helped to foster this work from beginning to end. More importantly, his critical and imaginative engagement with the troubling questions both of Scripture and of life has given a voice to my own search. For a better supervisor I could not have hoped.

I am grateful to my examiners, Professors Joel Kaminsky and David Janzen, whose constructive feedback has made my argument both more coherent and more rounded.

My regular trips to England would not have been possible without the support of those in Durham who opened their homes and hearts, and whose friendships have helped me to find there yet another home: Philip and Michelle Davies, Ben and Sarah Johnson, Zoltán and Kati Schwáb, Richard and Melody Briggs, Rachel Davies, and Jerry Lofquist.

The local Cirkev bratská church in Bratislava, Slovakia, where I spent those years during which I was working on my thesis, was a wonderful and exciting place to live out the Christian faith openly and honestly in the midst of the opportunities and complexities of our secular age. I am thankful to the ever-optimistic board of elders for their continuous understanding and support in my ongoing need to study, write, and travel, and especially its two successive chairmen, Dušan Číčel and Vladislav Matej. My colleagues Daniel Pastirčák and Matěj Hájek have shaped my thinking more than I can fully recognize. My deep appreciation goes also to Jonathan McCormick, whose watchful proofreading has made my writing if not eloquent, then at least readable.

I began to work on this project around the time that our younger son was born. I have often wondered what my sons would think, when they were older, of their old dad going to school. Now Simon and Luke are big boys, and even though they still cannot understand why they so often hear the words "I need to study" as an excuse, they have coped with this ambiguity with amazing resilience. Lynette, you were the one who not only believed that I could do it, but also that I should. You have been a steady support throughout, and I am glad you are my partner in life.

This work is dedicated to the memory of my friend whose life story has set my feet on the path of the unfavored—both as a small token of the connection we had, and as a reminder that the semi-technical study on the following pages has a real and painful counterpart in everyday life.

1

Introduction

The Troubling Concept of Election

The biblical notion of election sits rather uncomfortably within current philosophical and theological discourse. How can one believe in a God who chooses some and rejects others, when the dominating intellectual framework stresses the equality of all persons? The force of the contemporary critical stance towards monotheism in general, and divine favoritism in particular, has been felt across the scholarly literature. The works of Cott, Lüdemann, and Schwartz,[1] for example—from different perspectives but with a common agenda—challenge the notion of election by pointing out its dominance within the Bible (particularly in the Old Testament)[2]—and by arguing that election is, in some situations, connected with the rejection or obliteration of those who are portrayed as standing in the way of God's chosen people. Election, with its corresponding disfavor towards the unchosen, remains a troubling notion in our contemporary understanding.

Nevertheless, it remains to be asked whether this is all that can be said about the concept of chosenness, and whether the idea itself does not contain some positive aspects that might prove valuable for the life of faith in our modern age. In recent years, a number of scholars have attempted to approach the thorny issue of God's election and its troubling legacy from this direction.

First, two Jewish scholars in particular, Levenson and Kaminsky,[3] have done much to illuminate the notion of God's election in the Hebrew Bible.

---

1. Jeremy Cott, "The Biblical Problem of Election," *JES* 21 (1984): 199–228; Gerd Lüdemann, *The Unholy in Holy Scripture: The Dark Side of the Bible*, trans. John Bowden (London: SCM, 1997); Regina M. Schwartz, *The Curse of Cain: The Violent Legacy of Monotheism* (Chicago: University of Chicago Press, 1998).

2. When referring to the first part of the Christian canon, I use the traditional description "the Old Testament." Despite its problematic connotation for Jewish-Christian dialogue, I think it retains from the Christian point of view something valuable about the relationship between the testaments after the arrival of Jesus Christ. However, when I describe the works of Jewish authors, out of respect for their tradition I will use the designation "the Hebrew Bible."

3. Jon D. Levenson, *The Death and Resurrection of the Beloved Son: The Transformation of Child Sacrifice in Judaism and Christianity* (New Haven: Yale University Press, 1995); Joel S. Kaminsky, *Yet I Loved Jacob: Reclaiming the Biblical Concept of Election* (Nashville: Abingdon, 2007).

Levenson investigates Israel's chosenness in the foundational stories of
the book of Genesis, since in the Hebrew Bible Israel functions as God's
first-born – the one upon whom God has an absolute claim.[4] This allows
Levenson to argue that the life of the elect is marked not only by their
dominance, but also by the undergoing of a certain humiliation—an
integral part of the chosen's maturing process—in order that the one who
experiences God's favor uses it not to rule over others harshly, but rather
for their benefit.[5] Similarly, as Levenson points out, the unchosen faces a
comparable challenge: one must accept this subordinate role and use it for
the common good.[6] Kaminsky's most innovative idea consists in developing the heuristic categories of elect, non-elect, and anti-elect.[7] While
the elect are favored by God, it is only the anti-elect that are, for various
reasons, annihilated by God's command. Although such cases and the
texts dealing with them remain disquieting both for Jews and Christians,
Kaminsky observes that they represent only a limited number of people or
situations in the Hebrew Scripture. The non-elect, on the other hand, cover
a vast range of foreigners in the Bible, who, while remaining a separate
group of people not needing to be converted to Israel's faith, occupy a
significant place in the divine logic of election; they often receive their
blessing in the course of working out their relation to the elect.[8]

Second, a number of other scholars have focused more specifically on
how the unchosen are portrayed in the Old Testament, and have offered
studies that probe more deeply this neglected aspect of its narratives.[9]
While admitting that in some limited cases election does involve the mistreatment of non-Israelites, these scholars have argued that a majority of
the less favored persons or nations in the Old Testament enjoy some level
of relationship with God, and have certain duties and requirements that

---

4. Levenson, *Death*, 12–17, 60. Levenson argues that the enigmatic clause in Exod
22:28 (ET 22:29), "You shall give me the first-born among your sons," testifies to the
existence of a tradition within early Israel, which expressed an ideal that an Israelite father
should either sacrifice his first-born son to the deity or offer a substitute in his place. See,
for example, the summary paragraph in Levenson, *Death*, 36.

5. Levenson, *Death*, 96, 152.

6. This pronouncement is made in connection with Judah (Levenson, *Death*, 155).

7. Kaminsky, *Jacob*, 107–36.

8. Kaminsky, *Jacob*, 121–22.

9. See especially Frank Anthony Spina, *The Faith of the Outsider: Exclusion and Inclusion in the Biblical Story* (Grand Rapids: Eerdmans, 2005); Volker Haarmann, *JHWH-Verehrer
der Völke: die Hinwendung von Nichtisraeliten zum Gott Israels in alttestamentlichen Überlieferungen*, ATANT 91 (Zurich: TVZ, 2008); Joel N. Lohr, *Chosen and Unchosen: Conceptions of
Election in the Pentateuch and Jewish–Christian Interpretation*, Siphrut 2 (Winona Lake, IN:
Eisenbrauns, 2009); Bradford A. Anderson, *Brotherhood and Inheritance: A Canonical Reading
of the Esau and Edom Traditions*, LHBOTS 556 (New York: T&T Clark, 2011); and John T.
Noble, *A Place for Hagar's Son: Ishmael as a Case Study in the Priestly Tradition* (Minneapolis:
Fortress, 2016).

follow from this relationship. Furthermore, those unchosen characters in the Old Testament who demonstrate their faith in YHWH often surpass their counterparts from Israel.

The present study, then, tries to situate itself within this framework, as it attempts to elucidate the concept of election from yet another angle.

Approaching the Unchosen in Israel

General Focus: The Unchosen Within Israel

The above-mentioned studies illustrate a growing interest in the biblical grounding of the doctrine of election, particularly as it concerns the fate of those who are not favored by God. Nevertheless, this has been undertaken primarily from the vantage point of individuals outside of Israel. This approach is understandable, since non-Israelites present a prime example of those who are not elected by YHWH. I would contend, however, that approaching the topic of election from this viewpoint does not exhaust the manner in which it is portrayed in the Old Testament. The dynamic of unchosenness can also be seen in the stories of those *within* Israel who did not receive God's favor in the way it was bestowed on their more fortunate brothers or neighbors. A good example of this phenomenon can be found in the case of Joseph's brothers, who are portrayed as not favored in the story and yet are part of Israel. Kaminsky calls them the "unchosen chosen" and reasons that the act of God's choosing remains operative even within the tribes of Israel.[10]

Two examples of the "unchosen chosen" will be the focus of my study. This approach has, I think, one advantage over those works that deal specifically with non-Israelites. The Old Testament is mainly interested in the story of the people of Israel. The nations and individuals outside of Abraham's seed receive only scant attention in the biblical text. Therefore, looking at the unchosen within Israel provides a greater volume of material to be examined, which, in turn, could lead to a more rounded portrayal of the dynamics of God's favoritism, thus perhaps supplementing what has been accomplished in this field so far.

Specific Focus: Joseph and Judah; David and Saul

Furthermore, I hope that my study can supply an extension of the work of Levenson and Kaminsky, who provided me with the impetus to pursue my own interest in the wider topic of election. Specifically, my study begins in a region that also occupied their attention: the story of Joseph and his brothers.

---

10. Kaminsky remarks: "The election of the nation does not lead to a cessation of all further acts of divine favoring" (Kaminsky, *Jacob*, 59, n. 1).

Joseph and Judah

Both Levenson and Kaminsky, who ground their assessment of the theological significance of chosenness in the brotherly rivalry found in the patriarchal stories, view the Joseph cycle in Gen 37–50 as the culmination of the topic of election in the book of Genesis.[11] This extended narrative, painting a picture of the family tension between Joseph and his brothers, is thus a good candidate for trying to see more clearly the contours of election in Genesis and for this reason it will be the focus of the first half of my discussion. Although I will also pay attention to Joseph's development in the story, in particular I am interested in the manner in which the biblical story portrays Judah, who is not favored by his father or by the deity at the beginning of the narrative, but who rises to a place of prominence among his brothers later in the story, eventually occupying a position rivaling even that of Joseph. In what ways does this story portray the role of the one not favored by the deity?

David and Saul

My second study focuses on David and Saul in 1 Samuel. The rise of Israel's monarchy brought to the throne a young man from the tribe of Benjamin, who concentrated in his person Israel's hopes, but who also experienced the empowering and blessing of YHWH. However, Saul is rejected by the deity and his prophet shortly into his reign because he was considered unfaithful to God's commands in his battles with the Philistines and Amalekites (1 Sam 13–15). Saul's rejection then led to a search for a leader who would in a more suitable way represented God's ideal for a monarch. Eventually, David replaced Saul as Israel's new king.

The stories of Israel's first kings can be seen as connected with the narratives about Joseph and Judah. The fatherly blessing, which both Judah and Joseph receive at the end of the Joseph cycle (Gen 49:8–12 and 22–26), logically points beyond itself. It seems that the tension between Israel's first two monarchs, Saul and David, may thus present a natural extension of the rivalry between Joseph and Judah. While David comes from the tribe of Judah (1 Sam 17:12), Saul is a Benjamite (1 Sam 9:1–2). Benjamin, Jacob's last son and the second son of his beloved wife Rachel, functions in the Joseph cycle as the son on whom Jacob's special affection and favor focus, especially during the period when Benjamin's older sibling Joseph is lost (Gen 44:27–31).[12] Saul, a descendant of Benjamin who inherits the privileged position of Rachel's sons,

---

11. Levenson, *Death*, 143; Kaminsky, *Jacob*, 78.

12. The tribe of Benjamin, located between Judah in the south and Manasseh and Ephraim in the north, is portrayed in the Old Testament as originally connected with its northern neighbors (e.g. Num 2:18–24). Only after the division of the united monarchy did Judah include Benjamin in its kingdom (1 Kgs 12:20–21), which eventually assured its survival of the fall of the divided kingdom (Esth 2:5). For an overview of Benjamin's

thus stands in contrast to David, who comes from the tribe of Judah, unfavored in the Joseph cycle.

Nevertheless, the way the topic of election is narrated in these stories of Saul and David is in a sense opposite to how it is narrated in the story of Judah and Joseph. Although both complex narratives defy simplification, it could be said that Judah began his journey as unfavored, both by his own father and by God, but his character at the end of the book of Genesis, especially when viewed towards the future, bears the marks of chosenness. Saul, on the other hand, starts as a chosen king, selected by the people and by the deity. However, he is rejected by the deity in the course of two episodes involving his military endeavors in 1 Sam 13–15. As a consequence, a king better suited to the task, namely David, is chosen by YHWH as Saul's successor. Saul's failure and his later replacement by David raise questions corresponding to those asked above regarding the Joseph narrative.

The characters of Judah and Saul (in Gen 37–50 and 1 Sam 13–15) will thus serve as two examples from within Israel which will reveal something about the nature of, and the relationship between, chosenness and unchosenness, and which consequently might deepen our understanding of the issue of election in general.

Purpose: Theological and Hermeneutical Concerns

My study has two overreaching concerns: a theological and hermeneutical one. Even though the theological interest remains an ultimate goal of this book, the hermeneutical concern will provide the crucial backbone, so to say, for the structure of the following chapters.

Hermeneutical Concern: Conducting a Thought Experiment

In the following study, my effort is to understand the received text in its canonical form. In aiming to achieve this, however, I do not wish to disregard the findings of historical criticism, but rather to employ them in order to read theologically. As Brevard Childs remarks: "To work with the final stage of the text is not to lose the historical dimension, but it is rather to make a critical, theological judgment regarding the process. The depth dimension aids in understanding the interpreted text, and does not function independently of it."[13] A canonical reading thus builds on the results of historical criticism and reconceives the

tradition as a tribe see Yigal Levin, "Joseph, Judah and the 'Benjamin Conundrum'," *ZAW* 116 (2004): 223–41. For a suggestive proposal that the tension between the Benjamite Saul and the Judean David continued into exilic and post-exilic times, consult Joseph Blenkinsopp, *David Remembered: Kingship and National Identity in Ancient Israel* (Grand Rapids: Eerdmans, 2013), esp. 28–41.

13. Brevard S. Childs, *Introduction to the Old Testament as Scripture* (Philadelphia: Fortress, 1979), 76.

various tentative layers of the text as "a kind of commentary on the text's prehistory."[14] Historical-critical work, therefore, is a necessary but provisional step in interpretation; it serves as a prerequisite for further theological assessment.

My own reading of the biblical narratives suggests that the texts in question illustrate well something of the issues at stake. Certain portions of the Joseph cycle (Gen 37–50) and the narratives of Saul's failure (1 Sam 13–15) have long been puzzling to readers. The segments comprising Gen 38 and 1 Sam 13:7b–15a, and to a lesser degree also Gen 49, feel awkward and/or intrusive in the narratives in which they are placed. Interestingly, these passages play an important role in developing the portrayal of the unchosen. Genesis 38 and 49 (more precisely Gen 49:8–12) focus on Judah, the former describing his failure within his own family and the latter narrating his blessing, which rivals even that bestowed on the chosen Joseph. These two chapters, then, could be saying something valuable about the personal growth of Judah and the potential effects of this development on a possible change in his unchosen status. On the other hand, the account of Saul's first rejection in 1 Sam 13:7b–15a presents an important step in his transition from a person privileged both by the people and by God, to a character rejected by the deity. The remainder of the narratives of Saul's failure lies in the shadow of this episode, which strengthens the impression that these textual units, if seen as additions both to the Joseph cycle and the Saul narrative, cohere with the crucial stages of the progress (or regress) of those persons, who at some point in their life do not enjoy God's favor.

The main portion of my analysis, then, will be devoted to a hermeneutical thought experiment. I will read the two narratives first without and then with the segments that are seen as likely additions to the biblical text, in order to see what difference these segments—focusing on Judah's rise and Saul's demise respectively—make to the overall interpretation of the narrative, and how they inform a theologically robust reading of these stories, especially as they pertain to the topic of chosenness.[15] I recognize that there are smaller passages within Gen 37–50 and 1 Sam 13–15, and

14. Christopher R. Seitz, "Canonical Approach," in *Dictionary for Theological Interpretation of the Bible*, ed. Kevin J. Vanhoozer et al. (Grand Rapids: Baker, 2005), 100–102, esp. 100.

15. This approach is not dissimilar to that employed by R. W. L. Moberly in his discussion of the Flood narrative, where he focuses especially on the awkward position of the "evil-thought clause," as he calls it, found in Gen 8:21. Moberly understands this clause as a later gloss incorporated into the text of Gen 6–9, but his observation is further used for theological evaluation of the final version of the story. See R. W. L. Moberly, "On Interpreting the Mind of God: The Theological Significance of the Flood Narrative (Genesis 6–9)," in *The Word Leaps the Gap: Essays on Scripture and Theology in Honor of Richard B. Hays*, ed. Ross J. Wagner et al. (Grand Rapids: Eerdmans, 2008), 44–66; and R. W. L. Moberly, *The Theology of the Book of Genesis* (Cambridge: Cambridge University Press, 2009), 102–20.

larger units outside of these texts, that may also be considered as possibly stemming from a later editorial hand. Clearly, a more rounded redactional study would require considering other passages that may also have been included in the redactional activity within these two books. However, the scope of my argument allows me to focus my thought experiment only on those segments that more obviously interrupt the stories under consideration, and which more directly relate to the topic of election. My aim is to use certain redactional findings only insofar as they illuminate the final form of the text in terms of its theological significance.

Consequently, I will argue that the canonical account of these two narratives seems to testify to the freedom felt by the editors of the biblical text to modify the earlier traditions in order to guide the reader towards those elements of Israel's religious and political life that revolve around the identity of the chosen king. Eventually, Israel's most famous monarch is to come from the tribe of Judah, and the house of David, and this is reflected both in the Joseph story and the tale of Saul's reign and rejection. Genesis 37–50 hints that despite Joseph's special position during Israel's sojourn in Egypt, Israel's king will not belong to the tribe of Ephraim, the favored of Joseph's two sons, but will be of Judah's offspring. In a similar way, Saul's rejection in ch. 15 of 1 Samuel concerns him only personally, and therefore Saul's son Jonathan—who has just exemplified courage and faith in an important battle with Israel's eponymous enemy, the Philistines—could still be a viable candidate to be his successor. But when 1 Sam 13:7b–15a has already signaled that YHWH has rejected Saul's dynasty, the reader is tacitly prepared to look for Saul's successor beyond the narrative portrayed so far. The surprising election of David in the second half of 1 Samuel is so crucial that even the earlier stories lie in its shadow.

Theological Concern: The Fate of the Unfavored Ones
My main aim is to present a theological assessment of the idea of God's favoritism based on the stories of Joseph and Judah, and of Saul and David. I am aware that these texts, as with other parts of the Old Testament, have undergone a complex literary and historical development, but I wish to examine them in the form in which they were received by the church (or the synagogue). Thus, I am positioning myself within the broader stream of contemporary theological interpretation, approaching the biblical text within a canonical frame of reference, with the desire to see what these texts, when read as Scripture, can say about matters of life under God. It is my conviction that the fruitfulness of theological interpretation should be tested precisely in those portions of Scripture which present difficulties in terms of understanding both their message and their contemporary relevance for the life of faith. I hope that my study can contribute something valuable in this direction by presenting a more rounded depiction of election, of which Levenson and Kaminsky are the representatives.

Election within Israel is exemplified in those offices that are endowed with leadership function.[16] More specifically, in the biblical narratives examined in this study, election concerns kingship. This is obvious in the case of 1 Samuel, where both David, and to a lesser degree Saul, are presented as God's choices for leading Israel. Similarly, Joseph's special position in Gen 37–50 also revolves around leadership—he is chosen to save both his clan and the wider world from the disastrous effects of famine. Nevertheless, despite his success as Israel's protector and provider, the future monarch will not come from Ephraim's tribe, but will be a Judahite.

This implies that election in Israel is not static. One may alter one's status—as either elect or non-elect—but the change takes effect only in the lives of one's children. In terms of the kingship, both Joseph's and Saul's descendants are passed over in favor of their more fortunate counterparts. This aspect also, I will argue, has some bearing on the portrayal of the unfavored. Saul's fault especially is magnified in order to highlight the election of David later in 1 Samuel. The character of Saul is overshadowed by the choice of Israel's most beloved king and the canonical text makes this feature even more palpable.

The bulk of my study will be devoted to a detailed exposition of my thought experiment. I turn first to the account in Genesis, and afterwards to that of Saul's rejection in 1 Samuel.

---

16. As Williams points out, "election within election" in Israel typically concerns kingship and priesthood. See Stephen N. Williams, *The Election of Grace: A Riddle without Resolution?* (Grand Rapids: Eerdmans, 2015), 47.

2

Judah in Genesis: Framing the Study

The sequence of the sibling-rivalry stories in the book of Genesis forms the bedrock of the larger part of the book spanning from ch. 12 to the end. These replacements of a firstborn by a younger sibling, which contribute significantly to the establishing of Israel's identity, find their climax in the rich narrative of Joseph and his brothers.[1] As Levenson points out:

> The story of Joseph in Genesis 37–50 is not only the longest and most intricate Israelite exemplar of the narrative of the death and resurrection of the beloved son, but also the most explicit. In it is concentrated almost every variation of the theme that first appeared in the little tale of Cain and Abel and has been growing and becoming more involved and more complex throughout the Book of Genesis.[2]

While Joseph, the beloved son of Jacob, is the chosen character in Gen 37–50, it is Judah who becomes in the course of the narrative the prime unchosen character within the brotherly circle and whose development demonstrates well the challenges and possibilities faced by the unchosen in Genesis.[3] If one wants to discover the rich matrix of this theological concept within the Old Testament, then the story of Joseph seems a natural place to begin.[4]

---

1. Other notable studies of the brotherly dynamic in the book of Genesis and in the Old Testament include: Roger Syrén, *The Forsaken First-born: A Study of a Recurrent Motif in the Patriarchal Narratives*, JSOTSup 133 (Sheffield: Sheffield Academic, 1993); Frederick E. Greenspahn, *When Brothers Dwell Together: The Preeminence of Younger Siblings in the Hebrew Bible* (New York: Oxford University Press, 1994); Christopher R. Heard, *Dynamics of Diselection: Ambiguity in Genesis 12–36 and Ethnic Boundaries in Post-exilic Judah*, SemeiaSt 39 (Atlanta: SBL, 2001); Benedikt Hensel, *Die Vertauschung des Erstgeburtssegens in der Genesis: Eine Analyse der narrativ-theologischen Grundstruktur des ersten Buches der Tora*, BZAW 423 (Berlin: de Gruyter, 2011).

2. Levenson, *Death*, 143. Similarly Kaminsky, *Jacob*, 72.

3. See Levenson, *Death*, 155.

4. Nevertheless, one needs to add a word of caution. It is only in the book of Deuteronomy where the concept of the election of Israel achieves its mature formulation. Deuteronomy encapsulates Israel's special status before God in several passages (e.g. Deut 4:37–38; 7:6–7; 10:14–15), where it also employs the Hebrew term בחר in a theological sense, as an expression of God's loving and careful choice of Israel. See Dale Patrick, "Election (Old Testament)," *ABD* 2:434–41, esp. 436. This mature idea of God's chosenness, together with its unique terminology, is not present in the previous books of the

The Position of Chapters 38 and 49 in the Joseph Narrative

To say that the reading of the Joseph cycle—potentially to clarify the issue of unchosenness—should focus on the character of Judah, follow his development, and take into consideration his interaction with Joseph in terms of Jacob's favor is to draw attention precisely to those features in the narrative that appear intrusive in the story. Except for Gen 44, it is in chs. 38 and 49 that Judah appears at his lowest and his highest points in the narrative, and where he receives significant narratival space. As Nahum Sarna puts it in his commentary, when he prefaces his comments regarding Gen 37–50: "The rest of the Book of Genesis is devoted to the story of Joseph—except for the abrupt and puzzling intrusion of the episode of Judah and Tamar (chap. 38) and Jacob's moving last testament (chap. 49)."[5] The position of these two chapters within the Joseph cycle, crucial for understanding the role of Judah in the narrative, and formative for the conducting of my thought experiment, thus needs to be examined at the outset.

Genesis 38

There are several reasons why ch. 38 does not fit seamlessly into the flow of the Joseph cycle. First, the events narrated in ch. 38 do not concern Joseph, who is the main protagonist of the extended story in Gen 37–50. The beginning of this portion of the book of Genesis begins with the last occurrence of the headline that is usual in the book, which separates the individual literary units within the narrative: אֵלֶּה תֹּלְדוֹת יַעֲקֹב, "this is the family history of Jacob" (Gen 37:2).[6] This phrase typically transitions the book into the next story, which within Gen 12–50 opens up segments that focus on a favored son of a particular patriarch. It is evident that in some cases this *toledot* formula introduces the story of the father and all his sons,[7] as in the case of the family history of Isaac (25:19), where the passage 25:19–35:29 deals not only with the favored Jacob, but also with his older brother Esau. But the events of the life of Esau, described in the *toledot* of

---

Pentateuch, including Genesis. The patriarchal stories may indeed be read as an outworking of God's mysterious choice (see Neh 9:7), but this reading utilizes the categories of election as a specific hermeneutical strategy that might illuminate certain features in the text and suppress others. MacDonald speaks in a similar vein in Nathan MacDonald, "Did God Choose the Patriarchs? Reading for Election in the Book of Genesis," in *Genesis and Christian Theology*, ed. Nathan MacDonald et al. (Grand Rapids: Eerdmans, 2012), 245–66. For a slightly different approach, which uses the brotherly rivalries including the Joseph story to tease out possible contours of the doctrine of election spanning both testaments, see Gary A. Anderson, *Christian Doctrine and the Old Testament: Theology in the Service of Biblical Exegesis* (Grand Rapids: Baker Academic, 2017), 75–91.

5. Nahum M. Sarna, *Genesis: The Traditional Hebrew Text with the New JPS Translation*, JPSTC 1 (New York: Jewish Publication Society of America, 1989), 254.

6. Unless stated otherwise, all translations from Hebrew and Greek are mine.

7. See, for example, Gordon J. Wenham, *Genesis 16–50*, WBC 2 (Waco, TX: Word, 1994), 344–45.

Isaac, are narrated only in so far as he interacts with Jacob. It is surprising, then, to find in the Joseph cycle a whole chapter devoted solely to Judah and his endeavors, which is in no obvious way connected to the rest of the narrative, and where Joseph is not named at all.

This is closely connected to my second point. Chapter 38 brings up places and characters that do not feature substantially in the rest of Gen 37–50. Judah's friend, Hirah, the Adullamite, and Judah's father-in law, Shua, the Canaanite, are not mentioned elsewhere in the Joseph cycle. Judah's sons Er, Onan, and Shelah, and his grandsons Perez and Zerah are named only in Gen 46:12, where they are included in the list of Jacob's descendants upon his transition to Egypt to join Joseph. Even Tamar, who in an important sense resolves the family issue in ch. 38, is not mentioned anywhere else in Gen 37–50.[8]

Moreover, the names of certain geographical places and main protagonists would fit better within the narratives of David than in a story where Joseph is the main hero. David hid in the cave of Adullam (e.g. 1 Sam 22:1; 2 Sam 23:13), which could be associated with the city of Adullam belonging to the tribe of Judah. Similarly, the other geographical places mentioned (Chezib, Timnah, Enaim) could possibly be located in Judean territory.[9] Furthermore, Tamar is the name of David's daughter who was raped by her half-brother Amnon (2 Sam 13), and Bath-shua (the daughter of Shua [שׁוּעַ] in Gen 38:2), whom Judah took for a wife, might also evoke the name of Uriah's wife, with whom David committed adultery and who later became the mother of David's beloved son Solomon (2 Sam 11)— especially when her more common name Bathsheba (בַּת־שֶׁבַע e.g. in 2 Sam 11:3) is given in the MT of 1 Chr 3:5 as Bath-shua (בַּת־שׁוּעַ).[10] The reference to Tamar suggests that although there are resonances between Judah's family troubles in the Joseph cycle and the so-called Succession Narrative (2 Sam 9–20),[11] a more sustained comparison might be made between Gen

---

8. For a similar argument regarding the absence of the characters of Gen 38 from the rest of Gen 37–50, see Jürgen Ebach, *Genesis 37–50*, HThKAT 3 (Freiburg: Herder, 2007), 119.

9. Westermann argues that Chezib could possibly be identified with Achzib (Josh 15:44; Mic 1:14), located 5 km south of Adullam. See Claus Westermann, *Genesis 37–50: A Commentary*, trans. John J. Scullion, CC (Minneapolis: Augsburg, 1986), 51. Timnah (Josh 15:57) is 7 km northeast of Adullam and Enaim might be a small village near Timnah— perhaps it is Enam mentioned in Josh 15:34 (Westermann, *Genesis 37–50*, 53). A similar observation is made also by Sarna, *Genesis*, 264; and John A. Emerton, "Some Problems in Genesis 38," *VT* 25 (1975): 338–61, esp. 344. However, the geographical locations mentioned in Gen 38 may also carry a symbolic meaning. For this possibility consider Mark Leuchter, "Genesis 38 in Social and Historical Perspective," *JBL* 132 (2013): 209–27, esp. 220–22.

10. The name of David's wife in 1 Chr 3:5 could be influenced by the occurrence of Bath-shua, Judah's wife in 1 Chr 2:3.

11. Several authors helpfully illuminate the connection between Judah's story in the Joseph narrative and 2 Sam 9–20. See Gary A. Rendsburg, "David and His Circle in

38 and 2 Sam 13 and their immediate literary contexts.[12] In both stories the main heroine is called Tamar, who engages in improper sex, after which she never has sexual relations again. Genesis 38 speaks of Judah and his sons, whereas 2 Sam 13 tells of David and his sons. Judah had a friend (רֵעַ) Hirah (Gen 38:12) and Amnon had a friend (רֵעַ) Jonadab (2 Sam 13:3), each of whom plays a supporting role in the story. Sheep shearing is also reported to take place in both chapters (Gen 38:12–13; 2 Sam 13:23). These parallels, among others, thus bring out the close relationship between Judah's story in Gen 38 and David's family troubles in 2 Sam 13.

The relationship between the two texts may, of course, be evaluated from various angles. At the source-critical level, the connection between them can be used to put forward various hypotheses regarding the possible origin and dependence of both narratives.[13] In terms of the overall structure of the narrative, however, it is perhaps enough to note that ch. 38 introduces themes connected with the royal lineage of King David, who is a descendant of Perez, born at the end of ch. 38. As Rendsburg puts it, when one reads Gen 38 "we should understand it to refer more to David and his family than it does to Judah and his."[14] Similarly, when Ho mentions one of the possible effects of the narrative of Judah's family troubles, he remarks: "Perhaps this is the intended effect and that is enough for our purpose— the author of Judah's story wants the reader to read the Judah story with the David story in mind."[15] Undoubtedly, there are other ways one might explore the connections between Judah's and David's story, but Ho's suggestion will at this point be sufficient for my purposes. For the reader familiar with the Old Testament, the story of Judah and his sons brings echoes of

---

Genesis 38," *VT* 36 (1986): 438–46, esp. 441–44; Craig Y. S. IIo, "The Stories of the Family Troubles of Judah and David: A Study of Their Literary Links," *VT* 49 (1999): 514–31, esp. 515–23; A. Graeme Auld, "Tamar between David, Judah and Joseph," *SEÅ* 65 (2000): 93–106. On the other hand, for an argument that somewhat weakens the attempts to establish a connection between Judah's story and the Succession Narrative, see Paul R. Noble, "Esau, Tamar, and Joseph: Criteria for Identifying Inner-biblical Allusions," *VT* 52 (2002): 219–52, esp. 222–28.

12. Besides the authors mentioned above, my list has been influenced by helpful comparisons by the following authors: Joseph Blenkinsopp, "Theme and Motif in the Succession History (2 Sam. xi 2ff) and the Yahwist Corpus," in *Volume du congrès, Genève, 1965*, VTSup 15 (Leiden: Brill, 1965), 44–57, esp. 53; Edward L. Greenstein, "The Formation of the Biblical Narrative Corpus," *AJSRev* 15 (1990): 151–78, esp. 165–66; and Kaminsky, *Jacob*, 74–75.

13. Some authors argue that Gen 38—with its less known characters, some of whom are otherwise not attested—was composed in accordance with incidents involving the more famous David and his children. See Rendsburg, "David," 444–46; Ho, "Stories," 523–26; and Auld, "Tamar," 97–103. Alternatively, Leuchter proposes that both narratives could be drawn from a common stock of traditions (Leuchter, "Genesis," 226–27).

14. Rendsburg, "David," 441, similarly also 444.

15. Ho, "Stories," 526.

the story of David and his children. Genesis 38 thus evokes themes from a different literary context, which only strengthens the impression that the chapter interrupts the flow of this last portion of the book of Genesis, which is focused mainly on Joseph and his adventures.[16]

Third, even on a quick reading it seems that the events of ch. 38 could hardly have taken place during the years spanning from Joseph's descent into slavery, to the arrival of his brothers in Egypt. Yet this is what the opening clause of ch. 38 seems to indicate when it says: "It happened at that time (בָּעֵת הַהִוא) that Judah went down from his brothers" (Gen 38:1). Since the phrase "at that time" follows Joseph's transition to Egypt, in which Judah played his part, the natural way to read ch. 38 is to understand it as taking place between Joseph's descent to Egypt and his brothers' visit there. In Gen 37:2 we are told that Joseph is seventeen, and thus one can calculate that he is thirty-nine when the whole family relocates to Egypt (Gen 41:46; 45:11), which means that the whole narrative of ch. 38 had to have happened in twenty-two years. Sarna, for example, argues that this is indeed possible, but the scenario he proposes shows the unlikelihood of the whole construct:

> The phrase ["about that time"] clearly intends to connect, in time, the sale of Joseph with the marriage of Judah. However, the events here described can be compressed into the twenty-two years that elapsed between the sale of Joseph and the descent to Egypt, only on the assumption that Er was born about a year after Judah's marriage and that Onan and Shelah followed in successive years. Er would then have been about eighteen when he married Tamar and died soon after, and Onan about seventeen when he repeated the experience of his brother. If Tamar waited a year in vain for Shelah before taking the initiative, the twins Perez and Zerah would have been born about twenty-one years after Judah's original marriage, which had taken place soon after the sale of Joseph. Thus they would have been about a year old upon their arrival in Egypt.[17]

Even though it is possible that all these events could take place in a manner suggested by Sarna, the probability of these coincidences seems small.[18]

---

16. The story of Jacob and his sons may thus be compared with the narrative of David and his sons, in order to explore the notion of chosenness in the Old Testament from yet another angle.

17. Sarna, *Genesis*, 264–65. Similarly also Hillel I. Millgram, *The Joseph Paradox: A Radical Reading of Genesis 37–50* (Jefferson, NC: McFarland, 2012), 225–27.

18. Another possibility, of course, is to propose a different understanding of the phrase "at that time." Benno Jacob, for example, compares Gen 38:1 with the second occurrence of this expression in Genesis (Gen 21:22), and suggests that the phrase "at that time" does not coincide with the end of the previous event (thus ch. 37), but with the beginning of the preceding section of the narrative. On this reading the saying would refer back to Gen 35:27—that is, to the moment when Jacob joined his father Isaac in Mamre, before the latter died—which could add another ten years to the overall time span of the events

These three factors contribute to the awkwardness with which one views the placement of ch. 38 in the overall narrative of Joseph's story. In being preoccupied with Judah and his endeavors, the chapter distracts the reader's attention from Joseph in a manner that is unprecedented in the rivalry stories of the book of Genesis. Echoes of the Succession Narrative in general, and of 2 Sam 13 in particular, increase one's inclination to read this episode with David in mind, which introduces a different set of themes and echoes. Finally, the action-packed narrative in Gen 38 seems to require more time to transpire than the chronological span between Joseph's descent into Egypt and the later family reunion allows.

All these arguments point to the suggestion that this chapter was originally an independent narrative. This does not mean, however, that Gen 38 is disconnected from the surrounding canonical context. The story of Judah and Tamar is in fact artfully incorporated into the extended narrative of Joseph and his brothers and several literary studies have focused especially on uncovering these verbal ties and similarities of theme between Gen 38 and the surrounding text.[19] Nevertheless, in order to perceive more clearly how ch. 38 effects the meaning of the overall narrative, I will initially set aside this likely once-independent segment,[20] and read the narrative first without it, and then subsequently again with its inclusion. However, before attempting this, we need to look at ch. 49, where one finds another substantial piece of text about Judah. What is the position of Jacob's blessing in the structure of the narrative?

Genesis 49

Although the awkwardness of the placement of ch. 49 within the Joseph cycle is not as pronounced as was the case with ch. 38, one can notice several ways in which Jacob's blessing upon his sons feels disconnected from its canonical context.

First, the testament of Jacob (Gen 49:1–28) does not contain any direct reference to its surrounding context. The blessings pronounced upon the twelve sons of Jacob do not move forward the flow of the Joseph story in any obvious way. Rather, they follow up on the happenings that took place before the Joseph cycle began, and point to events that lie beyond

---

occurring in Gen 38. See Benno Jacob, *Der erste Buch der Torah Genesis* (Berlin: Schocken, 1934), 710. A similar proposal is suggested also by Ebach, although for a different reason: to allow for Rachel's presence during Joseph's second dream and in order to bring the actions involving Reuben (Gen 35:22), and Simeon with Levi (Gen 34) closer to Gen 37–50 (Ebach, *Genesis*, 672).

19. Alter's study is especially important in this regard: Robert Alter, *The Art of Biblical Narrative* (New York: Basic Books, 1981), 3–12. The threefold connection between the two chapters using the verb "recognize" (נכר) has been put forward by Umberto Cassuto, *Biblical and Oriental Studies*, vol. 1 (Jerusalem: Magnes, 1973), 30–31.

20. For a concise statement concerning the ambiguity of Gen 38, see Leuchter, "Genesis," 211–12.

the contours of the book of Genesis. The first two blessings—the one upon Reuben (Gen 49:3–4) and the one given to Simeon and Levi (Gen 49:5–7)—may refer back to certain incidents in which these three oldest sons of Jacob behaved in ways which, here in ch. 49, seem to bring them reproach, or even a curse. Reuben slept with his father's concubine Bilhah (Gen 35:22), while Simeon and Levi killed every male inhabitant of the city of Shechem in retaliation for the mistreatment of their sister Dinah (Gen 34:25–26). All the other blessings—especially the two longest ones, given to Judah (Gen 49:8–12) and Joseph (Gen 49:22–26)—seem to anticipate something of the future settlement in the land, which will unfold later in the Old Testament. Brueggemann captures this tension well:

> As we have seen, chapter 48 has appropriate connections to the narrative and advances the plot. By contrast, the poem of chapter 49 seems to have no important connection with its context. It is inserted here to serve different purposes. The function of the narrative of 48:1–22 is to deal with the issue of transition in the narrative itself. It confines itself to the Joseph tribes which are the core of early Israel. Chapter 49, by contrast, ignores the dramatic movement of the narrative and presents an unrelated statement on the power relations of the tribes (sons?) at a later time when Judah-David is preeminent.[21]

Jacob's blessing is thus not directly connected to the events of the Joseph cycle, and contributes no significant information to the development of Gen 37–50.

The second way in which Jacob's testament feels disconnected is that the blessing of Joseph (Gen 49:22–26) comes somewhat as a surprise after Gen 48, where Jacob's blessing is delivered to Joseph's two sons, Ephraim and Manasseh, as they are adopted by Jacob as his own sons (Gen 48:5–6). With this in mind, the blessing Jacob pronounces upon Joseph in ch. 49, without any reference to his sons, comes as unexpected.[22] One would anticipate Jacob speaking to Ephraim and Manasseh, rather than to Joseph, when the chapter is read in sequence after Jacob's deathbed conversation in ch. 48.[23]

Third, the bulk of Gen 49:1–28 is written in poetic style, characterized by parallelism, with each blessing clearly delimited in the MT by separation markers.[24] This is unusual for the Joseph narrative and this poetic style with its small units sets this section apart from its literary context.

---

21. Walter Brueggemann, *Genesis*, IBC (Louisville, KY: Westminster John Knox, 1982), 365–66. Similarly also Ebach, *Genesis*, 580.

22. Similarly Hermann Gunkel, *Genesis*, trans. Mark E. Biddle, MLBS (Macon, GA: Mercer University Press, 1997), 380.

23. See also Gunkel, *Genesis*, 380.

24. The poetic structure of Gen 49:1–28 is examined in Raymond de Hoop, "Genesis 49 Revisited: The Poetic Structure of Jacob's Testament and the Ancient Versions," in *Unit Delimitation in Biblical Hebrew and Northwest Semitic Literature*, ed. Marjo Korpel and Josef Oesch, Pericope 4 (Assen: Van Gorcum, 2003), 1–32.

For the above reasons, even though Gen 49 does not feel quite so intrusive in the overall narrative as does ch. 38, its placement there is frequently considered secondary. Jacob's testament does not contribute in a substantive way to the plot of the Joseph cycle, it stands in a tension with ch. 48 by not including Ephraim and Manasseh, and it is written as a long poem, which is unusual for the extended narrative of the book of Genesis.

Summary

I have argued that chs. 38 and 49 of Genesis, although they are part of the canonical text, seem intrusive in their literary context. Next, and following upon the above remarks, I will first read Gen 37–50 without chs. 38 and 49. The concept of chosenness will provide a suitable lens for reading this biblical material in order to illuminate those facets of the narrative which focus primarily on the unfavored Judah and his interaction with his favored brother Joseph.[25]

---

25. Notable book-length studies on the Joseph cycle include: Lothar Ruppert, *Die Josephserzählung der Genesis: Ein Beitrag zur Theologie der Pentateuchquellen*, SANT 11 (Munich: Kösel, 1965); Donald B. Redford, *A Study of the Biblical Story of Joseph: Genesis 37–50*, VTSup 20 (Leiden: Brill, 1970); Eric I. Lowenthal, *The Joseph Narrative in Genesis* (New York: Ktav, 1973); Herbert Donner, *Die literarische Gestalt der alttestamentlichen Josephsgeschichte*, SHAW 2 (Heidelberg: Carl Winter, 1976); Horst Seebass, *Geschichtliche Zeit und Theonome Tradition in der Joseph-Erzählung* (Gütersloh: Gütersloher Verlagshaus, 1978); Ludwig Schmidt, *Literarische Studien zur Josephgeschichte*, BZAW 167 (Berlin: de Gruyter, 1986); W. Lee Humphreys, *Joseph and his Family: A Literary Study* (Columbia: University of South Carolina Press, 1988); Walter Dietrich, *Die Josephserzählung als Novelle und Geschichtsschreibung: Zugleich ein Beitrag zur Pentateuchfrage*, BThSt 14 (Neukirchen-Vluyn: Neukirchener, 1989); Robert E. Longacre, *Joseph: A Story of Divine Providence; A Text Theoretical and Textlinguistic Analysis of Genesis 37 and 39–48* (Winona Lake, IN: Eisenbrauns, 1989); Norbert Kebekus, *Die Josefserzählung: Literarkritische und redaktionsgeschichtliche Untersuchungen zu Genesis 37–50*, Internationale Hochschulschriften (Münster, New York: Waxmann, 1990); Barbara Green, *What Profit for Us? Remembering the Story of Joseph* (Lanham, MD: University Press of America, 1996); Yiu-Wing Fung, *Victim and Victimizer: Joseph's Interpretation of His Destiny*, JSOTSup 308 (Sheffield: Sheffield Academic, 2000); Rüdiger Lux, *Josef: der Auserwählte unter seinen Brüdern*, BG 1 (Leipzig: Evangelische Verlagsanstalt, 2001); Ron Pirson, *The Lord of the Dreams: A Semantic and Literary Analysis of Genesis 37–50*, JSOTSup 355 (London: Sheffield Academic, 2002); Hans-Jochen Boecker, *Die Josefsgeschichte (Genesis/1. Mose 37–50): Mit einem Anhang über die Geschichte der Tamar (38, 1–30) und die Stammessprüche (49, 1–28)* (Neukirchen-Vluyn: Neukirchener, 2003); Lindsay Wilson, *Joseph, Wise and Otherwise: The Intersection of Wisdom and the Covenant in Genesis 37–50*, PBM (Carlisle: Paternoster, 2004); André Wénin, *Joseph ou l'invention de la fraternité: Lecture narrative et anthropologique de Genèse 37–50*, Le livre et le rouleau 21 (Brussels: Lessius, 2005); Ebach, *Genesis*; Michael Fieger and Sigrid Hodel-Hoenes, *Der Einzug in Ägypten: Ein Beitrag zur alttestamentliche Josefsgeschichte*, Das Alte Testament im Dialog 1 (Bern: Peter Lang, 2007); Pete Wilcox, *Living the Dream—Joseph for Today: A Dramatic Exposition of Genesis 37–50* (London: Paternoster, 2007); Millgram, *Paradox*.

3

Genesis 37

The Rivalry Stories in Genesis Culminate in the Joseph Cycle

When one uses the framework of election to illuminate the Joseph story, certain aspects come to the forefront. First of all, the opening chapter of the Joseph cycle may be seen as tying the story of Jacob and his sons to other rivalry stories in the book of Genesis.

Favoritism and Hatred

The first connection with the previous rivalry stories can be detected in the atmosphere of special love and unchecked hatred within the family. The *toledot* of Jacob focuses on Joseph, about whom we are told that Israel loved him more than all his sons, which the father demonstrated by making him a special robe (Gen 37:3). Although we cannot be sure about the exact appearance of this piece of clothing,[1] the connection with Israel's preferential love towards Rachel's firstborn son shows that the robe expressed outwardly what Jacob felt inwardly—Joseph was his most beloved son.[2] When Joseph's brothers saw this sign of their father's special affection, they began to hate Joseph and could not speak peacefully with him (37:4).[3]

---

1. It is not clear what this piece of clothing (כְּתֹנֶת פַּסִּים), mentioned in Gen 37:3, 23, and 32, looked like. While כְּתֹנֶת indicates a "shirt-like tunic" (*HALOT* 1:505), פַּס is ambiguous. The LXX translates the whole phrase as χιτών ποικίλος (similarly Vulg.), which gave rise to "a tunic made from different pieces of colored material." The same phrase occurs only here and in 2 Sam 13:18 and 19, where it belonged to Tamar, the royal princess, and where the LXX reads χιτών καρπωτός—"a robe reaching to the wrists and the ankles." Spurrell points out that פַּס means in Aramaic "the extremities of the hand and foot" (Dan 5:5, 24), which would concur with the LXX translation in 2 Sam (G. J. Spurrell, *Notes on the Hebrew Text of the Book of Genesis: With Two Appendices* [Oxford: Clarendon, 1896], 272–73). Nevertheless, this interpretation has been recently challenged by Görg, who proposes that the word פַּס may come from the Egyptian verbal root *psj*, meaning "cooking" or "dyeing" a piece of fabric. The presence of other Egyptian words in the Joseph cycle would thus make the translation of this phrase as "a colorful tunic" possible again, and could even hint at Joseph's Egyptian identity later in the story. See Manfred Görg, "Der gefärbte Rock Josefs," *BN* 102 (2000): 9–13.

2. Westermann expresses this notion well: "[Jacob] was raising the boy to a level above that of his brothers." See Claus Westermann, *Joseph: Eleven Bible Studies on Genesis*, trans. Omar Kaste (Minneapolis: Fortress, 1996), 6.

3. The one to whom the siblings were not able to speak a peaceful word (Gen 37:4) was later sent to inquire about their peace (Gen 37:14).

Their hatred and jealously only intensified when Joseph told his brothers his dreams (Gen 37:8, 11), which eventually led to their attempt to murder their more favored brother (37:20).

The themes of love and hatred resonate with the other rivalry stories in the book of Genesis.[4] Jacob's preferential treatment of Joseph resembles his own preferential love for Rachel (29:30), the maternal favor showed by Rebekah to Jacob himself (25:28), and the special position of Abraham's son Isaac, who was also called the "son of his old age" (בֶּן לִזְקֻנָיו in 21:2; בֶּן־זְקֻנִים in 37:3),[5] and who was also loved in a special way (22:2; 37:3). Jacob's family thus continues the rivalry depicted in his own life and the lives of his ancestors, and Joseph stands in the line of those sons who were not firstborn, but who were favored by their parents at the expense of the other siblings.

Likewise, the hatred of Joseph's brothers and their attempt to kill him recall similar situations in the lives of other unfavored characters in Genesis. Cain was angry because YHWH had not accepted his sacrifice and as a result killed his more favored brother Abel (4:8).[6] Esau also responded with hatred and intended to murder Jacob (27:41). Joseph's brothers thus stand in a long procession of the unchosen characters in the book of Genesis who reacted with hatred and murderous thoughts to the preferential treatment of their younger siblings.[7]

---

4. A suggestive interpretation of the sibling rivalry stories in Genesis that intends to read them for generating less violent relationships among the monotheistic religions can be found in Jonathan Sacks, *Not in God's Name: Confronting Religious Violence* (New York: Schocken, 2015), 107–73. Sacks highlights that when "love" is mentioned in Genesis it often produces conflict. Love, in itself, is not unproblematic (Sacks, *Not in God's Name*, 145, 165).

5. Benjamin, who seems to be only acted upon within the Joseph cycle and thus functioning merely as a child, is called similarly the "child of [Jacob's] old age" (יֶלֶד זְקֻנִים) in Gen 44:20. For this view of Benjamin's role in the narrative consult, for example, Humphreys, *Joseph*, 70–71. For an interesting extension of Benjamin's role, which views the tension between Joseph and Judah, and the latter's taking control over the former, as reminiscent of the position of Benjamin's tribe between the Northern and Southern Kingdom, see Levin, "Benjamin," 232–41.

6. Westermann mentions an interesting aspect of such rivalries. The hatred is not directed towards the one who prefers one over another (God, father, husband), but toward the chosen one (Westermann, *Genesis 37–50*, 37). Even though Hamilton suggests that the text allows for seeing the brothers' hatred as directed to Jacob (וַיִּשְׂנְאוּ, "they hated him," Gen 37:4), it seems to me that the parallels with other rivalry stories and the natural flow of the text warrant Westermann's observation. See Victor P. Hamilton, *The Book of Genesis: Chapters 18–50*, NICOT 2 (Grand Rapids: Eerdmans, 1995), 409.

7. One extension of this topic might be the unlikely occurrence involving the Ishmaelites in the course of ch. 37. It is interesting that both Esau's and Joseph's brothers' moment of hatred and murderous intent is accompanied in the story by the appearance of Ishmael's descendants (Gen 28:9; 37:25, 28; 39:1). At the time that they contemplate getting rid of the favored one, the unchosen brothers unite with the unchosen descendants, emphasizing perhaps the negative tendency that unchosenness entails.

Divine Favoring

Jacob's preferential love for Joseph at the expense of his other sons is not the only expression of Joseph's unique position in ch. 37. What may be seen as an unhealthy pattern of behavior passed by Jacob on to his children,[8] is accompanied in 37:5–11 by the two dreams that similarly highlight Joseph's role vis-à-vis his brothers. Dreams are a backbone of this narrative—they move the events in the Joseph cycle forward and therefore deserve close attention.[9] In ch. 37 it is Joseph who is given these dreams, and they speak favorably of him, mirroring perhaps Jacob's preference for Joseph. What is more important, Joseph's depiction of the dreams, manifesting God's special place for him within the family, were as much a source of his brothers' hatred as was the robe showing Jacob's favoritism. The MT emphasizes the brothers' reaction by stressing, even before the first dream is narrated, that the brothers "hated him even more" (37:5).[10] Verse 8, then, which seems to bring both of Joseph's reports together and to summarize the brothers' response to the dreams, similarly states: "And they hated him even more because of his dreams and his words" (37:8).[11] The text thus highlights that Joseph's brothers reacted in a similar manner both to Jacob's special love as demonstrated in Joseph's unique clothing (37:3) and to the dreams as they were expressed by Joseph (37:5, 8).

Moreover, both features may play some role when Joseph's brothers' first notice that their younger brother came to meet them in Dothan: "And they saw him from a distance, and before he came near to them, they conspired to kill him. They said to each other: 'Here comes this dreamer'" (37:18–19). It is possible that it was precisely Joseph's special robe, which the brothers took away from him later (37:23), that distinguished his figure in the distance and alerted the brothers that it was he who was

---

8. The special treatment Joseph accepts from his father is often criticized by commentators (see Hamilton, *Genesis: 18–50*, 407).

9. Weeks, for example, highlights the role of the dreams as the driving force in the narrative (Stuart Weeks, *Early Israelite Wisdom* [Oxford: Clarendon, 1994], 102–9). Similarly also Brueggemann who points out that dreams hide YHWH's work (Brueggemann, *Genesis*, 298).

10. The phrase וַיּוֹסִפוּ עוֹד שְׂנֹא אֹתוֹ ("and they hated him even more") does not appear in the LXX. It is often considered a later gloss (see, e.g., Westermann, *Genesis 37–50*, 34; or Gunkel, *Genesis*, 389), but Becking argues that it may be part of a literary technique of "flashbacks" (*Nachholende Erzählung*), which states upfront the result that the following episode depicts in the narrative. See Bob Becking, "'They Hated Him Even More': Literary Technique in Genesis 37:1–11," *BN* 60 (1991): 40–47.

11. The plural of both nouns (עַל־חֲלֹמֹתָיו וְעַל־דְּבָרָיו, "because of his dreams and his words") is surprising, given that this response comes only after the narration of the first dream. It may again be considered a gloss (Redford, *Study*, 29) or as a means joining vv. 3–4 with vv. 5–11 (Westermann, *Genesis 37–50*, 39). Perhaps another option is to take the brothers' statement as summarizing their opinion concerning both dreams. After the second dream is told, the narratival space to voice questions is given to Jacob. This would be yet another instance of "flashbacks," as proposed in Becking, "They Hated."

approaching them. The robe and the dreams, the signs of both human and divine favoritism, continued to be sources of the brothers' animosity towards Joseph.[12]

On the one hand, this aspect of divine favoring continues the trajectory from previous patriarchal stories. Abraham's offspring would come from Isaac and not Ishmael (Gen 21:12), and the fates of the twins in Rebekah's womb were determined even before they were born (25:23). The human aspect of chosenness is interwoven with a divine preference for the younger sibling. On the other hand, the negative reaction of Joseph's brothers warrants our modern criticism. Election, at least at the outset of this story, creates frictions, estrangement, and rivalry between people. But, since we are only at the beginning of the story, perhaps the characters may yet move beyond this painful and troubling aspect of chosenness.

What Is Different about This Sibling Rivalry?

Inner-Israel Conflict

So far, I have attempted to show that the story of Joseph and his brothers both continues and brings to a climax the brotherly struggles of previous narratives in the book of Genesis. But the aspect of chosenness in the Joseph cycle is also significantly different. Whereas in the preceding patriarchal stories both the deity and humans favored the seed that eventually led to the birth of Israel as a nation, and did not favor those characters whose descendants in many cases were to become nations inhabiting the land around Israel, the Joseph narrative, on the contrary, describes a struggle among brothers—all of whom belonged to the chosen nation. While up until this point in the book of Genesis the concept of election established the distinction between Israel and other nations, the chosenness in Gen 37–50 is portrayed from the inner-Israel perspective.[13] If this is the case, then one must still ask: What does this chosenness within Israel entail?

It seems to me that the dreams in ch. 37 might point a way forward. They portray Joseph's dominance over his brothers who show their respect towards their younger brother by bowing down before him (37:5–11). The first dream takes place on earth, specifically in the field, where Jacob's sons were binding sheaves. Suddenly Joseph's sheaf rose and stood up while the brothers' sheaves bowed down to it (37:6–7). The stage for the second dream is set in the sky where the sun, the moon, and the eleven stars were bowing to Joseph (37:9).

---

12. See also Wilson, *Joseph*, 57–67, esp. 67.
13. Hensel, whose book is concerned with the replacement of the firstborn in Genesis, helpfully distinguishes between the inter-national perspective of Gen 1–35 and the inner-Israel perspective of Gen 36–50 (Hensel, *Vertauschung*, 284–91).

Joseph's dreams contain some interpretative difficulties[14] and their interpretation is not self-evident.[15] The meaning of the dreams is posed only as questions,[16] stemming from Joseph's family, while Joseph himself is conspicuously silent about their understanding, though one may read his telling them as indicative. Since it is Joseph who interprets the rest of the dreams in Gen 37–50 (41:12, 15), one should perhaps wait until this favored son of Jacob shares his more mature view of how and why the dreams unfolded as they did (see perhaps 45:5–8 and 50:19–20). Nevertheless, these first exclamations of Joseph's family members may show how *they* perceived his purported special role in their clan.

---

14. A major hermeneutical problem exists in the second dream, where Joseph's mother and also his younger brother Benjamin seem to be included among those who come to bow down before Joseph. According to Gen 35:16–20, Rachel died while giving birth to Benjamin. Therefore, to put it plainly, only one of them could be envisioned as making obeisance to Joseph. Interpreters throughout the ages have proposed various solutions to this puzzle: the young Benjamin needed a mother and so another of Jacob's wives became his stepmother. Gen. Rab. 84:11 proposes Bilhah; Sarna suggests Leah (Sarna, *Genesis*, 257). Ebach proposes that the dreams in Gen 37 could have taken place when Rachel was still alive, which would also allow enough time for the happenings in Gen 38 (Ebach, *Genesis*, 70, 672). Rashi reasons that Jacob's question could be, in fact, ironic. Since Joseph's mother is dead, even the reminder of the dream is absurd (M. Rosenbaum and A. M. Silbermann, eds., *The Pentateuch with the Commentary of Rashi: Genesis* [Jerusalem: Silbermann, 1972], 181). Pirson offers an interesting proposal, in which the heavenly bodies in the second dream stand for the number of years (thirteen) until the brothers will meet Joseph again and bow down before him (Pirson, *Lord*, 42–59). Jörg Lanckau offers an innovative suggestion that connects the situation of the Egyptians under Joseph's government, expressed, for example, by their obeisance in Gen 41:43, with Joseph's second dream in Gen 37:9. Lanckau brings to the picture Deut 4:19, in which "the sun, the moon, and the stars" are told to be given to other nations to worship. He reasons, then, that the second dream, contrary to the first one, does not signify Joseph's dominance over his family, but predicts that the Egyptians would bow down before Joseph, who would be raised to this position by God. See Jörg Lanckau, *Der Herr der Träume: Eine Studie zur Funktion des Traumes in der Josefsgeschichte der Hebräischen Bibel*, ATANT 85 (Zurich: TVZ, 2006), 169–73. In my opinion, the imagery of the second dream goes beyond those who showed hatred towards Joseph and represents Jacob's family as a whole, including those who might have been dead (Rachel), those who might have not have been born yet (Benjamin), or Jacob himself (who did not bow down to Joseph explicitly, but rather a puzzling gesture in Gen 47:31 could be interpreted this way). Eventually all Israel will owe a debt to Joseph.

15. In view of four other dreams in the Joseph cycle that are not obviously straightforward, I wonder how Fritsch can say that "[the dreams] need no special interpretation, for both Joseph and his family recognize their meaning." Charles T. Fritsch, "'God Was with Him': A Theological Study of the Joseph Narrative," *Int* 9 (1955): 21–34, esp. 24.

16. Döhling rightly stresses that the meanings of the dreams are posed as questions (Gen 37:8, 10), which invite further reading, and perhaps suggest that their interpretation is questionable. Jan-Dirk Döhling, "Die Herrschaft erträumen, die Träume beherrschen: Herrschaft, Traum und Wirklichkeit in den Josefsträumen (Gen 37,5–11) und der Israel-Josefsgeschichte," *BZ* 50 (2006): 1–30, esp. 3–8.

Whereas the brothers' accusing questions, "Are you indeed to rule over us (אִם־מָשׁוֹל תִּמְשֹׁל בָּנוּ)?," in Gen 37:8 has some merit within the narrative—since the verbal root מָשַׁל occurs in connection with Joseph in Gen 45:8 and 26, where he is referred to as a "ruler (מֹשֵׁל) of all the land of Egypt"—the verb מלך in "Are you indeed to reign over us (הֲמָלֹךְ תִּמְלֹךְ עָלֵינוּ)?" introduces a concept from within a different framework. Although certain preceding narratives mention that kings will come from the promised seed (Gen 17:6, 16; 35:11), the establishment of the monarchy still lies far in the future (1 Sam 8). But perhaps this royal theme—which follows yet another reflection on kingship, in Gen 36:31, where the narrator records that the kings of Edom reigned before any king reigned over the sons of Israel[17]—highlights what is so unique about the topic of chosenness in the Joseph story. On the one hand, the concept of election in this last section of the book of Genesis focuses on an individual who will gain preeminence among his brothers. On the other hand, however, the story of Joseph and his brothers is also about one whose descendants are chosen to reign over his kin and occupy Israel's throne, when the time for the establishment of the monarchy is ripe. The story seems to signal royal connotations.

It is evident that the possibility of this reading is only hinted at the outset of Joseph's story.[18] Nevertheless, some elements present in ch. 37 could support this view. Clearly, the act of prostration, expressed by the verb חוה (Gen 37:7, 9, 10), could be a greeting or an act of respect, offered to anyone who is in a higher position,[19] and as such it is closely connected with the idea of lordship, functioning as a keyword for the whole narrative.[20] Nevertheless, people also bowed down to monarchs, as the story of King David shows that he regularly received this kind of tribute (1 Sam 25:23–24, 41; 2 Sam 1:2; 9:6, 8; 14:4, 22, 33). The dreams seem to predict that Joseph will rise to a place above his brothers, who will look up to him with similar respect as the one given to a ruler or a king.

Further, Joseph's father is introduced under his less usual name "Israel" when the text reports that he loves Joseph more than any of his other sons (Gen 37:3), and when he sends him to check on his brothers at

---

17. Both Döhling and Ebach notes that it is possible to recognize an assonance between Gen 36:31 and 37:8 (Döhling, "Herrschaft," 8–9; Ebach, *Genesis*, 74).

18. Nonetheless, some commentators note this theme. See Westermann, *Genesis 37–50*, 38, and Ebach, *Genesis*, 73. On the other hand, however, von Rad warns that the Joseph narrative is not primarily about the relationship of the tribes to one another; only Joseph could possibly represent northern Israel. See Gerhard von Rad, *Genesis: A Commentary*, trans. John H. Marks, rev. ed., OTL (Philadelphia: Westminster John Knox, 1972), 434.

19. See, for example, *HALOT* 1:296; Horst Dietrich Preuss, "חוה," *TDOT* 4:248–56, esp. 251.

20. For example, Döhling says: "Das dreimal gebrauchte חוה gibt das Thema der Herrschaft deutlich zu erkennen und fungiert als Leitwort der gesamten Erzählung" (Döhling, "Herrschaft," 6).

Shechem (37:13). Since the narrative seems to prefer using "Israel" rather than "Jacob" when it portrays the dealings of Rebekah's favorite son with Joseph, this could heighten the impression that Joseph is seen as preeminent as a clan in Israel.[21]

In addition, given the reference to kingship in the brothers' response to Joseph's first dream, the opening statement about Joseph—describing his role in the company of his brothers "[Joseph] was shepherding the flock with his brothers" (רֹעֶה אֶת־אֶחָיו בַּצֹּאן)—could acquire another meaning, since the preposition אֵת might also be read as the definite direct object marker.[22] The sentence would thus allow for the reading: "Joseph was shepherding his brothers with the flock." According to Hamilton, this could be an example of anticipatory paranomasia, where "what Joseph is doing during his teen life is exactly what he will be doing in his adult life—caring and providing for those who are dependent on him."[23] The verb רעה has resonances with the royal task of taking care of and providing for the people,[24] as it is used at least in the case of David, who is called to "shepherd" or to be a "shepherd" of God's people Israel (2 Sam 5:2; 7:7).[25]

In stating the above-mentioned considerations I do not wish to imply that the topic of kingship is the main theme of the Joseph narrative. But the hint of an overseeing responsibility of Joseph vis-à-vis his brothers, and their fear or puzzlement that he might reign over them, suggest that the idea of monarchy might create an undercurrent which will become more important later in the Old Testament. At the outset of the Joseph story, it is Joseph who is the chosen character favored by his father and by God and who—when read in our experimental version without chs. 38 and 49 – is assigned the leadership role both within Gen 37–50 and in the tribal history of Israel that is to follow.

---

21. Besides ch. 37, the reference to "Israel" in circumstances relating to Joseph in the experimental version of the text occurs in Gen 46:29, 30; 47:29, 31; 48:2, 8, 10, 11, 13 (×2), 14, 20, 21; 50:2. The name "Jacob" is used in a direct connection with Joseph only in Gen 47:7 (×2); 48:2 (however, here "Israel" appears as well), and 48:3. Wenham suggests that the title "Israel" tends to be used when the context speaks of Jacob as the head of the clan or in those scenes where Joseph is present (Wenham, *Genesis 16–50*, 351).

22. This possibility is strengthened by another instance of the verb רעה in ch. 37. Genesis 37:12 mentions a situation in which the brothers went "to shepherd their father's flock in Shechem" (לִרְעוֹת אֶת־צֹאן אֲבִיהֶם בִּשְׁכֶם), where אֵת stands for the direct object marker. See also Pirson, *Lord*, 29.

23. Hamilton, *Genesis: 18–50*, 406, following Duane L. Christensen, "Anticipatory Paronomasia in Jonah 3:7–8 and Genesis 37:2," *RB* 90 (1983): 261–63, esp. 263.

24. The noun "shepherd" (רֹעֶה) is also used within the Joseph cycle as an epithet for God used in the context of God's relationship with Jacob and Joseph (Gen 48:15; 49:24).

25. Levenson points out that Joseph shares the act of "shepherding," both literal and metaphorical, with Moses and David (Levenson, *Death*, 144–45).

Differentiation among the Unchosen: Reuben and Judah

The second difference between this sibling rivalry and those that preceded it, is the differentiation that takes place among the unchosen characters in the narrative. Since Joseph's narrative focuses on the twelve sons of Jacob, this allows for a more nuanced portrayal of those who are favored neither by people nor by God.

Until the moment at Dothan when the brothers spotted Joseph's unmistakable figure on the horizon and decided to kill him (Gen 37:18–20), they had acted as an unified group. But at this key moment in the narrative, two of the brothers stood out among their siblings. When Reuben heard about the brothers' plot, he made two entreaties to spare Joseph's life—"Let us not take his life!" and "Do not shed his blood!"—and suggested that he be thrown into a pit in the wilderness instead (37:21–22). While to the brothers the idea of lowering Joseph into an empty cistern may have sounded as a less violent, and thus more acceptable, proposal as to how to take Joseph's life, the narrator discloses that Reuben's true intention was to bring Joseph back to his father. His suggestion prevailed and thus Reuben saved Joseph's life.[26]

Reuben voices his plea before Joseph arrives and when the latter finally reaches his brothers he does not get a chance to speak, nor does he speak throughout the scene.[27] The brothers strip off his exceptional robe and lower him into the cistern (37:23–24). Then they sit down to eat,[28] presumably some distance away from the cistern containing their brother, and see a caravan of Ishmaelites on their way to Egypt (37:25). This prompts Judah to suggest yet another plan as to how to deal with Joseph. On the one hand, he also is concerned about shedding the blood of somebody who is their kin. On the other hand, however, he wonders what profit the killing would bring, and therefore proposes to sell Joseph to the Ishmaelites (37:26–27).

The following verse, however, further complicates the sequence of the events when it states: "When the Midianite merchants passed by, they pulled Joseph up, lifting him out of the cistern and sold him to the Ishmaelites for twenty pieces of silver. And they took Joseph to Egypt" (Gen 37:28).

---

26. Before Reuben speaks, the text contains this straightforward expression: "When Reuben heard it, he delivered him (וַיַּצִּלֵהוּ) from their hands" (Gen 37:21). Although Westermann suggests that this should be translated as the conative imperfect—"he would deliver him from their hands" (Westermann, *Genesis 37–50*, 34)—this could be another instance where the text at the outset reveals the result of the upcoming action. Joseph was not killed on the spot, but Reuben's proposal to throw him into the cistern eventually saved his life. Similarly also Ebach, *Genesis*, 90, 95.

27. The story is narrated in a detached, almost cold, manner, which does not open up any window into Joseph's feelings, even though the brothers later recall his anxious plea for mercy (Gen 42:21). He is simply a passive object of the brothers' plot in Gen 37:18–36.

28. The food motif in the Joseph cycle is examined in Katie M. Heffelfinger, "From Bane to Blessing: The Food *Leitmotif* in Genesis 37–50," *JSOT* 40 (2016): 297–320.

The sudden appearance of yet another caravan is the main problem as to why the fast-paced narrative in 37:21–30 seems to elude any easy explanations that might offer a coherent understanding of Joseph's transition to Egypt.

From a source-critical point of view, the reference to two caravans provides a good basis for discerning two variants underlying our present text.[29] Undoubtedly, the suggestion to discern two possible layers beneath the text offers a valuable contribution towards understanding the possible prehistory of the text. Nevertheless, the question remains: how can one make sense of the story in its present form? One common move is to notice that Judg 8:22–24 suggests that the Midianites are also called the Ishmaelites, and to propose that both names are used in Gen 37 interchangeably.[30] On this interpretation, the brothers are made the subject of the two middle verbs. Genesis 37:28 then reads: "So when the Midianite merchants came by, *his brothers* pulled Joseph up out of the cistern and sold him for twenty shekels of silver to the Ishmaelites" (NIV). This reading has the obvious advantage of smoothing out the otherwise convoluted text. Nevertheless, the narrative in Genesis does not prepare the reader to understand the Midianites and the Ishmaelites as one and the same group. This, coupled with the observation that the Midianites are the more obvious subject for pulling Joseph up and lifting him from the cistern in v. 28, persuades me to take them as separate peoples.[31] It is also noteworthy that Joseph later mentions that he was stolen from the Hebrew land (Gen 40:15), which would support that it was the Midianites who lifted him from the cistern and sold him to the Ishmaelites.[32] Even though this view does not solve all the difficulties present in Gen 37:21–36,[33] it is a viable

---

29. Typically, in this understanding, Judah and the Ishmaelites are considered to be a part of the J layer of the text, while Reuben along with the Midianites represent the E layer. A verse-by-verse division concerning the putative sources is offered by S. R. Driver, *The Book of Genesis with Introduction and Notes*, 10th ed. (London: Methuen, 1916), 324–25.

30. The Ishmaelites, for example, could be seen as a broad term and the Midianites as an ethnic referent. Consult Longacre, *Joseph*, 29–30; Hamilton, *Genesis: 18–50*, 423; and E. J. Revell, "Midian and Ishmael in Genesis 37: Synonyms in the Joseph Story," in *The World of the Aramaeans I: Biblical Studies in Honour of Paul-Eugène Dion*, ed. P. M. Michèle Davian et al., JSOTSup 324 (Sheffield: Sheffield Academic, 2001), 70–91.

31. NRSV, NJPS, or ESV also keep the Midianites as those who drew Joseph out of the cistern.

32. Joseph's words that his brothers sold him to Egypt in Gen 45:4 may be due to Joseph's overhearing the brothers' guilt-driven memories in Gen 42:21–22.

33. This interpretation leaves unanswered the reference to the Midianites who sold Joseph to Egypt according to Gen 37:36. Possibly this verse can be understood in a way that the Midianites initiated the whole transaction, which does not exclude the possibility of the Ishmaelites acting as a middle agent. But, admittedly, there is no obvious solution to this difficulty. Nevertheless, reading the story without chs. 38 and 49 allows me to leave out 37:36 and include only 39:1 in the experimental version of the text.

option, which highlights the irony that the brothers were not able to get rid of their favored sibling regardless of how much they tried.[34] Despite Judah's plan, it was the Midianite travelers who drew Joseph out of the pit and sold him, gaining a profit of twenty pieces of silver.

This interpretation might also explain Reuben's puzzlement over an empty cistern and his distressed words when he returns to his brothers: "The boy is not there. And I, where can I turn?" (Gen 37:29–30). This prompts us to consider the interplay between the firstborn Reuben and the fourth-born Judah, and to evaluate their twin proposals and the different outcomes of their plans. I will make several points in this regard.

First, Reuben's reaction to the brothers' idea to kill Joseph, as well as his shock when he discovers the empty cistern at the end of this passage, show his emotions and personal involvement in this endeavor. This could stem from his concern as the older brother to protect his younger sibling,[35] or possibly from his desire to gain his father's favor, which at this moment rested on Joseph, but which would normally have belonged to the first-born.[36] Whereas Reuben responds with words that betray his attachment to Joseph's case and possibly display his sensitivity, Judah's suggestion seems more detached, but also more realistic. Judah is a practical man, and this could be another reason why he becomes the representative of the brothers in the story.[37] The narrator has a special proclivity towards wisdom-like elements in the story, as Joseph is often understood as a man of wisdom (Gen 41:39),[38] and Judah seems to act with prudence and diplomacy—a skill we will later admire in his dealings with the now lost Joseph—while Reuben's noble plans fall apart.

---

34. Similarly also Paul Borgman, *Genesis: The Story We Haven't Heard* (Downers Grove, IL: InterVarsity Press, 2001), 181–82; Edward L. Greenstein, "An Equivocal Reading of the Sale of Joseph," in *Literary Interpretations of Biblical Narratives*, ed. Kenneth R. R. Gros Louis and James S. Ackerman (Nashville: Abingdon, 1982), 114–25; and Levenson, *Death*, 147.

35. Thus, for example, Hugh C. White, "The Joseph Story: A Narrative Which 'Consumes' Its Content," *Semeia* 31 (1985): 49–69, esp. 65.

36. Goldin, for example, suggests that Reuben's attempt in ch. 37 could be driven by his desire to remedy his previous act of sleeping with Jacob's concubine Bilhah (Gen 35:22). See Judah Goldin, "Youngest Son or Where does Genesis 38 Belong?," *JBL* 96 (1977): 27–44, esp. 40. Similarly also Kaminsky, *Jacob*, 60; and Hensel, *Vertauschung*, 198.

37. Berlin states in this regard: "Judah can hardly be accused of having a soft spot for Joseph. He appears less emotional than Reuben, and more logical. He sees an opportunity, perhaps even a profitable one, to solve a problem and he seizes it. Judah is the practical one in the family" (Adele Berlin, *Poetics and Interpretation of Biblical Narrative*, BLS 9 [Sheffield: Almond Press, 1983], 121).

38. Joseph as the model of wisdom and the Joseph cycle as the wisdom narrative was famously asserted by Gerhard von Rad, "The Joseph Narrative and Ancient Wisdom," in *From Genesis to Chronicles: Explorations in Old Testament Theology*, ed. K. C. Hanson, trans. E. W. Trueman Dicken (Minneapolis, MN: Fortress, 2005), 75–88. A recent critique of von Rad's proposal can be found especially in Weeks, *Wisdom*, esp. 92–102. Redford, on the other hand, does not consider Joseph to be a model of wisdom (Redford, *Study*, 100–105).

Second, neither Reuben nor Judah seems to have the family's best interests in mind. This is obvious in the case of Judah, who coldly suggests earning twenty shekels of silver for selling Joseph to slavery.[39] However, although Reuben's spirited attempt to rescue Joseph and bring him back to his father by temporarily lowering him into the pit sounds pious, it may have produced a deep rupture in the already strained relationships within the family. White helpfully points out this difficulty:

> If Reuben is successful, and Joseph returns to Jacob with a report of these happenings (as it clearly must be assumed that he would do), the communication in the family will be irreparably shattered and the moral ambiguity which has colored each of the parties until now will be overcome by the polarization of the absolutely good against the absolutely evil.[40]

Even though I do not think it is necessary to frame the possible outcome of Joseph's return home in terms of absolute good and evil, White usefully points out that Reuben's pious-sounding ideas were not especially wise and could have had disastrous consequences for the family dynamics.

Third, the narrative portrays Reuben as being more removed from the circle of brothers than is Judah. Verses 21–22 portray him as acting independently from and against the will of his siblings. Verses 29–30 picture him walking alone to the cistern and wondering what consequences the disappearance of Joseph might have for him. On the other hand, not only does Judah make reference to Joseph being their own flesh and blood, but also seems to speak from within the group as one of them,[41] which may have played some part in his winning the agreement of his brothers (Gen 37:26–27).[42]

In the end, even though one may discern some differences between the actions of the two main unchosen brothers, hinting as to why it was Judah whose plan succeeded, it needs to be stressed that the text does not spell

---

Wilson takes a middle position and argues for the presence of "wisdom-like elements" in the Joseph story (Wilson, *Joseph*, esp. 35–37). Moberly helpfully shows how von Rad's argument may have some heuristic value for reading the Joseph cycle today in Moberly, *Genesis*, 225–45.

39. Kaminsky further suggests that Judah could have been motivated by his desire to usurp the right of the firstborn (Kaminsky, *Jacob*, 60).

40. Hugh C. White, "'Where Do You Come From?' Genesis 37, 39–45, 50," in *Narration and Discourse in the Book of Genesis*, ed. Hugh C. White (New York: Cambridge University Press, 1991), 232–75, esp. 250.

41. Hensel views Judah positively in this regard: "Im Gegensatz zu Ruben zeigt Juda immerhin, dass er in Kategorien von Brüderlichkeit zu denken und zu handeln versucht. Er steht damit relative gesehen besser da als Ruben. Was jedoch wahre Brüderlichkeit innerhalb Israels bedeutet, muss Juda noch erlernen" (Hensel, *Vertauschung*, 199).

42. A broader argument for the difference between Reuben and Judah in terms of the relationship to the rest of the brothers can be found in Pirson, *Lord*, 66–68.

out explicitly why one prevailed and the other did not. The most important thing to note from their interplay in ch. 37 is *that* Judah's plan is the most successful,[43] and *not why*.

Chosen Remains Chosen

Chapter 37 ironically ends where it began—with Jacob's preoccupation with Joseph. His physical disappearance did nothing to change this in Jacob's heart. In rich terms, the text describes Jacob's mourning his beloved son, and that cannot be comforted by any of his sons or daughters (Gen 37:34–35). The chosen son cannot be replaced by the unchosen. Rather, Joseph's disappearance, which was hidden from Jacob's eyes, endangers his father's life. Jacob seems to imitate Joseph's descent; he is ready to go down to Sheol in mourning, and Jacob's desperate words testify to the intricate connection between the father and his beloved son. As Levenson aptly remarks: "To be separated from Joseph is, for Jacob, to be dead, and to be together with him is to live again."[44]

Therefore, the brothers did not succeed in assuming Joseph's position, nor were they able to dissociate Jacob from his favorite son. On the contrary, they brought disaster on their father and unwittingly set Joseph's destiny in motion. Joseph was sold to Potiphar, who was himself connected with the Pharaoh (Gen 37:36), and Joseph thus landed in close proximity to a much greater place of power than his brothers had imagined. In the remainder of the story one truly sees "what comes of his dreams" (Gen 37:20).

Summary

This extensive discussion of ch. 37 comprises an important part of my study, since the opening section of the Joseph cycle connects this story with the previous episodes of sibling rivalry, and simultaneously opens up new themes that both deepen and somewhat modify the predictable pattern from the preceding narratives. The tale of Jacob and his sons stands in a long line of stories that favor the younger son over his older sibling. In this case it was Joseph who was loved by his father more than his siblings and who was repaid for this preferential treatment with his brothers' hatred, which eventually led to their attempt to kill him. Human favoritism is then interwoven with divine favoritism as his dreams reveal that Joseph would have a special position in the family, making his brothers bow down to him.

---

43. Some authors stress, however, that Reuben's construal is not in fact overshadowed by Judah. Syrén, for example, sees Reuben in a positive light as the one who was more compassionate than the others and was finally vindicated in Gen 42:21–22 (Syrén, *First-born*, 130–33).

44. Levenson, *Death*, 151.

The story, however, also shows some traits different from those stories which precede it. Joseph's special position among his brothers points to an inner-Israel conflict. When one takes the brothers' fear that Joseph would reign over them, together with those texts indicating that it was "Israel" who endowed Joseph with this special privilege, then one may suggest that what we have here prefigures in some way Israel's tribal history extending to the establishment of the monarchy. Similarly, the presence of the ten unchosen brothers gives us opportunity to see how the various brothers react to their non-special fate. In the interplay between two of them, it is not the firstborn Reuben, but the fourth-born Judah, whose plan prevails, which may be a sign of his future important role in the story.

4

Genesis 39–42

Joseph's Descents and Ascents

The opening chapter of the Joseph cycle ends on a sad note, as Jacob mourns the loss of his beloved son.[1] On my experimental reading, this verse constitutes both an appropriate closure to Gen 37 and a fitting bridge to ch. 39.[2] As Jacob desired to go down (ירד) to Sheol to be with Joseph (Gen 37:35), so Joseph was brought down (ירד) to Egypt by the Ishmaelites (Gen 39:1). Joseph's several descents and ascents in chs. 39–42, which eventually leave Joseph in a high position in Egypt, will be the subject of the first portion of this chapter.[3] The second part of the chapter will be devoted to the brothers' first trip to Egypt and the evaluation of Joseph's treatment of his siblings.

YHWH Is with Joseph

When Joseph is bought by Potiphar from the hand of the Ishmaelites (Gen 39:1), he becomes the first Hebrew slave[4] in a land that is famously characterized in Scripture as "the house of slavery" (i.e. Exod 13:3, 14; 20:2; Deut 5:6; 6:12; 7:8).[5] Egypt thus becomes the setting in which most of the remainder of the Joseph narrative takes place. The beginning of the chapter (Gen 39:1–6), however, focuses not on Joseph's slavery in Potiphar's house, but rather on his transition from having being bought "from the hand of the Ishmaelites" (מִיַּד הַיִּשְׁמְעֵאלִים, 39:1) to a place where Potiphar

---

1. Undoubtedly, there are other ways to outline the Joseph cycle. I divide the story according to several texts that employ the image of death and are associated with beloved sons (Gen 42:38; 45:28; 50:26). They serve to keep my discussion of the narrative closely connected with the concept of chosenness.

2. Of the two conflicting references to Joseph's transition into slavery in Gen 37:36 and 39:1, I retain the latter, which takes the Ishmaelites to be those who sold Joseph to Potiphar.

3. Levenson considers Joseph to be an exemplar of a symbolic death and resurrection. His descent into the pit, his slavery in Egypt, and his imprisonment after the incident with Potiphar's wife represent several downward steps that have a transforming effect on Joseph's life (Levenson, *Death*, 150–52).

4. For this suggestion, see Ebach, *Genesis*, 162.

5. One of the purposes of the Joseph cycle is to provide an explanation for Israel's transition to slavery in Egypt. For a larger argument on this issue, see George W. Coats, *From Canaan to Egypt: Structural and Theological Context for the Joseph Story*, CBQMS 4 (Washington, DC: Catholic Biblical Association of America, 1976), esp. 3–9.

"appointed him over his house (עַל־בֵּיתוֹ) and all that he had, he put in his hand (בְּיָדוֹ)" (39:4).[6] This unexpected, and from the narratival point of view, rapid change, was due to YHWH's being with Joseph and making everything that was in his hand prosper (39:3). The story thus stresses in several different ways that "YHWH was with Joseph," this being discerned even by the Egyptian master, who left almost everything in Joseph's care and who himself had concern only for the food he ate (39:6a).[7] In turn, God's blessing remained on all that Potiphar possessed (39:5).

A similar scenario repeats itself at the end of the chapter, in Gen 39:21–23. Joseph is thrown into prison after he escapes the sexual advances of Potiphar's wife and leaves his cloak in her hand (בְּיָדָהּ, 39:13), but the chief jailor quickly discovers that whatever Joseph does prospers, because YHWH is with him, and so the jailor,[8] as Potiphar before him, leaves the whole "house of prison" (בֵּית הַסֹּהַר) in Joseph's hand (בְּיַד־יוֹסֵף) (39:22). Several comments with regard to these two paragraphs in ch. 39 are in order.

First, God's name "YHWH" is unusual in the Joseph cycle. In fact, when one reads the narrative without chs. 38 and 49,[9] it appears only in these two passages just discussed (Gen 39:1–6 and 21–23). The appearance of "YHWH" in these sections could be explained on source-critical grounds,[10] but Westermann helpfully reorients the issue towards the text's function. He suggests that the reference to YHWH may create a theological introduction to the Joseph story, through which the narrator highlights that YHWH was the source of Joseph's achievements.[11] Even in the hardships of a foreign land, Joseph was accompanied by YHWH.[12]

---

6. The word "hand" (יָד) is one of the keywords in Gen 39:1–6 (×4), and also in Gen 39:21–23 (×2). See Ebach, *Genesis*, 161.

7. Westermann agrees with Ruppert, who claims that the designation of the "food that he ate" in Gen 39:6a might be an expression indicating his private affairs generally (Ruppert, *Josephserzählung*, 46; and also Westermann, *Genesis 37–50*, 640). If this is along the right lines, it could be another reason why Joseph regarded Potiphar's wife as excluded from his oversight (Gen 39:9).

8. The person in charge of Joseph is called a "chief jailor" (שַׂר בֵּית־הַסֹּהַר) in Gen 39:21, 22, and 23, but a "captain of the guard" (שַׂר הַטַּבָּחִים) in Gen 40:3, 4, which is the same term used for Potiphar in Gen 37:36. For this reason Ebach, for example, suggests that chs. 39 and 40 both take place in Potiphar's palace (Ebach, *Genesis*, 164–65).

9. It appears here eight times. God's name "YHWH" can also be found in Gen 38:7 (×2), 10, and 49:18.

10. Genesis 39 is often thought to continue to use both the J and E layers of the story, where J, with its usage of "YHWH," comprises the bulk of the chapter. For a succinct summary, see Driver, *Genesis*, 332; and Gunkel, *Genesis*, 404–5.

11. Westermann, *Genesis 37–50*, 62.

12. Ebach emphasizes that the story of YHWH's being with Joseph in Egypt could have provided a strong encouragement for the Israelites in exile (Ebach, *Genesis*, 166). Somewhat similarly, and with one eye on the possibility a believer's having used the story, Moberly asks whether, by using the term "YHWH" in Gen 39, the storyteller may have interpreted the narrative at a key moment "so as to appropriate it for Yahwistic readers so

Second, both Joseph's success and YHWH's being with him call to mind David at the beginning of the so-called History of David's Rise (1 Sam 16– 2 Sam 5). For one thing, a similar series of statements underscoring YHWH's being with someone similarly chosen can be found in 1 Sam 16–18, where David finds his way into both Saul's court and his family (1 Sam 16:18; 18:12, 14, 28). The narrator's repeated affirmations that "YHWH was with David" prepare the reader for the rest of 1 Samuel, in which David is a fugitive and Saul remains on Israel's throne, in a way similar to the Joseph cycle: YHWH works behind the scenes to bring his chosen person to a position of authority and responsibility. Additionally, Joseph's physical appearance and managerial abilities are not only important for the flow of the story in ch. 39 (Gen 39:6), but they also might have some points of contact with David's description in 1 Sam 16–18, where the text portrays a similarly ideal young man. David has beautiful eyes and is handsome (1 Sam 16:12; 17:42) and is introduced to Saul as a suitable person to relieve his torments by these words: he is "skillful in playing, a man of valor, a warrior, prudent in speech, and a man of good presence; and YHWH is with him" (1 Sam 16:18).[13] These references to the beauty and skill both of Joseph and David may thus serve to invite the reader to accept these persons as those who are favored by God and equipped to achieve the role for which they were chosen.[14]

Third, Joseph's transition from being in the "hand" of somebody else to a place where almost everything was in his "hand," in each of the two houses in ch. 39 paints a picture of the slave becoming master, in spite of such restrictive circumstances as his. Joseph's rise to the position of major-domo both in Potiphar's house and in prison testifies to the fact that God's blessing remained on his chosen one even when he found himself in difficult situations. Although Joseph sojourned in Egypt involuntarily and as a slave, his dreams were not forgotten. Rather, even in the midst of these unforeseen difficulties, they seemed to be slowly coming true.

The two segments Gen 39:1–6 and 21–23 thus seem to draw attention to YHWH as the source and guarantor of Joseph's destiny. Joseph is handsome and successful, which further underscores his special status,

---

that they can see that YHWH may be present with the believer even in times of unmerited adversity." See R. W. L. Moberly, *The Old Testament of the Old Testament: Patriarchal Narratives and Mosiac Yahwism*, OBT (Minneapolis: Fortress, 1992), 178–79, esp. 179.

13. Von Rad also suggests a connection between the description of Joseph and that of David in 1 Sam 16:18 (von Rad, *Genesis*, 364). Similarly also Ruppert, *Josephserzählung*, 46–47; and Ebach, *Genesis*, 166–67.

14. However, this does not mean that the gifts given to the chosen cannot be misused or misunderstood by others. For example, Reno points out the possibly negative effects of Joseph's and David's good looks. They both had to face sexual temptations. See R. R. Reno, *Genesis*, BTC (Grand Rapids: Brazos, 2010), 268.

visible to those to whom he is subordinate—each of whom quickly makes him the overseer of his respective realm of responsibility. The connection between Joseph and David and their relevant attributes at the outset of their stories not only stresses the privileged statuses of each, but further tightens the link between Joseph's narrative and the establishment of the monarchy in Israel.

Master of the Dreams

In Genesis 40 and 41, which describe Joseph's ascent from the position of an imprisoned slave to a place of stewardship over the whole land of Egypt, dreams play an important part. Joseph is truly a master of dreams, not only because his own two dreams portray him as lord, but also because he "masters" the interpretation of other people's dreams at the very moment when this is critically needed (40:8a; 41:8). To be sure, Joseph reminds his listeners that it is God who gives the interpretation (40:8b; 41:16, 25, 28); nevertheless, it is through Joseph that God explains the hidden meaning of these nocturnal visions. Dreams, and not God's self-revelation as in the case of the patriarchs,[15] are the means through which Joseph's ascent is achieved. Nevertheless, since both the dreams and Joseph's interpretation of them come from God, this is yet another way in which the narrative highlights the hand of God behind Joseph's transition to the top of the Egyptian hierarchy.

When Joseph interprets Pharaoh's two dreams in ch. 41, and adds some practical advice on how to deal with the upcoming crisis in Egypt (Gen 41:33), Pharaoh decides that Joseph himself is the right man for this task and appoints him to rule over his kingdom with these words: "You shall be over my house (עַל־בֵּיתִי)" (41:40). Pharaoh excludes only his throne from Joseph's jurisdiction. We do not find here any sentence that would say that everything would be given into Joseph's *hand*, but 41:42 mentions that Pharaoh took a ring from his hand—possibly a signet ring carrying Pharaoh's authority[16]—and put it on Joseph's hand (עַל־יַד יוֹסֵף). Joseph also receives a special garment of fine linen,[17] and a gold necklace placed around his neck (41:42)—all three items probably signifying Pharaoh's granting his power to Joseph.[18] This procedure—together

---

15. Von Rad connected this feature of sparse incidents of divine revelation and theological comments with early wisdom literature (von Rad, "Joseph," 77–78).

16. A similar incident takes place in Esth 3:10–12 and 8:2, 8, 10, where the bearer of the ring acts in the king's name and with his authority. Similarly also Westermann, *Genesis 37–50*, 95; and Ebach, *Genesis*, 248–49.

17. Clothing in the Joseph narrative signals a status change and in this case it underscores Joseph's new role as an Egyptian officer. See Victor H. Matthews, "The Anthropology of Clothing in the Joseph Narrative," *JSOT* 65 (1995): 25–36.

18. See Lanckau, *Herr*, 271.

with Joseph's new name and the priest's daughter he was given to marry (41:45)—seems to secure Joseph's leadership position and new identity as an Egyptian lord.[19] The references to "hand" and "house" connect the happenings at Pharaoh's court with the two situations depicted in ch. 39, and help the reader get the core message of these chapters even on a quick reading. Joseph now finds himself a third time in the position of running somebody else's house—this time, however, the house comprises the whole of Egypt.[20]

When Joseph rides in a chariot as the second-in-command in Egypt, and the people are asked to bow down before him (Gen 41:43), one gets the impression that certain elements from the opening chapter of the Joseph cycle are back again, albeit now in a different fashion: Joseph is clothed in special garments, and the people around him show their honor by bowing down to him in a manner reminiscent of Joseph's dreams. Joseph has achieved what the dreams hinted at—yet those who are subject to him are foreigners. Those missing from the scene are Joseph's brothers. However, before we turn to their portion of the story, we need to examine whether his sojourn in Egypt has in any way changed Jacob's favorite son.

Joseph's Development

Chapter 39 focused on YHWH's blessing upon Joseph and his ability to run a large household, whereas ch. 40 demonstrated that Joseph possessed God's gift of interpreting dreams. These characteristics come together in Gen 41, where Joseph explains Pharaoh's two dreams and becomes his vice-regent over Egypt, due to the Egyptian king's recognizing his discernment, wisdom, and connectedness with God (41:38–39). This is Joseph's final ascent,[21] which he experiences at the age of thirty

---

19. For a comparison of Joseph's Egyptian identity in Gen 41 and Daniel's more reserved attitude to assimilation in Dan 2, see Matthew S. Rindge, "Jewish Identity under Foreign Rule: Daniel 2 as a Reconfiguration of Genesis 41," *JBL* 129 (2010): 85–104.

20. The all-encompassing nature of Joseph's governance over Egypt is expressed by the word כֹּל, occurring in Gen 41:40–57 sixteen times. Similarly also Brueggemann, *Genesis*, 328.

21. Joseph is brought from the "pit" in Gen 41:14, which is the third reference to בּוֹר in the narrative (also in Gen 37:20–29; 40:15). The narrative contains several features that appear three times. To my previous observation that Joseph oversaw three different houses, may be added Joseph's being brought low three times (to the cistern, to slavery in Egypt, to the prison), three pairs of dreams in the story, and three journeys of the Israelites down to Egypt (42:3; 43:15; 46:3–4). On a more miniscule level, Sherman's essay finds this threefold pattern also in Gen 40: Miriam Sherman, "Do Not Interpretations Belong to God? A Narrative Assessment of Genesis 40 as it Elucidates the Persona of Joseph," in *Milk and Honey: Essays on Ancient Israel and the Bible in Appreciation of the Judaic Studies Program at the University of California, San Diego*, ed. Sarah Malena and David Miano (Winona Lake, IN: Eisenbrauns, 2007), 37–49. Such elements both heighten the suspense of the story and increase its depth.

(41:46a)[22]—a good point at which to look back at his journey since the day he left his father's house for Shechem, and to say something about his character.

It should be stressed at the outset that the narrative gives more weight to the role that God plays in Joseph's ascent than to Joseph's own achievements. Nevertheless, one may, perhaps, sketch at least a tentative appraisal of Joseph's attitude and behavior. One fruitful approach may be to take a closer look at Joseph's ability to withstand the temptation to engage in inappropriate sexual relations with Potiphar's wife. Joseph's own response to Potiphar's wife, in one of her attempts to seduce him, is to point out that everything in his master's house, except his wife, is under his care (Gen 39:8–9a). Then Joseph adds: "How can I do this evil thing and sin against God?" (39:9b). Commentators sometimes recognize in Joseph's answer a twofold reason for refusing the woman's request (breaching Potiphar's trust and sinning against God). Ebach, for example, asserts that "loyalty to Potiphar carries a greater weight,"[23] but spends a whole paragraph looking for a possible pentateuchal ordinance that would see adultery as a sin.[24] However, these final words of Joseph do not seem to be adding a new reason for his self-control. Rather, they seem to be summing up what he has already said and what is in line with the characterization of the narrator in Gen 39:1–6—that is, that Joseph's success in Potiphar's house is directly related to YHWH's blessing. Joseph's sin against God can be seen, then, as a move in the same direction as a betrayal of Potiphar: overstepping Potiphar's instructions would transgress also God's commands.[25]

This insight is both in line with Joseph's own deference to God as the sole source of dreams and their interpretation, and more embedded in the story as such—both of which might hint at something that Joseph's attitude displays in these chapters about the topic of chosenness. They signify that an important part in the life of the chosen is to recognize that in order to rule, one needs to accept a certain level of subordination. Joseph is the second-in-command both in Potiphar's house and in Pharaoh's court, and

22. Since priests entered the priestly service at the age of thirty (Num 4:2–4), the reference to Joseph's age in Gen 41:46a is sometimes thought to betray the P source (see Westermann, *Genesis 37–50*, 96). On the other hand, this is yet another point of contact with David, who at the same age became king (2 Sam 5:4). See also Lanckau, *Herr*, 137.

23. "Doch obwohl die religiöse Komponente in Josefs Worten durchaus zur Sprache kommt, *trägt die Loyalität gegenüber Potifar das Hauptgewicht*" (Ebach, *Genesis*, 180, emphasis mine).

24. Deut 22:22 offers the most suitable pretext (Ebach, *Genesis*, 180.)

25. Similarly also Westermann, *Joseph*, 26–27. Moreover, my proposal is reinforced when Joseph's respect towards his master is contrasted with the attitude of the chief cupbearer and chief baker who "sinned against their master, the king of Egypt" (Gen 40:1).

in both cases a few things are excluded from his oversight. The power of the chosen is thus not limitless. It has certain boundaries, which should be respected.

The Brothers' First Trip to Egypt

When a famine strikes the land and the text reports that "all the earth came to Joseph in Egypt to buy food" (Gen 41:57), the story naturally transitions back to Canaan, to Jacob's family in need, who decide to go to Egypt to purchase grain there (42:1–3). This first visit is undertaken without Benjamin, whom Jacob keeps at home for fear that something terrible might happen to him on the journey (42:4)—the first hint in the narrative that Benjamin, in his father's eyes, has assumed the place of absent Joseph, at least in some respect.

The Brothers Tested

When the ten brothers came to Joseph, who was in the position of an Egyptian lord, they "bowed down before him with their faces to the ground" (Gen 42:6). The gesture of "bowing down" from those who called Joseph "lord" and themselves his "servants," together with Joseph's role of a ruler and food provider,[26] echo Joseph's dreams, which were immediately remembered[27] by him (42:9).[28] Although this may be taken as an early sign of the dreams' realization, the continuation of the narrative shows that much has to happen on both sides for the deeper fulfillment to take place.[29]

---

26. Joseph's position of a "ruler" (הַשַּׁלִּיט) and "provider of food" (הַמַּשְׁבִּיר), used in Gen 42:6, further harkens back to his two dreams in ch. 37, which depict the sheaves of grain and the heavenly objects that may be viewed as ruling the day and night. For the connection between the two chapters, see, for example, Hamilton, *Genesis: 18–50*, 518–19.

27. The twin themes of "remembering" and "forgetting" play a significant role in the narrative. When we hear that the chief cupbearer "did not remember Joseph; he forgot him" (Gen 40:23), the narrative signals that Joseph will remain in prison. But when the cupbearer remembers Joseph (41:9), the events begin to move forward. Similarly, although Joseph forgets the hardship in his homeland (expressed when he named his son Manasseh in 41:51), everything changes when he see his brothers bowing down before him and remembers his dreams (42:9).

28. Jacob notices the unusual way in which Gen 42:9 refers to Joseph dreams: "Joseph remembered the dreams that he dreamt regarding them (לָהֶם)," and argues that the memory brings back the notion that the dreams were dreamt for the brothers' benefit: to save their lives for which they will bow down to Joseph, thanking him (Jacob, *Genesis*, 766).

29. For the view that Gen 42 might trick the reader to expect an imminent fulfillment of the dreams, but then shows that the denouement of the story is further on, see James S. Ackerman, "Joseph, Judah, and Jacob," in *Literary Interpretations of Biblical Narratives*, ed. Kenneth R. R. Gros Louis and James S. Ackerman (Nashville: Abingdon, 1982), 85–113, esp. 86–87. Döhling also expresses caution. He reasons that the purpose of the dreams, not their fulfillment, is of interest here. Joseph wants to bring both Benjamin and Jacob to Egypt (Döhling, "Herrschaft," esp. 15).

Since Joseph recognized his siblings but they did not recognize him (42:8), it provided for him an opportunity to instigate a long series of events that would eventually bring to Egypt Joseph's younger brother Benjamin (42:15, 20).

Joseph's harsh words to his brothers accusing them of spying (Gen 42:7, 30),[30] and his plot to get Benjamin to Egypt—which included imprisonment, lying, and threats—do not play well with most contemporary readers. The text itself is ambiguous as to the intentions of Joseph when he assigns his brothers different tasks and involves them in various trials, and so one needs to infer a possible answer from the narrative as a whole. One plausible reading allows for seeing Joseph's methods as imposing punishment on his siblings. For example, Weeks says: "Given the considerable anguish and humiliation which Joseph inflicts upon his brothers, it is hard to believe that there is no element of punishment present, and this is never denied in the narrative."[31] Joseph's harsh measures may point to at least some level of chastisement on his part.

On the other hand, the positive portrayal of Joseph in the rest of the story, and his own words in Gen 42:16–17, may point to the interpretation that Joseph constructed a test to see whether the brothers would act the same way towards Benjamin as they had acted towards him. Von Rad, for example, sees it this way:

> The sufferings that come upon the brothers are not "fate." They are initiated by Joseph; they are not even punishment, let alone reprisal; they are a test. That is what Joseph says in one of those ambiguous statements that our narrator loves: Therein I will test you (Gen. 42:16). He does not test whether they are spies. He knows that they are not. He tests whether they are the same old brothers or whether perhaps an inner change has occurred in them.[32]

Arnold, similarly, argues that the most plausible scenario is that Joseph wants to see whether his brothers have changed over the years:

> Joseph simply does not trust his brothers. And why should he? Perhaps Benjamin is not standing with them now because they have also sold him into slavery or worse. Perhaps Jacob too is dead. Joseph at first seems

---

30. For the suggestion that the phrase וַיְדַבֵּר אִתָּם קָשׁוֹת in Gen 42:7 (and similarly in 42:30) should be translated "he spoke harsh words to them," and should be connected with Joseph's accusation of spying, see Jean Louis Ska, "Judah, Joseph, and the Reader (Gen 42:6–9 and 44:18–34)," in *Das Alte Testament—Ein Geschichtsbuch?*, ed. Erhard Blum et al. (Münster: LIT, 2005), 29–30.

31. Weeks, *Wisdom*, 94. Gunkel, for example, states bluntly: "Joseph wants to punish his brothers" (Gunkel, *Genesis*, 424). Miscall calls Joseph "a ruthless, arbitrary despot" (Peter D. Miscall, "The Jacob and Joseph Stories as Analogies," *JSOT* 6 [1978]: 28–40, esp. 34). Similarly, replete with psychological insights, Wilcox, *Dream*, 57.

32. Gerhard von Rad, "The Story of Joseph," in *God at Work in Israel*, trans. John H. Marks (Nashville, TN: Abingdon, 1980), 19–35, esp. 30.

merely to stall for more time while he sorts out what he should do. Then he seems intent to ensure that Benjamin and Jacob are not also mistreated by this lot, and wants only to discern whether these ten can be trusted.[33]

Von Rad and Arnold argue that Joseph's long procedure, which is certainly open to various interpretations, could have served two concerns—to see whether the brothers have truly changed and to reveal the fate of those who were dear to Joseph's heart: Benjamin and Jacob. On an existential level it could also testify to the complexities of forgiveness and reconciliation. Such situations are not resolved lightly, and they are not cheap. They require a certain change, which at least on the part of a perpetrator often requires the ability to see things from the perspective of the wronged party.

It should be noted, however, that one cannot be sure about Joseph's attitudes with respect to the trial that he initiated. In the end, the procedure which the brothers undergo impacts also Joseph himself. Even he is caught in the interwoven web of actions that test one's relationship to the chosen. The examination of the effect that these events had on Joseph, however, needs to wait until the next chapter. At this point one needs to look at Jacob's oldest son.

Reuben

Chapter 42 ends up in Canaan, because Jacob refuses to send Benjamin down to Egypt, even if that means Simeon needs to stay in prison. Benjamin's loss would be a blow that would end Jacob's life (Gen 42:38). This prompts another reaction from Reuben. Unfortunately, this is the last occasion of him speaking up in the narrative.

Reuben's first speech in the chapter came when Joseph urged his brothers to bring Benjamin to him and they sensed that this hardship came as a result of their mistreatment of Joseph earlier in the story. Reuben reproached them: "Did I not tell you not to sin against the boy? But you would not listen. So now there comes a reckoning for his blood" (Gen 42:22). His words again betray his personal engagement and feelings of remorse. On the other hand, a comparison with 37:21–22 shows that his recollection seems to blend his intention (to save Joseph) with his actual words to his brothers (to put him into a cistern instead of shedding his blood).[34] Furthermore, Reuben again singles out himself as guiltless or less guilty than his brothers.[35]

---

33. Bill T. Arnold, *Genesis*, NCBC (New York: Cambridge University Press, 2009), 353.

34. With Ebach, *Genesis*, 295–96, and against Gunkel, who emphasizes that Reuben's words in Gen 42:22 are "an approximate citation of 37:22" (Gunkel, *Genesis*, 425).

35. Pirson reasons: "[Reuben] again takes a stance in opposition to his brothers" (Pirson, *Lord*, 79). Similarly also Ackerman, "Joseph," 101.

Reuben's second speech comes towards the end of the chapter, where he offers to let Jacob kill his two sons if he does not bring Benjamin back (Gen 42:37). This passage shows again Reuben's willingness to solve the situation, even if it costs him the lives of his children.[36] This may again be problematic for most readers, but from the point of view of the narrative it appears as both noble and courageous, even though possibly not especially wise. Jacob's own concerns, expressed in the preceding verse (42:36), highlight how much he worries about his children. Furthermore, the subsequent narrative emphasizes that something needs to be done to protect Israel's "little ones" (43:8). In light of this, Reuben's proposal to let Jacob kill his two sons does not seem the most prudent solution to ensure the continuity of life.[37] Nonetheless, one must be careful not to criticize Reuben too harshly. Perhaps, given the happenings in Canaan, Jacob simply needed more time to process the situation and to realize that further action is needed to guarantee the survival of his clan.[38]

Summary

YHWH is with Joseph in Egypt, and through a series of pitfalls, Joseph ends up overseeing the whole of Egypt. It is not clear whether Joseph has actually changed since ch. 37, but the qualities I have discussed stand somewhat in contrast to Joseph's description at the beginning of the narrative, where he is at the center of the family and enjoys the unrivaled favor of his father. Mature Joseph is more capable of submission and is able to use his gift of dreams for others.

Chapter 42 depicts the difficult condition of Jacob's sons in Egypt. The brothers' first journey to Egypt only temporarily solved their problem with grain. The strange command of an unknown Egyptian lord, on the one hand, and the unwillingness of their father to send Benjamin with them, on the other, stalled any progress toward making their life-threatening situation any better. Something needed to change within the family concerning their relationship to a beloved son.

---

36. Gen 42:37 creates the impression that Reuben has only two sons. Genesis 46:9, however, names four.

37. Koepf-Taylor's book argues that the value of children in Ancient Israel was primarily economical, assuring the survival of the community. See Laurel W. Koepf-Taylor, *Give Me Children or I Shall Die: Children and Communal Survival in Biblical Literature* (Minneapolis: Fortress, 2013).

38. Hensel suggests that Jacob might still be mourning the loss of Joseph and hence Reuben's proposal might have been rather cynical (Hensel, *Vertauschung*, 205).

5

Genesis 43–45

Jacob's family in Canaan were in a dire situation. The famine in the land was not letting up and the food, which had been brought from Egypt, was gone (Gen 43:1–2a). It was at that moment that Judah's plan prevailed once again, as he convinced his father Jacob to let Benjamin accompany his brothers on their second journey to Egypt.

Judah Convinces Jacob to Send Benjamin

The lack of food for Jacob's clan prompted his response: "Go again, buy us a little more food" (Gen 43:2b). Jacob's request is surprising. Did he forget that the next trip to Egypt could take place only in the company of Benjamin, whom he did not want to let go? Judah reminds Jacob of this piece of information with a series of persuasive comments. He repeats twice that Joseph warned them: "You will not see my face unless your brother is with you" (43:3, 5),[1] and states that if Jacob sends Benjamin, *their brother*, with them, they will go down and buy food, but if he does not send him, they will not go down (43:4–5). Judah emphasizes their common family tie,[2] and puts the responsibility for the survival of the whole clan into Jacob's hands.[3] Jacob needs to let his beloved son go in order to ensure that his other children and grandchildren will have something to eat.

After the brothers explain to the troubled father that they could not have known that the Egyptian vizier would demand Benjamin's presence (Gen 43:7), Judah recommends the following plan:

> Send the boy with me, and we will arise and go, so that we may live and not die—we and you and our little ones. I myself will be surety for him; you may seek him from my hand. If I do not bring him back to you and set him before your face, then let me bear the blame forever, for if we had not delayed, we would now have returned twice. (Gen 43:8–10)

---

1. Judah's words, repeated by him in Gen 44:23, do not precisely correspond to Joseph's words in Gen 42:15–16, but seems to get to the essence of Joseph's message. For a similar opinion, see Ebach, *Genesis*, 318. For a list of possible views, including the one that Judah might have embellished Joseph's words, see Hamilton, *Genesis: 18–50*, 540.

2. Joseph's request to bring Benjamin ("your youngest brother" in Gen 42:15) may stand behind Judah's reference to "our brother" in Gen 43:4. A rift between Rachel's son and the sons of Jacob's other wives is beginning to heal. See also Ebach, *Genesis*, 317–18.

3. Rashi sums up well the force of Judah's argument: "As for Benjamin it is doubtful whether he will be seized or whether he will not be seized, but as for us, we shall certainly all die of hunger if we do not go" (Rosenbaum and Silbermann, eds., *Rashi: Genesis*, 213).

Judah's suggestion calls for several comments. First, in comparison to Reuben's proposal, Judah's centers on life, specifically on the life of Jacob's descendants, including those most vulnerable and dependent.[4] Not only is Judah more optimistic, focusing on life, not death, but he also does not propose any killing.[5] He is willing to bear the blame forever, but, in line with his aiming at life, he does not propose a death penalty for himself even if he fails to bring Benjamin back. Again, Judah might be less noble than Reuben, but he seems more practical.

Second, although Judah does not show his personal feelings, he is willing to accept responsibility for Benjamin's security, which stands in marked contrast to Judah's earlier attitude toward Joseph in ch. 37. There he attempted to get rid of Joseph, while here he accepts that he will bear the guilt forever if he fails to protect the brother loved more than him.[6]

Third and lastly, Judah stresses the urgency of the situation. It was not necessary to wait so long. They could have been back twice by now, so they should waste no more time. Jacob agrees, and before he falls into his usual lament of self-pity concerning his children, he sends the brothers on their way with an ample supply of gifts for the Egyptian governor (Gen 43:11–14). Judah succeeds again, and, as the narrative relates, from this point on he becomes the leading voice among his unchosen siblings. He has persuaded his father to release his favored son. The beloved one needs to go down to a foreign country and risk his life so that the life of their father's other children, including the little ones, might be saved.

Judah Acknowledges His Guilt

When the brothers arrive in Egypt, they are led into Joseph's house to eat, where they again bow down before him (Gen 43:26, 28). On this occasion Joseph comes close to disclosing his identity, as he inquires of them about Jacob's fate (43:27), and—moved by the sight of his younger brother Benjamin—expresses his affection for him by giving him five times more food than he gives the other brothers (43:34). Nevertheless, Joseph's brothers do not recognize Joseph, which allows him to implement the final part of his test: he orders his steward to put a silver cup into Benjamin's sack (44:2) and to instigate a situation in which his younger brother will be caught with a stolen item among his possessions when leaving Egypt (44:12).

---

4. Wenham stresses that the term ףַט, which often appears in the plural, and which I translate here as "little ones" (Gen 43:8; 45:19; 46:5; 47:12, 24; 50:8, 21), refers to the "dependent and vulnerable younger generation, whom the parents have a particular duty to protect" (Wenham, *Genesis 16–50*, 421).

5. Similarly Ackerman, "Joseph," 103.

6. Hensel considers Judah's emphasis on brotherhood an important element in his portrayal (Hensel, *Vertauschung*, 244–45).

When the text mentions that it was "Judah with his brothers" (Gen 44:14)[7] who were brought to Joseph and fell before him with their faces to the ground, this signals that Judah is now to be viewed as the leader of the whole group. This is confirmed when it is he who responds to Joseph's accusation. Interestingly, Judah speaks for the group as a whole when he acknowledges that "God has found out the guilt" of the brothers, and offers that they all become Joseph's servants (44:16). This behavior suggests a change of attitude in Judah. For one thing, he does not try to justify their actions or to blame Benjamin, but is true to his word and attempts to protect Benjamin by suggesting that they should all be made Joseph's servants. In contrast to his behavior in ch. 37, he does not allow the more loved son of his father to go to slavery, but instead he is willing to accept that fate for himself and his siblings. Additionally, he does not shy away from acknowledging their guilt, which recalls the brothers' earlier admission of their past wrongdoing (42:21), but which is in stark contrast to Reuben's words of accusation in 42:22. Judah does not blame: he accepts their guilt and yet tries to protect Benjamin.

Since it is clear to the reader that the brothers are not guilty of stealing Joseph's cup, one is compelled to think of a different crime that the brothers committed. The iniquity of selling Joseph into slavery immediately springs to mind. It was Judah who had then proposed selling Joseph into Egypt, and it is Judah who now confesses their guilt. In both situations the brothers appear to follow him, thus adding to the impression that Judah is the primary unfavored character in the Joseph cycle.

Judah Accepts the Special Bond between the Father and His Chosen Son

Joseph, however, does not accept Judah's proposal, and wants to enslave only Benjamin. This leads to Judah's lengthy speech (Gen 44:18–34), which is, in fact, the longest speech in the narrative and in all of Genesis.[8] It is not only a masterful example of persuasive verbal communication, structured and delivered so as to achieve its purpose, but it is also a demonstration of Judah's changed attitude both towards his father and towards Jacob's beloved son. Judah first places himself in a low position, calling himself, his brothers, and even his father "your servant/s" (e.g. 44:18, 21, 27), and Joseph "a lord" who is equal to Pharaoh himself (44:18). Then he proceeds to explain to the Egyptian vizier the special relationship that exists between Judah's father and Benjamin.

---

7. Genesis 44:14 highlights Judah's role by using the verb "come" in the singular form: וַיָּבֹא יְהוּדָה וְאֶחָיו.

8. Thus argues Westermann, *Genesis 37–50*, 134.

The word "father" appears fourteen times in the speech,[9] which indicates its significance for Judah's argument. Judah is worried about his father's wellbeing, mentioning several times that Jacob might die if Benjamin does not return (Gen 44:22, 29, 31). He has personally guaranteed Benjamin's safe return to his father in Canaan and offered himself as surety for him, and so now needs to persuade the foreign lord to let this youngest of Israel's sons go home. Judah also recognizes something that might still be eluding Joseph—that the special bond between the chosen son and his father should not be broken. Otherwise it could endanger the father's life. Judah refers to Jacob's special love towards Benjamin in a way that highlights the unique bond between them over and above Israel's relationship with his other sons. Judah says, "and his father loves him" (44:20); and a little later, "The boy cannot leave his father or his father will die" (44:22), and reports Jacob's insensitive words that his wife bore him only two sons (44:27).[10] Towards the end of this powerful speech Judah describes their father's life as being "bound up with the boy's life" (44:30).

Although both Jacob's special love for Rachel's children and the disastrous effect Joseph's disappearance had on him were quite obvious to his children (Gen 37:34–35; 42:38), Judah's acceptance of this bond may be more subtle to discern, yet the repetition of this concept in the chapter may further our understanding. Judah has somehow learned that protecting this special relationship between father and the chosen son is to the benefit of the whole family. The attempt to get rid of the favored one did not help the situation, as none of the unfavored brothers was elevated to this privileged position, and so now Judah is ready to accept his unfavored status and do whatever he can to save the chosen son and thus also protect the father. Alter's words point out eloquently this change in Judah's attitude in comparison with his stance in ch. 37:

> It is a painful reality of favoritism with which Judah, in contrast to the earlier jealousy over Joseph, is here reconciled, out of filial duty and more, out of filial love. His entire speech is motivated by the deepest empathy for his father, by a real understanding of what it means for the old man's very life to be bound up with that of the lad. He can even bring himself to quote sympathetically (verse 27) Jacob's typically extravagant statement that his wife bore him two sons—as though Leah were not also his wife and the other ten were not also his sons. Twenty-two years earlier, Judah

---

9. Noted in Wilson, *Joseph*, 113.

10. This might be a reference to Jacob's words in Gen 42:38, where he truly speaks like he had only two sons. Alter's comments on this verse are helpful: "The extravagant insensitivity of Jacob's paternal favoritism continues to be breathtaking. He speaks of Benjamin as 'my son' almost as though the ones he is addressing were not his sons" (Robert Alter, *Genesis: Translation and Commentary* [New York: Norton, 1996], 251).

engineered the selling of Joseph into slavery; now he is prepared to offer himself as a slave so that the other son of Rachel can be set free. Twenty-two years earlier, he stood with his brothers and silently watched when the bloodied tunic they had brought to Jacob sent their father into a fit of anguish; now he is willing to do anything in order not to have to see his father suffer that way again.[11]

Alter remarks that Judah is now "willing to do anything" to protect Benjamin for the sake of his father. This "anything" includes offering himself as a substitute for Benjamin (Gen 44:33) and going into slavery, which symbol-izes death in the story.[12] Judah is willing to assume Benjamin's place in order to save the lives of his brother and his father, even if it might cost him his.[13] That Judah is able to do this to protect his younger sibling is extraordinary.[14] The unfavored brother has reached a point where he is able to take a punishment for a brother privileged by their father, and this moment becomes a turning point in the narrative.

Judah Contributes to Joseph's Unmasking and the Family's Reconciliation

When Judah reaches the point in his speech where he repeats that enslaving Benjamin might endanger Jacob's life (Gen 44:34), Joseph cannot control himself any longer. Judah's willingness to suffer for his preferred brother, and his eloquent speech, thus significantly contributed to Joseph's unmask-ing.[15] He sends everyone else away and then, alone in the presence of his siblings, weeps for the third time (45:1–2).[16] On two previous occasions (42:24; 43:30) he was able to control himself, but this time, the Egyptian court and Pharaoh himself hear his emotional outburst, even though he orders everyone to leave his presence. Furthermore, Joseph's willingness to weep in front of the members of his family continues throughout the narrative (45:14; 46:29; 50:1, 17) and thus seems to play an important role

---

11. Alter, *Art*, 175.

12. Harris's article emphasizes the contrast between death and life in Judah's speech. See J. S. Randolph Harris, "Genesis 44:18–34," *Int* 52 (1998): 178–81.

13. Westermann reminds us that "[h]ere, at the climax and turning point of the Joseph story, the Bible speaks for the first time of vicarious suffering" (Westermann, *Genesis 37–50*, 137).

14. See Meir Sternberg, *The Poetics of Biblical Narrative: Ideological Literature and the Drama of Reading* (Bloomington: Indiana University Press, 1985), 308.

15. O'Brien's article stresses that Judah's speech was a crucial element in Joseph's will-ingness to reveal his true identity to his brothers. See Mark A. O'Brien, "The Contribution of Judah's Speech, Genesis 44:18–34, to the Characterization of Joseph," *CBQ* 59 (1997): 429–47. Similarly also Ska, "Judah," 34.

16. An intriguing comparison between instances of weeping in the Joseph cycle and in the *Odyssey,* based on attachment theory, can be found in David A. Bosworth, "Weeping in Recognition Scenes in Genesis and *Odyssey*," *CBQ* 77 (2015): 619–39.

in the reconciliation of the brothers. Ebach, for example, suggests that Joseph's self-control is connected with his control over his brothers.[17] If this is the case, then it is possible that a capacity to come to terms with emotions connected to the past pain seems to be a significant element in one's ability to cope with previous hurts. Joseph is defenseless and more vulnerable, which seems to feature positively in his dealing with those who have previously harmed him.

Only after Joseph weeps does he reveal his true identity to his stunned brothers: "I am Joseph" (Gen 45:3, 4). There are two aspects to this confession. First, when Joseph finally utters his name, he immediately connects it with the question of whether his father is still alive (45:3), which is subsequently developed in his eagerness to bring Jacob and the rest of his family down to Egypt as soon as possible. Joseph, in cooperation with Pharaoh, will allow them to settle in the best portion of the Egyptian land (45:9–11, 17–18), and escape the tragic consequences of the continuing famine. Second, Joseph affirms his identity more specifically with the statement "the one you sold to Egypt" (45:4)—not to reproach them for their past wrongful action but to explain its deeper meaning for the future. The brothers need not be distressed, because it was God all along who was sending Joseph ahead in order to preserve the lives of the Israelites (45:5, 7).[18]

The revelation of Joseph's identity has overarching consequences. On the one hand, what did not happen between Cain and Abel, and what was only partially accomplished between Jacob and Esau when the latter welcomed his deceiving younger brother with some benevolence (Gen 33:1–17), achieves fuller shape here. The emotional and private moment between the long-estranged brothers shows that reconciliation has begun to take place. On the other hand, however, there are yet signs of a continuing rift between Rachel's sons and the sons of Jacob's other wives. After Joseph points to the divine ordering of events (45:4–13), he embraces Benjamin and weeps, and Benjamin does the same in return (45:14). When he kisses his other brothers, however, and weeps over them, they only "talk with him" (45:15). This might express that the response of these brothers lacked the reciprocity appropriate to their renewed relationship, but on the other hand it might also testify to the reversal in their

---

17. See Ebach, *Genesis*, 384–86. On the issue of Joseph's emotional development, consider Fred Guyette, "Joseph's Emotional Development," *JBQ* 32 (2004): 181–88. Joseph's vulnerability is explored in David Zucker, "Seize the Moment," *JBQ* 37 (2009): 197–99.

18. Jacobs employs the concepts of good and evil for his examination of the Joseph narrative and argues that "good" in the Joseph story is defined as the preservation of life. See Mignon R. Jacobs, "The Conceptual Dynamics of Good and Evil in the Joseph Story: An Exegetical and Hermeneutical Inquiry," *JSOT* 27 (2003): 309–38, esp. 317.

attitude from 37:4.[19] Additionally, it seems that the fundamental difference between Joseph's relationship with Benjamin and his relationship
with the rest of his brothers prevails. Benjamin receives money and five
sets of clothes, as compared to only one set of new clothing for each of the
remaining brothers (45:22).

The continued difference between Joseph's relationship with Benjamin,
and that with his other brothers, as well as Joseph's concern that they might
quarrel on the road (Gen 45:24), point to at least two suggestions. First,
reconciliation is not fully achieved at this stage of the narrative, which is
in line with the way the story has been told so far. It is a prolonged tale in
which the main features of the story require time to play out in detail. And
of course, no major split in interpersonal relationships heals in a moment.
The narrative thus portrays forgiveness and reconciliation in a realistic way,
occurring in stages and needing time to reach completeness.[20] Second, the
unequalness of Joseph's behavior towards his brothers shows that reconciliation within Jacob's family does not level all differences. Quite the contrary,
chosenness continues to play a vital part in the life of Jacob's clan and of
Israel as a whole, becoming the prime vehicle through which God achieves
his purposes for his people.

Summary

To conclude this chapter, I will summarize the most important lessons
learned concerning the role of Judah in the story. The story never explains
why Judah succeeds and Reuben does not, but Gen 43 shows that Judah
focuses on saving the life of Israel's children, and acts with both responsibility and urgency. When he and his brothers go to Egypt the second time,
Jacob's family is close to death. Surprisingly, it is the unchosen Judah who
alters the family's future and brings life out of death, precisely because
he is willing to risk his own life. He values the bond between Jacob and
his beloved Benjamin, and hence offers himself in substitution for the
brother more loved than himself. In addition to this, Judah's wise and
persuasive words show Joseph that he is, in effect, now doing the very
same thing his brothers did to him. Joseph might have brought his father
down to Sheol in sorrow by his plan to enslave Benjamin. Judah's speech
thus prompted Joseph to reveal himself to his brothers and moved the
whole family towards reconciliation. Judah represents a kind of climax in
the line of unchosen brothers in the book of Genesis. He is instrumental

---

19. For the first position, see Kaminsky, *Jacob*, 71, for the latter, see Coats, *Canaan*, 47;
and White, "Joseph," 58.

20. Wilcox takes this position, stressing that a fuller reconciliation could be realized
only at the end of the Joseph story: Wilcox, *Dream*, ix, 57, 71. Schimmel arrives at a similar
conclusion from a more psychological angle: Sol Schimmel, "Joseph and His Brothers: A
Paradigm for Repentance," *Judaism* 37 (1988): 60–65, esp. 64–65.

in effecting a fuller reconciliation than that which occurred between Esau and Jacob, and accomplishes something that Cain failed to do—be his brother's keeper (4:9).[21]

---

21. See Reno, *Genesis*, 281. Similarly also P. J. Berlyn, "His Brother's Keeper," *JBQ* 26 (1998): 73–83, esp. 83. Alternatively, Joseph's ability to provide for the brothers during the famine could indicate that he might be seen as his brothers' keeper. Thus, for example, Matthew R. Schlimm, *From Fratricide to Forgiveness: The Language and Ethics of Anger in Genesis*, Siphrut 7 (Winona Lake, IN: Eisenbrauns, 2011), 267–82, esp. 281.

6

Genesis 46–48 and 50

The final section of the Joseph narrative, as it appears in my hypothetical version of the text without chs. 38 and 49, is found in Gen 46–48 and 50. This segment centers on the transition of Jacob's clan into Egypt and the events surrounding the deaths of the patriarch and his beloved son. I will focus on the important events of this segment directly relating to Joseph or Judah, and especially on Jacob's blessing to Joseph's two sons.

Jacob's Family Settles in Egypt

Chapter 46 opens up with themes that seem to come from a different literary context.[1] Israel offers sacrifices to the God of his father Isaac and God assures him of his presence in visions of the night. YHWH will go with Jacob down to Egypt where he will become a great nation,[2] but will also bring them up again to Canaan (Gen 46:1–4). Encouraged by the promise of God's continuing presence, and that it would be his beloved son Joseph who would close Jacob's eyes (46:4), Jacob embarks on the journey to Egypt together with all his offspring.[3] Judah retains his important place within the group of Jacob's sons not born to Rachel, as it is he who is sent ahead to prepare the journey to Goshen (46:28).[4] The one who notably

---

1. This instance of directly hearing the voice of God, unusual in the Joseph narrative, seems to connect the tale of Jacob and his sons both with the earlier patriarchal stories and with Israel's later slavery in Egypt. See Wenham, *Genesis 16–50*, 440.

2. The phrase גּוֹי גָּדוֹל in Gen 46:3 is the same as in Gen 12:2, where the promise to become a "great nation" is announced to Abraham. See, for example, Jamie Viands, *I Will Surely Multiply Your Offspring: An Old Testament Theology of the Blessing of Progeny with Special Attention to the Later Prophets* (Eugene, OR: Wipf & Stock, 2013), 56.

3. The totality of Jacob's family is underscored both by the repeated reference to "all of his offspring" (כָּל־זַרְעוֹ) who journey to Egypt (Gen 46:6, 7), and by the round number "seventy" (see also Exod 1:5 and Deut 10:22). The concluding remarks in Gen 46:26–27 make a distinction between those who moved to Egypt (66 persons) and the final number of the Israelites there (70), but it is unclear who is counted and who is left out. Von Rad suggests that the list originally included all male descendants, but that the narrator recognized that Joseph and his two sons were born in Egypt, and that Er and Onan died in Canaan. Therefore the number "seventy" could be calculated by adding Joseph and his two sons, Jacob, and Dinah to the final count (von Rad, *Genesis*, 402–3).

4. The verb signifying Judah's task in Gen 46:28 is the Hiphil infinitive construct from ירה ("teach," or "instruct"), but without a direct object, which is unusual. The NRSV

contributed to Joseph's self-revealing is trusted to lead the way towards a family reunion.

Besides this brief remark about Judah, however, the narrative remains focused upon Jacob and his favorite sons. Benjamin and Joseph are again introduced in the list of Jacob's offspring as "the sons of Jacob's wife Rachel" (Gen 46:19), which emphasizes Jacob's special relationship to his beloved wife. Furthermore, Benjamin's tribe is depicted as the most fruitful one (46:21).[5] Joseph welcomes his father to Goshen and then, based on his advice, Israel secures a habitation in the area considered to be the best portion of the land (47:6, 11)—presumably made possible because it was pasture land and shepherding was an "abomination" for the Egyptians (46:34). The transition of the whole clan to Egypt then enables Joseph to provide for them during the most severe years of the famine (47:12).

Joseph Enslaves the Egyptians

Israel's settlement in Egypt seemed to change, at least from the narrative point of view, the dynamics between the Egyptians and Israel's family. It is Jacob who blesses Pharaoh (Gen 47:7, 10),[6] which seems to indicate that elderly Jacob is a more important person than the head of the most powerful empire of that time. More significantly, however, the growing difficulties caused by the famine resulted in Joseph's selling grain to the Egyptians— first for money (47:14), then for their livestock (47:17), and then for their service and land (47:19–26). Pharaoh thus gained control over the land— with the exception of the land of the priests—reaping one-fifth of the people's harvest (47:26).[7] Joseph's agrarian policy may be evaluated from various angles,[8] but perhaps the most fruitful way in terms of my study is

---

translates: "to lead the way before him into Goshen." The LXX uses here συναντῆσαι αὐτῷ, which means "to meet him [Joseph]." For a good discussion of this problem, see Westermann, *Genesis 37–50*, 162; or John W. Wevers, *Notes on the Greek Text of Genesis*, SBLSCS 35 (Atlanta: Scholars Press, 1993), 787.

5. However, the reference to Benjamin's sons is problematic on several levels. It is unlikely that Benjamin, who is described as only a "boy" in the narrative (e.g. Gen 44:22), could be at the same time a father of ten sons (Gen 46:21). Moreover, a comparison with Benjamin's genealogy in Num 26:38–40 and 1 Chr 8:1–5 reveals that the list in Gen 46:21 likely counts Benjamin's grandsons as his children. Consult also Ebach, *Genesis*, 453–54.

6. McKenzie's article argues that Jacob's blessing of Pharaoh finds its fulfillment in Joseph's agrarian policy. See Brian A. McKenzie, "Jacob's Blessing on Pharaoh: An Interpretation of Gen 46:31–47:26," *WTJ* 45 (1983): 386–99.

7. The passage in Gen 47:13–26 is often considered an interpolation serving an etiological purpose. The law concerning a fifth of the produce being given to Pharaoh was valid "to this day" (Gen 47:26). See, for example, Westermann, *Genesis 37–50*, 173; and Gunkel, *Genesis*, 442.

8. Joseph's administration might be, of course, evaluated negatively. Lerner, for example, suggests that Joseph treated the Egyptians harshly because he was too absorbed in trying to achieve the most for Pharaoh (Berel Dov Lerner, "Joseph the Unrighteous,"

to note the contrast between the enslavement of the suffering Egyptians and Israel's ability to acquire the best region in the land.[9] Whereas the Egyptians spent all their money (47:14) and traded all their livestock (47:17), Joseph's family had the money they used to pay for the grain returned (42:25), and they not only brought to Egypt all their animals (46:6), but also remained shepherds during their sojourn there (46:32; 47:6).[10] In short, while the Egyptians suffered and had to sell their land (47:19), Israel was able to acquire land in Goshen, where they "were fruitful and multiplied" (47:27). This phrase both echoes the primeval blessing given to humankind,[11] and shows how Israel's wider family, through Joseph's help, retains its separate identity, and despite difficult circumstances thrives in the land where they settle.[12] Joseph's position as an Egyptian vizier thus secures Israel's future.[13]

Jacob's Last Wishes and His Death

Genesis 47:28 begins the last section of the Joseph narrative, concerned with the death of Jacob and his beloved son Joseph.[14] The most significant

---

Judaism 38 [1989]: 278–81). Fung notes that Joseph continues the favoritism in the story and privileges his own family over the Egyptians (Fung, *Victim*, 38). Wildavsky views Joseph as acting towards the Egyptians contrary to moral law (Aaron Wildavsky, "Survival Must Not Be Gained through Sin: The Moral of the Joseph Stories Prefigured through Judah and Tamar," *JSOT* 62 [1994]: 37–48). On the other hand, it should be noted that Joseph enslaved the people in response to their own proposal (47:19) and the Egyptians viewed this action as saving their lives (47:25). In this regard, see, for example, von Rad, *Genesis*, 410–11. It may be noteworthy to point out that Joseph saved both groups who exclaimed that they wanted to "live, not die" (וְנִחְיֶה וְלֹא נָמוּת, 42:2; 47:19), but that his treatment of his own family was preferential.

9. Thus Weimar, who also sees Jacob's blessing of Pharaoh and the enslavement of the Egyptians as highlighting the contrast between the fates of the Egyptians and Israel under Joseph's rule: Peter Weimar, "Gen 47, 13–26—ein irritierender Abschnitt im Rahmen der Josefsgeschichte," in *Auf dem Weg zur Endgestalt von Genesis bis II Regum: Festschrift Hans-Christoph Schmitt zum 65. Geburtstag*, ed. Ulrike Schorn and Martin Beck, BZAW 370 (Berlin: de Gruyter, 2006), 125–38.

10. See Brian O. Sigmon, "Shadowing Jacob's Journey: Gen 47:13–26 as a Sideshadow," *BibInt* 19 (2011): 454–69.

11. Genesis 1:28 presents this divine speech to the humans: "God blessed (ברך) them, and God said to them: 'Be fruitful (פרה) and multiply (רבה) and fill the earth.'" Genesis 47:27 mentions Israel's possession of the land, where they were fruitful (פרה) and multiplied (רבה), which was preceded by Jacob's blessing (ברך) of Pharaoh (Gen 47:7, 10).

12. Egypt thus could be seen as a new promised land for Jacob's family, as expressed in Dany Nocquet, "L'Égypte, une autre terre de salut? Une lecture de Gn 45, 1–46, 7," *ETR* 84 (2009): 461–80.

13. Although one may also argue that Joseph's enslavement of the Egyptians was reversed later on, as the book of Exodus recounts.

14. Although the opening phrase in Gen 48:1, "it happened after these things," might be viewed as marking a new beginning in the narrative (thus, for example, Wenham, *Genesis 16–50*, 449), both Gen 47:28–31 and 48:1–22 are structured around the theme of Jacob's approaching death, and thus they belong together. For this conclusion, see, for

passage concerns Jacob's last wishes before his death, where Joseph's special status vis-à-vis his brothers is highlighted. For this reason, it will be thoroughly examined.

Jacob Asks Joseph to Bury Him in Canaan (Genesis 47:29–31)

Jacob is 147 years old and so, in preparation for his death, he calls for Joseph, in order to request that he be buried with his ancestors in Canaan (Gen 47:28–30). His words and gestures towards Joseph are full of unusual respect. First, he makes this request: "If I have found favor in your eyes, put your hand under my thigh and promise to deal kindly and loyally with me. Do not bury me in Egypt" (47:29).[15] The phrase "If I have found favor in your eyes" (אִם־נָא מָצָאתִי חֵן בְּעֵינֶיךָ) is often used in a context when an inferior asks somebody in a superior position for an act of kindness,[16] even though the biblical text includes cases where the situation may be evaluated differently.[17] Nevertheless, it is uncommon to find a father addressing his son with such words. Although Jacob's reverent attitude likely results from his strong wish to be buried in Canaan,[18] the fulfillment of which solely depends on Joseph's will and abilities,[19] this plea highlights Joseph's significant role after Jacob's death.

Second, after Joseph swears that he will take his father's body and bury him in Canaan, Jacob performs an interesting action. The Hebrew text, which famously puzzles interpreters, contains this description: וַיִּשְׁתַּחוּ יִשְׂרָאֵל עַל־רֹאשׁ הַמִּטָּה. The NRSV, which closely follows the Hebrew text here, translates: "Then Israel bowed himself on the head of his bed" (Gen 47:31).

---

example, Horst Seebass, "The Joseph Story, Genesis 48 and the Canonical Process," *JSOT* 35 (1986): 29–43, esp. 30.

15. Jacob's request that Joseph put a hand under his thigh reflects Abraham's wish in Gen 24:2, where he asked his servant to do the same before the latter's journey to find a suitable wife for Isaac. This ritual, where the person asked to fulfill a wish likely touches the patriarch's genitals, is clouded in mystery, but in both cases it concerns the desire of an aging patriarch related to the land promised by God, and family matters. Thus also Hamilton, *Genesis: 18–50*, 139; and Meir Malul, "More on *pachad yitschāq* (Genesis 31:42, 53) and the Oath by the Thigh," *VT* 35 (1985): 192–200, esp. 197–98. For a possibility that touching one's genitals evokes the deity, see R. David Freedman, "'Put Your Hand under My Thigh'—Patriarchal Oath," *BAR* 2 (1976): 3–4, 42.

16. Thus *TWOT* 694a. In the immediate proximity of the passage under investigation consider Gen 47:25.

17. Hamilton mentions that besides the present verse there are two other examples in the Old Testament where a person in a superior position asks for favor from the inferior: in the cases of David and Jonathan (1 Sam 20:3), and David and Nabal (1 Sam 25:8) (Hamilton, *Genesis: 18–50*, 621, n. 4). Nevertheless, it is unclear whether these situations truly present cases where the superior addresses the inferior. David is a fugitive there, and not yet a king.

18. Similarly Westermann, *Genesis 37–50*, 183.

19. This is similar to Jacob's entreaty of Esau—in that case persons of equal status— where we also find the above-mentioned phrase. Jacob expects a hostile reaction from Esau, and therefore he sends ahead gifts to ensure Esau's kind welcome (Gen 33:8, 10).

There are several different ways that one may explain the meaning of this gesture. For example, Westermann, who takes his inspiration from a similar movement performed by David on his deathbed in 1 Kgs 1:47–48, views Jacob here as bowing down to God.[20] Other interpreters see in Jacob's gesture an act of gratitude without a clear recipient.[21] Yet another possibility is that the act of bowing down is not an expression of worship or gratitude but the picture of an aging Jacob bending down toward the head of his bed.[22] In any case, in all these interpretations either the object of Jacob's prostration is God, or it is an unidentified act of gratitude or a mere sign of tiredness and old age.

Nevertheless, Jacob's action might also be interpreted differently, namely as a prostration to Joseph. This is the position taken by Raymond de Hoop in his article dealing with Gen 47:31.[23] He points out that in 1 Kgs 1:47 an aging David asks for favor from God and then bows to God, while here Jacob asks for favor from Joseph.[24] Further, he uses the Peshitta and the LXX to show that Joseph himself might be the object of Jacob's reverence. The Greek text, "and Israel bowed to the top of his staff" (καὶ προσεκύνησεν Ισραηλ ἐπὶ τὸ ἄκρον τῆς ῥάβδου αὐτοῦ), shows that the consonants of the Hebrew word at the end of the clause might be vocalized either as הַמִּטָּה ("bed"), which is how it is understood by the MT, or as הַמַּטֶּה ("staff"), which is reflected in the LXX.[25] This latter possibility—coupled with the observation that the verb "bow down," for example, in 2 Sam 16:4, is used in connection with the phrase "find favor in one's eyes"—supports in de Hoop's view the conclusion that it is Joseph who is the object of his father's reverence.[26]

---

20. Westermann, *Genesis 37–50*, 183–84. Similarly also John Skinner, *A Critical and Exegetical Commentary on Genesis*, 2nd ed., ICC (Edinburgh: T&T Clark, 1930), 503; and Ruppert, *Josephserzählung*, 168.

21. See von Rad, *Genesis*, 414; Bruce Vawter, *On Genesis: A New Reading* (New York: Doubleday, 1977), 451; and Ephraim V. Speiser, *Genesis*, AB 1 (New York: Doubleday, 1964), 357.

22. Thus Wevers, *Genesis*, 806; and Arnold, *Genesis*, 372.

23. Raymond de Hoop, "'Then Israel Bowed Himself . . .' (Genesis 47.31)," *JSOT* 28 (2004): 467–80. De Hoop develops van der Merwe's suggestion that Gen 47:29–48:22, at least, depicts Joseph as Jacob's successor. See B. J. van der Merwe, "Joseph as Successor of Jacob," in *Studia Biblica et Semitica: Theodoro Christiano Vriezen qui Munere Professoris Theologiae per XXV Annos Functus est, ab Amicis, Collegis, Discipulis Dedicata*, ed. W. C. van Unnik and A. S. van der Woude (Wageningen: H. Veenman & Zonen, 1966), 221–32.

24. De Hoop, "Israel," 470.

25. De Hoop, "Israel," 468–69. The Greek translation's rendering found its way into the New Testament's letter to the Hebrews where we read: καὶ προσεκύνησεν ἐπὶ τὸ ἄκρον τῆς ῥάβδου αὐτοῦ, "and he bowed down to the top of his staff" (Heb 11:21).

26. De Hoop, "Israel," 471. 2 Sam 16:4b reads: "And Ziba said: 'I bow down; may I find favor in your eyes, my lord the king'." De Hoop's argument is further strengthened by the view expressed in *TDOT* that "find favor in one's eyes" "[is] not uncommonly accompanied by bowing and prostration," citing Gen 33:3, 6, 7; 2 Sam 14:22; 16:4; Ruth 2:10; Ps 31:10 [ET 31:9] as examples. See David N. Freedman et al., "חָנַן," *TDOT* 5:22–36, esp. 27.

Since the Hebrew word מַטֶּה could mean either a "staff" or a "tribe,"[27] de Hoop concludes that Jacob "bowed down to the head of the tribe," indicating thus that Joseph may be seen here as the new *pater familias*.[28]

De Hoop's proposal is not without its difficulties,[29] but presents a plausible interpretation of this difficult verse, useful especially here where my attempt is to read the Joseph narrative without chs. 38 and 49.[30] Jacob strongly wishes to be buried in Canaan, and for this reason he approaches Joseph. Joseph's position as the vizier in Egypt makes him a more appropriate figure than Jacob's other sons to deal successfully with his father's wish. Moreover, Jacob's special love for Joseph might also be in view here. After all, it is Joseph who was mentioned earlier in the narrative in connection with the patriarch's death, as Jacob wished to "go down to Sheol" (e.g. Gen 37:35) to mourn his son's sudden disappearance. Both sons of Rachel were closely linked with their father's life, and so it seems understandable that it is long-lost Joseph who will be called on to fulfill his father's last desire. Finally, however, Joseph's special position with regard to the future—as somebody who will become Jacob's successor—might also be in view here, especially when this brief episode of 47:29–31 is read together with Jacob's blessing upon Ephraim and Manasseh.

The Blessing of the Progeny and the Land (Genesis 48:1–7)

Genesis 48 begins with the report of Jacob's illness or weakness, which was partially overcome by news of Joseph's arrival, where Israel "strengthened himself and sat upon his bed" (48:2).[31] The opening verses of the chapter thus present the picture of a distance between the father and his beloved son—each of whom needs to be told about the other's doings[32]—and of Jacob's illness, which is temporarily surmounted by Joseph's appearance at his father's bedside together with his two sons, Manasseh and Ephraim.[33]

---

27. See, for example, *HALOT* 1:573.

28. De Hoop, "Israel," 473–74.

29. Probably the most significant difficulty lies in the observation that the continuation of the story also portrays Jacob on the bed (Gen 48:2) and that the verb חוה in Hishtaphel is usually accompanied by לְ, and not by עַל when it expresses the notion "bow down to" (see *HALOT* 1:295–96, esp. 296).

30. Joseph's position in the final form of the text, which also concerns de Hoop, "Israel," 475–79, must be left for a later part of my study.

31. The reference to Jacob sitting upon his bed may recall his father's posture when he conferred upon Jacob his blessing (Gen 27:19). See also Joshua Berman, "*Mishneh bereshit*: The Form and Content of Genesis 48," *Tradition* 25 (1990): 28–41, esp. 28–29.

32. The distance between Joseph and Jacob during Israel's settlement in Egypt is elaborated upon in Jeffrey M. Cohen, "Joseph under Suspicion," *JBQ* 29 (2001): 186–89.

33. Manasseh and Ephraim are mentioned in this order only at the beginning of the chapter (Gen 48:1). This sequence is reflected, for example, in Num 26:28–37.

Both main protagonists thus take the initial steps towards what is, as the further narrative will show, the key issue of Gen 48:1–22, namely, the blessing.[34]

Jacob first recounts the blessing that he received from God Almighty in Canaan, when he promised him fruitfulness and a land to be acquired for his descendants (Gen 48:3–4).[35] Given the tenor of the preceding narrative, focusing on Joseph, one would naturally expect that this favored son will be the promised and blessed descendant here, but the story quickly turns its attention to Ephraim and Manasseh, born in Egypt (they are mentioned by Jacob in this order, anticipating perhaps the reversal of the primogeniture later in the narrative), as they are adopted or legitimated by Jacob as his own sons in v. 5.[36] They are to be counted as Jacob's own sons, similar to Reuben and Simeon, while their brothers born after them will be Joseph's (Gen 48:5–6).[37] The reference to Reuben and Simeon in the present text seems to indicate that the aging patriarch wants to give Ephraim and Manasseh the first and second places in the hierarchy of his sons, which is in congruence with 1 Chr 5:1–2 where Joseph's sons are described as receiving Reuben's birthright.[38]

---

34. The verb ברך occurs seven times in the chapter (Gen 48:3, 9, 12, 15, 16, 20 [×2]). Ruppert reasons that ch. 48 has three main goals: the adoption of Joseph's sons, preeminence of Ephraim, and allocation of Shechem (Ruppert, *Josephserzählung*, 165). My examination follows approximately this outline.

35. The reference here is probably to Gen 35:11–12, but it does not make any use of "kings who would come from his body" (35:11). However, it is also possible that Jacob echoes several blessings he has received on his journey. For example, Berman argues that the original blessing given in 28:3–4 is the closer parallel (Berman, "Mishneh," 29–31).

36. Westermann proposes that the inclusion of Ephraim and Manasseh by Jacob should be viewed as legitimation (Westermann, *Genesis 37–50*, 185), Sarna sees it as adoption (Sarna, *Genesis*, 325). Regardless of what label we give it, the act established that Ephraim and Manasseh will be counted as Jacob's full heirs.

37. The Bible is silent about any other sons of Joseph, which seems to indicate that Joseph, after his first two sons were adopted by his father, remained childless. This is emphasized by Raymond de Hoop, *Genesis 49 in Its Literary and Historical Context*, OtSt 29 (Leiden: Brill, 1999), 338. Nachmanides, on the other hand, proposes that the Scripture's silence is less indicative than Jacob's prophetic insight here; Joseph will have more children because the aging patriarch foresees it. Nachmanides, *Commentary on the Torah: Genesis*, trans. C. Chavel (New York: Shilo, 1999), 576.

38. The section of Gen 48:1–7 finishes with a seemingly marginal note on Rachel. Jacob recalls that his beloved wife and the mother of Joseph died on the way to Ephrata and was buried there (48:7). This verse, possibly an insertion in the text (thus Vawter, *Genesis*, 452), can be viewed as connected with the surrounding narrative in at least two ways. First, Rachel died young, and the impossibility of her bearing more children may be rectified by Jacob, for whom her death was a terrible loss, in the adoption of Manasseh and Ephraim (see, e.g., Sarna, *Genesis*, 326). Second, Rachel's death and burial, as well as the blessing, which Jacob is about to bestow on his newly adopted sons, are associated with the land of Canaan (see, e.g., Nachmanides, *Genesis*, 573).

The Preeminence of Ephraim (Genesis 48:8–20)

The story now continues with an unusual piece of text in which Jacob expresses his puzzlement concerning Joseph's two sons: "When Israel saw Joseph's sons, he said, 'Who are these?'" (Gen 48:8). Not only had Manasseh and Ephraim just arrived together with Joseph (48:1), but they were, a moment before, the subject of Jacob's speech in 48:5–6, and so Jacob's question about their identity naturally puzzles the reader. One possible way to make sense of this anomaly is to take the comment made shortly afterward in 48:10, about Jacob's failing sight, and use it as a possible explanation for the surprising need to reintroduce Joseph's sons to the aging patriarch in 48:8.[39] In the flow of the narrative, this comment likely prepares the reader for the reversal of the blessing, which occurs several verses later (though the allusion to Jacob's near blindness also reminds us of a similar condition that Jacob's father Isaac suffered, mentioned in 27:1, at the outset of the pericope in which Isaac unwittingly blesses Jacob instead of Esau).[40] Nevertheless, as an interpretative strategy the reference to Jacob's failing sight can be used retrospectively to explain why Joseph had to introduce his sons to his father: Jacob was perhaps not aware of the arrival of Manasseh and Ephraim or he did not recognize them even though he was making reference to them when speaking of their adoption.

Joseph responds to his father's desire to bless his sons with three simple acts (Gen 48:12–13). First, he removes his sons from his father's knees (48:12a).[41] The Hebrew word used for a "knee" (בֶּרֶךְ) creates a possible wordplay on the verb "bless" (ברך), which might indicate that being seated on Jacob's knees in some way prepares the boys to receive Jacob's

---

39. Another possible solution is to suggest that the passage in Gen 48:8–10 comes from an earlier stage in the narrative, perhaps soon after Jacob moved to Egypt, when Joseph possibly introduced to his father his two sons, born to him during his sojourn in Egypt (see von Rad, *Genesis*, 415). Another possibility is to follow the LXX rendering of this question (τίνες σοι οὗτοι, "Who are these *to you*?"), which might indicate that Jacob does not ask about the identity of the two boys but rather he is seeking after their relationship towards Joseph (see Sarna, *Genesis*, 325). Alternatively, it is also plausible to suggest that the inconsistency in Jacob's character may be due to his aged mind (thus Kaminsky in a personal communication).

40. The echo of Isaac's blessing of the younger son is developed in Karin Schöpflin, "Jakob segnet seinen Sohn: Genesis 49,1–28 im Kontext von Josefs- und Vätergeschichte," *ZAW* 115 (2003): 501–23, esp. 516.

41. It should be noted that the Hebrew text is ambiguous here. It says: "and Joseph brought them out from his knees" (וַיּוֹצֵא יוֹסֵף אֹתָם מֵעִם בִּרְכָּיו). Although the third person suffix attached to the noun "knees" in a sentence where Joseph is the subject would more naturally point to the image of Joseph lifting the boys from his own knees, the wider context seems to favor Jacob as the person having Ephraim and Manasseh on his knees.

blessing.[42] It is also interesting that verbal parallels can be found between this piece of text and other instances in which newborn babies are placed on the knees of the person who regards them as his or her own.[43] The blessing, adoption, and the emphasis of the continuation of the patriarchal line are thus all connected here.

Second, Joseph bows down to Jacob (48:12b), which complements Jacob's prostration in 47:31, possibly before Joseph, and likely shows Joseph's reverence to his father and gratitude for the blessing of his sons that is about to follow. On the one hand, this gesture might somewhat complicate the straightforward meaning of Joseph's dreams in ch. 37. It was Joseph's family who were projected to bow down before Joseph, not vice versa. On the other hand, however, Joseph's journey through Potiphar's house, the prison, and the Egyptian court have demonstrated that the favored one needs to learn a certain sort of submission in order to be blessed. The actions of the mature Joseph appear to fulfill the dreams in a way that is life-giving, because they respect the authorities given into his life.

Third, Joseph positions his older son closest to Jacob's right hand—the suitable place, it would seem, for receiving the greater blessing (48:13).[44] But the reaction of the old patriarch shows that not only was his inner sight stronger than his physical sight, but also that he did not need Ephraim on his right side in order to bestow on him greater blessing: Israel crosses his hands (Gen 48:14), and pronounces the following blessing:[45]

---

42. The image of the boys sitting on their grandfather's knees suggests that presumably they are very young, which does not fit with the overall chronology of the narrative, according to which Manasseh and Ephraim should now be over seventeen years old (Gen 47:28; 48:5). This is one of several puzzling instances in Genesis where grown-up children are presented by the narrative as babies or small children (see, e.g., 21:14).

43. Most notably Rachel spoke in this way about Bilha's future son, who would be placed upon her knees right after his birth (Gen 30:3). Note also a similar phrase describing a possible act of adoption of Manasseh's grandsons by Joseph: "the children of Machir son of Manasseh were also born on Joseph's knees" (Gen 50:23).

44. The importance of the "right hand," for example, is echoed in the parable of the sheep and the goats in Matthew's Gospel (Matt 25:31–46), where the sheep, the righteous ones, are positioned on the right hand of the Son of Man, symbolizing their status as inheritors of the promised kingdom (Matt 25:33–34). See also the place of honor on the right hand in Ps 110:1.

45. The blessing is prefaced with the following words: "And he [Jacob] blessed Joseph" (Gen 48:15a). The LXX, which contains the translation "and he blessed them" seems to be harmonizing the blessing's introduction with its content and its two recipients (thus, for example, Wevers, *Genesis*, 815; and Westermann, *Genesis 37–50*, 189). The MT text, however, seems to alternate between Joseph and his sons (see also Gen 48:20), which might indicate that Joseph is blessed with and through his sons. For this emphasis, see also Ebach, *Genesis*, 551.

The God before whom my fathers Abraham and Isaac walked,
the God who has been my shepherd[46] all my life to this day,
the angel who has redeemed me from all evil,
may he bless the boys;
and in them may my name be called,
and the name of my fathers, Abraham and Isaac;
and may they grow into a multitude in the midst of the earth. (Gen
48:15–16)

In these two verses the tripartite reference to the provider and deliverer of
Jacob's life is matched by the tripartite request for the future of the boys.
The blessing of God the Shepherd focuses on the perpetuation of the names
of the three main patriarchs into the future, and also concerns the fruitfulness of the boys. The image evokes the importance and perhaps even
supremacy of Joseph's two sons over against their uncles, with Ephraim
playing an even greater role than his older brother.

Joseph's attempt to reverse his father's blessing that privileged the
younger Ephraim over the older Manasseh is not effective (Gen 48:17–19).
If for a while Joseph thought that Jacob was redeemed from all evil except
for this one[47]—the misguided act of skipping the older son in the final
blessing—he was quickly reminded that the poorly seeing father in fact saw
something of greater importance, which Joseph did not yet comprehend. "I
know, my son, I know," says Jacob calmly (48:19), and the double reassur-
ance, if taken in the literary context of the whole book of Genesis, signals
that the preeminence of the younger sibling was not a mistake in the case
of Joseph's sons, just as it was not in the earlier stories of Genesis.

Although the precise interpretation of the difference between the two
sons is difficult to specify, the preeminence of Ephraim over Manasseh
seems to be one of degree: Ephraim will be greater and his seed will
become a group of nations (Gen 48:19).[48] As in the case of Esau, who also
tried hard to rectify his father's blessing (27:37–38), the present blessing

---

46. The image of shepherding brings back Joseph's task in Gen 37:2. It might also be
closely tied to the idea of walking before God and following God as it is explored in Pierre
van Hecke, "Shepherds and Linguists: A Cognitive-Linguistic Approach to the Metaphor
'God is Shepherd' in Gen 48,15 and Context," in *Studies in the Book of Genesis: Literature,
Redaction and History*, ed. André Wénin, BETL 155 (Leuven: Peeters, 2001), 479–93.

47. Verse 17 says that the act of the crossing of Jacob's hands, which gave Ephraim
preeminence, was "evil in Joseph's eyes" (וַיֵּרַע בְּעֵינָיו). The use of the verb רעע resonates
with the previous verse where Jacob mentions that the angel redeemed him from all evil
(מִכָּל־רָע).

48. The specific difference, as spelled out in Gen 48:19, is between Manasseh's ability
to become a "people" (עַם), and Ephraim's capacity to become a "group of nations" (מְלֹא־
הַגּוֹיִם). Something of this distinction can be observed in the numerical difference referenced
in Deut 33:17. For a creative handling of a similar distinction—that between Abraham and
Ishmael in Gen 17:4–6 and 17:20—see Noble, *Place*, 73–78.

is not reversible, as both Jacob's additional blessing and the narrator's comment demonstrate: "And he blessed them on that day saying: 'In you [singular] Israel will invoke blessing saying: May God make you like Ephraim and Manasseh.' So he put Ephraim ahead of Manasseh" (48:20). This verse not only continues the tension between plurality and singularity in Jacob's blessing, but also reverberates with echoes of the blessing conferred upon Abraham in 12:3.[49] The Abrahamic blessing is thus carried into the future through the house of Joseph. Joseph's sons, and especially Ephraim, will become important peoples who will be acknowledged as such by Israel.[50]

The important section Gen 48:8–20, where the blessings upon Ephraim and Manasseh form the centerpiece of the whole unit, focuses on the continuation of the promised, chosen line which began with Abraham and Isaac, and brings to the fore once again the theme of election. While it is true that both boys are blessed, the placement of Jacob's right hand on Ephraim's head acquires for him a more significant blessing, resulting in a greater stature and greater fruitfulness than that of Manasseh. The favoring of the younger son seems to be a part of a larger purpose for the people of Israel.[51] In addition to the privileging of Ephraim, Joseph seems also to be included in the blessing of his two sons, as the narrative frequently switches between Jacob's act of blessing directed toward Joseph and that directed toward his two sons.

The Allotment of Shechem (Genesis 48:21–22)

The final portion of ch. 48 contains encouraging words to Joseph. He is assured that God will visit him and bring him to the land of his ancestors (Gen 48:21). Joseph is also given a special inheritance that seems to mark him off vis-à-vis his brothers (48:22). Apart from the factual problem consisting in the supposition that Jacob wants to give to Joseph a place situated in Canaan while he sojourns in Egypt—and thus his rights to Shechem and his ability to deal with this piece of property are called into

---

49. The phrase "in you (sg.) will Israel invoke blessing" (בְּךָ יְבָרֵךְ יִשְׂרָאֵל) in Gen 48:20 resembles Gen 12:3, "and in you (sg.) all the families of the earth will be blessed" (וְנִבְרְכוּ בְךָ כֹּל מִשְׁפְּחֹת הָאֲדָמָה). Thus Rosenbaum and Silbermann, eds., *Rashi: Genesis*, 49; and also Berman, "Mishneh," 37.

50. Of course, Gen 12:3 has been often interpreted differently, hinting at the universality of salvation through Abraham's seed (see Paul's appropriation in Gal 3:6–9; or von Rad's proposal in von Rad, *Genesis*, 152–54). For an alternative construal, stressing that God's blessing might be given for Abraham's sake, see Moberly, *Genesis*, 141–61.

51. Sternberg, who highlights the tension between the failing physical sight and the clear inner vision of Jacob, says in a similar vein: "Acting in the spirit of the divine logic of election manifested in the past, the blind patriarch shows an insight into the future denied to his clear-sighted (and occasionally clairvoyant) but for once earthbound son" (Sternberg, *Poetics*, 353).

question[52]—the actual meaning of the verse is ambiguous. The MT says here: וַאֲנִי נָתַתִּי לְךָ שְׁכֶם אַחַד עַל־אַחֶיךָ אֲשֶׁר לָקַחְתִּי מִיַּד הָאֱמֹרִי בְּחַרְבִּי וּבְקַשְׁתִּי. There are two main possibilities as to how it can be understood.[53]

The first suggestion understands the reference to שְׁכֶם as an allusion to the ancient town of Shechem, which figures both in the book of Genesis in general and in the Joseph cycle in particular (e.g. Gen 12:6–7; 33:18–20; 34:1–31; 37:12–15).[54] The NAB captures this meaning when it reads: "As for me, I give to you, as to the one above his brothers, Shechem, which I captured from the Amorites with my sword and bow." Given the importance of Shechem in early and later Israelite history and the fact that it was the place where Joseph was buried (Josh 24:32), there is a good case for taking the word as an indication of the geographical area. However, Jacob's comment that he captured the place from the Amorites with his sword and bow does not fit the description given earlier in the book of Genesis and repeated later in Joshua, where we read that Jacob purchased the plot of ground for a "hundred pieces of silver" (Gen 33:19; Josh 24:32).[55] A major setback for this theory, however, lies in the fact that the text does not contain the word Shechem in isolation, but in combination with אֶחָד. Read together, then, the text speaks of "one Shechem."

The second possibility is to take שְׁכֶם as a reference to a "mountain range" and thus by extension signifying an additional portion of the land given to Joseph. Here one can take the word אֶחָד either as an indication of Joseph's special role vis-à-vis his brothers (as translated, for example, by the NIV: "And to you, as one who is over your brothers, I give the ridge of land"), or it can be understood in connection with the word "Shechem" (as expressed in the NRSV: "I now give you one portion more than to your

---

52. Speiser captures well the difficulty the verse presents when he states: "V.22, in particular, not only presupposes a version of the capture of Shechem different from any found elsewhere, but it is out of harmony with the situation in which the words are assumed to have been uttered. For it is scarcely credible that Jacob should have referred thus to a conquest which he had subsequently lost, and which would have to be recovered by force of arms before the bequest could take effect" (Speiser, *Genesis*, 507).

53. Another possibility is proposed by Alter who—making use of the same phrase used in Zeph 3:9—suggests to interpret it figuratively as "one accord" (Alter, *Genesis*, 291). However, Zeph 3:9 emphasizes that the peoples will serve YHWH with one accord, whereas in Gen 48:22 the subject is only Jacob, which makes the use of the same idiom more unlikely. Second, even though the presence of an unmarked object in the sentence is possible, one would more naturally expect the object of "what I took from the hand of the Amorites" to be introduced by אֶת אֲשֶׁר.

54. Note also the importance of Shechem at the time of the establishment of the Northern Kingdom (1 Kgs 12:1–19, 25).

55. See, for example, von Rad, *Genesis*, 419. Nevertheless, it is possible to argue that if Jacob acted as the ruler of the Israelite clan, then it is plausible that he viewed the actions of his sons/people as his own actions. See John Calvin, *Commentary on Genesis*, trans. John King, 2 vols. (Grand Rapids: Baker, 1996), 2:324.

brothers"), which is suggested by the use of the conjunctive accent marks in the *BHS*.[56] This meaning fits well with the episode in Josh 17:14–18, where the tribe of Joseph receives one additional lot (גּוֹרָל אֶחָד) or portion (חֶבֶל אֶחָד) of the hill country because it is too numerous. In relation to Ephraim and Manasseh, this latter meaning might also indicate that the extension of Jacob's blessing beyond Joseph to his two sons exemplifies a double portion, which is otherwise kept for the firstborn (Deut 21:15–17).[57] The obvious problem with this (otherwise compelling) theory is that the metaphorical meaning of שְׁכֶם is, as recognized by Westermann himself,[58] only found here in the Old Testament.

In my opinion, these two main possibilities do not need to be seen as mutually exclusive. Joseph is promised a portion of the land associated with the hill country around Shechem, which privileges him against his brothers. As Jacob wants to be buried in Canaan, where his dear wife passed away and is laid to rest, there will also be a place for Joseph. The continued persistence of the theme of the chosen line in the promised land seems to be confirmed by v. 22: Joseph's chosen status may continue on indefinitely, and this seems to be secured by granting Joseph an additional portion of the Cannanite land, reflecting the numerousness of Joseph's descendants.

Jacob's and Joseph's Death

Jacob's Death and Funeral

Our experimental version of the text then continues with Jacob's charge to bury him with his ancestors in the field at Machpelah, near Mamre, in Canaan (Gen 49:29–32). When Jacob finished giving this command to his sons,[59] he breathed his last and was gathered to his people (49:33). Genesis 50:1–14 goes on to describe the events leading up to Jacob's funeral. Joseph is deeply touched by his father's death. He weeps again and then gives orders to prepare his father's body in an Egyptian fashion

---

56. The LXX emphasizes the special nature of the land given to Joseph. It says: ἐγὼ δὲ δίδωμί σοι Σικιμα ἐξαίρετον ὑπὲρ τοὺς ἀδελφούς, "and I give you Sicima, a special portion beyond that of your brothers." See Wevers, *Genesis*, 819.

57. This interpretation is in accordance with Merwe, "Joseph," 226.

58. See Westermann, *Genesis 37–50*, 192

59. I acknowledge that the section Gen 49:29–33 does not fit seamlessly into the text without Jacob's last testament in 49:1–28. While the clause "Then he charged them, saying to them" in 49:29 could be addressed to Joseph and his two sons (following perhaps the plural in 48:20), this is harder to imagine in Gen 49:33: "When Jacob finished his charge to his sons." Here the text seems to presuppose the presence of Jacob's sons. One can easily conjecture redactional activity here. Generally speaking, I follow Westermann's argument for including the segment 49:28b–33 in the last section of Gen 37–50 (Westermann, *Genesis 37–50*, 195–97).

for burial (50:1–3).[60] With Pharaoh's approval a large procession of Egyptian dignitaries joins Joseph and his brothers on the journey to Canaan, where—with much lamentation and mourning—they bury Joseph's father in the grave he had chosen.

The funeral bears all the marks of Egyptian custom, as was recognized even by the Canaanites observing it (Gen 50:11). On the one hand, this further confirms Joseph's thoroughly Egyptian identity. On the other, however, the largeness and pomp of the funeral, together with the lengthy period of the lamentation, point to the importance of Jacob as a person both for Joseph's family and for Egypt as a whole.[61] Someone greater than Pharaoh has died here and the whole land remembers his passing.

It should also be noted that it is Joseph who takes a lead in organizing Jacob's funeral. Joseph went up to bury his father (Gen 50:7), while his brothers joined him (50:8). The whole company held "a very great and sorrowful lamentation," while Joseph "observed a time for mourning for his father seven days" (50:10). Further, the emphasis on *his* father, *his* brothers, and all who had gone up with *him* points to Joseph's important role in administering Jacob's last wish (50:14). While on one level it is the task of all siblings to bury their father, on the other level it is Joseph who has greater responsibility in the whole affair. Joseph is the only brother (besides his children) mentioned by name beyond ch. 48 and he also acts as the new head of the family by playing a large part in organizing his father's funeral, and in assuring his distressed brothers about his loyalty. Jacob's death and funeral confirm Joseph's special status.

Further Reconciliation within the Family

The fatherly figure of Jacob played an indispensable role both in Judah's speech in Gen 44:18–34 and in Joseph's unmasking sometime later. Jacob's close bond to his favorite sons was the source of Judah's willingness to risk his life, as well as the occasion for Joseph's revealing his identity. His first words were: "I am Joseph. Is my father still living?" (45:3). It is natural, therefore, now when the father is no longer alive,[62] that the brothers begin to fear that the powerful Joseph might act toward them with revenge.

---

60. Berman argues that the way Joseph organizes Jacob's funeral and the surrounding arrangements takes a middle ground between Jacob's request and an Egyptian cultural norm. See Joshua Berman, "Identity Politics and the Burial of Jacob (Genesis 50:1–14)," *CBQ* 68 (2006): 11–31, esp. 22.

61. Gen 50:3 says that the Egyptians mourned for Jacob for seventy days. This is an extraordinary long period of lamentation, compared to only thirty days of mourning for Aaron and Moses (Num 20:29; Deut 34:8). See, for example, Ebach, *Genesis*, 646.

62. Naumann's work stresses Jacob's importance in the Joseph narrative: Thomas Naumann, "Der Vater in der biblischen Joseferzählung: Möglichkeiten einer Charaktermodellierung in biblischen Erzählungen," *TZ* 61 (2005): 44–64.

The brothers thus send a message to Joseph in what is portrayed as Jacob's words:[63] "Thus you will say to Joseph: 'I beg you, forgive the offense of your brothers and the sin they did in harming you. Now please forgive the offense of the servants of the God of your father'" (Gen 50:17). When Joseph hears this message, he weeps. Afterwards the brothers themselves appear before Joseph,[64] fall on their faces and say: "We are your slaves" (50:18). The brothers' request and their encounter here with Joseph bring back several themes from chs. 44–45. Not only does Joseph weep again (as also in 45:2, 14), but a cluster of words occurring here (50:18) that also occur in 44:14–16—"they fell before his face" (וַיִּפְּלוּ לְפָנָיו), "here we are" (הִנֶּנּוּ), and "servants" (עֲבָדִים)[65]—make it evident that the brothers continue to struggle with guilt, and therefore are willing to present themselves as Joseph's servants. The brothers' prostration before Joseph, even though it does not contain the same term חוה in Hishtaphel as in ch. 37 (see 37:7, 9, 10), also recalls Joseph's dreams. Here one can find the fulfillment of the narrative device that set the story in motion.[66] Joseph's brothers reflect on their guilt, bow down before their younger sibling, and are willing to serve him.

Yet Joseph does not accept their servantship, refusing to exercise dominion over them. He sees himself as subservient to God (Gen 50:19), and his power not as a means to rule over his siblings but as God's way of providing for them in a time of crisis. He is able to perceive God's hand even in his brothers' merciless act towards him, an act which eventually resulted in much good for many (50:20). He does not speak harshly to his brothers any more (42:7) but reassures and comforts them (50:21), which further rectifies the hostile relationship which began in 37:4.[67]

---

63. If the message really comes from Jacob himself, then he at this point already knew about his sons' involvement in selling Joseph into slavery. The text itself does not answer this question. I lean towards the opinion that the message is fabricated (similarly Hamilton, *Genesis: 18–50*, 703); however, there are authors who think otherwise (see, e.g., Lowenthal, *Joseph*, 151–55).

64. The MT has וַיֵּלְכוּ ("and they went"). The textual apparatus of the *BHS* proposes that it could be וַיִּבְכּוּ ("and they wept"), which is followed in the NRSV, because it likely understands the brothers to be already in Joseph's presence.

65. To these exact parallels one may add also a thematic link between "guilt" (עָוֹן) in Gen 44:16, and "offense" (פֶּשַׁע) and "sin" (חַטָּאת) in Gen 50:17. For all these references, see Ebach, *Genesis*, 657.

66. Although Schmid, for example, in his compositional study argues for the strong structural coherence of Gen 37–45, he nevertheless acknowledges that this unit of text does not offer a sufficient resolution of the tension introduced in ch. 37. This is in the canonical version of the story concluded only in Gen 46–50. See Konrad Schmid, "Die Josephsgeschichte im Pentateuch," in *Abschied vom Jahwisten: Die Komposition des Hexateuch in der jüngsten Diskussion*, ed. Jan Christian Gertz et al., BZAW 315 (Berlin: de Gruyter, 2002), 83–118, esp. 95–106.

67. For this comparison, see Kenneth A. Matthews, *Genesis 11:27–50:26*, NAC 1B (Nashville: Broadman & Holman, 2005), 923.

The scene presents a final denouement of the drama of brotherly rivalry in the Joseph cycle. Even though the unfavored brothers shield themselves behind the authority of their father, nevertheless they in some sense acknowledge their guilt and come to ask for forgiveness. In contrast to ch. 44, where Judah spoke for all the brothers and admitted their wrong to the Egyptian vizier, here the brothers act together and approach Joseph as their brother. Moreover, while in ch. 44 the confession was related to the fabricated robbery of Joseph's silver cup, here it concerns a real offense that the brothers had committed. This recognition brings further reconciliation within the family. The brothers are prepared to live differently than when the story presented them the first time.[68]

Nonetheless, Joseph's words in Gen 50:19–21 show that even he has changed. He will not usurp a position that belongs rightfully only to God—which might have led to crude dominance and retaliation—but instead responds to his brothers in an attitude of service and provision. His dreams at the outset of the story are thus interpreted in a life-enhancing way at the story's end.[69]

Joseph's Death

The remainder of the Joseph narrative describes the events leading to Joseph's death. He, together with Jacob's family, remains in Egypt and is able to see his children and their children, down to the fourth generation (Gen 50:22–23), thus exemplifying the image of the blessed man who fears God (Job 42:16–17; Ps 128:6). His last wish continues the trajectory begun with the patriarchs: he wants to be brought out of Egypt and buried in the land promised to his ancestors by YHWH (Gen 50:24–25).[70] His future burial in Canaan, however, is only anticipated here. Joseph dies at the age of 110, and his body is placed in a coffin in Egypt (Gen 50:26), thus preparing for the continuation of Israel's story in the book of Exodus.

---

68. Kaminsky helpfully notes: "Reconciliation does not necessarily entail full erasure of the past or newly perfected characters. Rather, it involves a commitment to live the relationship differently than one did in the past" (Kaminsky, *Jacob*, 72).

69. Similarly Döhling, who stresses that the dreams are fulfilled through the actions of the narrative's heroes (Döhling, "Herrschaft," 30).

70. When God visits the Israelites, Joseph says, and brings them out (עלה) of Egypt (Gen 50:24), they should also bring out (עלה) Joseph's bones (Gen 50:25). Israel's fate is bound with that of Joseph. Further, Ebach helpfully summarizes this tendency to seek one's final resting place in the land of Canaan this way: "Man kann in Ägypten überleben und auch leben—auch für längere Zeit—doch das Israelland (auf der Ebene der erzählten Zeit: Kanaan) bleibt Heimat und soll Israel wieder zur Heimat werden" (Ebach, *Genesis*, 694).

Summary

Chapters 46–47 describe Israel's transition to Egypt and their settlement and prosperity thereof despite the continuous famine and the bitter ordeal that the impoverished Egyptians have to endure. The important ch. 48 then highlights Joseph's uniqueness.[71] He appears to be approached by Jacob with special reverence. His two sons are adopted by his father, thereby gaining the positions of the first- and second-born instead of Reuben and Simeon. Ephraim is privileged above his brother, which continues the important theme of chosenness in the book of Genesis. Finally, Joseph is given a specific portion of the Canaanite land, which further sets him apart from his siblings. The emphasis upon the future fruitfulness of Ephraim and Manasseh and the special place of Joseph among his brothers both seem to point towards a future leadership role for Joseph's clans within Israel. This seems to be confirmed in Joseph's instrumental role in Jacob's burial and in the forgiveness that he offered to his brothers in spite of their former crime against him. When this is connected with Joseph's dreams in ch. 37, which in some sense predicted Joseph's capacity to rule over his brothers, one is led to imagine that Ephraim, Joseph's more favored son, will be the tribe which will give Israel its future king.[72]

---

71. For a similar conclusion, highlighting the role of Joseph in ch. 48, see, for example, Schöpflin, "Jakob," 511.

72. Within the framework of the Old Testament the connection between Joseph and kingship is most evident in the establishment of northern Israel under Jeroboam who is from Ephraim (1 Kgs 11:26) and who makes Shechem his base (1 Kgs 12:25). For the connection between ch. 48 and northern Israel, see also Ebach, *Genesis*, 526. However, see also Leuchter's argument that Jeroboam might be presented as a Davidic king in Mark Leuchter, "Jeroboam the Ephratite," *JBL* 125 (2006): 51–72. Nevertheless, Jeroboam is clearly associated with the Northern Kingdom.

7

Genesis:
Evaluation of the Experimental
Reading

In the next chapter I will summarize the main ideas from the preceding study that concern the persons of Joseph and Judah in the Joseph cycle when read without chs. 38 and 49. I will give particular attention to those features of the text that might illuminate the concept of election.

Joseph

Favored

When the narrative is read without chs. 38 and 49, Joseph, the firstborn son of Rachel, is the main hero of the tale comprising the last portion of Genesis. He is the favored son of his father and the one chosen by God for the special task of saving his family and the wider world from famine. This is evident in the story from beginning to end. In ch. 37, Jacob shows his special love for his son by making him a unique garment, and towards the end of the narrative favors his sons with a special blessing. The bulk of the narrative is occupied with Joseph's descents into various "pits" and his unexpected rise to the top of the Egyptian hierarchy. Joseph's agrarian strategy plays a key role in helping to overcome this famine, both in Egypt and for his family. The transition of Jacob's clan to Egypt secures their survival and even prosperity.

The dreams are the backbone of the narrative. From the outset they hint at Joseph's prominent place within the family, and—given the image of Joseph ruling over the others (37:8)—possibly within the future Israel. Joseph is rather sarcastically called by his siblings a "master of dreams" (37:19), yet his gift of interpreting other people's dreams and suggesting a wise course of action becomes one of Joseph's most important assets, eventually contributing to his success. In the end, not only the Egyptians (41:43) but also his own brothers (44:14; 50:18) bow before Joseph, and this, eventually, is done voluntarily and with full acknowledgment that the person to whom they are paying such respect is their younger, and (at first) possibly immature, brother. The development of the story implies that the dreams are not to be taken woodenly, but rather that they need to be interpreted in a way that reflects God's character: with grace, wisdom, and maturity.

Leader

Joseph has the leadership position among his brothers. At the outset, it is not evident how the dreams prefiguring Joseph's position of authority might come true, but the remainder of the story portrays how Joseph moves into a place of power and responsibility, and what this position entails. Joseph might be judged at times as too harsh or strict, especially when making his brothers the subjects of a prolonged trial, or when enslaving the Egyptians. But he may also be viewed as wise when saving the people from famine, and generous when dealing with his own family. Finally, Jacob's blessing upon Ephraim and Manasseh suggests that Joseph's house might play a leadership role even in the future Israel. A future king might well be expected to come from Joseph's house.

Development

Joseph's forgiving and life-giving attitude towards the brothers who once attempted to kill him might be contrasted to his perhaps boastful telling of the dreams in ch. 37. At the end of the story one encounters a Joseph who is likely different from the one we first saw in his father's house in Canaan. The mature Joseph seems to have changed. One aspect worth noticing is his willingness to be submissive to the authorities in his life, be it Potiphar, the jailor, Pharaoh, or even the deity. At the end of the story, he does not use his position to dominate—at least not his own family (the approach towards the Egyptians might be evaluated differently)—but to serve and to save many lives with his influence and his means.[1] Another important character trait that the story reveals is Joseph's openness to his own feelings and vulnerability. His weeping goes hand in hand with his soft approach toward those who have hurt him in the past. These may be important qualities that the favored one needs to learn in order to use his favor and leadership position with an attitude towards others that strengthens life and does not diminish it.[2] As Levenson points out, the story of Joseph is a story of legitimation of the favor of God (among other things).[3] The progression of the story demonstrates that God's favor comes to a person who puts it to right use.

Unfavored Judah

As compared to Joseph, Judah is very much the opposite. At the beginning of the story he is there as one of the unfavored brothers, then gets his chance to influence the course of action when the brothers contemplate

---

1. Levenson also emphasizes the notion of service in Joseph's story (Levenson, *Death*, 168–69). Similarly also Kaminsky, *Jacob*, 69.

2. I have further developed these themes as viewed within the framework of one's vocation and purpose in Josef Sykora, "The Mission that Transforms: A Development of Joseph's Character in Genesis 37–50," *CTR* 4 (2015): 11–18.

3. Levenson, *Death*, 167–68.

dispossessing Joseph. Judah's most important moment comes when he promises to protect Benjamin on the second journey down to Egypt, culminating in a moving and masterful speech that eventually changes almost everything within the family. After this episode, however, Judah recedes again into obscurity. The end of the tale describes the group of brothers (none of them mentioned by name), acting in unison and being submissive to Joseph. Judah remains an unfavored character throughout.

Nevertheless, Judah is the most significant brother among those not born to Rachel. On two occasions—in which he competes, so to say, with Reuben—he exemplifies practical thinking and an orientation towards the future. Although the narrative is silent as to the reasons why Judah's proposals eventually prevail, these moments lead to his becoming the spokesman for his brothers. His speech in ch. 44 is the high point of his role. Judah here shows that he respects the unique bond between their father and his beloved son Benjamin, accepts his own unfavored status, and is willing to risk his life for the brother loved more than him.[4] This brave act contributes to Joseph's revealing his identity, and, when compared with the other rivalry stories in the book of Genesis, demonstrates well the set of challenges that an unchosen person faces. Judah becomes the main unfavored person not only in the Joseph story, but possibly one of the main unchosen characters in the whole book of Genesis—both Esau and Judah in different ways have mastered the beast of unchosenness (Gen 4:7).[5]

Summary

Joseph is the chosen character, and Judah is the main unfavored person, when Gen 37–50 is read without its intrusive chapters. However, one must ask how different their appraisals would be if one were to read the narrative not only with ch. 38, where Judah is at his lowest, but also with ch. 49, where he is given a blessing comparable to that of Joseph. For this reason, I will first suggest an interpretation of the tale centering on Judah and Tamar in ch. 38. Then I will turn to Gen 49, paying close attention to the blessing given to Judah and Joseph. These two steps will aid me in offering an interpretation of the canonical text that will highlight the difference between the two readings.

---

4. Similarly Kaminsky, *Jacob*, 68.
5. For an analogous perspective, see Anderson, *Doctrine*, 82.

8

Genesis 38

The beginning of Gen 38,[1] a chapter which has occupied interpreters down the centuries,[2] depicts Judah on a similar journey as that undertaken by Joseph: he goes down (ירד), away from his brothers (38:1). This, together with the phrase "at the time" (38:1), may be taken as suggestive that the story of Judah, which interjects the narrative at this point, might be read alongside Joseph's journey.

Judah's Downward Journey

Nevertheless, contrary to Joseph's overall upright stature in ch. 39, this beginning of Judah's little tale bears certain not-so-positive marks concerning his character and actions.[3] First, his connection with Hirah is introduced by the verb נטה (Gen 38:1). Although the verb likely signifies the movement of turning aside[4] or settling down[5] near his Adullamite friend, its double occurrence in the chapter (38:1, 16)—always preceding dubious sexual activity on Judah's part—might evoke the image of turning aside from the proper path. Second, Judah marries a woman from Canaan, which is an action, at least according to the preceding narratives, that does not have the approval of the patriarchs (24:3–4; 28:1–2). The sons of Abraham should

---

1. There is an abundance of secondary literature on Gen 38. A helpful list of recent works can be found in Ebach, *Genesis*, 117–19.

2. Valuable books focusing on the history of interpretation of Gen 38 are: Esther Marie Menn, *Judah and Tamar (Genesis 38) in Ancient Jewish Exegesis: Studies in Literary Form and Hermeneutics*, JSJSup 51 (Leiden: Brill, 1997); Peter Weimar, *Die doppelte Thamar: Thomas Mann's Novelle als Kommentar der Thamarerzählung des Genesisbuchs*, BthSt 99 (Neukirchen-Vluyn: Neukirchener, 2008); Esther Blachman, *The Transformation of Tamar (Genesis 38) in the History of Jewish Interpretation*, CBET 71 (Leuven: Peeters, 2013).

3. Judah's description in the chapter is not overtly negative. Menn, for example, says: "As a rule, the negative evaluation of Judah in Gen 38 appears in the subtle form of ironic understatement and implication" (Menn, *Judah*, 36).

4. *HALOT* 1:693 indicates that when the verb נטה describes motion, it could mean "turn aside" (see, e.g., Num 20:17; 21:22), which might also be understood metaphorically (as in 2 Sam 19:15 [ET 19:14]), where it is used in connection with the human heart). For von Rad this "turning aside" is related to Judah's intermarriage with the Canaanites (von Rad, *Genesis*, 357).

5. The verb נטה is often used in Genesis in connection with the noun אֹהֶל ("tent"), meaning "pitch a tent" (see, e.g., Gen 12:8; 26:25; 33:19; 35:21). Therefore Westermann takes Gen 38:1 as the abbreviated version of the same action (Westermann, *Genesis 37–50*, 51) and the NRSV translates the sentence: "and [he] settled near a certain Adullamite."

find women within the circle of their relatives. However, one should also note that Joseph as well marries a foreign woman (41:45), and so this piece of information provides yet another link with the story of Joseph. Third, the narrative hints that Judah's attitude towards his wife and family may not be the most intimate one. The text says that when Judah "saw there (וַיַּרְא־שָׁם) a daughter of a certain Canaanite whose name was Shua, he took her and went in to her (וַיָּבֹא אֵלֶיהָ)" (38:2). The woman is not named and the description of their union is rather abrupt, stressing the sexual aspect based merely on Judah's seeing the woman, an element functioning also in his sexual encounter with Tamar later on.[6] Finally, the short narrative describing the succession of three sons born from the union between Judah and the daughter of Shua might be read as indicating an increasing distance between the two. When the first son is born, Judah gives him a name (38:3). The second son, however, is named by Judah's wife (38:4). The third son is also named by her, and the MT (וְהָיָה בִכְזִיב בְּלִדְתָּהּ אֹתוֹ) might be read: "he was in Chezib when she bore him" (38:5).[7] Although these are minor indicators,[8] they may suggest a growing estrangement between Judah and his family.[9]

Even if the opening verses of ch. 38 may not suggest that the establishing of Judah's own family has negative overtones, the real trouble begins when Judah's firstborn Er marries Tamar (Gen 38:6), likely another Canaanite woman.[10] Both Er and later Onan, who marries Tamar according to the levirate law (Deut 25:5–6),[11] did what YHWH considered evil and

---

6. Gen 38:15 says: "When Judah saw her" (וַיִּרְאֶהָ יְהוּדָה), and Gen 38:18 describes that later Judah "went in to her" (וַיָּבֹא אֵלֶיהָ).

7. It could also be an impersonal construction "it was in Chezib." The NRSV translates here: "She was in Chezib when she bore him," which partly follows the LXX: αὐτὴ δὲ ἦν ἐν Χασβι ἡνίκα ἔτεκεν αὐτούς ("She was in Chezib when she bore them").

8. Emerton looks at the textual complexities involved in vv. 3–5, in Emerton, "Problems," 339–41.

9. Spina argues along similar lines: Spina, *Faith*, 39–41.

10. The narrative never mentions whether Tamar is a Canaanite, but given Judah's place of settlement, her non-Israelite origin seems likely. See Westermann, *Genesis 37–50*, 51; Gunkel, *Genesis*, 397; or more fully John A. Emerton, "Examination of a Recent Structuralist Interpretation of Genesis 38," *VT* 26 (1976): 79–98, esp. 90–93.

11. The levirate law concerns the situation where a married man dies without a son, in which case it was the duty of a brother or other near relative to marry the widow. Their son would then be reckoned as the son of the first husband. The pentateuchal reference can be found in Deut 25:5–10 and an example of this practice in Ruth 4:1–10. Ruth also includes the recollection of Tamar (Ruth 4:12) as well as the genealogy beginning with Perez and concluding with David (Ruth 4:18–21). The intertextuality between Ruth and Tamar is the subject of a study by E. J. van Wolde, "Texts in Dialogue with Texts: Intertextuality in the Ruth and Tamar Narratives," *BibInt* 5 (1997): 1–28. For a study that argues that a later development of the levirate law allowed for the living brother to refuse conceiving an heir for his deceased sibling, see Dvora E. Weisberg, "The Widow of Our Discontent," *JSOT* 28 (2004): 403–29.

therefore they died (Gen 38:7, 10). The cause of their death is explained to
the reader, but remains hidden to the characters in the narrative: they are
killed by YHWH. The reference here to "YHWH" is unique in the Joseph
cycle, as is the use of God's covenantal name in Gen 39,[12] and may frame
the story in a similar way: YHWH is active even during Judah's detour
to Canaan, even though YHWH's presence is made manifest in the most
horrific way—in the terrible death of Judah's first two sons.[13] Judah's story
thus bears further resemblance to Joseph's journey. Both are separated from
their father and go down to live in a foreign country, yet YHWH is active
in the lives of both. However, in contrast to the upright Joseph, Judah's
behavior is depicted in darker colors, and this becomes even clearer as the
story progresses.

Tamar Acquires a Son

Judah, who understandably suspects that Tamar is somehow connected
with the death of his two sons, decides to withhold his youngest from
her. He sends her to her father's house and promises to give Shelah to her
when he reaches maturity (Gen 38:11). When Tamar eventually becomes
aware that this is only a stratagem on Judah's part,[14] she orchestrates a
plan as to how to acquire the awaited descendant. When Judah goes to
a sheep-shearing festival[15] with his friend Hirah, having been comforted
over his wife's recent death (38:12),[16] Tamar disguises herself with a veil[17]
and sits by the road to Timnah, by the entrance to Enaim,[18] hoping that

---

12. The reference to "YHWH" is one of the reasons why ch. 38 (and also the major
part of Gen 39) is attributed to the J source. See, for example, Gunkel, *Genesis*, 395, 404.

13. This is contrary to Coats's remark: "No important theological observations can
be made about Yahweh, the God who kills levirate dodgers." George W. Coats, "Widow's
Rights: A Crux in the Structure of Genesis 38," *CBQ* 34 (1972): 461–66, esp. 462.

14. This incident is one of several in the chapter where the knowledge of one person is
concealed from another. An exploitation of this theme appears in Jean Louis Ska, "L'ironie
de Tamar (Gen 38)," *ZAW* 100 (1988): 261–63.

15. Sheep-shearing is mentioned four times in the Old Testament—besides here also
in Gen 31, 1 Sam 25, and 2 Sam 13. Three of these references are associated with David,
and the remaining one, Gen 31, reads, according to Geoghegan, like 1 Sam 25. See Jeffrey
C. Geoghegan, "Israelite Sheepshearing and David's Rise to Power," *Bib* 87 (2006): 55–63,
esp. 58–59.

16. Alter suggests that the reference to Judah being comforted (Gen 38:12) may be
contrasted with Jacob's refusal to be comforted by any of his children (Gen 37:35). See
Alter, *Art*, 7; and also Wenham, *Genesis 16–50*, 364.

17. Huddlestun makes use of the addition at the end of Gen 38:15 in the LXX, which
says, "and he did not recognize her" (καὶ οὐκ ἐπέγνω αὐτήν), and argues that the veil did
not mark Tamar as a prostitute but was her way of concealing her identity from Judah.
See John R. Huddlestun, "Unveiling the Versions: The Tactics of Tamar in Genesis 38:15,"
JHebs 3 (2001): art. 7, pp. 1–18, 10.5508/jhs.2001.v3.a7.

18. Enaim (עֵינַיִם) could be Enam (עֵינָם) mentioned in Josh 15:34 (see, e.g., Driver,
Genesis, 326; or Westermann, *Genesis 37–50*, 53). For a discussion concerning the

Judah will notice her (38:14). Her chances seem slim. Why would Judah use this opportunity for sex shortly after his wife's death? Would he not recognize his daughter in-law in such an intimate situation? Could Tamar hope to conceive a child in a one-night sexual encounter? But perhaps Tamar knew better that the sight of a woman would entice Judah's interest and her intuition was proved right. Judah saw her (וַיִּרְאֶהָ, 38:15), turned away a second time (וַיֵּט, 38:16), and, after promising her a kid from his flock and giving her certain tokens of his identity—his signet, cord, and staff[19]—he went in to her (38:18). And thus on the night of sheep-shearing, Tamar conceives.

Judah intends to keep his promise and sends the woman a kid so that he can retrieve his personal items. Yet his friend Hirah, now in the role of his messenger, cannot find any "cult prostitute" on the road to Timnah (Gen 38:20–23). Whereas in 38:15 Judah thought he spotted by the road a "prostitute" (זֹנָה), Hirah now looks for a "cult prostitute" (קְדֵשָׁה)[20] when searching for Tamar (38:21), and reporting back to Judah about his unsuccessful search (38:22).[21] This peculiarity has given rise to several suggestions as to how to explicate this exchange of terms.[22] One option is that Tamar, in fact, was a cult prostitute, which would, for example according to Astour, better explain Judah's resolution to burn her as a punishment for

---

topography of the locations found in Gen 38, see Detlef Jericke, *Die Ortsangaben im Buch Genesis: Ein historisch-topographischer und literarisch-topographischer Kommentar*, FRLANT 248 (Göttingen: Vandenhoeck & Ruprecht, 2013), 230–35. Nonetheless, the designation Enaim is also a good example of a larger point, that place names in Gen 38 may be taken symbolically. The phrase "by the entrance to Enaim" (בְּפֶתַח עֵינַיִם) might then suggest the opening of the eyes (Rosenbaum and Silbermann, eds., *Rashi: Genesis*, 187), or it could be translated "the beginning of the flowing waters" since עַיִן means an "eye" or a "spring" (see Leuchter, "Genesis," 221).

19. Westermann notes: "The signet ring or cylinder seal is used to sign contracts; the staff has markings carved on it which are peculiar to the owner. The seal was carried on a cord around the neck" (Westermann, *Genesis 37–50*, 53).

20. A recent monograph-length study of cult prostitution in the Old Testament by Christine Stark comes to the conclusion that this phenomenon comes only from late Greek sources. Stark argues that the various terms derived from קדשׁ refer only to cult personnel. The biblical association between the cult personnel and harlotry may be explained metaphorically: the biblical authors viewed cult practices as disloyalty to YHWH. The only problematic text, according to Stark, is Gen 38 where the connection between זֹנָה and קְדֵשָׁה is clear. This text, however, might be late and in any case does not function in a cultic context. See Christine Stark, *"Kultprostitution" im Alten Testament? Die Qedeschen der Hebräischen Bibel und das Motif der Hurerei*, OBO 221 (Fribourg: Academic Press, 2006), esp. 183–203.

21. Although the LXX has the same word πόρνη in all three verses (Gen 38:15, 21 [×2], 22).

22. Deuteronomy 23:17–18 (ET 23:17–18) stipulates that none of the men or women of Israel should be a male (קָדֵשׁ) or female cult prostitute (קְדֵשָׁה). They are named among the abominations in the land in such passage as 1 Kgs 14:24; 15:12; 22:47 (ET 22:26); and 1 Kgs 23:7.

her pregnancy.[23] The other possibility is that the difference in these terms might be due to the differing perspectives of the two men. Whereas the narrator uses the inner-Israelite term "prostitute" when depicting Judah's thoughts about Tamar, Hirah—when speaking to and in connection with "the people of the place" (Gen 38:21)—uses the description known to him from the Cannanite culture.[24] Finally, and along similar lines, the difference could be viewed as a juxtaposition between Judah's private thought ("he thought her to be a prostitute," Gen 38:15) and the publicly suitable designation of קְדֵשָׁה.[25]

These suggestions are not mutually exclusive, but perhaps a more fruitful approach might be to ask about the possible function of this idiosyncrasy for the overall characterization of Judah in the narrative. Here the position of Spina, who notes that Judah does not correct Hirah's designation of קְדֵשָׁה in his dialogue with him (Gen 38:22–23), might be instructive:

> Ironically, from a strictly Israelite standpoint, consorting with a *zônāh*-prostitute would have been less abominable than engaging a *qĕdēšāh*-prostitute. To be sure, being with a *zônāh*-prostitute was a blatant violation of one of YHWH's commandments; nevertheless, this transgression did not necessarily negate one's relationship, however sinned against, with YHWH. But consorting with a *qĕdēšāh*-prostitute was more than a sexual sin, for it presupposed a relationship with a deity other than YHWH: thus it was an act of worship directed toward another God.[26]

Perhaps the narrative, in including this exchange of terms, is hinting that Judah's encounter with Tamar is not only problematic sexually, but a sign that Judah's lifestyle is indistinguishable from Canaanite practices. This would, on the one hand, only darken Judah's portrayal in the narrative, but, on the other hand, would bring Judah yet closer to Joseph, who, especially towards the end of the Joseph story, behaves like an Egyptian.[27]

Judah eventually ends his search, because, as he says, he does not want to become a laughingstock (Gen 38:23). As Spina again remarks, Judah seems to care more about his reputation within the Cannanite culture where he lives, than about the continuation of his clan, which at this point

---

23. Michael C. Astour, "Tamar the Hierodule: An Essay in the Method of Vestigial Motifs," *JBL* 85 (1966): 185–96.

24. See, for example, Hans-Jochen Boecker, "Überlegungen zur 'Geschichte Tamars' (Gen 38)," in *"Ihr Völker alle, klatscht in die Hände!": Festschrift für Erhard S. Gerstenberger zum 65. Geburtstag,* ed. Rainer Kessler et al., EZ 3 (Münster: LIT, 1997), 49–68, esp. 57.

25. See, for example, Phyllis A. Bird, "The Harlot as Heroine: Narrative Art and Social Presupposition in Three Old Testament Texts," *Semeia* (1989): 119–39, esp. 125–26. I have followed the convenient summary of these three positions found in Ebach, *Genesis,* 139.

26. Spina, *Faith,* 47.

27. Joseph is dressed like a high Egyptian official (Gen 41:42), and speaks like an Egyptian (Gen 42:23). Additionally, Jacob's funeral, administered by Joseph, has all the signs of an Egyptian rite (Gen 50:2–3, 11).

is in the immediate danger.[28] Judah's lax attitude towards his own family and his preoccupation with his good reputation thus stand in contrast to the unconventional action of Tamar, who risked her own reputation in order to acquire a son who would carry on Judah's family line.

Tamar More Righteous than Judah

Tamar's pregnancy was kept secret for three months, but then Judah was told that his daughter-in-law expected a child. Specifically, the message that Judah hears evokes once again the image of prostitution: "You daughter-in-law has played (זָנְתָה) the prostitute; moreover, she is pregnant as a result of prostitution (זְנוּנִים)" (Gen 38:24). The verbal root זנה stands behind two words in this verse, which connects this report with Judah's own thoughts about Tamar when he saw her by the road (Gen 38:15).[29] Paradoxically, when previously the sighting of a prostitute prompted Judah to sleep with Tamar, on this occasion he wants to burn her.[30] However, Tamar sends him the items which he left with her on the fateful night with a request: "Recognize, please (הַכֶּר נָא), whose these are, the signet, the cord, and the staff" (Gen 38:25). The opening phrase here connects this chapter with the situation in which the brothers brought back to Jacob Joseph's bloody tunic (Gen 37:32),[31] and thus creates another link with Joseph's endeavors. Within ch. 38 itself, however, this sentence brings the story to its pivotal moment. Judah recognizes his personal items and exclaims: "She is more in the right than I; for I did not give her Shelah, my son" (Gen 38:26). This acknowledgment, together with the remark that they did not have any further sexual encounters, rounds out Judah's encounter with Tamar. Judah recognizes that Tamar is less guilty than he,[32] because, despite her pretending to be a prostitute in order to gain an heir from her father in-law,

---

28. See Spina, *Faith*, 47–48.

29. Undoubtedly, however, there is a difference between the two situations, at least from Judah's vantage point. Bird explains it helpfully: "In the first instance, the term *zônâ* describes the woman's position or profession (prostitute) as well as the activity on which it is based. Thus, it serves as a class or status designation. In the second instance, the verb describes the activity of one whose socio-legal status makes it a crime" (Bird, "Harlot," 124).

30. It is unclear why the death penalty was burning, presumably outside of the city gates (Gen 38:24). Astour argues that this was perhaps a suitable death for a cult prostitute because fire was used to execute those who were considered holy (Lev 21:8–9). See Astour, "Tamar," 194.

31. Bosworth thinks that the phrase "Recognize, please!" points to a larger theme of deception in the story. See David A. Bosworth, *The Story within a Story in Biblical Hebrew Narrative*, CBQMS 45 (Washington, DC: Catholic Biblical Association of America, 2008), 47.

32. This seems to be the idea behind the phrase צָדְקָה מִמֶּנִּי in Gen 38:26. Interestingly, NRSV translates a similar sentence in Jer 3:11 (צִדְּקָה נַפְשָׁהּ מְשֻׁבָה יִשְׂרָאֵל מִבֹּגֵדָה יְהוּדָה) as "faithless Israel has shown herself less guilty than false Judah."

she cared for the preservation of Judah's family line. The focus on the seed, visible already in vv. 9–10 where Onan is killed for spilling his seed on the ground, comes to the foreground again. Israel's future is saved through an unlikely candidate—a foreign woman—and through the improper sexual relations with her father-in law. Despite this impropriety, and based on the logic of Judah's words, his reluctance to give up his youngest son is deemed less righteous than Tamar's improper sexual act. In contrast to Onan, she risks her own name and reputation in order that Judah's family may continue.

Judah's Favored Progeny

The story in ch. 38, however, does not conclude with Judah's acknowledgment of Tamar's greater righteousness, but with a depiction of the birth of Tamar's children (Gen 38:27–30), which provides the real climax of the chapter.[33] Within the chapter itself, the birth of Perez and Zerah contrasts with the death of Er and Onan.[34] In a larger perspective, however, the birth of the twins, and the fact that the son who initially appears to be coming out first is associated with the color red (Gen 38:28), both recall the birth of Esau and Jacob in Gen 25:24–26.[35] As with Jacob and Esau, it is Perez who gains preference over Zerah, even though it appeared that Zerah would come out of the womb first (Gen 38:28–30). This conclusion to the chapter, which connects Gen 38 with the earlier brotherly rivalry, calls for at least two remarks. First, as patterned in previous patriarchal stories, here also the same preference for the younger son is displayed. In spite of the usual human actions and conventions,[36] the descendants of Judah and Tamar continue the recognizable pattern of God's chosenness, crucial for the people of Israel.[37] Second, this same Perez is later in the Old Testament associated with King David (Ruth 4:18–22). Perez is thus not only one of the sons of Israel, but *the* son of Israel, since Israel's most famous king is to be counted among his offspring.

---

33. Coats stresses that the fulfillment of Tamar's plan in the framework of a levirate law was the conception of a child (Coats, "Rights," 461–66). This is asserted against von Rad's contention that the chapter finishes somewhat unsatisfactorily since it is unclear whether Tamar became married to Judah or Shelah (von Rad, *Genesis*, 356).

34. See Hensel, *Vertauschung*, 249. Goldin suggests that the birth of Perez and Zerah in place of Er and Onan is a sign that Judah has been forgiven (Goldin, "Son," 30).

35. Menn lists several parallels between both stories (Menn, *Judah*, 90–91). Additionally, Gen 38:27 is similar in words and content to that of Gen 25:24 (see also Westermann, *Genesis 37–50*, 55).

36. Emerton, who searches for a possible context where the story could have originated, reasons that since the story is critical, but not hostile, towards Judah, it could have circulated among those Canaanites living close to the tribe of Judah. See John A. Emerton, "Judah and Tamar," *VT* 29 (1979): 403–15.

37. On Gen 38 in connection with the preference for the younger son, see Goldin, "Son," 27–44.

Summary

There are several ways in which the tale of Judah and Tamar in Gen 38 may affect the reading of the Joseph story. I will focus on the lesson learned by Judah in ch. 38 and the role it may play in his protection of Benjamin, and on the effect the positioning of the chapter may have for the way in which one reads the rest of the narrative.

Judah's Experience in Chapter 38 Might Further Explain His Protection of Benjamin

When one attempts to envisage the influence of ch. 38 on the rest of the Joseph story, this subplot may be viewed as having a bearing upon the situation endangering Benjamin in chs. 43–45. It is possible that Judah's emphasis on the continuation of Israel's family line and his understanding that the life of the youngest might need to be risked in order to ensure the future (Gen 43:8) might be seen as stemming from Judah's own experience in ch. 38. His willingness to be a surety for Benjamin (Gen 43:9) may further show that he wanted to prevent a similar scenario happening again. This facet is well captured by Ackerman:

> In chapter 38 Judah learned the crucial importance of the continuation of the family. He is able to bring Jacob back to his senses by demonstrating that his protective favoritism for Benjamin will destroy the future generation of the family of Israel. Judah demonstrates to Jacob that Israel must live into the future. Whereas he left personal items in pledge to Tamar until the kid be brought, he now pledges himself to Jacob until Benjamin be returned home safely.[38]

The emphasis upon the "pledge" helps Ackerman to highlight the connection between Gen 38 and 43.[39] Judah's encounter with Tamar could be viewed as what is behind his persuading of Jacob to let Benjamin join his brothers on the trip to Egypt, which culminates in Judah's ultimate willingness to fulfill the vow that he gave to his father. This larger perspective, which connects both episodes, is pointed out by Levenson with both nuance and clarity:

> That it is Judah who effects this total reversal is a point of high significance. From the historian's vantage point, this is undoubtedly to be associated with Judah's role as the preeminent tribe of the south, the tribe from which kings of the House of Jesse hail.... From the vantage

---

38. Ackerman, "Joseph," 105. Similarly also Reno, *Genesis*, 266.

39. The word "pledge" (עֵרָבוֹן) used in Gen 38:17, 18, 20 is derived from the verb "stand surety for" (ערב) in Gen 43:9 and 44:32. This link is also noted by Bosworth, *Story*, 47–48; and Jan P. Fokkelman, "Genesis 37 and 38 at the Interface of Structural Analysis and Hermeneutics," in *Literary Structure and Rhetorical Strategies in the Hebrew Bible*, ed. L. J. Regt et al. (Assen: Van Gorcum, 1996), 152–87, esp. 180.

point of narrative analysis, however, the key point is that it is Judah's experience in Genesis 38, the incident with Tamar, that prepares him to play the great substitutionary role that reverses the decline in the family fortune. He can empathize with Jacob—indeed, take his place—because his own loss of two sons and his unwillingness to surrender the third have taught him a lesson. Moreover, it is in chapter 38 that he first learns to play the role of a substitute, taking the place of Shelah with shameful results as he will, six chapters later, take the place of Benjamin with the most honorable of results—the healing of a family gravely wounded, the family chosen by God and wounded by his very act of choosing. Whereas Reuben offered the lives of his two *sons* as surety (42:37), Judah, as always more realistic and more effective, offered *himself*. He has, in the process, accepted in the name of the brothers the very prospect that first evoked their fateful conspiracy against Joseph. He has freely accepted Joseph's rule and his own status as the unfavored brother doing obeisance to the beloved son.[40]

Levenson offers a view that takes into consideration both historical and narratival perspectives, of which the latter, at this point, is of interest to me. He suggests that Judah has learned something from his decision not to give his youngest son to Tamar in marriage, since he believed that this situation would endanger Shelah's life. This fear, however, might have been fateful for Judah's family fortune, since, were it not for Tamar's unconventional course of action, he would likely have remained childless. Instead, he unwittingly became a substitute for his youngest son, which may have influenced his willingness to offer his own life in order to save that of Jacob's youngest son and guarantee the continuity of the clan. Perhaps it is only a certain kind of risk and vulnerability—exemplified here by Judah and also by Jacob, when, persuaded by Judah, he is willing to release Benjamin—that is able to move a family forward. Risking one's life or the life of a son, when facing an imminent danger of death, may be the only way to gain life.[41]

Chapter 38 thus brings a greater richness to the Joseph story by deepening its portrayal of the unfavored Judah.[42] When one reads the story in Gen 38 in connection with the rest of the narrative, the significance of the unchosen characters comes to the foreground. Both Jacob's openness

---

40. Levenson, *Death*, 163–64, emphasis his.

41. The motifs of life and death in Gen 38 are explored in M. E. Andrew, "Moving from Death to Life: Verbs of Motion in the Story of Judah and Tamar in Gen 38," *ZAW* 105 (1993): 262–69.

42. Clifford states the matter more forcefully: "Without ch. 38, the extraordinary change in Judah's character is inexplicable." Richard J. Clifford, "Genesis 37–50: Joseph Story or Jacob Story?," in *The Book of Genesis: Composition, Reception, and Interpretation*, ed. Craig A. Evans et al., VTSup 152 (Leiden: Brill, 2012), 213–29, esp. 221. The development of Judah is also traced in Anthony J. Lambe, "Judah's Development: The Pattern of Departure–Transition–Return," *JSOT* 83 (1999): 53–68.

to let go of his beloved Benjamin, and Joseph's self-revelation—two key events that contribute to family reconciliation—were influenced by the unfavored Judah, who was in turn influenced by Tamar, a person who came to Israel's family as an outsider. The favored characters of the second half of the book of Genesis (Jacob and Joseph) need the presence and actions of those less privileged in order to accomplish transformations that are seen as crucial for the future of Israel's clan.

Judah's Royal Offspring Overshadows Joseph's Portrayal of Leadership

Genesis 38 is skillfully incorporated into its literary context and shares several parallels with Joseph's story. To touch on a few of them: both Joseph and Judah go down to a foreign country and marry foreign wives. Both face sexual temptation,[43] and towards the end of their stories each has two sons in whose lives may be observed the peculiar twist of God's chosenness. Both stories also attest to YHWH's presence and activity, unusual for the Joseph cycle. Both Judah and Joseph seem to be portrayed as accepting customs and patterns indigenous for the foreign culture in which they live. How can this resemblance be evaluated?[44]

One may say that by inserting this little tale of Judah and Tamar immediately after Joseph's being sold into Egypt, the composers of the book of Genesis have achieved extraordinary effect. By depicting, albeit briefly, Judah's family history in Canaan, they have marked him as a second main character of Gen 37–50, leading some commentators to suggest that the traditional designation of the "Joseph cycle" should be exchanged for a different one that would better express Judah's role in the story.[45]

But perhaps the most important aspect of this story's inclusion is a changed perspective on Israel's kingship. Even though Joseph's dreams in ch. 37 might hint at a future role for Joseph as Israel's king, the subsequent narrative, which ends with the birth of the twins and Perez's preeminence, turns reader's attention elsewhere: it will be Judah's descendants who will occupy Israel's throne. Judah's two sons stand in tension with Joseph's two sons (who are emphasized in ch. 48), as God's favoring alters their destiny.

---

43. A comparison between the seduction of Potiphar's wife and the motives of Tamar can be found in James McKeown, *Genesis*, THOTC 1 (Grand Rapids: Eerdmans, 2008), 167.

44. Among authors who note the connection between ch. 38 and the remainder of the Joseph story, the most innovative proposal, in my opinion, comes from Bosworth who likens the chapter to a *mise-en-abyme*, which he defines as "a device in which a part reduplicates the whole" (Bosworth, *Story*, 1). In his view, Gen 38 reduplicates the Joseph cycle (Bosworth, *Story*, 37). Somewhat similarly, see also Jonathan Kruschwitz, "The Type-scene Connection betwen Genesis 38 and the Joseph Story," *JSOT* 36 (2012): 383–410.

45. Hensel, for example, thus opts for the designation of the "Joseph-Judah-Narrative" (Hensel, *Vertauschung*, 190–91).

The inclusion of ch. 38 may thus be seen as a putting forward of Judah. With the tale of Judah and Tamar inserted *before* the events of Joseph's life in Egypt—where he rises from a lowly state to the position of a high-ranking Egyptian official with his own family—the reader is first of all given a succinct overview of Judah's own family history. Joseph's journey is prefaced, so to say, with Judah's own story, which bears stronger royal overtones. When ch. 38 finishes with a suggested preference for Perez, who is later in the Old Testament associated with King David, the narrative effectively distances Joseph from the link with kingship.[46] Joseph might have an indispensable role to play in saving Israel from famine in Gen 37–50, but a future deliverance, connected with the future kingdom, is reserved for Judah's descendant.

---

46. This could be an example of "revision through introduction," as brought forward in Sara J. Milstein, *Tracking the Master Scribe: Revision through Introduction in Biblical and Mesopotamian Literature* (New York: Oxford University Press, 2016).

9

Genesis 49:
Judah

Chapter 49 is perhaps the most enigmatic chapter in the whole of the book of Genesis, as it confronts the reader with several puzzling issues.[1] First, it contains significant textual difficulties, and thus the interpreter needs to choose the best received text for him or her to study.[2] Second, the meaning and relevance of the individual blessings[3] pronounced in poetic fashion are far from obvious. They abound with enigmatic metaphors and unusual similes—far removed from the ordered narrative world of Gen 37–50—and their meaning is thus inherently open to various interpretations. Third, while Jacob first addresses his sons as a group (49:1–2) and then by name in the individual blessings,[4] the end of his testament[5] makes it clear that the oracle is pronounced upon the twelve tribes of Israel (49:28). Furthermore, the opening of his testament stresses that Jacob discloses to his sons what will happen "in the days to come" (בְּאַחֲרִית הַיָּמִים). This phrase seems to

---

1. Two recent monographs that deal specifically with Gen 49 are: de Hoop, *Genesis*; and Jean-Daniel Macchi, *Israël et ses tribus selon Genèse 49*, OBO 171 (Göttingen: Vandenhoeck & Ruprecht, 1999).

2. My reference to the "best received" text reflects Brevard Childs' attempt to navigate between the original and the received text in its canonical form: Brevard S. Childs, *The New Testament as Canon: An Introduction* (London: SCM, 1984), 518–39, esp. 525.

3. Genesis 49 has been often examined together with similar lists in Deut 33 and Judg 5 in order to highlight their similarities and differences and to argue for their possible common origin as tribal sayings. See, for example, Antonius H. J. Gunneweg, "Über den Sitz im Leben der sog. Stammessprüche (Gen 49, Dtn 33, Jdc 5)," *ZAW* 76 (1964): 245–55; or Hans-Jürgen Zobel, *Stammesspruch und Geschichte: Die Angaben der Stammessprüche von Gen.49, Dtn 33 und Jdc 5 über die politischen und kultischen Zustände im damaligen "Israel"*, BZAW 95 (Berlin: Töpelmann, 1965). Especially the comparison with Deut 33 is telling: in both situations the oracles are pronounced by Israel's dying leaders who will not go back/ enter into Canaan.

4. The use of the term "blessing" might be viewed as puzzling since the oracle given to Reuben resembles more a curse than a blessing, and the one addressed to Simeon and Levi even declares itself to be such (Gen 49:7). For a helpful discussion see Helmuth Pehlke, "An Exegetical and Theological Study of Genesis 49:1–28" (Ph.D. diss., Dallas Theological Seminary, 1985), 58–62.

5. For a defense of this designation, see Eckhard von Nordheim, *Die Lehre der Alten II: Das Testament als Literaturgattung im Alten Testament und im Alten Vorderen Orient*, ALGHJ 18 (Leiden: Brill, 1985), 29–51. I will use both the term "blessing" and "testament" interchangeably.

denote a period that still lies in the future.[6] The future horizon of the poem, in some sense, overshadows the present context of the Joseph cycle. This future-oriented posture is present especially in Judah's oracle while the aspect of blessing is most visible in the saying upon Joseph.[7]

The positive nature of Judah's blessing is strengthened by its placement after Jacob's sayings that are addressed to Reuben and to Simeon and Levi together. The firstborn Reuben will no longer be exalted, because he defiled his father's bed (Gen 49:3–4), which seems to be connected to his sleeping with Jacob's concubine Bilhah (35:22).[8] Similarly, Simeon and Levi are rebuked for the violence and anger with which they killed men (49:5–7), which recalls the massacre at Shechem (34:25–26). The two sayings diminish the role of the first three of Jacob's sons vis-à-vis Judah,[9] which may even be interpreted as disqualifying them from the status of firstborn son.[10] Jacob's words pronounced upon Judah thus acquire special importance. Since the blessing contains numerous textual and interpretative complexities, I will deal with each verse individually.

Verse 8

In contrast to the two previous sayings, which compiled various negative comments about Jacob's first three sons, the blessing on Judah begins with a wordplay on Judah's name:[11] "You are Judah (יְהוּדָה), your brothers will praise you (יוֹדוּךָ)."[12] This saying, by which Jacob addresses his fourth-born

---

6. This phrase also occurs in several other places in the Old Testament (see, e.g., Num 24:14; Deut 31:29; Ezek 38:16; Dan 10:14), where the image to which the phrase is attached also points beyond the horizon of the text. Similarly John T. Willis, "The Expression *be' acharith hayyamin* in the Old Testament," *ResQ* 22 (1979): 54–71. More specifically, Huddleston focuses on the occurrence of this phrase in the Pentateuch (Gen 49:1; Num 24:14; Deut 31:29) and suggests that "these parallel poems serve to confirm the notion that the Pentateuch is presenting the scope of history from the very beginning to the very end." Jonathan Huddleston, *Eschatology in Genesis*, FAT 57 (Tübingen: Mohr Siebeck, 2012), 218.

7. For a similar conclusion, see Schöpflin, "Jakob," esp. 505–6.

8. Absalom listened to Ahithophel's advice and went into his father's concubines in 2 Sam 16:20–23, which was intended to challenge David's authority. Reuben's action could be understood as analogous to this (Macchi, *Israël*, 53).

9. Sparks, for example, suggests that the sayings upon Reuben, Simeon, and Levi have been reworked in order to grant the preeminence to Judah. See Kent Sparks, "Genesis 49 and the Tribal List Tradition in Ancient Israel," *ZAW* 115 (2003): 327–47, esp. 330–32. Macchi argues that all sayings not included in Gen 49:13–21 stem from a later hand: Macchi, *Israël*, 301–6.

10. Thus, for example, Hensel, *Vertauschung*, 191–97; or Arnold, *Genesis*, 379.

11. Some authors suggest that Gen 49:8 provides, as does Gen 29:35, an etymology for Judah's name. See, for example, Gunkel, *Genesis*, 456. My view of it, however, is that rather than offering an etymology, the connection with "praise" is a wordplay (Westermann, *Genesis 37–50*, 227; or Sarna, *Genesis*, 335) similar to Matt 16:18.

12. Alternatively, the first clause can be translated: "Judah—you will your brothers praise" (see Arnold, *Genesis*, 381).

directly,[13] captures the image of Judah's brothers appreciating him and bowing down (חוה) before him. The reason for these acts of reverence is given in the middle clause, which says: "Your hand is on the neck (עֹרֶף) of your enemies." The image expressed by these words seems to be taken from the context of close combat and conveys a man's domination over his adversaries.[14] This is strengthened by a similar depiction in 2 Sam 22:41, which is repeated almost verbatim in Ps 18:41 (ET 18:40), where David praises God similarly: "you have given me the neck of those who hated me, and I destroyed them."[15] Even though the text does not specify this, one can reasonably infer that Judah's enemies might be also his brothers' enemies, and thus Judah's victory over them might naturally lead to the brothers' appreciation of Judah.

Given the fact that receiving an act of bowing down is reserved to Joseph in Gen 37–50 (Gen 37:7, 9, 10; 42:6; 43:26, 28; possibly also 47:31), it is striking here to read that in the future the brothers will prostrate themselves before Judah. Furthermore, this special position of Judah also reminds us of Jacob's own privileged position expressed in Isaac's blessing upon him in 27:29, where one can hear echoes of God's blessing of Abraham (12:1–3):

> Let peoples serve you,
> and nations bow down to you.
> Be lord over your brothers,
> and may your mother's sons bow down to you.
> Cursed be those who curse you,
> and blessed be those who bless you. (Gen 27:29)

In contrast to the emphasis on Joseph and his unique role earlier in the narrative as Jacob's son who receives the special reverence of his siblings, in Gen 49:8 it is Judah who seems to be singled out to continue the patriarchal line that carries the divine blessing, which will enable him to be victorious over his enemies and praised by his brothers.

Verse 9

Animal imagery is employed in describing Judah's special position in v. 9. Judah is compared to a lion: first to a small cub (גּוּר אַרְיֵה), then to a male (אַרְיֵה), and finally to a female lion (לָבִיא)[16] who got up from or with her

---

13. Reuben, Judah, and Joseph are addressed directly in Gen 49:1–28. See Ebach, *Genesis*, 577.

14. Similarly also Kevin Smyth, "The Prophecy Concerning Juda: Gen. 49:8–12," *CBQ* 7 (1945): 290–305, esp. 291.

15. A similar phrase can also be found in the book of Job, where Job complains about God that "he broke me in two; he seized me by the neck (עֹרֶף) and dashed me to pieces; he set me up as his target" (Job 16:12 NRSV).

16. For a thorough discussion of leonine imagery, see Brent A. Strawn, *What Is Stronger than a Lion? Leonine Image and Metaphor in the Hebrew Bible and the Ancient Near East*, OBO 212 (Gottingen: Vandenhoeck & Ruprecht, 2005).

prey.[17] The last sentence describes the challenge posed by a lion to those surrounding him: he crouched (כָּרַע)[18] and laid down to rest, so who will dare to rouse him up?

The metaphor of a lion[19] devouring his prey and then resting where one had better not rouse him is developed in two instances in the book of Numbers, where Balaam, in a poetic form, prophesies concerning Israel (Num 23:24; 24:9). There the bearer of this extraordinary strength and power is Israel who has already defeated the Amorites and was approaching Moab (Num 21:21–22:4a). The imagery of a lion in connection with its prey thus might indicate that Judah is someone who has already accomplished something significant with regard to his enemies.[20] Even though he rests now, he terrifies those who would come close to him.[21]

Verse 10

Verse 10 is undoubtedly the most difficult verse in the blessing of Judah and perhaps in the whole of ch. 49, mostly because of the uncertainty as to the meaning of the obscure "Shiloh" in the middle of the verse. I will first

---

17. The LXX version contains an interesting divergent text in the second line: "from the sprout, my son, you have grown up" (ἐκ βλαστοῦ υἱέ μου ἀνέβης). As Wevers comments: "What [the Greek text of Genesis] has achieved by using a word from the plant world is to get rid of the notion of Judah ferociously tearing at his prey" (Wevers, *Genesis*, 825). Similarly also Martin Rösel, "Die Interpretation von Genesis 49 in der Septuaginta," *BN* 79 (1955): 54–70, esp. 61.

18. Ackerman suggests that the verb כרע may carry sexual overtones, especially when viewed in connection with the staff between Judah's feet in Gen 49:10. He evaluates these references as reminding the reader of Judah's sexual encounter with Tamar in Gen 38. See Ackerman, "Joseph," 111. However, out of the forty-five occurrences of this root in the Old Testament, only in Job 31:10 is it used with unambiguously sexual connotations.

19. The image is used in several contexts. In Deut 33:20, 22 it is applied to Gad and Dan.

20. Although the link between the image of a lion and a monarch is frequently made in ancient Near Eastern contexts, Strawn cautions against this connection within the Old Testament where "apart from 1 Sam 17 and 2 Sam 1:23 such a motif is entirely absent from the narrative traditions about the Israelite monarchy" (Strawn, *Lion*, 242–43). Nevertheless, he does not completely rule out this idea with regard to Gen 49:9 (Strawn, *Lion*, 243, n. 41). From the New Testament comes the interesting reference to "the lion of the tribe of Judah" (Rev 5:5).

21. Some authors try to connect Gen 49:8–12 with the wider context of Gen 37–50. The noun "prey" (טֶרֶף) serves this purpose well since it has appeared in the Joseph cycle before—always when Jacob is evaluating Joseph's disappearance (37:33; 44:28). Good follows this trajectory when he suggests that the second line of v. 9 might read, "From the prey *of my son* you have gone up," understanding the phrase בְּנִי as objective genitive and not as vocative, as it is normally taken. See Edwin M. Good, "'Blessing' on Judah, Gen 49:8–12," *JBL* 82 (1963): 427–32, esp. 429. Similarly Calum M. Carmichael, "Some Sayings in Genesis 49," *JBL* 88 (1969): 435–44, esp. 439; or Rosenbaum and Silbermann, eds., *Rashi: Genesis*, 245. However, the Hebrew text does not contain any indication—such as the nouns being in a construct state, or via conjunctive marks—that would support such a reading.

look closely at the meaning of Gen 49:10a together with 10bβ, and then summarize my findings in order to assess a probable significance of Judah's blessing before the "Shiloh" question is even raised.

Its opening bicolon has a parallelism which assigns to Judah a special role: "The staff (שֵׁבֶט) will not turn away from Judah, nor the scepter (מְחֹקֵק) from between his legs." The image that these two clauses invoke is quite straightforward, since both שֵׁבֶט and מְחֹקֵק signify a position of leadership that in some situations may also carry royal connotations.[22] Judah is promised a leadership authority[23] that will be enduring: Judah's descendants—those who will come from "between his legs"[24]—will reign over and for his people. This leadership position naturally recalls the Davidic dynasty: especially, as Benno Jacob notes, when the promise given to David in 2 Sam 7, expressed in contrast to the fate of Saul, contains the same words as Gen 49:10—the staff "will not turn away" (לֹא־יָסוּר) from Judah and God's "steadfast love" (חֶסֶד) "will not turn away" (לֹא־יָסוּר) from David's son (2 Sam 7:15).[25]

Verse 10bβ can be translated: "the obedience of the peoples is his." The sentence contains the unusual word יְקָהָה whose likely meaning is that of obedience.[26] According to v. 10 Judah will have authority and leadership among his own, until something extraordinary happens that will cause other peoples to submit to him.[27]

---

22. The two words seem to function as synonyms (Westermann, *Genesis 37–50*, 230; Gunkel, *Genesis*, 456; or Zobel, *Stammesspruch*, 13). The word "staff" (שֵׁבֶט) occurs in Balaam's fourth oracle in Num 24:17, where it is paired with the image of a "star" that will rise out of Israel and dominate the surrounding nations. It is used in a context with royal overtones in Ps 45:7 (ET 45:6). The second term, מְחֹקֵק, is a Poel participle, meaning "one who makes a decree" and thus a leader (see *HALOT* 1:114; Wevers, *Genesis*, 825–26). It can be found, for example, in Num 21:18, or, with possible reference to Judah's kingship, in Ps 60:9 (ET 60:7).

23. The LXX expresses this more explicitly: οὐκ ἐκλείψει ἄρχων ἐξ Ιουδα καὶ ἡγούμενος ἐκ τῶν μηρῶν αὐτοῦ ("a ruler will not be wanting from Judah, nor a leader out of his loins"). See Wevers, *Genesis*, 825; and Rösel, "Septuaginta," 62–63.

24. For Ackerman, the ruler's staff from "between his feet" is a sexual euphemism that may be a subtle reminder of Judah's staff which he gave to Tamar for her sexual service (Ackerman, "Joseph," 111). Verses such as Judg 3:24; 1 Sam 24:3; or Isa 7:20 indicate that the term "feet" is sometimes used as a symbol for the private parts (see Wenham, *Genesis 16–50*, 477). Although the phrase more readily evokes the image of a ruler in a seated position with a staff held between his legs, it might also, especially when taken together with the permanency of Judah's leadership role, point to the idea of one's descendants (as in Deut 28:57). See André Caquot, "La parole sur Juda dans le testament lyrique de Jacob (Gen 49:8–12)," *Sem* 26 (1976): 5–32, esp. 18.

25. Jacob, *Genesis*, 901.

26. The word occurs only here and in Prov 30:17. See also *TWOT* 902a and *HALOT* 1:430. The translators of the LXX likely thought that the Hebrew word comes from the root קוה, and hence they translated the clause: "and he is the expectation of the nations" (καὶ αὐτὸς προσδοκία ἐθνῶν).

27. The preposition "until" (עַד or עַד כִּי) may mean that something is valid only up to this point, and not afterwards. This understanding of "until" in Gen 49:10 is expressed,

Before we proceed to elaborate upon the obscure word "Shiloh," it helps here to summarize my findings up to this point. Verses 8–10a, together with 10bβ, speak in positive terms of Judah, who will be honored and respected by his kin for his ability to fight against his—and hence presumably their – enemies. Judah's clan is compared to a powerful lion who should be left undisturbed lest he proves dangerous for those surrounding him. Finally, the image of leadership, and of the ability to prevail over one's enemies, is carried further in v. 10. Here it is promised that Judah's tribe will permanently hold a position of respect and power. This depiction of Judah's future is portrayed in the blessing even before the mysterious "Shiloh" enters the discussion.[28]

But what will accomplish this progression of events, that in turn will result in the increase of Judah's role? The answer to this question is hidden in the third line of v. 10, where the Hebrew text reads: עַד כִּי־יָבֹא שִׁילֹה, which is literally translated: "until Shiloh comes." But who or what is "Shiloh"? And what does the phrase mean? This question already puzzled ancient interpreters and remains problematic until today. My aim is not to recount exhaustively the various interpretative positions focusing on this enigmatic phrase, but rather simply to group and summarize the most important of them into four basic approaches.[29]

Person

The expectation that Shiloh would be a person—which is expressed, for example, in the NASB ("until Shiloh comes")—comes rather naturally, since the blessing so far has been focused on the person of Judah. In addition to this, שִׁילֹה is by conventional syntax readily construed as the subject of יָבֹא. Read this way, the sentence speaks of a ruler who comes after Judah, who until now has been the primary subject of the blessing.

Who, however, is this mysterious Shiloh? Since neither the book of Genesis nor the Old Testament know of anyone with such a name, scholars have come up with differing suggestions, either involving a supposed

---

for example, in Treves, who argues that a Judean king in fact ruled in Israel "until a man of Shiloh came," which happened in 1 Kgs 11:29 when Ahijah the Shilonite appeared on the scene and his instigation played a role in dividing the kingdom (see Marco Treves, "Shiloh [Genesis 49:10]," *JBL* 85 [1966]: 353–56). But "until" could also signal a change in degree or intensity, as in Judg 4:24; 1 Kgs 17:17; or Ezek 34:21. This inclusive view of the preposition עַד and its Greek counterpart ἕως in A. M. Honeyman, "Matthew V.18 and the Validity of the Law," *NTS* 1 (1954): 141–42. See also Otto Eissfeldt, "Silo und Jerusalem," in *Volume du Congrès: Strasbourg 1956*, ed. G. W. Anderson, VTSup 4 (Leiden: Brill, 1957), 138–47, esp. 141; and Zobel, *Stammesspruch*, 13.

28. Westermann argues that Judah's leadership position is already contained in v. 10a (Westermann, *Genesis 37–50*, 230). On the contrary, von Rad considers "Shiloh" to be the aphorism "upon the understanding of which almost everything depends" (von Rad, *Genesis*, 424).

29. For a succinct yet more thorough discussion of the various proposals, see de Hoop, *Genesis*, 124–35; and Macchi, *Israël*, 99–109.

connection with other ancient Near Eastern languages, or based on an emendation of the MT. These can be divided into three groups.

First, in what is probably the simplest solution, certain authors have noted that the consonants of the word Shiloh (שׁלה) are precisely the same as those contained in the name of Judah's son Shelah.[30] Second, and unsurprisingly, several attempts have been made to elucidate this perplexing term from cognate languages. Nötscher, for example, has argued that שׁילה might be connected to the Akkadian word *šēlu*, which, when used about persons, means a "ruler" or "prince."[31] Seebass, on the other hand, seeks a possible explanation in the Egyptian language and suggests a link with the Egyptian word for "prince"—*śr*, which developed into *śjr(w)*.[32] Third, another possibility is to suggest that a certain conso-nant has been lost during the transmission of the text. Thus Westermann, for example, proposes that the opening מ has dropped out and the text may have originally read משׁלה, understood either as a substantive or a participle.[33] The clause would in this case read: "until his ruler comes,"[34] which would fit quite naturally into the whole blessing. Another sugges-tion is that מ might be inserted into the word itself, resulting in שׁלמה ("Solomon")—whose reign provides a natural climax for Judah's royal line.[35]

Although the supposition that "Shiloh" refers to a person is readily attractive, the suggested solutions have their own sets of problems. To understand it as referring to Shelah might make some sense within Gen 37–50, but much less so in the rest of the Old Testament where he does not feature substantially. And as I have already pointed out, propos-als to illuminate the term from its purported connection with cognate languages have their own sets of problems. Finally, there is no textual

---

30. See, for example, Good, "Blessing," 430. Several more attempts tending in the same direction are listed in John A. Emerton, "Some Difficult Words in Genesis 49," in *Words and Meanings: Essays Presented to David Winston Thomas*, ed. Peter R. Ackroyd and Barnabas Lindars (Cambridge: Cambridge University Press, 1968), 81–93, esp. 84–85.

31. Friedrich Nötscher, "Gen 49,10: שׁילה = akk. *šēlu*," *ZAW* 47 (1929): 323–25. Before him also Godfrey Rolles Driver, "Some Hebrew Roots and their Meanings," *JTS* 23 (1921): 69–73, esp. 70. However, Moran critiques Nötscher, arguing that his position is based on ambiguous references, while in the vast majority of occurrences of the word *šēlu* means "hole" (William L. Moran, "Gen 49,10 and Its Use in Ez 21,32," *Bib* 39 [1958]: 405–25, esp. 405–7).

32. Horst Seebass, "Die Stämmesprüche Gen 49:3–27," *ZAW* 96 (1984): 333–50, esp. 346. Nevertheless, de Hoop points out that a more natural connection might be found between the Egyptian *śr* and the Hebrew שׁר. See de Hoop, *Genesis*, 125, n. 272.

33. Westermann, *Genesis 37–50*, 231. This also entails omitting the י.

34. Westermann, *Genesis 37–50*, 218; see also von Rad, *Genesis*, 425.

35. See, for example, Joseph Klausner, *Messianic Idea in Israel: From Its Beginning to the Completion of the Mishnah* trans. W. F. Stinespring (New York: Macmillan, 1955), 29–30; or Caquot, "Juda," 27–28, 31–32.

witness that would justify the emendation of the word's spelling in the way proposed above.

Place

The second option is to begin with the larger context of the Old Testament in mind, in which "Shiloh" is a well-known village in Ephraimite territory, which at some point functioned as a cultic center. The sentence would then read: "until he comes to Shiloh," where the final ה from שִׁילֹה could be understood as "*he*-locale,"[36] or the whole word taken as indicating direction even without a preposition (likely אֶל).[37]

This emphasis on Shiloh the village may be construed in several different ways. For example, Lindblom tries to reconstruct a specific historical situation in which David would come to the cultic center at Shiloh to accept formally the servitude of other Israelites.[38] Alternatively, some authors have tried to date the event at Shiloh at an earlier period—the book of Judges providing fertile ground in this regard as it narrates certain episodes which hint at a situation in which one tribe wanted to achieve some kind of preeminence over the others.[39] However, there is no biblical evidence that Shiloh played any important role among Judah's descendants.[40] Rather, it is the *destruction* of Shiloh that the choice of Judah and the rejection of Ephraim are linked with in the later biblical tradition (Ps 78:56–68; Jer 7:12–15; 26:4–9).[41] Furthermore, when we return to Gen 49:10, the *Qere*

---

36. See de Hoop, *Genesis*, 126.

37. Schley in his monograph argues that the Old Testament knows instances where the preposition is left out. He cites Josh 18:1: וַיִּקָּהֲלוּ כָּל־עֲדַת בְּנֵי־יִשְׂרָאֵל שִׁלֹה ("and the whole congregation of the sons of Israel assembled *at* Shiloh"); and Josh 18:9: ־וַיָּבֹאוּ אֶל־יְהוֹשֻׁעַ אֶל הַמַּחֲנֶה שִׁלֹה ("and they came back to Joshua to the camp *at* Shiloh"). See Donald. G. Schley, *Shiloh: A Biblical City in Tradition and History*, JSOTSup 63 (Sheffield: JSOT Press, 1989), 161–62. Steiner adds that in 1 Sam 4:12 one finds an almost identical phrase to Gen 49:10: וַיָּבֹא שִׁלֹה בַּיּוֹם הַהוּא ("and he came to Shiloh on that day"). See Richard C. Steiner, "Poetic Forms in the Masoretic Vocalization and Three Difficult Phrases in Jacob's Blessing: *yeṭer śě'ēt* (Gen 49:3), *yěṣû'î 'ālāh* (49:4), *yābō' šîlōh* (49:10)," *JBL* 129 (2010): 209–35, esp. 219.

38. In his understanding, the poetic saying in Judah's blessing is a prophecy about David's arrival at Shiloh, the central place in Israel, to assume leadership over the rest of the Israelite tribes. See Johannes Lindblom, "The Political Background of the Shilo Oracle," in *Congress Volume Copenhagen*, ed. G. W. Anderson, VTSup 1 (Leiden: Brill, 1953), 78–87. But there is no indication that Shiloh maintained its cultic role after the ark was captured by the Philistines (1 Sam 4:1–10).

39. Eissfeldt cites Judg 8:1–3 and 12:1–6, where the tribe of Ephraim acts in this way. He also refers to Mic 5:1–3, which mentions such a dominance for Judah, and which, in Eissfeldt's understanding, may be based on an older tradition (Eissfeldt, "Silo," 141).

40. Zobel, however, suggests that Gen 49:10 may be portraying Judah's unrealized wish (Zobel, *Stammesspruch*, 75–76). Since the biblical text does not testify to a situation in which Judah's tribe gain preeminence over the other tribes or surrounding nations in Shiloh, yet another possibility is to posit such an occurrence in the future (see Jacob, *Genesis*, 907–8).

41. In this regard I wonder whether the phrase in Gen 49:10 could not be understood as a reference to an event that took place at Shiloh. For example, Ps 78:56–68 hints that

שִׁילוֹ indicates that the final ה in שִׁילֹה was understood by the Masoretes, in accordance with v. 11, as an ancient masculine third-person singular ending.[42] These features lead us to consider the other interpretative positions regarding the enigmatic "Shiloh."

"That Which Is Reserved for Him"

The third option is, in fact, suggested by the LXX. The Greek text reads: ἕως ἂν ἔλθῃ τὰ ἀποκείμενα αὐτῷ καὶ αὐτὸς προσδοκία ἐθνῶν, which can be translated: "until there should come the things laid up (i.e. held in reserve) for him, and he is the expectation of the nations."[43] The sentence seems to refer back to the "staff" in the beginning of v. 10 and announces the coming of the promised ruler to whom the staff belongs and who is the hope of the people. This rendering presupposes the division of "Shiloh" in the Hebrew into two words: שֶׁ (conjunction "which") and לֹה ("for him").

The Old Testament itself supports this reading in Ezek 21:32 (ET 21:27), which presents us with a verse similar to our passage:

> Thus says the Lord YHWH: Remove the turban, take off the crown; things will not remain as they are. Exalt that which is low and abase that which is high. A ruin, a ruin, a ruin I will make it! This also has not happened until he comes whose judgment it is; to him I will give it (עַד־בֹּא אֲשֶׁר־לוֹ הַמִּשְׁפָּט וּנְתַתִּיו). (Ezek 21:31–32 [ET 21:26–27])

Even though it is unclear whether the expected figure is to bring to Judah restoration or judgment,[44] for our purposes it is important to note that Ezek 21:32 possibly echoes Gen 49:10 by substituting the conjunction אֲשֶׁר for שֶׁ. Although this reconstruction of the Hebrew text has found several supporters[45] and is attested in a few modern translations (notably

---

Israel's past could be viewed as a series of rebellious acts culminating in the departure of God's presence from Shiloh and the rejection of Ephraim, which was followed by God's choice of David and Jerusalem. Similarly, but with a different rhetorical purpose, also Jer 7:12–15 and 26:4–9. Frolov's recent proposal to read "Shiloh" as a reference to a place seems to venture in a similar direction: Serge Frolov, "Judah Comes to Shiloh: Genesis 49:10bα, One More Time," *JBL* 131 (2012): 417–22, esp. 420.

42. De Hoop also points out that the spelling שִׁילֹה can be found only here in the Old Testament. See de Hoop, *Genesis*, 126–27. שִׁילוֹ occurs ×3 in the Old Testament (×2 in Judg 21:21 and ×1 in Jer 7:12), שִׁלֹה is found ×22, and שִׁלוֹ ×8.

43. For a discussion of the Greek rendering, see Wevers, *Genesis*, 826; or Rösel, "Septuaginta," 63–64.

44. For a good discussion of this issue, see Walther Zimmerli, *Ezekiel 1: A Commentary on the Book of the Prophet Ezekiel, Chapters 1–24*, trans. Ronald E. Clements, Hermeneia (Philadelphia: Fortress, 1979), 447–48.

45. For example, Skinner adopts this version, but is nevertheless careful to point out the divergent options that the phrase allows—he mentions both a reference to the Davidic kingdom and a coded name for the Messiah (Skinner, *Genesis*, 522–24). See also Smyth, "Prophecy," 298; Matthews, *Genesis*, 895; or Ebach, *Genesis*, 570, 603. Perhaps also Sabottka's unconvincing proposal should be mentioned in this category. He reads עַד as

the NIV), it faces its own difficulties. First, the expected parallelism of the last two sentences of v. 10, which one would expect to form another bicolon, is thus broken. The emphasis on the expectation of the nations does not parallel the coming of the leader to whom the scepter belongs. Second, this suggestion does not adequately explain why the Hebrew word שִׁילֹה contains יֹ.

"A Tribute to Him"

In recent years Moran has proposed that the text could be read: עַד כִּי־יָבֹא שַׁי לֹה, meaning "until tribute is brought to him."[46] He divides the ambiguous term into two words: the noun שַׁי ("tribute") and the prepositional phrase לֹה ("for him"). The word שַׁי can then be found three more times elsewhere in the Old Testament: in Isa 18:7, Ps 68:30 (ET 68:29), and 76:12 (ET 76:11), strengthening the validity of Moran's proposal.[47] In all three cases the verb indicating that the "tribute" is brought to God or the temple is יבל, different from the verb בוא used in Gen 49:10, but de Hoop, who attempts to reinforce Moran's proposal, argues that the word מִנְחָה ("gift") covers almost the identical semantic field as שַׁי, which then serves for him as a backdrop for suggesting that not only יבל but also בוא and other verbs can be used within this semantic category.[48] Furthermore, Steiner has recently argued that שַׁי, as a version of שַׁי, likely existed in the Old Canaanite, and that the verbal form יָבֹא makes perfect idiomatic sense in Hebrew.[49] Thus in the end both de Hoop and Steiner significantly tighten up Moran's argument, which is commendable mostly for its suggestion of an option that provides the fourth line of our verse with the expected parallelism: the descendant of Judah will reign until the tribute is brought to him and people obediently come to him. Nevertheless, I wonder if the resulting parallelism does not read awkwardly in Hebrew: עַד כִּי־יָבֹא שַׁי לֹה וְלֹו יִקְּהַת עַמִּים. The occurrence of לֹה/לֹו next to each other seems unusual.

Summary of Various Positions

As we have seen, the interpreters are divided with respect to what the enigmatic term "Shiloh" means, but they all point in the direction of a greater influence for Judah's descendants. Thus, the fundamental meaning of the

---

a "throne" and translates: "his throne will truly come to Shiloh." See Liudger Sabottka, "Noch einmal Gen 49:10," *Bib* 51 (1970): 225–29.

46. Moran, "Gen 49,10," 412–14. Moran's proposal has been widely accepted by scholars (e.g. Speiser, *Genesis*, 366; Wenham, *Genesis 16–50*, 478; Sarna, *Genesis*, 336; or de Hoop, *Genesis*, 129–39), is reflected in the NRSV and NJPS, and has even made its way into a popular handbook of exegesis as an example of the usefulness of orthography. See Douglas Stuart, *Old Testament Exegesis: A Handbook for Students and Pastors*, 3rd ed. (Louisville, KY: Westminster John Knox, 2001), 54–55.

47. Moran, "Gen 49,10," 413.

48. See, for example, Ps 96:8.

49. Steiner, "Forms," 222–26.

blessing of Judah is unaffected by the puzzling reference to "Shiloh," as in any case this seems to indicate that his role will only increase.

Verse 11

The imagery of the eleventh verse is again different. The text[50] refers to a person that will bind his donkey to a vine, and will wash his garment[51] in the grapes. Both actions seem unreasonable. A donkey would likely eat the grapes of the vine to which it is bound, and one can readily imagine a better use of wine than to wash clothes with it. Nevertheless, these irregular procedures are likely cases in point. As Wenham points out, the images carry the overtones of abundance:

> There will be so many vines that the ruler will not worry about his ass eating the choicest vines, as it surely would if tethered to them.... There will be such an abundance of grapes that those trampling them in the wine press will not just splash their garments (cf. Isa 63:1–3) but soak them. Or the image may be of such a surplus of wine that people will not worry about using it to wash clothes in![52]

Verse 11 thus suggests that the surplus of the fruit of vine will be lavishly used for purposes far from ordinary.[53] Judah's leadership position will usher Israel, and possibly the wider world, into a life that overflows with good things.

Verse 12

The last verse of Judah's blessing addresses his physical qualities.[54] The text says: "his eyes are darker[55] than wine (יָיִן) and teeth whiter than

---

50. The Masoretes indicate again that the closing word in the first and the fourth lines should be read עִירֹו and סוּתֹו respectively. This ending is likely an earlier version of the third person singular, which was replaced with a later one (similarly also "Shiloh" in v. 10). See Joüon §266.

51. For a survey of patristic interpretations of the concept of clothing in Gen 49:11, see Carmelo Granado Bellido, "Simbolismo del vestido: Interpretación patrística de Gen 49:11," *EstEcl* 59 (1984): 313–57.

52. Wenham, *Genesis 16–50*, 478–79.

53. Caquot recalls that just as the absence of vines and the lack of wine are signs of judgment (Isa 16:10; Jer 8:13), so their abundance points to the restoration of Israel (Amos 9:13–14). See Caquot, "Juda," 29.

54. Zobel highlights that the whole blessing personifies Judah's tribe by mentioning his feet (v. 10), teeth, and eyes (v. 12). See Zobel, *Stammesspruch*, 12.

55. The adjective חַכְלִיל has its only counterpart in the Old Testament in the noun found in Prov 23:29 (חַכְלִלוּת). Westermann follows Kapelrud and takes the root of the verb to be חכל, with a meaning similar to Akkadian and Arabic signifying "to be dark." See Westermann, *Genesis 37–50*, 219; and Arvid S. Kapelrud, "Genesis xlix 12," *VT* 4 (1954): 426–28. However, *HALOT* derives the root from כחל and assumes metathesis of the first two consonants. The proposed meaning is then "sparkling" or "shining," which fits quite well with wine as the cause (*HALOT* 1:313; also Bruce K. Waltke, *Genesis: A Commentary* [Grand Rapids: Zondervan, 2001], 609, n. 197). Even though both possibilities probably

milk (חָלָב)."[56] On the one hand, this parallelism seems to continue the resonances of abundance from the previous verse, as the image of milk echoes the "land overflowing with milk (חָלָב) and honey" (e.g. Deut 26:9). Similarly, both milk and wine are present in Isa 55:1, where God promises an age of great plenty symbolized by people's ability to "buy wine (יַיִן) and milk (חָלָב) without money and without price." On the other hand, v. 12 seems to visualize beauty and health, as for example in Song 4:1–2, which describes the beauty of a lover using similes focusing on the eyes, hair, and teeth.

Verses 11–12 thus abound with images of wealth, beauty, and health. The focus since the beginning of the blessing has changed. Judah, who is strong against his enemies and respected by his brothers, has achieved significant progress in his rule. At the end of the blessing, his reign is portrayed in extravagant terms that evoke prosperity and wellbeing.

Summary

The blessing Jacob gives to Judah stands in sharp contrast to the much harsher words delivered to his older brothers. Unlike those first two, the blessing upon Judah portrays him as a leader of his people. He is revered by his brothers and like a powerful animal poses a threat to his enemies. His reign will eventually increase, leading to the atmosphere of abundance and bliss of unusual proportion. The blessing thus depicts a situation that will take place in the days to come, pointing beyond the contours of the Joseph cycle and naturally thrusting itself into the future.[57]

---

signify a state of happiness and joy, I think that the image of "dark eyes" fits better the context where it is contrasted with "white teeth." See also Aaron Demsky, "Dark Wine from Judah," *IEJ* 22 (1972): 233–34. The LXX contains χαροποί ("flashing"), which probably comes through haplography from χαροποιοί, which is retained in some manuscripts, and means "gladdening." See Wevers, *Genesis*, 827; or Rösel, "Septuaginta," 65.

56. The preposition מִן should probably be understood comparatively here (thus also de Hoop, *Genesis*, 142; or Caquot, "Juda," 30). The LXX already points to this interpretation in the second part of the verse: λευκοὶ οἱ ὀδόντες αὐτοῦ ἢ γάλα ("his teeth whiter than milk"). See Wevers, *Genesis*, 827.

57. This forward-looking orientation of the oracle, together with its mysterious reference to Shiloh, has proved to be fertile ground for various messianic interpretations down the ages. For a thorough representation of both Jewish and Christian appropriations up to Middle Ages, see Adolf Posnanski, *Shiloh: Ein Beitrag zur Geschichte der Messiaslehre* (Leipzig: Ginrichs, 1904). See also Alfred Marx, "'Jusqu'à ce que vienne Shiloh': Pour une interprétation messianique de Genèse 49,8–12," in *Ce Dieu qui vient: Études sur l'Ancien et le Nouveau Testament offertes au professeur Bernard Renaud à l'occasion de son soixante-cinquième anniversaire*, ed. Raymond Kuntzmann, LD 159 (Paris: Cerf, 1995), 95–111.

10

Genesis 49:
Joseph

Having looked at Judah's blessing in Gen 49:8–12, I now need to attend closely to Jacob's other lengthy oracle—the one devoted to Joseph (Gen 49:22–26). As in the previous case, I will discuss this complicated saying verse by verse. This approach is further necessitated by the unusual number of grammatical and syntactical problems that Joseph's oracle contains.

Verse 22

Already the opening verse of the blessing, which in Hebrew reads בֵּן פֹּרָת
יוֹסֵף בֵּן פֹּרָת עֲלֵי־עָיִן בָּנוֹת צָעֲדָה עֲלֵי־שׁוּר, bristles with textual difficulties. First, the vocalization of פֹּרָת in the double occurrence of the construct chain בֵּן
פֹּרָת indicates that it could be the Qal feminine singular participle from the root פרה, "be fruitful." However, conventional grammar usually requires that the first word should be in the construct form בֶּן־.[1] Additionally, one wonders what the phrase "son of a fruitful (one)" might indicate. Second, the noun בָּנוֹת ("daughters") in the third colon is in the plural, but it is followed by the verb צָעֲדָה in the singular, and thus there is no agreement between the noun and verb. Third, and perhaps most importantly, this verb seems to come from the root צעד, which means "walk," "stride," or "march."[2] What are then some possible interpretative proposals that may make this verse intelligible?[3]

---

1. See, for example, GKC §89. It is conceivable that in rare cases the first word in the construct chain would also be in the absolute state. However, HALOT mentions in this regard only בֶּן with maqqēp̄, and this construction is found only in 1 Sam 22:20 and Ezek 18:10 (see HALOT 1:137).

2. See, for example, HALOT 2:1040; or TDOT, which suggests that these verbs are "frequently used in elevated, poetic expressions." See D. Kellermann, "צעד," TDOT 12:421–24, esp. 422.

3. The Greek text does not seem to offer much help here. It contains: υἱὸς ηὐξημένος Ιωσηφ υἱὸς ηὐξημένος ζηλωτός υἱός μου νεώτατος πρός με ἀνάστρεψον ("A grown up son is Joseph, a grown up enviable son. My youngest son, turn to me!"). The perfect passive participle ηὐξημένος of the verb αὐξάνω ("increase") seems to focus on one possible aspect of what the Hebrew text describes metaphorically: Joseph is fruitful, which could be taken as that he has grown up (see Wevers, Genesis, 831). Similarly also Marguerite Harl, La Genèse, BdA 1 (Paris: Cerf, 1986), 312. Whereas Wevers states that "the origins of ζηλωτός 'enviable' are inexplicable" (Wevers, Genesis, 831), Caquot suggests that it could come

Traditional Interpretation

Traditionally the verse has been interpreted as referring to a fruitful tree, as it is expressed, for example, in the NRSV:

> Joseph is a fruitful bough,
> a fruitful bough by a spring,
> his branches run over the wall.

To begin with, this rendering could explain some of the textual complexities of v. 22. First, the participle from the root פרה is found also elsewhere in the Old Testament, where it refers to "fruitful branches" or a "fruitful vine."[4] It is thus plausible that the phrase בֵּן פֹּרָת may denote a "young fruit tree." Second, the textual difficulty involving the presence of the noun בֵּן in its absolute, rather than construct, state is defended as required by the rhythm, which would have been destroyed if the noun בֵּן in the first two lines had lost its stress and was connected by a *maqqēp̄* with the following word.[5] Third, the problematic form פֹּרָת, which appears to be the feminine singular participle, may be understood as a noun with the rare feminine ending *āt*.[6] Fourth, the noun בָּנוֹת, ("daughters") in the third colon may be taken symbolically as a tree's limbs climbing or running over a wall.[7]

---

from a transliteration of the last phrase as עֲלֵי עָיִן, meaning "on whom the eye is," which might denote envy. See André Caquot, "Ben Porat (Genèse 49:22)," *Sem* 30 (1980): 43–56, esp. 46, n. 1. The rendering "my youngest son" perhaps took the obscure phrase בנות צעדה as בני הצער (thus Wevers, *Genesis*, 831). Finally, the surprising imperative ἀνάστρεφον, calling Joseph to return to Jacob, likely read the final שׁור as שׁוב. See Wevers, *Genesis*, 832; or Harl, *Genèse*, 312. A concise discussion can be found also in Rösel, "Septuaginta," esp. 67. The LXX text is thus a good example of the difficulties that the MT text poses and the creativity which needs to be employed to make it intelligible.

4. The feminine participle פֹּרִיָה occurs in connection with "branches" in Isa 17:6, or with a "vine" (גֶּפֶן) in Ps 128:3; Isa 32:12; and Ezek 19:10–14. Zobel also highlights Hos 10:1—"Israel is a luxuriant vine (גֶּפֶן) that yields its fruit (פְּרִי)" (NRSV)—as an echo of Gen 49:22 (Zobel, *Stammesspruch*, 21).

5. The construct chain would in this case create one phonetic unit and the rhythm would be broken. Thus, for example, Skinner, *Genesis*, 529; and de Hoop, *Genesis*, 181, n. 654. De Hoop also points out that when we look up construct forms of other monosyllabic nouns, such as שֵׁם, we discover that in cases where the word preserves its stress, it is often vocalized שֵׁם and not שֶׁם. Only in Genesis can this form be found, for example, in Gen 2:13, 14; 4:17, 19, 21; 10:25, or 11:29. This strengthens the possibility that בֵּן can be written similarly (de Hoop, *Genesis*, 185–86).

6. Thus Joüon §89n. Alternatively, פֹּרָת could be understood as a masculine noun with an unusual ending (similar to מוֹדַעַת applied to Boaz in Ruth 3:2), which signifies an intensification of certain characteristics. Seen this way, the phrase might mean an "especially fruitful tree." See Shelomo Morag, "ומתערה כאזרה רענן (Psalms xxxvii:35)," *Tarbiz* 41 (1971): 1–23 (in Hebrew), esp. 6, n. 22, and the summary of this proposal in Stanley Gevirtz, "Of Patriarchs and Puns: Joseph at the Fountain, Jacob at the Ford," *HUCA* 46 (1975): 33–54, esp. 36.

7. Calvin nicely captures the reasoning behind this interpretation: "I suppose the tender and smaller branches to be called daughters" (Calvin, *Genesis*, 2:346). Nevertheless,

Fifth, the disagreement between the subject and predicate may be a feature that is sometimes reflected in other parts of the Old Testament where plural abstract nouns or names of animals or plants take a singular feminine verb.[8]

Additionally, this interpretation fits the thematic world of the book of Genesis.[9] The Joseph narrative itself culminates the story of the human race within the book of Genesis that begins with the opening commandment: פְּרוּ וּרְבוּ, "be fruitful and multiply" (Gen 1:28). This command is echoed in several places towards the end of the book. It appears when the narrator recounts Israel's experience in famine-stricken Egypt where Israel was "fruitful and multiplied" (וַיִּפְרוּ וַיִּרְבּוּ, 47:27), and when Jacob recollects his own experience with God, who promised to make him "fruitful and numerous" (מַפְרְךָ וְהִרְבִּיתִךָ, 48:4). It also resonates with the name given to Joseph's second-born Ephraim, who is named this way because, as Joseph said: "God has made me fruitful (הִפְרַנִי) in the land of my misfortunes" (41:52).[10] Viewed in this framework, the opening verse of the blessing upon Joseph presents the patriarch in line with the narrative that precedes it: fruitful and increasing in stature.[11]

A More Recent Interpretation

Nevertheless, although textual difficulties may indeed be solved by reference to irregularities in the language, such a large number of irregularities nevertheless raises suspicion. Additionally, in addressing his sons Jacob's blessing frequently employs animal images, and Gen 49:22 would be the only instance where we encounter a floral imagery.[12]

Kugel reminds us that a creative rabbinic interpretation surmised that the phrase perhaps speaks of young women climbing the wall to see Joseph's beauty. James L. Kugel, *The Bible As It Was* (Cambridge, MA: Harvard University Press, 1997), 280–81.

8. GKC §145k, for example, cites, besides Gen 49:22, also Job 12:7; Jer 12:4; and Joel 1:20. Similarly Joüon §150g. Alternatively, the verb could in fact be plural, where the final ה is misspelled for ו under the influence of Aramaic (also Joüon §42f).

9. Wenham also highlights the connection between fruitfulness and Psalms in Wenham, *Genesis 16–50*, 484.

10. Spurrell notes that Ephraim might mean "double fruitfulness," and thus the connection with Joseph's more favored son creates a natural allusion in Gen 49:22 (Spurrell, *Notes*, 352). Similarly Zobel, *Stammesspruch*, 21–22.

11. Probably the most notable, albeit cautious, modern proponent of this view is Westermann, *Genesis 37–50*, 219–20, 236–37. See also von Rad, *Genesis*, 420, 427; Matthews, *Genesis*, 904; and Ebach, *Genesis*, 569. This rendering is also adopted by the NIV and NRSV.

12. Also, the words בֵּן and בָּנוֹת are not commonly used in connection with plants, but rather with humans or animals. De Hoop states that בֵּן "is never used for plants" (de Hoop, *Genesis*, 184). He substantiates his argument by referring, among other things, to the exhaustive listing in *DCH* 2:186–26, esp. 207–8. *TDOT* mentions only Gen 49:22 as possibly referring to a "bough" or " sprout." See Jan Bergman et al., "בֵּן," *TDOT* 2:145–59, esp. 150.

Although certain scholars have tried to ease some of the difficulties and thus keep the botanical imagery a viable interpretive option,[13] a recent opinion, which has gained significant acceptance among some interpreters, finds a solution in understanding v. 22 as employing an animal metaphor. Although interpreters differ considerably in their suggestions that the oracle likens Joseph to an animal, two basic approaches might be distinguished.[14]

First, Joseph might be seen as resembling a "wild ass." The reference to cognate languages has proved helpful in this case, as Arabic *banāt ṣaʿdat*—"wild asses"—has been suggested as being very similar to the obscure phrase בָּנוֹת צָעֲדָה in the third colon.[15] Perhaps the most succinct proposal of this sort can be found in Speiser's commentary, where he suggests connecting פֹּרָת with פֶּרֶא, "ass,"[16] and offers this translation of the whole verse:

> Joseph is a wild colt,
> a wild colt by a spring,
> wild asses on a hillside.[17]

This suggestion, however, also has its weaknesses. Besides the unusual change from singular in the first two cola to the plural in the third colon, the chief objection lies in the observation that although שׁוּר might indeed denote a "wall" in a more poetic sense, this is still quite far removed from the description of a "hillside."[18]

Second, Joseph might be depicted poetically as a "cow."[19] In this regard one might understand פֹּרָת as derived from פָּרָה and the phrase may be re-vocalized as בֶּן פָּרֹת, "son of cows," especially when the fuller version

---

13. See especially Caquot, "Ben," 52; and Emerton, "Words," 91–93.

14. Macchi's succinct summary of the various approaches has been most helpful in this regard (Macchi, *Israël*, 189–95).

15. The connection with Arabic is noted in Arnold B. Ehrlich, *Randglossen zur Hebräischen Bibel: Textkritisches, Sprachliches and Sachliches*. Vol. 1, *Genesis und Exodus* (Leipzig: Hinrichs, 1908), 250.

16. Speiser, *Genesis*, 367–68. Perhaps it may be an archaic feminine form (Macchi, *Israël*, 189).

17. Speiser, *Genesis*, 363. This proposal seems to be reflected in the NJPS translation.

18. Gevirtz tries to remedy this weakness by pointing out that שׁוּר in connection with עַיִן ("spring") can also be found in Gen 16:7, where the angel of YHWH visits Hagar and Ishmael "by the spring on the way to Shur" (עַל־הָעַיִן בְּדֶרֶךְ שׁוּר). Since Ishmael is described similarly to Joseph in Gen 16:12—he is called a "wild ass of a man" (פֶּרֶא אָדָם)—Gevirtz considers the image in Gen 49:22 a geopolitical pun associating Joseph with Ishmael and the area of Negeb, and ventures to explore its possible implications (Gevirtz, "Puns," 41–44). A comparison between Ishmael and Joseph is also explored in Noble, *Place*, 41–43.

19. Ehrlich already hints at this when he notes that Deut 33:17 uses the imagery of a "bull" (Ehrlich, *Randglossen*, 250). Yet Joseph's designation here is not פָּרָה, but שׁוּר. The metaphor using פָּרָה in relation to Northern Israel can be found, however, in Hos 4:16 and Amos 4:1.

פָּרוֹת ("cows") has appeared previously in the Joseph cycle (Gen 41:2, 3, 18, 19). The last word in the oracle might also be vocalized differently, as שׁוֹר, "bull." One possible interpretation then might be as follows:

> Joseph is a son of cows,
> a son of cows near a spring.
> Daughters (of cows) marched towards the bull.[20]

An appealing modification of this view is presented in Korpel's brief note in her study on Hebrew and Ugaritic metaphors of the divine.[21] First, she suggests that the word בָּנוֹת does not mean "daughters," as is commonly assumed, but should be changed into בְּנוֶה, meaning "in the meadow," where נוֶה is a noun with a primitive feminine ending.[22] Second, she takes the word שׁוֹר, "bull," as a metaphor for the divine being.[23] Finally, Korpel proposes reading v. 22 together with the first colon of v. 23, where she interprets the first verb וַיְמָרֲרֻהוּ based on Ugaritic as "strengthen," for which the bull is the subject, and the second verb וָרֹבּוּ as "make numerous."[24] Her final translation thus offers this reading:

> A son of a cow is Joseph,
> a son of a cow next to a well,
> in the meadows she strode towards the Bull,
> and he made him strong, so that they became numerous.[25]

Korpel's translation thus brings God into a picture by suggesting that the reference to the "Bull" in the third colon of v. 22 continues into v. 23. God is, in this way, a source of Joseph's strength and the unusual numerousness of his descendants.[26]

---

20. Thus Macchi, *Israël*, 185. Similarly Gunkel, *Genesis*, 459–60; Bruce Vawter, "Canaanite Background of Genesis 49," *CBQ* 17 (1955): 1–18, esp. 7–9; J. Coppens, "La bénédiction de Jacob: Son cadre historique à la lumiére des paralléles ougaritiques," in Anderson, ed, *Volume du Congrès: Strasbourg 1956*, 97–115, esp. 100–101; and Vello Salo, "Joseph, Sohn der Färse," *BZ* 12 (1968): 94–95.

21. Marjo C. A. Korpel, *A Rift in the Clouds: Ugaritic and Hebrew Descriptions of the Divine*, UBL 8 (Münster: Ugarit, 1990), 532–34.

22. Korpel, *Rift*, 532, n. 58.

23. Korpel, *Rift*, 532, n. 60. For more on the bull metaphor in the Old Testament based on a comparison with Ugaritic, see A. H. W. Curtis, "Some Observation on 'Bull' Terminology in the Ugaritic Texts and the Old Testament," in *In Quest of the Past: Studies on Israelite Religion, Literature, and Prophetism*, ed. A. S. van der Woude (Leiden: Brill, 1990), 17–31.

24. Korpel suggests that the root מרר, which in Ugaritic means "strengthen," is often used in connection with blessings (Korpel, *Rift*, 533, n. 61; also de Hoop, *Genesis*, 191).

25. Korpel, *Rift*, 532–33.

26. The change from masculine to feminine in Gen 49:22c, however, is problematic. De Hoop, who otherwise accepts Korpel's argumentation, picks up this issue and proposes that the verb may be the infinitive construct with the archaic third masculine singular (צָעֲדֹה) meaning "his striding" (de Hoop, *Genesis*, 193–94).

Summary

I have recounted several suggestions as to how Gen 49:22 may depict an animal metaphor. This was done in order to demonstrate the ways in which they vary in terms of how the verse might be understood in its entirety. Their strength comes precisely from the ability to draw on cognate languages in order to show that the text can refer to a "wild ass" or a "heifer," which would fit nicely with the rest of Jacob's blessing where animal images abound.[27] However, besides the fact that no single rendering among them has gained unanimous acceptance so far,[28] their major weakness lies in their shifting of the problem away from the obscure words and onto the common ones. When unclear phrases, such as the clause בָּנוֹת צָעֲדָה or the verb מרר, are explained with reference to Arabic or Ugaritic, the problem then moves to other words whose meaning was previously unquestioned. Thus, even though this series of proposals has been quite influential among recent interpreters, and is attractive in terms of its continuing the sequence of animal metaphors in Jacob's blessing, it creates its own specific set of problems. In my opinion, the burden of proof still rests with the more recent view, which should elucidate more effectively how the presence of the animal metaphor makes greater sense of Gen 49:22 as a whole. Although I am aware that on any reading of 49:22 the problem resists easy solutions, the picture of a fruitful bough seems to fit well with the portrayal of Joseph in the preceding narrative, which focuses on Joseph's unique role in ensuring and embodying Israel's fruitfulness.

Verse 23

Although v. 23, which in the Hebrew reads: וַיְמָרֲרֻהוּ וָרֹבּוּ וַיִּשְׂטְמֻהוּ בַּעֲלֵי חִצִּים, does not present the reader with difficulties of the scale and importance of those in the preceding verse, it nevertheless contains several problems of its own. First, the subject of all three verbs in the series—בַּעֲלֵי חִצִּים, "masters of arrows," and thus "archers"—occurs only at the end of the whole verse, which is quite unusual in terms of word order.[29] Second, the perfect aspect of the second verb of the three stands in contrast to the imperfect of the other two verbs, which would again be quite uncharacteristic for verbs written in such a sequence.[30] Third, although the verb רֹבּוּ might be regarded as the Qal perfect third person plural of the root רבב

---

27. See Hamilton, *Genesis: 18–50*, 683.

28. Ebach, *Genesis*, 624, comes to a similar conclusion.

29. If the subject of a sentence functions for both cola, it is normally introduced already in the first colon as, for example, in vv. 19 and 20.

30. Macchi calls attention to the series of verbs in *wayyiqtol* in Gen 49:15 (Macchi, *Israël*, 197).

or רבה, meaning "shoot,"[31] one would expect that the appropriate form would be רָבוּ and not רֹבוּ.[32]

The traditional understanding of the verse regards the construct chain בַּעֲלֵי חִצִּים as the subject of the clause, even though it occurs only at the end of the whole verse.[33] Further, the second verb might be taken as the imperfect וַיְרֹבּוּ, as suggested by the textual apparatus of the *BHS*, which would fit better into the series of the present verse's three verbs. Finally, the unusual pointing of רֹבוּ instead of the expected רָבוּ is defended for example by GKC, which points out that such forms may occur in situations where verbs denote states or qualities.[34] The whole verse might thus be interpreted in this way: "The archers embittered him[35] and shot [at him,] they were hostile towards him."

Although the more traditional understanding faces some criticism,[36] it offers, in my opinion, the best explanation of the present crux. Seen in this light, v. 23 portrays an image of Joseph or his tribe under attack. On the one hand, one may espy some resonances here with the rest of the book of Genesis. The third verb in the verse, שׂטם, meaning to "be at enmity with" or to "be hostile towards,"[37] is used in Genesis regarding

---

31. See *HALOT* 2:1175; or BDB, 8852 with its additional reference to Ps 18:15 (ET 18:14), where one finds: "And he sent his arrows and scattered them; he shot his lightnings and routed them (וּבְרָקִים רָב וַיְהֻמֵּם)."

32. SP has וַיָּרִיבָהוּ, from the root ריב, meaning "and they strove with him" or "entered into controversy with him," which is likely reflected in the LXX ἐλοιδόρουν (the only word of this verse where the LXX diverges from the MT), "they were reviling." See Wevers, *Genesis*, 832; or Macchi, *Israël*, 199.

33. Westermann suggests that "it is possible that some words have fallen out before" the first verb (Westermann, *Genesis 37–50*, 220).

34. GKC says: "In the perfect, isolated examples are found with ō in the first syllable, which it is customary to refer to triliteral stems with middle ō." GKC mentions alongside our present verb also, for example, רֹמּוּ, "they are exalted" in Job 24:24 (GKC §67m). However, if the word carries the meaning "they shot," then the force of the verb is active. For this reason Joüon opines that this rules out the possibility of a stative verb, and thus it is hard to explain (Joüon §82l).

35. The verb וַיְמָרֲרֻהוּ may be categorized as the Piel imperfect third masculine plural with the third masculine singular suffix from the verb מרר, meaning "they made him bitter." See Heinz-Jozef Fabry and Helmer Ringgren, "מרר," *TDOT* 9:15–19; or *HALOT* 1:638. However, it has been argued that, based on Ugaritic and Arabic, the verb מרר may also mean "be strong" or "strengthen." See, for example, Laurence A. Kutler, "A 'Strong' Case for Hebrew *Mar*," *UF* 16 (1984): 111–18; or Hamilton, *Genesis: 18–50*, 679, n. 6.

36. Korpel and de Hoop read the first colon of v. 23 together with v. 22 (see p. 95). They take the obscure רֹבוּ as coming from the common root רבה or רבב meaning "make many/great" (see *HALOT* 2:1174–75; 2:1176–78). However, the perfect of וְרֹבוּ seems awkward in its placement in the sequence of the three verbs, and its form is not typical even for the supposed root רבב. Also, the change from the singular "he will make him strong" to the plural "they will become numerous" seems unnatural, and one wonders who is meant by the subject *they*.

37. See *HALOT* 2:1316.

Esau hating Jacob (Gen 27:41), and also in regard to Joseph's brothers' fear concerning their formerly estranged brother, in Gen 50:15.[38] On the other hand, the imagery in v. 23 may point to some future situations in which Joseph's descendants are attacked by enemies. After the opening verse of the blessing, which describes Joseph in positive terms, we are faced with the image of opposition. Joseph is a fruitful son but his prosperity provokes enmity. The resulting picture may be appropriately applied both to Joseph as a character in Gen 37–50, and to the subsequent history of the tribes that bore the names of his two sons.

Verse 24

Verse 24 can be divided into two parts. The first portion of the verse (וַתֵּשֶׁב בְּאֵיתָן קַשְׁתּוֹ וַיָּפֹזּוּ זְרֹעֵי יָדָיו) may be translated as follows: "His bow remained taut,[39] and the arms of his hands[40] were agile."[41] The first colon then describes a bow that is constantly firm, while the second portrays the arms of an archer that remain active. Skinner summarizes well the main thrust of the first half of v. 24: "[it] suggests a fine picture: the bow held steadily in position, while the hand that discharges the arrows in quick succession moves nimbly to and fro."[42] The idea thus seems straightforward.[43] Joseph

---

38. Further, the image of archers shooting at Joseph may be understood meta-phorically, as is suggested, for example, by Rashi, who mentions that Joseph's brothers, Potiphar, and his wife all dealt bitterly with Joseph (Rosenbaum and Silbermann, eds., *Rashi: Genesis*, 250). The imagery of tongues as arrows can be found in Ps 120:3–4; Prov 25:18; 26:18–19; and Jer 9:2 (ET 9:3). See also, for example, Gen. Rab. 98.19, and Wenham, *Genesis 16–50*, 485.

39. The meaning of the image seems to be clear even though the precise meaning of the adjective אֵיתָן is not altogether certain (*HALOT* 1:44–45, suggests that it means "constant" or "continual"), and the preposition בְּ occurs in connection with it only here in the Old Testament out of its twenty-two occurrences. As a phrase it might be translated "in firmness." See Spurrell, Notes, 396; and Westermann, *Genesis 37–50*, 238.

40. The construct chain זְרֹעֵי יָדָיו ("arms of his hands") occurs only here in the Old Testament. Driver suggests that arms "regulate and control the movements of the hands" (Driver, *Genesis*, 391). Similarly BDB, 2744.

41. The verb וַיָּפֹזּוּ comes from the root פזז, probably meaning "be nimble, agile, quick moving," and occurs in Qal only here (*HALOT* 2:921; Spurrell, *Notes*, 396). The second occurrence of this word in the Old Testament, which describes David "leaping (מְפַזֵּז) and dancing before YHWH" (2 Sam 6:16), is in Piel.

42. Skinner, *Genesis*, 530.

43. However, the LXX presents a different interpretation of likely the same text (thus Wevers, *Genesis*, 832), when it says: "and their bows were broken with force, and the tendons of the arms of their hands became weary." The Greek text thus effectively links God, who becomes the source of Joseph's strength later in the saying, more directly to Joseph's victory in battle. Similarly Magne Sæbø, "Divine Names and Epithets in Genesis 49:24b–25a: Some Methodological and Tradition-historical Remarks," in *History and Traditions of Early Israel: Studies Presented to Eduard Nielsen*, ed. André Lamaire and Benedikt Otzen, VTSup 50 (Leiden: Brill, 1993), 115–32, esp. 117–18.

displays here a "courageous resistance: steadfastness and dexterity with weapon, arm, and hand"[44] when attacked by his enemies.

The second part of v. 24, which reveals God as the source of Joseph's strength, begins a series of divine epithets, which continue into the following verse. The occurrence of several untypical designations of God in Gen 49:24–25 is surprising, and signals that Joseph's clan retains not only a close connection with Joseph's father, but through him also with the God of the patriarchs.[45]

The first phrase is מִידֵי אֲבִיר יַעֲקֹב ("by the hands of the Mighty One of Jacob"). The word אֲבִיר means "strong" or "powerful" and as an epithet for the deity it occurs six times in the Old Testament: five times (Gen 49:24; Ps 132:2, 5; Isa 49:26; 60:16) with "Jacob," and once (Isa 1:24) with "Israel."[46] The phrase in a poetic way depicts the identity of the source behind Joseph's triumph: his hands were made strong by the hands of Jacob's mighty God.

The two other divine names contained in the last colon of the verse—which reads מִשָּׁם רֹעֶה אֶבֶן יִשְׂרָאֵל, and may be translated "by the name[47] of the Shepherd, the Rock of Israel"—carry distant echoes of earlier parts of Genesis. Jacob's sons are introduced to the Pharaoh as shepherds (Gen 47:3), and Jacob himself refers to God as a Shepherd when he blesses Joseph (Gen 48:15).[48] The divine name רֹעֶה, the "Shepherd," which famously appears also in the opening of Ps 23 (and also in Ps 80:2 [ET 80:1]), seems therefore an appropriate term for God, who was guiding Jacob and is now evoked in the blessing of his most favorite son.

---

44. Westermann, *Genesis 37–50*, 238.

45. The divine names in Gen 49:24–25 have been used as providing a window into Israel's ancient religion. For the seminal study of this reconstruction, see Albrecht Alt, "God of the Fathers," in *Essays on Old Testament Religion*, trans. R. A. Wilson (Garden City, NY: Doubleday, 1968), 3–86. For a succinct discussion of the development of this argument up until modern times, see Matthews, *Genesis*, 56–60.

46. Vawter states in his article, which argues for the Canaanite background of Jacob's blessing, that the original meaning of the phrase was "Bull of Jacob" (Vawter, "Background," 11). However, as Köckert points out, this link is, at most, only indirect. See Matthias Köckert, "Mighty One of Jacob," in *Dictionary of Deities and Demons in the Bible*, ed. Karel Van der Toorn et al. (Leiden: Brill, 1999), 573–75, esp. 574.

47. The vocalization of the MT text suggests that the beginning of the phrase consists of מִן and שָׁם, which means "from there." This is also reflected in the LXX: ἐκεῖθεν ("thence, from there"). However, this would be quite unusual, given the apparent parallelism between the third and the fourth colon. For this reason a number of scholars propose to re-vocalize the phrase to מִשֵּׁם, so that it would express a similar notion as in the preceding phrase—"because of the name." Thus Westermann, *Genesis 37–50*, 219–20, 228; Wenham, *Genesis 16–50*, 458; and de Hoop, *Genesis*, 198.

48. Sæbø uses the link with Gen 48:15 to suggest that רֹעֶה might also be functioning as a participle, and translates: "from where the Stone of Israel is guarding/protecting" (Sæbø, "Names," 130).

The second epithet—אֶבֶן יִשְׂרָאֵל, "Rock of Israel"—occurs only here in the Old Testament, even though the same concept, but with a different wording—צוּר יִשְׂרָאֵל—can be found in several biblical passages, mainly in Psalms.[49] More importantly, one may perhaps recall Jacob's two experiences with YHWH after which he erected pillars of stone (Gen 28:18–22; 35:11–14). Especially the second occasion has a close affinity to our present passage, since it features God the Almighty charging Jacob with a commandment to be fruitful and multiply (35:11). The patriarch was further promised the land for his offspring, and the oracle also mentions kings coming from his seed (35:11–12). This web of resonances between the events at Bethel and the blessing given to Joseph shows that a reference to God as the "Rock" is plausible here.[50] It is a fitting catchphrase evoking God's stability in protection of Jacob and his favorite son.

Verse 25

Verse 25 continues the line of thought from the preceding verse, by adding more divine names that further characterize the God that helps and blesses Joseph, and by describing the scope of the blessing that Jacob's favored son receives. The source of Joseph's aid is here depicted by the expression אֵל אָבִיךָ וְיַעְזְרֶךָ.[51] There is some debate as to whether the phrase should be understood as the genitive "God of your father," referring to Jacob, or as two words in apposition "God/El, your father," where both nouns speak of the deity. Although the second option has its attractiveness, possibly being paralleled in other ancient texts,[52] the whole of ch. 49 deals with the blessing given by *Jacob* to his twelve sons, and thus it seems natural in this context to find a reference to the "God *of your father* who will help you."[53] Furthermore, the reference to "the blessings of your father" in the following

---

49. For example, 2 Sam 23:3; Pss 18:3 (ET 18:2), 32 (ET 31), 47 (ET 46); 28:1; 62:3 (ET 62:2), 7 (ET 6); 89:27 (ET 89:26); 94:22; Isa 30:29.

50. Some scholars disagree. For example, David N. Freedman proposes that אֶבֶן might be read as בְּנֵי with prosthetic *aleph*, expressing "sons" in the plural construct state. See David N. Freedman, "Divine Names and Titles in Early Hebrew Poetry," in *Pottery, Poetry, and Prophecy: Studies in Early Hebrew Poetry* (Winona Lake, IN: Eerdmans, 1980), 77–130, esp. 87. Another option is suggested by Sanmartín who thought that the word could have been a gloss, reading אֶבֶן—in itself possibly a defective form of אָבִינוּ—"our father." See J. Sanmartín, "Problemas de textologia en las 'Bendiciones' de Moises (Dt 33) y de Jacob (Gn 49)," in *El misterio de la palabra: Homenaje a Luis Alonso Schökel*, ed. Vicente Collado and Eduardo Zurro (Madrid: Ediciones Cristiandad, 1983), 75–96, esp. 89.

51. As before, the epithet is again introduced by the preposition מִן.

52. De Hoop stresses that in the Ugaritic "the Bull Illu is also called 'father'" (de Hoop, *Genesis*, 205–6, esp. 206). Similarly also Vawter, "Background," 12; Coppens, "Bénédiction," 102; or Korpel, *Rift*, 533.

53. The deity in Genesis is frequently introduced as the "God of your father" (אֱלֹהֵי אָבִיךָ), sometimes including the name of a particular patriarch or patriarchs (e.g. Gen 26:24; 31:29; 43:23; 46:3; 50:17). See also Macchi, *Israël*, 217–18.

verse makes the genitive construal more probable. The God known from the patriarchal stories, who was Jacob's protector and sustainer, is the same God who will help Joseph and his descendants.

Finally, the one who blesses Joseph is described as שַׁדַּי ("Almighty").[54] This is only appropriate, as noted by Wenham, because this epithet is consistently used in connection with blessing in Jacob's story (Gen 28:3; 35:11; 48:3).[55] The blessings falling upon Joseph's head, of which the counterpart can be found in Deut 33:13–16, are expressed here in three lines containing four areas of divine activity—heaven above, the deep that lies below, the breast, and the womb. The first two lines make a distinction between the sphere above and that which is below, when בִּרְכֹת שָׁמַיִם מֵעָל ("blessings of heaven from above") is contrasted with בִּרְכֹת תְּהוֹם רֹבֶצֶת תָּחַת ("blessings of the deep that lies below").[56] Both phrases resonate with the opening chapters of Genesis where, after the creation of the heaven (שָׁמַיִם) and the earth in Gen 1:1, we read about the void and formless earth and the darkness covering the face of the deep (תְּהוֹם) in Gen 1:2, which was later transformed by the fashioning and ordering activity of the Spirit of God. This sort of magnified and powerful blessing spanning the whole universe is available to Joseph.

The second instrument of divine help is spoken of as "breasts" and a "womb," which may offer a contrast to the curse of Gen 3:16, and which ensures that Joseph and his future generations will have divine help in establishing a lineage of many children. The whole image evokes a theme of fertility and fruitfulness, important throughout the book (1:22, 28; 9:1, 7; 17:6, 20; 28:3; 35:11; 48:4). From the standpoint of interpreting 49:22–26 it also strengthens the possibility that the opening verse of the blessing upon Joseph could be understood as speaking of a "fruitful bough." God Almighty, who revealed himself to his father, now blesses Joseph with blessings as rich as the realms above and below, and who makes his clan to be fruitful and multiply.

---

54. The title is introduced with the direct object marker and the connecting *waw*—וְאֵת. However, the direct object marker seems puzzling in this series of divine epithets, and thus interpreters propose the word should be either rewritten as וְאֵל, "God" (Driver, *Genesis*, 392; Westermann, *Genesis 37–50*, 219–20), or as the preposition אֵת, "by, with" (Hamilton, *Genesis: 18–50*, 682, n. 18). It seems to me that an interchange of ל for ת is less likely, and thus we may consider the first word to be the preposition אֵת, for which we have at least one, albeit similarly ambiguous, parallel in Gen 4:1: קָנִיתִי אִישׁ אֶת־יְהוָה ("I acquired a man with the help of YHWH"). See de Hoop, *Genesis*, 207.

55. Wenham, *Genesis 16–50*, 486. Not only can the Joseph's oracle be connected with the patriarchal blessings, but also with his blessing in ch. 48. See also Schöpflin, "Jakob," 511–16.

56. The LXX translates literally only the first blessing. The second one is rendered εὐλογίαν γῆς ἐχούσης πάντα ("blessing of the earth containing everything"), which does not correspond to the Hebrew text. It seems that the Greek translators wanted to contrast "heaven" with "earth" and not with the "abyss." See Wevers, *Genesis*, 833–34.

Verse 26

The abundant blessings of the heaven above and the deep below, the blessings of the breasts and the womb are in fact the "blessings of your father." The blessing which Jacob has received throughout his life (Gen 27:10, 25, 27–29) is now handed over to his son Joseph, and is further depicted as surpassing two other kinds of blessing. The first of these is captured by a peculiar phrase הוֹרַי.[57] The construction would then literally mean "those who have conceived me," or figuratively "my ancestors."[58] However, the root הרה normally describes a woman's conceiving (see, e.g., Gen 4:1, 17; 16:4). Moreover, since the next (and possibly parallel) line speaks of תַּאֲוַה גִּבְעֹת עוֹלָם ("desire of the eternal hills"), and the LXX translates ἐπ' εὐλογίαις ὀρέων μονίμων ("over the blessings of the lasting mountains"), it seems plausible to emend the Hebrew text to הָרֵי עַד ("steadfast mountains").[59] In all its tentativeness this seems the most plausible attempt to make sense of a difficult text, which would then express that the blessings given to Joseph exceed even "the blessing of steadfast mountains and the bounty of the eternal hills." Presumably the dynamic power of Jacob's blessing concerning his progeny is more precious than the static power and beauty of mountains and hills enduringly towering above the land.

The last thought in the blessing upon Joseph is captured by the two cola, which highlight the special role of Joseph among his brothers. In a passage, which is reminiscent of Deut 33:16b, we are told that these rich blessings "will be on the head of Joseph," while the parallel colon adds "on the head[60] of the one separated from his brothers." The word which I translate "the one separated from" is נָזִיר, which is normally used in the Old Testament as a technical term for a person consecrated to YHWH (see, e.g., Num 6:1–21).[61] Here, however, it probably denotes a person who in a more ordinary way is separated or set apart from his brothers,[62] which is an apt description of Joseph, who from the beginning was the son more loved by his father than his siblings (Gen 37:3), and who was separated from his family when he

---

57. It comes from הרה, being the Qal masculine plural participle with the first person singular suffix.

58. Sarna translates the first part of the verse: "The blessings of your father surpass the blessings of my ancestors, to the utmost bounds of the eternal hills" (Sarna, *Genesis*, 344).

59. Thus also SP. See also the version הָרֵי־עַד in Hab 3:6 and הַרְרֵי־קֶדֶם in Deut 33:15. Rendsburg suggests the form הורי may have a double meaning: expressing both "my fathers" and "steadfast mountains." See Gary A. Rendsburg, "Janus Parallelism in Gen 49:26," *JBL* 99 (1980): 291–93. See also Macchi, *Israël*, 228–29.

60. The Hebrew noun קָדְקֹד is used as a fitting substitution for the word "head" (רֹאשׁ), for example, in Pss 7:17 (ET 7:16) or 68:22 (ET 68:21). See also *HALOT* 2:1071.

61. When נָזִיר is used as a description of a person, the word appears in its non-technical sense in only three places: here, its echo in Deut 33:16, and Lam 4:7.

62. However, some authors, for example Gunkel, think otherwise (Gunkel, *Genesis*, 461).

was sold into slavery in Egypt (Gen 37:28–36). The blessing upon Joseph thus does not seem to diminish Joseph's special role. Were it not for the blessing bestowed upon his brother Judah, one might even take the term נָזִיר as expressing the idea of kingship.[63] In any case, even here Joseph is seen as maintaining his special status vis-à-vis his brothers. He is the recipient of a special blessing of his father and is made fruitful and successful due to the protective hand of the God of his father.

Summary

To summarize our discussion of Jacob's blessing given to the firstborn son of Rachel, Joseph is likened to a fruitful bough, which has wider resonances with the theme of fertility and blessing in the book of Genesis and beyond. He is the head of a future tribe that will be characterized by unusual productiveness. As Joseph's life was marked by the attacks of various enemies within his own family and among the Egyptian masters, so his subsequent descendants will face enmity as well. But as Joseph remained stable and strong, the same promise is given to those bearing his name, because the Mighty One of Jacob will be the Rock and Shepherd of Ephraim. He is the one who helps and blesses, with blessings echoing the creation of the world and of humankind. These blessings, which are in fact greater or perhaps more dynamic than the fortunes of steadfast mountains, will rest on the head of Joseph, who is still viewed as set apart from his brothers.

Comparison of the Blessing upon Judah and Joseph

Although any comparison of the two blessings can be at best only tentative, as the whole of ch. 49 is written in poetic form and therefore evokes various inferences, it might be useful to note certain similarities and differences between these two accounts.

In terms of similarities, both blessings describe Jacob's most renowned tribes in admirable terms, praising their strength when facing enemies. Judah is described as a crouching lion who should not be roused. Joseph's bow remains strong and his hands agile, as he fights back against those who attack him. It is also noteworthy that the other blessings in ch. 49 do

---

63. Swenson's article suggests that the reference to נָזִיר may hint at Joseph's royal position. See Kristin M. Swenson, "Crowned with Blessings: The Riches of Double-meaning in Gen 49,26b," *ZAW* 120 (2008): 422–25. Westermann, on the other hand, asserts that נָזִיר "never denotes a king" (Westermann, *Genesis 37–50*, 241). One should mention in this regard a post-biblical tradition that associates Joseph's descendant with one of the messianic figures (the other is the son of Judah) coming at the end times to die in a battle against God's enemies. See, for example, Charles C. Torrey, "The Messiah Son of Ephraim," *JBL* 66 (1947): 253–77; and the host of articles by Mitchell who associates this tradition with Deut 33:17, notably: David C. Mitchell, "Messiah ben Joseph: A Sacrifice of Atonement for Israel," *RRJ* 10 (2007): 77–94.

not contain any reference to fighting enemies. They are brief, at any rate in comparison to the blessings upon Judah and Joseph, but this only underscores the suggestion that the tribes bearing the names of Judah and Joseph will be most involved in protecting Israel's future.

Nevertheless, despite these similarities, the blessings also differ significantly—for example in the way they are interconnected with the rest of the Joseph cycle. The depiction of Joseph's blessing in Gen 49:22–26 is in many ways consistent with the way he is portrayed throughout the Joseph narrative.[64] Joseph is a fruitful son and his life is characterized by a corresponding fruitfulness. His success is repeatedly described as owing to YHWH's being with him (e.g. Gen 39:2). He becomes a source of blessing for others (e.g. Gen 39:5), and it is promised that his sons will become great nations (Gen 48:19–20). Joseph's prosperity, and his special connection with his father and with God, are carried over into his blessing where the ability to deflect the attacks of enemies comes from God, who is presented in the oracle with an abundance of divine epithets. Finally, at the end of the whole blessing, Joseph maintains his special status. He is set apart from his brothers in a way which evokes the memory of the special love that his father extended to him in his teenage years (Gen 37:3).

With respect to Judah, on the other hand, although the blessing given to him might be recognized as containing several echoes and resonances with parts of the Joseph story,[65] its main theme—focused upon Judah's leadership position within Israel—is not anticipated in Gen 37–50. It is only understandable then that from a historical-critical point of view this disconnectedness with the Joseph story has prompted interpreters to see in this the work of a later compositor, who has remolded the blessing upon Judah according to future developments in Israel, when David and his descendants were to occupy the Israelite throne.[66] Judah's blessing, as it is described in Gen 49:8–12, seems to depict something from beyond the horizon of the Joseph cycle itself, which reflects the dominant position of Judah's tribe in the later Israel.

Even if this historical assessment says something about the origin of the Judah blessing in ch. 49, one still may want to ask what the relationship might be between the favored Joseph and his unfavored sibling Judah, who receives in the canonical ordering of the text such a prominent position. This is the task of the final portion of my study of the Genesis material, to which I now turn.

---

64. Thus, for example, Brueggemann, *Genesis*, 366.

65. See, again, the works of Ackerman, "Joseph," 109–11; and Good, "Blessing," 427–32.

66. Gunkel, for example, concludes that the revision of Gen 49 stems from a Judean pen from the time of Judah's dominion over Israel (Gunkel, *Genesis*, 453). Similarly, but with more detail, David M. Carr, *Reading the Fractures of Genesis: Historical and Literary Approaches* (Louisville, KY: Westminster John Knox, 1996), 277–80, 303–5.

11

Genesis:
Evaluation of the Canonical
Reading

The appearance in the Joseph story of chs. 38 and 49, in which Judah plays a substantial role, affects the overall interpretation of this portion of the biblical material. Whereas the version of Joseph's narrative when read without these chapters focuses from beginning to end on Joseph—who was favored by his father Jacob and also by the deity—the incident with Tamar in Gen 38 and the laudatory blessing given to Judah in ch. 49 bring to the fore Joseph's older sibling. On the one hand, this ordering of the narrative corresponds to the way in which the story is introduced. In Gen 37:2 it is prefaced as "the story of Jacob's family" (אֵלֶּה תֹּלְדוֹת יַעֲקֹב). This framing of what traditionally has been called "Joseph's tale" allows for a greater role for Joseph's brothers, among whom the most important one is played by Judah.[1] On the other hand, however, the tension between Joseph, a person privileged and set apart from his brothers, and Judah, whose low moment is captured in his encounter with Tamar and who receives a lavish blessing in Jacob's testament, raises some hermeneutical and theological questions. First, one must try to suggest in what ways the canonical ordering might change one's reading of the story. Second, I will chart various models that attempt to conceptualize the manner in which the relationship between Joseph and Judah may be construed. Third, the concept of election needs to be revisited in order to see whether my analysis of these "intrusive chapters" in the Joseph cycle sheds any light on the idea of election as such.

The Perceived Need to Rationalize

It should be acknowledged at the outset that the way in which I have construed my thought experiment exerts a certain pressure on the biblical story at hand. The experimental reading, I believe, adds a greater depth

---

1. See a similar comment—but which highlights also the role of Reuben who is portrayed in contrast to Judah—by Ebach, *Genesis*, 685–86. Similarly also Friedemann W. Golka, "Genesis 37–50: Joseph Story or Israel–Joseph Story?," *CurBR* 2 (2004): 153–77; Clifford, "Genesis 37–50," 213–29; and Dohyung Kim, "Genesis 37–50: The Story of Jacob and His Sons in Light of the Primary Narrative (Genesis–2 Kings)," *ExpTim* 123 (2012): 486–93.

to the canonical interpretation of the Joseph narrative, as it highlights the difference made by chs. 38 and 49 in the overall understanding of the story. However, given such a scenario as I have outlined, it is only natural to revisit the Joseph cycle in order to look for possible reasons for Judah's exaltation (and Joseph's relative drop in importance). In other words, the tendency to rationalize as to what may have prompted such an unexpected change in the portrayal of biblical characters becomes in this case even more palpable. In order to probe this issue, I will first note various suggestions that might be made for this somewhat altered roles of Joseph and Judah, and then comment more broadly on certain hermeneutical questions related to this felt need to articulate reasons for the sudden favor or disfavor of biblical characters in texts related to the concept of election.

Diminishing Joseph

To begin with, the lofty position that is ascribed to Judah in the abundant blessing of Gen 49:8–12 may prompt one to look for possible reasons for a relativizing of Joseph's importance. A ready basis for Joseph's diminished role beyond the borders of the Joseph story itself may understandably be sought in those of Joseph's deeds that appear morally objectionable. One may note his remark upon the birth of his first son, Manasseh, that God has made him forget his father's house (41:51)—a saying that may explain why he has never contacted his family in Canaan. His harsh treatment towards the Egyptians (47:13–26) also does not feature well in Joseph's evaluation. Perhaps most controversial, however, is Joseph's Egyptian identity, which manifests itself in a range of actions: he looked (41:14, 42), spoke (42:23), and dined like an Egyptian (43:32). He organized his father's funeral in a typically Egyptian manner (50:2–3, 7, 11). Furthermore, some of his actions seem to compromise what later is part of Israel's religious way of life:[2] he married a daughter of an Egyptian priest (41:45), swore by the life of Pharaoh (42:15), and even stated that he was competent to divine (44:5, 15). Joseph's morally objectionable deeds and his Egyptian manners may form a basis for his diminished role beyond Genesis.[3]

---

2. Earl evaluates various interpretations of Joseph's Egyptian identity in Douglas S. Earl, *Reading Old Testament Narrative as Christian Scripture*, JTISup 17 (Winona Lake, IN: Eisenbrauns, 2017), 103–47. For the suggestion that Joseph's acceptance of Egyptian customs provides an example for the Israelites of the Persian period, see Hyun Chul Paul Kim, "Reading the Joseph Story (Genesis 37–50) as a Diaspora Narrative," *CBQ* 75 (2013): 219–38.

3. Pirson's study tries to discern why Joseph has lost his privileged status (Pirson, *Lord*, 3). In conclusion he lists reasons similar to those stated above (Pirson, *Lord*, 139–41, esp. 141).

However, it is not only Joseph's failures and suspicious activities that may have caused his retreat into the background of Israel's history. Joseph's successes and accomplishments may be interpreted similarly. For example, Jacob's adoption of Ephraim and Manasseh in Gen 48, which in the narrative read without chs. 38 and 49 may be viewed positively—possibly as his receiving a "double share" of what is normally assigned to the firstborn[4]—may, on the other hand, be subjected to a more negative twist. De Hoop focuses on this particular aspect when he says: "The consequence of Jacob's action is that now Joseph has no sons any more, and unless he would beget one later he would be childless. His name is wiped out completely because it will be the patriarch's name which will be called in them."[5] When de Hoop reads ch. 48 within its broader canonical context,[6] he is able to interpret Joseph's childlessness as a tragic outcome of Jacob's adoption of Joseph's two sons. This may be a plausible hermeneutical inference from the canonical ordering of Joseph's narrative.

Consequently, even Joseph's blessing in ch. 49 may be seen as perhaps too dangerous for an Israelite leader. Rusty Reno combines Joseph's more problematic traits and his positive treatment in Gen 49:22–26 in his theological evaluation of ch. 49 in this way:

> Nonetheless, the chapter as a whole epitomizes the eccentric status of Joseph in the clan. From the outset, his dreams, his vainglorious temperament, and his Egyptian ways keep him from fitting with his brothers. His very success in Egypt, which was absolutely crucial for the survival of his brothers, seems to compromise his identity and block a role for his name in the future of Israel. He is undoubtedly the crucial brother, the rescuer. We read of no brother harboring objections to Joseph's double portion. He seems to deserve a special status in the clan. Yet that special status puts Joseph's name outside the normal history of Israel. It is as if Joseph's success has made him too dangerous for the future of the clan, and he must be suppressed even as he is honored.[7]

---

4. See, for example, the studies by Merwe and Seebass, which are both synchronically and diachronically sensitive, and which argue that Joseph was originally depicted as Jacob's successor in ch. 48: Merwe, "Joseph," 225–29; Seebass, "Genesis 48," 30.

5. De Hoop, *Genesis*, 338.

6. De Hoop's tome on Gen 49 deals both with the diachronic and synchronic issues of this chapter and its surrounding material, and suggests that some older "pro-Joseph" material, which possibly originated in northern Israel, was remodeled with a later "pro-Judah" layer, possibly during the period of the united monarchy (de Hoop, *Genesis*, 569–74, 613–17). De Hoop is thus well aware of the depth of the narrative that these possible layers have developed.

7. Reno, *Genesis*, 286–87. Pirson similarly views Joseph's success as a hindrance to his future role when he notes that he is "striving to acquire a position for himself that borders on the realm of the divine" (Pirson, *Lord*, 141).

It is interesting that Reno not only views Joseph's "vainglorious temper-
ament and his Egyptian ways" as suspicious, but that he also questions
whether his success and his special status were not possibly too dangerous
for Israel's future, and thus "he must be suppressed even as he is honored."
I wonder if "suppression" is the most appropriate term for describing the
blessing upon Joseph in Gen 49:22–26, and if Joseph's success is truly
so unsafe that he needs to be, so to say, set aside. Nevertheless, Reno's
proposal is a good example of an interpretative strategy that tries to make
sense of Judah's precedence over Joseph in the Old Testament story, which
also makes the imaginative use of the supposition that the culmination of
a hero's journey may not always lead to a happy ending.[8]

Highlighting Judah

Judah's willingness to substitute himself for a brother more privileged than
himself and to suffer instead of him in slavery (Gen 44) creates a fitting
backdrop for Judah's rise in ch. 49. When our appreciation of this brave
act is deepened by Judah's previous acknowledgment of Tamar's greater
righteousness in ch. 38, one gets a storyline that might help to understand
why Judah is praised by Jacob so lavishly and why he is a good candidate
for a position of leadership.

A suggestive way to conceptualize this transformation of Judah and its
relationship to kingship has been offered by Benedikt Hensel in his book
investigating the supplanting of the firstborn in Genesis.[9] Hensel ties
together several themes in order to argue that Judah is a suitable candidate
for a royal dynasty. First, he uses the parallel phrase הַכֶּר־נָא in Gen 37:32 and
38:25 to suggest that whereas Joseph had to give up his special clothing—
associated in 2 Sam 13:18 with a "royal garment"—Judah received back his
seal, cord, and staff—the items considered by Hensel as "royal insignia."[10]
Second, Judah's reference to "righteousness" in Gen 38:26 brings forward
the topic intrinsically connected with kingship.[11] Third, and perhaps most
importantly, Judah's actions express what true brotherhood entails, and
brotherhood in Hensel's understanding is closely associated with Israel's
kingship since in Deut 17:15 a future king must be "from among your

---

8. One may, for example, think of The Lord of the Rings trilogy by J. R. R. Tolkien
and how Frodo's life's ended, after the climax of the story, at the Crack of Doom—a significantly gloomier ending than that of the merrier, and more ordinary, life of Sam Gamgee.
I am indebted to Walter Moberly for this literary parallel.

9. Hensel, *Vertauschung*, 217–23.

10. "In Josephs Fall hatte dieser die Zeichen seiner königlichen Würde endgül-
tig abstehen müssen. Juda dagegen erhält seine 'königlichen Insignien' wieder zurück"
(Hensel, *Vertauschung*, 220).

11. Hensel suggests that the connection is alluded to in the name of Melchizedek
(מַלְכִּי־צֶדֶק, "king of righteousness") in Gen 14:18 (Hensel, *Vertauschung*, 215, 220).

brothers."[12] Hensel can thus summarize that, as the Joseph story progresses, Israel being described as "Joseph and his brothers" (Gen 37:2) becomes "Judah and his brothers" (Gen 44:14), which may be seen as preparing Judah to be a recipient of his brothers' obeisance as mentioned in ch. 49.[13] By imaginatively interpreting several of the themes embedded in the narrative, especially the notion of brotherhood, Hensel is able to lay out reasons for Judah's elevated role as predicted in ch. 49.

Evaluation

I have recounted several alternative reasons that may be invoked in order to explain *why* Judah has risen to a prominent position within Israel, and why this development has somewhat tempered the special favor accorded to Joseph. They all represent plausible reading strategies that try to account for the unexpected progression seen both within the Joseph story and beyond Genesis. Nevertheless, one may ask whether this need to rationalize what the biblical text does not make clear is the best way forward. Perhaps the occurrence of this kind of shift in a story related to the concept of election should give one pause. It is indeed possible to find pieces of information in the text that darken Joseph's portrayal, or on the other hand that feature well with Judah. But one should bear in mind, for example, that Joseph's assimilation into the Egyptian way of life does not seem to trouble the biblical narrator. Also, ch. 38—where Judah fails but later acknowledges Tamar's greater righteousness—is not necessarily providing a reason for his loftier role later in the narrative. At least, the text never makes this connection explicit.

Perhaps it must be that a story containing such a rich texture of themes associated with the idea of chosenness will also include elements that remain unexplained, and thus will continue to provoke one's understanding and imagination. The nature of election itself defies rationalization. If one could find satisfying reasons for God's choice in a person's motives, words, or deeds, the choice would perhaps cease to be divine.[14] The tendency to rationalize and to find possible reasons for chosenness is

---

12. Hensel, *Vertauschung*, 220–21.

13. Hensel, *Vertauschung*, 221. A similar argument is put forward by Iain Provan in his recent introductory text on the book of Genesis, in which he also makes use of the intrusiveness of ch. 38, and to a lesser degree of ch. 49, in the Joseph story. Provan reasons that their inclusion in the narrative is due to the fact that "Judah's line is crucially important to the biblical story; ultimately it inherits the dream of lordship not only over the other brothers, but over the whole earth." See Iain W. Provan, *Discovering Genesis: Content, Interpretation, Reception* (Grand Rapids: Eerdmans, 2015), 185–88, esp. 187.

14. The present case is not dissimilar from that of Cain and Abel. Although Gen 4 does not mention reasons for God's decision not to look upon Cain's sacrifice, interpreters down the ages, including biblical writers (Gen 4:7 [LXX]; Heb 11:4; 1 John 3:12;

understandable, but it must be complemented, or perhaps preceded, by an acknowledgment that God's reasons for his choices may remain beyond human reach.

Judah and Joseph Having Different Roles

Having commented on the felt need to find reasons for the sudden change in the portrayals of Joseph and Judah, I will now offer a brief discussion of several ways in which the special position of Joseph, which is rivaled in the canonical version of the story by that of Judah, might be evaluated.

Kingship and Fertility

The first option is to distinguish between the two characters as pointing to differing concepts. Since the blessing upon Joseph abounds with natural blessings and Judah's position of authority aligns with kingship, one may view the difference between them as a distinction between a natural and a political realm. This is the opinion expressed, for example, in Kass's commentary on Genesis. After finishing his interpretation of Gen 49:22–26, he offers this comment:

> Despite the uncertainty of the translation, there can be no doubt that Jacob has reserved a full and handsome blessing for his beloved Joseph. Yet notwithstanding the single final reference to Joseph as a "prince— the consecrated one; *nazîr*—among his brethren," the entire blessing is more natural than political, a blessing for fertility and plenty, not for rule. Joseph is "a fruitful vine," not "a lion's whelp." Assailed by others, he endures but he does not conquer. His blessings are from the skies above and the deep below, from the breast and from the womb. They may crown his princely head, but they do not bring him praise or obedience from his brethren. He still has the love of his father, who backs his own blessing by calling down God's help for his naturally superior son, but not for supremacy in Israel. Joseph, master of the fertile place, gets the natural blessing; Judah, leader of his brothers, gets the national blessing. Joseph is blessed in the way of Egypt; but in the way of Israel, right is more important than beauty, justice more esteemed than natural gifts.[15]

Jude 1:11), have tried in various ways to account for Cain's disfavor. For an argument stressing the inexplicability of God's choice of Abel's offering in Gen 4, see Moberly, *Genesis*, 88–101; and R. W. L. Moberly, "Is Monotheism Bad for You? Some Reflections on God, the Bible, and Life in the Light of Regina Schwartz's *The Curse of Cain*," in *The God of Israel*, ed. Robert P. Gordon, UCOP 64 (Cambridge: Cambridge University Press, 2007), 94–112. For a discussion of the ways in which Heb 11:4 rationalizes the divine preference of Abel, see R. W. L. Moberly, "Exemplars of Faith in Hebrews 11: Abel," in *The Epistle to the Hebrews and Christian Theology*, ed. Richard Bauckham et al. (Grand Rapids: Eerdmans, 2009), 353–63.

15. Leon R. Kass, *The Beginning of Wisdom: Reading Genesis* (Chicago: University of Chicago Press, 2003), 648.

Although Kass, in my view unjustifiably, phrases his conclusion in terms of a polarity between the way of Egypt and the way of Israel, the distinction he draws between Joseph's natural riches and Judah's more political blessing is worthy of merit.[16] Both concepts arise from ch. 49 and may have some counterpart in Israel's subsequent history in which Judah's tribe gave Israel more kings but Ephraim was a larger and more numerous entity.

Kingship and the Status of a Firstborn

Second, Hensel, with whose work I have engaged before, suggests that the supplanting of the firstborn—a central theme of Genesis—becomes more complex in Gen 37–50. Whereas Judah receives political authority, Joseph is blessed as Israel's firstborn.[17] Again, Hensel mounts several supporting arguments for his interpretation.[18] Joseph is a son of Jacob's beloved, and barren, wife Rachel—and barren women were systematically mothers of patriarchs' firstborns. In the adoption of Ephraim and Manasseh by his father, he seems to receive a double portion of what is assigned to a firstborn. In Hensel's understanding the firstborn is responsible for the wellbeing of the family, which is precisely what Joseph accomplished through his provision of food. Furthermore, the distinction between Judah's political authority and Joseph's firstborn status is captured also in 1 Chr 5:2: "For Judah was most prominent among his brothers and a ruler came from him, yet the birthright belonged to Joseph."[19] This reference strengthens the possibility that this interpretation was already alive in biblical times.[20]

Although it is difficult for me to conceptualize what the difference between Judah's political power and Joseph's status of a firstborn precisely entails—as the task of providing for one's people seems also to be inherent in a king's responsibilities—the strength of Hensel's proposal comes from his ability to fill in with specific details what 1 Chr 5:1–2 only suggests with broad strokes: Judah is a ruler, but Joseph is a firstborn.

Kings over Different Areas of Israel

The third option is to focus solely on the idea of kingship and to propose that Joseph and Judah stand in some way for the Northern and Southern

---

16. A similar opinion is expressed by Swenson-Méndez, who sees the difference between the two longest blessings of ch. 49 this way: "Genesis 49:8–12 portrays Judah as exercising dominion; Gen 49:22–26 portrays Joseph as the image of fruitfulness and fertility." See Kristin M. Swenson-Méndez, "The Relationship of Judah and Joseph in Genesis 49" (Ph.D. diss., Boston University, 2001), 181.

17. See Hensel's summarizing comment: "Juda wird zwar politische Macht in Israel zugesprochen, doch den mit dem Erstlingstum verbunden Segen bekommt nur Joseph" (Hensel, *Vertauschung*, 223–25, esp. 223).

18. All of the following arguments are taken from Hensel, *Vertauschung*, 223–24.

19. Hensel, *Vertauschung*, 224, n. 644.

20. A similar suggestion can be found also in Schöpflin, "Jakob," 516–17.

Kingdoms respectively, in the period of divided monarchy in Israel. Ebach, for example, frequently points out that Jeroboam is a fitting candidate for a king coming from the house of Joseph.[21] When Jeroboam appears on the scene, he is introduced as an Ephraimite (1 Kgs 11:26) whose initial responsibility under Solomon was to be in charge of the labor force of the house of Joseph (1 Kgs 11:28). Since the Southern Kingdom consists mainly of the tribe of Judah, the suggestion that Joseph and Judah stand for respective kingdoms after the division of Israel's monarchy is an attractive one.

Kings at Different Times

Lastly, Joseph's governing position in Egypt where he oversaw practically the whole region could open up the possibility that the leadership role, predicted for him in his dreams, was exhausted by his reign in Egypt. This possibility was already proposed by Calvin, who, in contrast to Judah's permanent reign, viewed Joseph's as only temporary. Calvin offers this comment when he discusses Gen 49:8:

> The *double portion*, indeed which he recently assigned to his son Joseph, depended on the right of primogeniture; but because the kingdom was transferred to the tribe of Judah, Jacob properly pronounces that his name should be held worthy of praise. For the honor of Joseph was temporary; but here a stable and durable kingdom is treated of, which should be under the authority of the sons of Judah.[22]

According to Calvin, Joseph's authority was temporary—perhaps to preserve the life of the sons of Israel[23]—whereas Judah's leadership is stable and durable. This line of interpretation thus distinguishes between two periods in Israel's history. The Joseph story presents the period when Joseph provided for his kin and indeed the whole world, and they, in return, bowed down before him. But the subsequent history of Israel testifies that a similar act of obeisance will be coming to the descendants of Judah.[24]

Evaluation

My overview is not exhaustive and does not aspire to adjudicate among the proposed versions in a detailed way. They all present plausible readings that take seriously the depth of the tension between Joseph and Judah in the canonical version of the text, and provide useful examples of what fruitful theological reading of the biblical text might look like. Nevertheless, I

---

21. See, for example, Ebach, *Genesis*, 73, 687.
22. Calvin, *Genesis*, 2:335; emphasis his.
23. A similar distinction is made by de Hoop, *Genesis*, 324.
24. This line of interpretation, however, may be taken a step further. One may argue that Joseph's reign has not been limited only to his governing position in Egypt, but it may extend even up until the point when David is made Israel's king. Texts such as Ps 78:67–68; Jer 7:12–15, and 26:6 suggest that the choice of Judah replaces the election of Joseph, as the center of Israel's cultic life shifts from Shiloh to Jerusalem.

have given time and space to the question of whether Judah's leadership position within Israel may be seen as superseding the choice of Joseph's preeminence, since this option is linked with the second part of my study, in which I will look at the rivalry between Saul and David. It also presents a natural bridge to the concept of election in the canonical version of the Joseph story, which will occupy the following section.

Judah—The Unfavored Becoming Favored?

As we have seen, both Levenson and Kaminsky consider Joseph's story to be a culmination of the exposition of the concept of election in the book of Genesis.[25] Both authors engage with Gen 38 in their treatment of the roles of Joseph and Judah in Israel's chosenness; however, they do not incorporate findings from ch. 49 in any substantial way. It must be asked, then, in what ways might my study of the canonical shape of the Joseph story alter their conclusions.

One of the most significant adjustments might concern the supposition that one's chosenness does not change. Kaminsky deals with this issue when he carefully distinguishes that one's election is fulfilled by service, but that election exists prior to service and "appears to abide even through a failure to perform such service."[26] He adds:

> Thus, neither does Joseph earn God's favor through proper action, nor is his election canceled when he misunderstands and thereby misuses his special status. Rather, he *always was* God's specially elect one, due to God's mysterious choice of him as well as of his mother, Rachel, Jacob's favored younger wife. It seems likely that in at least one and possibly in two instances his failures led to various trials and tribulations that served as a type of punishment for misusing his divine favor, yet *the narrator makes clear that he never lost his chosen status* (Gen 39:2, 23).[27]

Thus, in Kaminsky's view, Joseph "always was God's special elect one" who "never lost his chosen status." I agree that the story does not explicitly alter Joseph's chosen status, yet Judah's portrayal in ch. 49, where he is depicted on a par with his more favored and divinely blessed brother Joseph,[28]

---

25. See p. 9, n. 2.

26. Kaminsky, *Jacob*, 63.

27. Kaminsky, *Jacob*, 63; emphasis mine.

28. Whereas Joseph is lavished with blessings from God, who is introduced in his blessing by several divine titles, Judah's blessing contains no explicit reference to God. This recognition stands behind Swenson-Méndez's suggestion (which would fare better as a heuristic proposal) that Joseph and Judah together embody the dynamic of human initiative and divine will: "Lacking any reference to God and illustrating the individuality and power that Judah achieves, Gen 49:8–12 is the picture of human initiative as Judah subdues his enemies and wields the ensigns of a monarch. Genesis 49:22–26, on the other hand, glorifies Joseph for his state of blessedness by God" (Swenson-Méndez, "Relationship," 181).

complicates the issue. Unchosenness, at least when it occurs within the elect group, may be dynamic rather than static, and the Joseph story, with the rivalry between these two brothers pointing beyond its horizon, may testify to this dynamic, unseen elsewhere in the Genesis material. As far as the Joseph story is concerned, Joseph does not lose his favored status, yet Judah seems to achieve a place that goes well beyond his unfavored position at the beginning of the narrative, which is later actualized in the stories of Judah's descendants. If the topic of election in the closing chapters of Genesis also revolves around the notion of kingship, then the situation in subsequent Old Testament narratives changes even more. Although Gen 48 may suggest that the future monarch will be an Ephraimite, Israel's most enduring dynasty will come from Judah.

12

From Genesis to 1 Samuel

The first part of my study focused on the extended narrative of Gen 37–50. When the text was read without the intrusive chs. 38 and 49, Joseph's favored position, and his possible association with future kingship, came to the forefront. However, the canonical version of the story increasingly puts forward Judah, who—at least towards the end of this beautiful tale—rivals Joseph and his special place within Israel. Since the book of Genesis forms the opening to both Jewish and Christian Bibles, and because Gen 49—with Jacob's two highly esteemed sons—presents a forward-looking aspect, it is only natural to look beyond the borders of Genesis for a possible future development of the tension between Judah and Joseph. It is my suggestion that the story of Israel's first two kings, Saul and David, is a good candidate for the continued development of this surprising twist occurring at the end of the Joseph cycle. I would contend that the book of 1 Samuel, which contains a complex narrative of the ups and downs of the beginnings of Israel's monarchy, is connected with the Joseph cycle on several levels.

Literary Connections

To begin with, the prolonged narratives about Israel's first two monarchs seem to be connected with the interplay between Judah and Joseph in the canonical shape of the Old Testament on a literary level. This is especially evident in terms of the connection between Judah and David. First, Gen 49:8–12 offers a picture of a leader who enjoys a special position among his brothers, and whose reign seems to reverberate with symbols of unusual prosperity. Among other things, Judah is promised to receive a gesture of obeisance which in the preceding narrative is promised only to Joseph. A ruler will come from his tribe who will reign over and fight for his people. While this image can undoubtedly be appropriated in several imaginable ways, David's kingship, placed at the beginning of the long line of Israel's kings, serves as a fitting fulfillment of Jacob's blessing given to Judah.[1]

---

1. Even Westermann, who argues that vv. 8–9 of the blessing likely originated during the period of judges, and thus do not need to presuppose royal connotations, states forcefully that by v. 10 "[o]nly monarchy can be meant" (Westermann, *Genesis 37–50*, 227–31, esp. 230).

Second, although the book of Ruth depicts its own storyline about the Moabite young woman who—despite her foreign origin and desperate living conditions—finds her way into the Israelite community and culture, the end of this short tale creates a bridge between the story of Judah and the story of David, as it reiterates the genealogy of Judah's son Perez (Gen 38:27–30), down through Boaz's son Obed, David's grandfather. Ruth 4:18–22 thus not only firmly places the local story of Ruth, Naomi, and Boaz into the larger framework of Israelite history, but also connects the open-ended trajectory of Judah's sudden favor in the Joseph cycle with the unusual election of David in the books of Samuel.[2]

Third, the stories of Saul and David may be read as continuing the tension between the descendants of Rachel and the other, less fortunate sons of Jacob. Although Saul is a Benjaminite (1 Sam 9:1–2) and not of Joseph's offspring,[3] nevertheless in the Joseph story itself, Benjamin, Rachel's second son, seems to function as Joseph's stand-in since Jacob's special love fixes itself upon Benjamin after Joseph's disappearance (Gen 42:38; 44:27, 30). I am hopeful, then, that the interplay between Saul and David may display characteristics similar to those which were exemplified by the tension between the unfavored Judah and the favored sons of Rachel.

Theological Similarities

The narratives of Saul and David also feature theological themes similar to those of the book of Genesis generally, and the story of Joseph and Judah in particular. First, 1 Samuel seems to present a pattern of displacement similar to that found in the book of Genesis. As Samuel displaces the corrupt line

---

2. Berlin notes this connecting function of Ruth's closing genealogy in terms of the story line from Genesis to Kings: Berlin, *Poetics*, 110.

3. It is Samuel who is portrayed in 1 Samuel as an Ephraimite (1 Sam 1:1), in contrast to 1 Chr 6:33–35, where he is assigned a Levitical descent. For an interesting proposal on this discrepancy, see, for example, Marvin A. Sweeney, "Samuel's Institutional Identity in the Deuteronomistic History," in *Construals of Prophecy in the Former & Later Prophets & Other Texts*, ed. Lester L. Grabbe and Martti Nissinen, ANEM 4 (Atlanta: SBL, 2011), 165–74. Furthermore, the designation אֶפְרָתִי sometimes designates Ephraim's tribal identity and sometimes the vicinity around Bethlehem, as in Ruth 1:2 and 1 Sam 17:12. See Kyle P. Jr. McCarter, *I Samuel: A New Translation with Introduction, Notes, and Commentary*, AB 8 (Garden City, NY: Doubleday, 1980), 303; or Robert P. Gordon, *1 & 2 Samuel: A Commentary* (Exeter: Paternoster, 1986), 155. Nevertheless, if Samuel is of Ephraim's tribe, then my above-proposed scenario would fit well with the suggestion of some authors who see Samuel and Saul (both descendants of Rachel) linked on several levels. Polzin, for example, argues that Samuel and Saul are connected in 1 Samuel by several interweaving features, including that both are the objects of a strong desire: Hannah desires a son and the Israelites desire a king. See Robert Polzin, *Samuel and the Deuteronomist: A Literary Study of the Deuteronomic History, Part 2: 1 Samuel* (San Francisco: Harper & Row, 1989), 22–26. It is peculiar, then, that Israel's first king and the prophet most associated with his reign both came from Rachel's seed.

of Eli and his sons (1 Sam 2:30–36), David gradually displaces Saul.[4] At the climax of the narrative it is not the first king, who enjoys divine and human favor, but instead the "younger," candidate, David—himself the youngest of Jesse's sons—who becomes God's and the people's chosen monarch. The usual preference in the book of Genesis for the younger, or later, contender seems to be retained in the first book of Samuel.[5]

Second, the two prominent sons of Jacob and the two first kings of Israel are in both cases individuals whose narratives also function etiologically. Perhaps more than anywhere else in the Joseph narrative, Gen 49:8–12 reveals the traits and characteristics of Judah acting as a *tribe*, which is the impression underlined by the closing summary of Jacob's testament: "all these are the twelve tribes of Israel, and this is what their father said to them when he blessed them" (Gen 49:28).[6] Something similar can be said about Saul and David and their respective stories when they become paradigms for the Northern and Southern Kingdoms respectively. For example, when commenting on Saul's fate, Barbara Green poses a fitting question: "Can a human character be a cipher for a more institutional problem?"[7] This question is further picked up by Keith Bodner, who answers it affirmatively:

> I will argue that this is indeed the case for Saul: Saul as a particular king represents the northern experience of kingship in general. Thus, Saul's personal story mirrors the national history. A growing number of scholars are arguing that Saul *is* a preview of kingship in Israel, and that his aborted reign presages the fate of kingship among the northern tribes.[8]

---

4. There are a number of parallels between the rejection of the Elides in 1 Sam 2–3 and Saul's rejection in 1 Sam 13–15. Both Saul's and Eli's family are initially chosen, yet they are rejected by YHWH through the prophetic word because of an issue involving sacrifice. Their rejection is final, which in turn brings severe consequences for both their families and Israel as a whole. Simultaneously, a person better suited for the task is appointed in their place. For some of these literary links, see Ulrich Berges, *Die Verwerfung Sauls: Eine thematische Untersuchung*, FB 61 (Würzburg: Echter, 1989), 27–30; and Peter D. Miscall, *1 Samuel: A Literary Reading* (Bloomington, IN: Indiana University Press, 1986), 20–21.

5. In making this comparison I do not wish to obscure the differences between the two accounts. For example, the narratives of Saul and David do not deal primarily with fraternal love. The book of Genesis is often about parental preference for the younger son, but 1 Samuel occupies itself with larger issues of kingship and nationhood. Although God, the source of election, stands behind both royal choices, the shape of chosenness is framed somewhat differently in Samuel's narratives.

6. One may think also of the unusual conclusion to the episode of Judah and Tamar, which centers on the birth of Zerah and Perez (Gen 38:27–30), and the preeminence of Ephraim in Jacob's blessing in ch. 48 (Gen 48:12–20). See, for example, Greenspahn who remarks in regard to these situations that they point toward the tribal history (Greenspahn, *Brothers*, 119–20).

7. Barbara Green, *How Are the Mighty Fallen? A Dialogical Study of King Saul in 1 Samuel*, JSOTSup 365 (Sheffield: Sheffield Academic, 2003), 113.

8. Keith Bodner, *1 Samuel: Narrative Commentary*, HBM 19 (Sheffield: Sheffield Phoenix, 2008), 116–17; emphasis his. Gordon spells out the issue this way: "Saul, in this

Bodner views Saul as symbolizing kingship in Israel in general, specifically prefiguring something from the experience of the Northern Kingdom. Bodner's stance, which as he asserts is becoming widespread among modern scholars, has a forerunner in Karl Barth's theological exposition of individual election in his *Church Dogmatics*, where he considers Saul largely a representative of God's negative stance towards the idea of kingship, whereas David typifies a paradigm for God's "yes" to monarchy.[9] In Barth's view Saul is the person who personifies the human ideal for kingship and also the human way of building up God's kingdom:

> Saul personally did both these things in what may be described as an almost or totally innocent manner. He did both with what was humanly a thoroughly respectable conviction and method. But in both he is an exact portrayal of the monarchy which has made itself independent of the kingdom of God, which is in competition with the latter both in what it does and what it does not do.[10]

Barth's creative interpretation is yet another example of Saul and David being seen as paradigms. While they certainly have a life of their own in 1 Samuel, and their stories are stories of their individual victories and failures, they also demonstrate in certain respects something of the nature of monarchy as such, and represent the fates of northern Israel and southern Judah. In this way they continue further the etiological functions present already in the Joseph cycle.

Third, the story of Saul and David seems to embody a trajectory opposite to that discerned in my study of Joseph and Judah. Whereas Judah is portrayed in Gen 37–50 as an unfavored character, and only in Gen 49 is depicted in terms that put him on a par with Joseph, Saul begins as a chosen king—first of all by the people, but also by God—and later loses God's favor and is rejected as king over Israel.

The study of Saul's fall from God's grace may thus present a useful companion to my research on Judah. A modification in terms of election is at the center of Saul's story as well, even though in his case it is a shift away from God's favor.

---

respect, may be taken as paradigmatic of kingship in Judah and Israel from the division of the kingdom to the exile." See Robert P. Gordon, *I & II Samuel* (Grand Rapids: Regency Reference Library, 1986), 10.

9. Karl Barth, *Church Dogmatics*, 4 vols. (Edinburgh: T&T Clark, 1957–75), 2.2:366–93. It should be noted, however, that Barth's theological appropriation of Saul's and David's story is far more complex than this simple short-hand dichotomy suggests.

10. Barth, *Church Dogmatics*, 2.2:371.

13

Saul in 1 Samuel: Framing the Study

Choosing the Text: 1 Samuel 13–15

Saul's story is relayed in the first book of Samuel: Saul himself plays an important role in chs. 9–31, while chs. 1–8 comprise a prologue to his reign that introduces significant themes of monarchy, the supplanting of one dynasty with another, and the issue of the divine presence in Israel. The house of Elides is rejected by YHWH, who promises to raise up a new and trustworthy priest in his place (1 Sam 2:35). The oracle concerning the priestly dynasty at Shiloh is fulfilled when the Philistines defeat Israel's army and capture the ark, the bearer and the symbol of the divine presence.[1] From the point of view of these early chapters of 1 Samuel, Eli is replaced with Samuel[2]—who leads the people back to YHWH and whose role in the narrative seems to serve a number of functions.[3] Nevertheless, not even Samuel is able to establish a dynasty, as his sons do not follow in his footsteps, their deeds perverting justice (1 Sam 8:3). The elders of Israel ask Samuel for a king who should govern them in a way similar to those of other nations (1 Sam 8:5).

When Saul appears on the scene, he is introduced as the son of a man whose delineated ancestry comprises four generations (1 Sam 9:1). Saul himself is described as a handsome young man who exceeds in height every other man in Israel (1 Sam 9:2).[4] Saul thus seems to be

---

1. Benjamin Sommer discusses various ways in which the divine presence is associated with the ark in 1 Sam 4–6 in Benjamin D. Sommer, *The Bodies of God and the World of Ancient Israel* (Cambridge: Cambridge University Press, 2009), esp. 102.

2. The view that Samuel is the fulfillment of 1 Sam 2:35 is defended, for example, by Lyle M. Eslinger, *Kingship of God in Crisis: A Close Reading of 1 Samuel 1–12* (Sheffield: Almond Press, 1985), 135–42; and Polzin, *Samuel*, 42–44.

3. Samuel seems to play more than one role in his ministry to Israel. Berges follows the lead of verses such as Jer 15:1 and Ps 99:6, likening Samuel to Moses. See Berges, *Verwerfung*, 25–27, also 63–66.

4. Saul's outstanding pedigree and his remarkable physical attributes, which make him a suitable candidate for the office of Israel's king, stand in contrast to the way David is portrayed in the story. The description in 1 Sam 17:12 of David's family of origin is quite brief (the extended genealogy can be found outside of 1 Samuel, in Ruth 4:18–21 and 1 Chr 2:1–15), and it is possible that, although David was handsome (1 Sam 16:12), he did

the embodiment the people's expectations of a king. He is the man for whom Israel is asking.[5]

However, Saul is a suitable candidate for Israel's throne not only from a human point of view, but he is also chosen by God. Samuel, having been instructed by YHWH, anoints Saul and sends him on a peculiar journey full of unusual signs—an excursion which also places the newly anointed leader under Samuel's tutelage.[6] These signs gradually locate Saul within the sphere of divine activity and in the end seem to transform him into a different kind of man (1 Sam 10:6, 9).[7] The Spirit's empowerment he experiences among a circle of prophets in 10:10–13 seems to be a foretaste of his Spirit-prompted action in ch. 11, where he rescues the inhabitants of Jabesh-Gilead from their Ammonite oppressors (11:6).

Saul's ascension to Israel's throne is narrated in several stages: he is privately anointed by Samuel (1 Sam 10:1), chosen by lot at Mizpah (10:17–27), and publicly proclaimed king at Gilgal (ch. 12). This last episode, at least from a canonical point of view,[8] establishes the existence of the monarchy within the covenantal system in Israel. The new monarch, as well as the people, is not exempted from the requirement to obey YHWH and his commands (12:13–15).

While both Saul's rise to the throne and the covenant renewal at Gilgal are important in terms of Saul's portrayal in 1 Samuel, the canonical text suggests that Saul's reign actually begins with his conflict with the Philistines in ch. 13, given that v. 1 contains a frequently used formula

---

not seem to exemplify an able fighter in the same class as Saul (1 Sam 16:11; 17:33, 42). The surprising choice of David is the subject of analysis in J. Randall Short, *The Surprising Election and Confirmation of King David*, HTS 63 (Cambridge, MA: Harvard University Press, 2010), 145–91, esp. 145–69.

5. Saul's name (שָׁאוּל) means "asked for," which may immediately raise the reader's expectation that Saul could be the person for whom the elders had asked in 1 Sam 8:10, in terms of their plea for a king. The verb also occurs seven times in chs. 1 and 2, during the episode in which the barren Hannah asks for a child—then receives, and later gives up again, Samuel (1:17 [×2], 20, 27, 28 [×2]; 2:20).

6. See, for example, David Jobling, *1 Samuel*, Berit Olam (Collegeville, MN: Liturgical Press, 1998), 111–25.

7. The nature of Saul's change is unclear. On the one hand, Saul may simply change his mind and—instead of thinking about the lost access—focus his thoughts on something related to the kingship. On the other hand, Saul's prophetic experience and the repeated references to the change of his heart might indicate that the young man from Benjamin experiences a deeper inner transformation. For the argument of the latter, see Walter Brueggemann, *First and Second Samuel*, IBC (Louisville, KY: John Knox, 1990), 77–78.

8. The canonical text of 1 Sam 8–12 may, of course, be a compilation of various pro-monarchical (9:1–10:16; 11:1–15) and anti-monarchical (8:1–22; 10:17–27; 12:1–25) layers, as has been observed, for example, by Julius Wellhausen, *Prolegomena to the History of Ancient Israel with a Reprint of the Article "Israel" from the Encyclopaedia Britannica*, trans. Sutherland J. Black and Allan Menzies (Edinburgh: A. & C. Black, 1885), 253–55; and Martin Noth, *The Deuteronomistic History*, 2nd ed., JSOTSup 15 (Sheffield: Sheffield Academic, 1981), 49–53.

for depicting a monarch's rule, albeit here in partial fashion.[9] In addition, although chs. 9–12 present a portrayal of Saul that is ambiguous, it is in chs. 13–15 that the reader encounters most of the morally problematic passages of the Saul narratives. Here Saul is rejected by the deity for reasons that are difficult to align with the image of a benevolent God described in other portions of Scripture and cherished in both Jewish and Christian tradition. In the first instance, in ch. 13, Saul is rejected by Samuel because he had overstepped the commandment of YHWH, presumably because Saul did not wait for the prophet as instructed and offered the sacrifice himself. Yet the text makes it clear that Saul did wait seven days, the time appointed by Samuel, and was still rejected by the deity. In ch. 15 Saul is rejected because he failed to fulfill another command, this time to annihilate another nation, Amalek. Saul had compassion on—that is, spared—the Amalekite king and the best of the spoils of the war. Furthermore, as my interest is in uncovering and constructing the notion of election in the Old Testament, it is in 1 Sam 13–15 where one can find statements and incidents that concern both Saul's rejection (13:13; 15:10, 22–23, 28) and David's election (13:14; 15:28).

For these reasons, although my examination of Saul's fall from God's favor could be enriched and supplemented by an account that would take into consideration the rest of Saul's story presented in 1 Samuel, for the sake of this study I will limit myself to a close reading of chs. 13–15. This is a portion of narrative that centers on Saul's rejection by YHWH and hints at his replacement with David. Besides, as in my study of the Joseph cycle, I will examine the impact of a segment of text that is generally considered to be intrusive in the story.

The Position of 1 Samuel 13:7b–15a in the Story of Saul's Reign

It is interesting that the narrative of chs. 13–15, where the two rejections of Saul are described, is at the same time also a portion of Scripture in which scholars have detected possible editorial work. It is the account of Saul's first rejection (in 1 Sam 13:7b–15a) that is seen as somewhat intrusive or awkward in the narrative. There are two prime reasons for regarding this first incident at Gilgal as possibly a later insert into the story.

Unnatural Move to Gilgal

The first reason consists in the observation that the narrative of Saul's rejection in ch. 13 unnaturally relocates Saul from the region of Michmash-Gibeah to Gilgal. The beginning of the chapter places Saul with two thousand men in Michmash and Jonathan with one thousand men across the valley in Gibeah (1 Sam 13:2). After Jonathan defeats the Philistine

---

9. For a closer look at this difficult verse (1 Sam 13:1), see below.

garrison, the Philistine army moves towards Michmash, which prompts some Israelites to run away in distress (13:6–7a). Then Saul suddenly appears at Gilgal, gathering more troops and offering sacrifice (13:7b–15a). This raises the question: Why would Saul, when facing imminent Philistine danger near Michmash in the hill country, retreat to Gilgal in the central region of Israel? Smith's commentary captures well this conundrum: "Saul's movement from Geba to Gilgal would be, from the military point of view, an insane step. The highlands were Israel's stronghold. To recover them once abandoned would be practically impossible."[10] The first reason for insisting that 13:7b–15a might be an insertion thus lies in the observation that after the text places Saul, quite naturally, in the midst of the battle at Gibeah, the detour to Gilgal does not seem to fit with prudent military tactics,[11] and appears to have been included in the narrative in order to connect it with the sacrifice and the sacrificial site at Gilgal, in ch. 15.[12]

The Narratival and Temporal Gap between the Command in 1 Samuel 10:8 and Its Fulfillment in 1 Samuel 13:8

The second main reason for attributing Samuel's first rejection of Saul in 1 Sam 13 to an editor consists in the observation that there is both a narratival and a temporal gap between Samuel's initial command (that Saul wait seven days at Gilgal) and its fulfillment. From the narrative point of view, much happens between Samuel's command in 1 Sam 10:8 (when Saul is anointed) and its potential fulfillment in 13:8—Saul is proclaimed king at Mizpah (10:17–27), he delivers the inhabitants of Jabesh-gilead from the Ammonite oppressors (ch. 11), and is present at the reestablishing and reconfiguring of the monarchy at Gilgal (ch. 12). Given this amount of information and the amount of progression in the story, the occurrence of a possible fulfillment of the command in 1 Sam 13 seems odd.[13]

---

10. Henry P. Smith, *A Critical and Exegetical Commentary on the Books of Samuel*, ICC (Edinburgh: T&T Clark, 1899), 93. And similarly, for example, Hans Joachim Stoebe, *Das erste Buch Samuelis*, KAT 8/1 (Gütersloh: Gütersloh Verlagshaus, 1973), 244.

11. To counter this argument, one may suggest that Saul likely left his army with Jonathan, and his own two thousand men to protect Gibeah in the hill country, while he descended to Gilgal to muster a larger constituency to face the imminent Philistine threat. For this suggestion see, for example, V. Philips Long, *The Reign and Rejection of King Saul: A Case for Literary and Theological Coherence*, SBLDS 118 (Atlanta, GA: Scholars Press, 1989), 47–48; or Hans Wilhelm Hertzberg, *I & II Samuel: A Commentary*, trans. John Bowden, OTL (London: SCM, 1964), 105.

12. As Wellhausen says: "This insertion is based on an older account of the breach between Samuel and Saul in 1 Sam. xv. Here also the matter of dispute is a sacrifice, and Gilgal is the scene; and this alone serves to explain how Gilgal is adhered to in xiii. 7–15 in spite of all impossibility, as being the right and necessary place for the occurrence" (Wellhausen, *Prolegomena*, 258).

13. Long somewhat tempers this issue of a narratival gap by proposing that the instruction in 1 Sam 10:8 is tied to the command in 10:7 to "do what your hand finds," which is

In addition to that, there is also a temporal gap between the two events. The story portrays Saul in 1 Sam 9:1–10:16 as a young man whose absence worries his father. But in 1 Sam 13 Saul has a son of his own who is able to fight in battle.[14] Thus, from the viewpoint of the story itself, in which the happenings between ch. 10 and ch. 13 overshadow the link between 1 Sam 10:8 and 13:8, and also from the viewpoint of the narrative's portrayal of Saul as in the first instance a young man and in the latter a king having his own family, the connection between 1 Sam 10:8 and 13:8 seems to be lost on the reader.[15]

Setting the Boundaries of the Passage

The remaining task is to establish the boundaries of the passage in ch. 13 that could be a later insert into the narrative. Smith is correct when, in the course of his discussion of this putative insertion, he remarks: "If it be taken as proved that we have here a separate document, the question arises: Exactly where does it begin? Its lower limit is evidently v. 15a. But the upper limit is not so plain."[16] Smith is correct that the incident at Gilgal finishes with the departure of both Samuel's and Saul's from the cultic site in the direction of Gibeah, which provides a natural continuation point for the subsequent events, at the forefront of the military action near Michmash. But the beginning of the passage is not so obvious. Perhaps the references to Gilgal at the end of v. 4 and in the middle of v. 7 may provide useful clues for delineating the boundaries of the passage for our purposes. While Smith regards the whole of 13:4–15a as editorial,[17] for the purposes of my thought experiment it seems better to read the narrative only without the section in 13:7b–15a, and from the remaining text merely leave out the location of "Gilgal" at the end

---

a signal that Saul is to challenge the Philistine presence in the land (in this Long follows Ludwig Schmidt, *Menschlicher Erfolg und Jahwes Initiative: Studien zu Tradition, Interpretation und Historie in Überlieferungen von Gideon, Saul und David*, WMANT 38 (Neukirchen-Vluyn: Neukirchener, 1970), 74–78). If Long is right, then the seven days, the time to set aside to wait for the prophet, begins not with Saul's anointing but with the moment when Saul (or his son) attacks the aggressor's garrison (Long, *Reign*, 51–66, esp. 65).

14. Thus, for example, McCarter, *I Samuel*, 228.

15. Firth recognizes that the gap between 1 Sam 10:8 and 13:8, both temporal and literary, creates a problem for seeing the link between the two verses. He refers to Long as solving the second difficulty leaving the first one, as far as I can tell, without an answer. David G. Firth, *1 & 2 Samuel*, ApOTC 8 (Grand Rapids: InterVarsity Press, 2009), 152–53. The problem of Saul's age is mentioned also by Tsumura and is left, again, without a sufficient answer. See David T. Tsumura, *The First Book of Samuel*, NICOT (Grand Rapids: Eerdmans, 2007), 340–41, esp. 340.

16. Smith, *Samuel*, 94.

17. Smith, *Samuel*, 95. This is indeed possible, but creates complications of its own when Smith needs to retain v. 5 in the older version of the story, in order to account for the mustering of the Philistine army, necessary for the upcoming conflict between the Israelites and the Philistines.

of v. 4.[18] Although one can make a case that would view Saul's detour to Gilgal as not completely unnatural, and its connection with the original instruction to wait seven days for Samuel tighter than I have argued, the historical-critical claim is supported by its usefulness—namely that without Saul's first rejection the text reads more smoothly than does the canonical version of the story. As Popović remarks: "The present unit ended as suddenly as it had begun. In fact the removal of the entire Gilgal episode in vv. 7b–15a, along with the mention of Gilgal in v. 4b, leaves a rather straightforward account."[19] My experimental version of ch. 13 will thus contain the text without vv. 7b–15a and the word "Gilgal" at the end of v. 4. In the second part of my study, I will first read 1 Sam 13–15 without and then with the awkward section 1 Sam 13:7b–15a in order to see how the first rejection of Saul influences one's interpretation of Saul's reign and how it affects the idea of election portrayed in these stories.

---

18. Wellhausen suggests that the possible insert is contained in 1 Sam 13:7b–15. See Julius Wellhausen, *Die Composition des Hexateuchs und der historischen Bücher des Alten Testaments* (Berlin: Georg Reimer, 1899), 245. Driver argues for 1 Sam 13:7b–15a. See S. R. Driver, *Notes on the Hebrew Text and the Topography of the Books of Samuel*, 2nd ed. (Oxford: Clarendon, 1913), 100.

19. A. Popović, "Saul's Fault in 1 Sam 13,7b–15a," *Anton* 68 (1993): 153–70, esp. 156.

14

1 Samuel 13

Chapter 13 is closely connected with ch. 14. They are both concerned with the war between Israel and the Philistines: ch. 13 presents the setting and an introduction to the battle, while ch. 14 describes the military conflict itself. The fight with the Philistines is further presented in the narrative as a token of Saul's reign as a whole, with the summary of Saul's kingship in 1 Sam 13:1 providing a fitting opening, and the review of Saul's military and familial endeavors in 1 Sam 14:47–52 representing an appropriate closure, for the whole story.

Saul's Brief Reign
(1 Samuel 13:1)

According to Samuel's words in 1 Sam 12, kingship in Israel can succeed only if both the king and the people listen to God's voice and follow his instructions (12:14–15). The renewal of kingship seems to present a fresh start for the monarchy in Israel, which creates a natural bridge for the introduction of Saul's reign. However, the summary of his reign—presented in a formula that is typical in the books of Kings—does not make much sense, as the Hebrew text says: "Saul was a year old (בֶּן־שָׁנָה) when he began to reign and he reigned for two years (שְׁתֵּי שָׁנִים) over Israel" (13:1). Although placing the beginning of Saul's kingship back to his infancy may possibly be interpreted metaphorically,[1] the grammar of the sentence suggests that some numbers are missing.[2] A similar difficulty arises when one considers the length of Saul's reign. The number "two" seems to be incomplete.[3]

---

1. An attempt to explain the number "one" by attributing innocence to Saul can be traced back to Targum: "As a one year old child, in whom there is no guilt, was Saul, when he became king; and he reigned two years over Israel." Eveline von Staalduine-Sulman, *The Targum of Samuel*, SAIS 1 (Leiden: Brill, 2002), 299–300, esp. 299.

2. A comparison between 1 Sam 13:1 and such passages as 1 Kgs 14:21, where one reads "Rehoboam was forty-one years old (בֶּן־אַרְבָּעִים וְאַחַת שָׁנָה רְחַבְעָם בְּמָלְכוֹ) when he began to reign," may indicate that the whole number has disappeared. See, for example, Driver, *Notes*, 96–97.

3. The phrase שְׁתֵּי שָׁנִים is not the regular Hebrew for "two years." One may encounter either שְׁתַּיִם שָׁנִים (e.g. 2 Sam 2:10) or the more common version שְׁנָתַיִם (e.g. 2 Sam 14:28). Smith stands for the majority of commentators when he considers this phrase corrupted; the number "two" was likely only a part of the whole amount (Smith, *Samuel*, 92).

Furthermore, the description of Saul's reign in the book of Samuel covers more than two years.[4]

This well known crux resists a clear solution. One option is to follow, for example, McCarter, who leaves out both numbers, arguing that the exact age of Saul and the length of his reign were not accessible to the Deuteronomistic historian.[5] When faced with such difficulties in a text, a solution like this presents itself as a sensible proposal. Another possibility is to supply the missing numbers from other sources. Some of the LXX manuscripts, such as the LXX[L], put Saul's age at thirty (υἰὸς τριάκοντα ἐτῶν) at the time when he assumed the kingship. With regard to the length of Saul's reign, a passage from the New Testament (Acts 13:21) mentions "forty years,"[6] which is also supported by Josephus.[7]

One way forward, and more along the lines of a literary approach, might be to accept the truncated text as it stands and to appropriate it as best one can in order to illuminate further the fate of king Saul. Thus, the incomplete summary and the short length of Saul's kingship, as given in the opening verse of ch. 13, may fit well with the brief period of Saul's reign *before he is rejected by God*, which could correspond to the two years mentioned in 1 Sam 13:1.[8] Nevertheless, the opening verse of ch. 13 remains—in a way corresponding to Saul's story as whole—puzzling.[9]

Jonathan's Attack on the Philistines
(1 Samuel 13:2–4)

The narrative section of the chapter begins with Saul being portrayed as a commander, possibly contemplating some sort of military action against the Philistines, whose army's presence in the area presented—at least according to 1 Sam 9:16—an external reason for the establishment of the

---

4. Thus, for example, Bar-Efrat, who notes that in 1 Sam 27:7 the narrative describes David as staying with the Philistines for one year and four months, all during Saul's reign. Shimon Bar-Efrat, *Das erste Buch Samuel: Ein narratologisch-philologischer Kommentar*, trans. Yvonne Szedlák and Walter Dietrich, BWA(N)T 176 (Bern: Kohlhammer, 2007), 191.

5. McCarter, *I Samuel*, 222–23. Similarly also Robert D. Bergen, *1, 2 Samuel*, NAC 7 (Nashville, TN: Broadman & Holman, 1996), 148. This proposal is followed, for example, by the NRSV.

6. The NIV takes the round number "forty," standing likely for a long reign, combines it unhelpfully with the Hebrew text, and arrives at "forty-two" years.

7. *Ant.* 6.14.9. But Josephus is not altogether consistent. Elsewhere he mentions "twenty years" (*Ant.* 10.8.4).

8. As Firth comments: "The 'two years' of reign ascribed to Saul may be the period when he is sanctioned by Yahweh as king" (Firth, *Samuel*, 153).

9. I say this in agreement with Bodner, who remarks: "After this corrupt start [of the chapter], the events of this chapter will only get worse for Saul, and thus the text-critical problem at the outset functions as a symbolically apt introduction for a king whose dynasty will not endure" (Bodner, *1 Samuel*, 119).

monarchy in Israel.[10] After Saul had chosen for himself three thousand men, he kept two thousand with him in Michmash, while the remaining thousand were deployed with Jonathan (interestingly not introduced here as Saul's son) in Gibeah (1 Sam 13:2). However, it is Jonathan, not Saul, who takes the next step, prefiguring his bold provocation a chapter later. He attacks the Philistine army in a location named Geba,[11] possibly assassinating the Philistine commander,[12] which causes an uproar on both sides. The Philistines naturally learn about the attack and take offence against Israel, while Saul announces it to the Hebrews[13] by blowing a

---

10. Robert Gordon, in search of the historical grounding of Samuel's narratives, considers the Philistine threat a plausible factor for the establishment of Israel's monarchy in Robert P. Gordon, "Who Made the Kingmaker? Reflections on Samuel and the Institution of Monarchy," in *Faith, Tradition, and History: Old Testament Historiography in Its Near Eastern Context*, ed. A. R. Millard et al. (Winona Lake, IN: Eisenbrauns, 1994), 255–69, esp. 257–60.

11. One wonders whether the location Geba (גֶּבַע) in v. 3 is identical to Gibeah (גִּבְעָה) in v. 2, and perhaps how these names are connected to Gibeath-Elohim (גִּבְעַת הָאֱלֹהִים) in 1 Sam 10:5. On the one hand, Albright has argued that Gibeah and Geba refer to separate locations. Gibeah stood for a modern-day Tell el-Fûl in the north and should be distinguished from Geba (likely modern Jeba). See W. F. Albright, *Excavations and Results at Tell El-Fûl (Gibeah of Saul)*, AASOR 4 (New Haven: ASOR, 1924), esp. 28–43. On the other hand, Miller argues that all these terms (not only Gibeah and Geba, but also Gibeath-Elohim and other variants) likely refer to the same site. See J. Maxwell Miller, "Geba/Gibeah of Benjamin," *VT* 25 (1975): 145–66. See also Patrick M. Arnold, "Gibeah," *ABD* 2:1007–9, esp. 1008. Although the conundrum is difficult to solve, the latter proposal makes good sense of the text in its received form.

12. The word used to describe the Philistine presence in 1 Sam 13:3, 4 and also in 10:5 is נְצִיב (the Greek text considers it a personal name Ναοιβ). However, a different noun, מַצָּב, can be found in 1 Sam 13:23 and throughout ch. 14 in vv. 1, 4, 6, 11, 15; and the feminine version מַצֵּבָה occurs in v. 12. All the designations probably come from the same verbal root נצב, meaning "stand, to take a stand." Perhaps, the change in terminology from נְצִיב that was attacked by Jonathan (1 Sam 10:5; 13:3, 4), to מַצָּב that advances to fight with Israel in ch. 14, might indicate that the former could signify the military commander, whom Jonathan assassinated, and the latter the whole military unit prepared for battle. For a distinction between נְצִיב and מַצָּב, see J. Reindl, "נצב/יצב," *TDOT* 9:519–29, esp. 526–27. For a similar conclusion, see Tsumura, *Samuel*, 336; and Long, *Reign*, 44.

13. An unusual term is used for the Israelites in 1 Sam 13:3—the Israelites are called here the "Hebrews" (עִבְרִים). This term most often designates the Israelites as viewed through the eyes of their neighbors, most often the Egyptians (e.g. Gen 39:14) or the Philistines (e.g. 1 Sam 4:6, 9; 14:11). But this is the case neither here nor in several other instances in chs. 13 and 14 (13:3, 7; 14:21), where the title is used either by Saul or the narrator. There have been several attempts to explain its occurrence here. From a sociopolitical point of view, Gottwald sees in this designation a remnant of the historical kernel of Israel's story before it was rewritten for theological purposes, where the designation "Hebrews" referred to the people *'apiru*, subdued by the Philistines but potentially capable of rebellion. See Norman K. Gottwald, *The Tribes of Yahweh* (Sheffield: Sheffield Academic, 1999), 419–25, esp. 422. Another possibility is that the "Hebrews" may represent a group distinct from the Israelites, one whom Saul wanted to join the ranks of

horn.[14] Thus the Israelites were called to Saul in order to face the Philistine oppressors in Israelite territory.[15]

It is interesting, however, that the Hebrew text of v. 4—which I am following at this point in my thought experiment, yet omitting the final word – says: "When all Israel heard that Saul had smitten the Philistine garrison and that Israel had become odious to the Philistines,[16] the people were called to follow after Saul." Even though it was Jonathan who had attacked the Philistine army, perhaps assassinating the Philistine commander, the Hebrews heard that the action was led by Saul.

There are various interpretative strategies as to how to make sense of this perplexing shift. A source-critical (or possibly redaction-critical) solution, could attribute these variants to the various layers present in the text: a version viewing Saul positively described him as a person who initiated the attack, whereas a later version favoring Jonathan, probably of Judean origin, attributed the provocation to him.[17] From the synchronic viewpoint it is possible to state that either Saul fabricated the news in order to show himself in a more positive light, or the messengers simply conjectured it was their king and leader who took this step against the Philistines.[18] Regardless of the exact answer to this puzzle, the contrast between Saul and Jonathan, exemplified at this point in the canonical version of the narrative, might signal their rivalry, which is only intensified in the next chapter.

Verses 2–4 prepare the reader for the military confrontation that is expected to follow without delay. By attacking the Philistine outpost, Jonathan started the conflict and news of this act—initiated by him, but credited to Saul—spread throughout both people's territories. The Philistines prepared to fight, and the Israelites followed Saul as their leader.

Israel. See Ralph W. Klein, *1 Samuel*, WBC 10 (Dallas: Word, 1983), 137; and McCarter, *I Samuel*, 241. From a literary perspective, the name can be interpreted as enhancing the portrayal of the Israelites in a way fitting for this section of the narrative. For example, as Fokkelman suggests that, by using this pejorative title, often found on Philistine lips, Saul could hope "to arouse his people's pride and fortify their will to resist." Consult Jan P. Fokkelman, *Narrative Art and Poetry in the Books of Samuel*. Vol. 2, *The Crossing Fates* (Assen: Van Gorcum, 1986), 30; see also Firth, *Samuel*, 154.

14. A similar custom is set out in Num 10:1–10.

15. Together with, for example, Hertzberg (*Samuel*, 104) I am following the MT of v. 3, even though the LXX, especially in light of Num 10:1–10, has some plausibility. The Greek text adds these words as Saul's announcement to Israel: "the slaves have revolted (ἠθετήκασιν οἱ δοῦλοι)." Similarly also 1 Sam 14:21. A contrary proposal is offered by McCarter, who prefers the Greek rendering since he thinks that the MT's sentence with the title "Hebrews" on Saul's lips is unnatural (McCarter, *I Samuel*, 224, also 225–26).

16. A phrase involving the verb באש ("become odious") often indicates that a certain action has brought about the worsening of a situation between two involved parties (e.g. Exod 5:21; 1 Sam 27:12; 2 Sam 10:6; 16:21).

17. See, for example, Arnold, "Gibeah," 2:1008.

18. Alternatively, Tsumura remarks that whatever Jonathan did might have been credited to his father and king (Tsumura, *Samuel*, 338).

Philistine Military Advantage
(1 Samuel 13:5–7a, 15b)

In reaction to Jonathan's attack, the Philistines gathered to fight Israel in extraordinary numbers. They occupied the position at Michmash formerly held by Saul: thirty thousand chariots, six thousand horsemen, and troops like the sand on the seashore in number (1 Sam 13:5). Although I am inclined to follow the LXX[L] and Syr. in terms of the number of chariots, which substitutes "three" for "thirty"[19]—this number being more reasonable for the military equipment of those days—the display of Philistine power simply demonstrates the overwhelming dominance of their army, which quite naturally created a panic in the Israelite camp.[20]

The people were hard pressed[21] and began to desert Saul. The text further details how the desertion took place: the people hid in places that were difficult to access—in caves, holes,[22] rocks, pits, or cisterns (1 Sam 13:6)—and the "Hebrews" crossed the Jordan to the territory of Gad and Gilead (1 Sam 13:7a). The number of people who remained with Saul was thus significantly diminished. Saul counted only six hundred people who stayed with him to face the now-increased numerical advantage of the Philistines (1 Sam 13:15b).

The Philistines Plunder the Land
(1 Samuel 13:16–18)

The continuation of the story intensifies the dire situation in which the Israelites found themselves. First, it recapitulates the positions at which both armies were encamped. The Israelites, led by Saul and his son Jonathan, were in Geba of Benjamin, while the Philistines faced them at Michmash, with the valley dividing the two camps (1 Sam 13:16). Second, whereas the Israelites remained inactive, the Philistines raided the country in three different directions (13:17–18). Tsumura summarizes the paths on which the plunderers traveled as towards the north, west, and east: with south – where Saul and his army were encamped—excluded.[23] Israelite territory being left unprotected, it becomes an easy prey to the raiding Philistines,

---

19. The three thousand chariots would also allow for two horsemen each to ride them. The Philistine numbers were astronomical even though the chariots may have been of little use in the hill country.

20. Klein compares the Philistine force of three thousand chariots to the nine hundred chariots of Sisera in Judg 4:3, and remarks how "exceedingly large" this army was (Klein, *1 Samuel*, 126).

21. The verb נגש occurs here and also in 1 Sam 14:24.

22. Together with many commentators, I emend ובחוחים, in thickets, to ובחורים, in holes." This conforms with 1 Sam 14:11: "The Hebrews are coming out of the holes (חֹרִים) where they hid themselves." Similarly NRSV, Bar-Efrat, *Samuel*, 193; and Tsumura, *Samuel*, 339. See, however, the dissenting voice of the NIV and McCarter, *I Samuel*, 226.

23. Tsumura, *Samuel*, 351.

which likely brought additional distress to Saul and his small group of soldiers.[24] Firth aptly summarizes the position of Saul and his men: "What is emphasized is that Saul's position is one where victory appears impossible. His small force is greatly outnumbered and completely surrounded. Philistine victory seems inevitable."[25]

The situation thus does not improve for Israel, as the Philistines flex their military muscle in the surrounding territory, displaying their control over the Israelites. While at this point one would have expected the narrative to proceed and depict the battle, the reader instead gets yet another look at Philistine dominance.

Philistine Technological Advantage
(1 Samuel 13:19–22)

Here the narrative suddenly pauses to describe the economic situation of both armies.[26] The reader learns that the Philistines on top of their numerical advantage had also a technological one, as they were the primary metalworkers in the area, upon whom the Israelites were dependent for acquiring and sharpening their tools.[27] These services were not cheap (1 Sam 13:21), and so on the day of the battle the only Israelites carrying swords or spears were Saul and Jonathan (13:22),[28] this occurring in spite of the Philistine intention to keep all the Hebrews without weapons (13:19).

On the one hand, this explanatory note prepares the reader for the action of the next chapter. Those having weapons at least comparable to those of the Philistines are Saul and Jonathan, and so one naturally expects for one or both of them to engage in some sort of combat with the Philistines. On the other hand, the inter-textual link with another instance in which "spear" (חֲנִית) and "sword" (חֶרֶב) appear together shows that, in the context of life under God, weapons do not play the decisive role in battle. On that occasion it was David who announced to the heavily armed

---

24. Thus Hertzberg, who reasons that the purpose of the raiders was "to increase the general fear and thus indirectly to damage the Israelite cause" (Hertzberg, *Samuel*, 107).

25. Firth, *Samuel*, 156. Similarly also Smith, *Samuel*, 99.

26. There are several textual problems in this paragraph, but they do not appear to bear any significance for my main thesis.

27. Kreuzer further draws on some archeological and sociological insights in order to argue that the Israelites most of the time had peaceful, albeit dependent, relations with their Philistine neighbors. See Siegfried Kreuzer, "'War Saul auch unter den Philistern?' Die Anfänge des Königtums in Israel," *ZAW* 113 (2001): 56–73, esp. 58–59.

28. Saul's reign as king is associated with the use of the spear, up until his death by the same weapon (1 Sam 18:11; 19:9, 10; 20:33; 22:6; 26:7, 8, 11, 12, 16, 22; 2 Sam 1:6), even though he also owned a sword (1 Sam 17:39). Jonathan, on the other hand, is known for giving his sword to David (1 Sam 18:4).

Philistine that "YHWH does not save by sword or spear; for the battle is YHWH's" (17:47),[29] and the narrative makes it clear that David's victory was indeed achieved without the use of any such weapons.[30] In the context of 1 Samuel, however, the technological advantage of the Philistines creates a bleak picture for Israel's success in the upcoming battle.[31]

The Sign of the Upcoming Conflict (1 Samuel 13:23)

The last verse of ch. 13 finally turns our attention back to the scene of the battle. The garrison of the Philistines went out southward, to the crossing at Michmash, which effectively prepares the scene for the action of the next chapter. The battle with Israel becomes imminent.

Summary

At least four things, I think, may be highlighted from this close reading of ch. 13 without the intrusive section of 1 Sam 13:7b–15a.

Overwhelming Dominance of the Philistines

"The purpose of the monarchy is to fight the Philistines,"[32] states Brueggemann in connection with the present chapter and I hope that my examination has brought to light some of the reasons why the Philistines presented such a threat to the Israelite kingship. They are described by the narrative as the oppressing force controlling Israelite territory. More specifically, the events of ch. 13 show that the Israelites near Gibeah and Michmash were in a dreadful situation. After the initial act of provocation carried out by Jonathan, they faced an army far larger than themselves, which caused some to hide or flee. The Philistines exploited this situation and plundered the rest of the land, leaving the Israelites in terror and panic. This, coupled with their technological dominance, comprised an enemy much stronger than the Israelites, and one they now had to face.

---

29. Similarly also 1 Sam 17:45.

30. This seems to be the meaning of the peculiar clause of 1 Sam 17:50: "so David prevailed over the Philistine with a sling and a stone, striking down the Philistine and killing him; there was no sword in David's hand," even though the text also portrays David as killing Goliath with Goliath's own sword. See Moberly's attempt to explain this conundrum by positing that v. 50 could be a pedagogical gloss trying to prevent the overtly wooden reading of the narrative. R. W. L. Moberly, "By Stone and Sling: 1 Samuel 17:50 and the Problem of Misreading David's Victory over Goliath," in *On Stone and Scroll: Essays in Honour of Graham Ivor Davies*, ed. James K. Aitken et al. (Boston: de Gruyter, 2011), 329–42.

31. Thus also Walter Dietrich, *Samuel*, BKAT 8/2 (Neukirchen-Vluyn: Neukirchener, 2011–12), 53.

32. Brueggemann, *Samuel*, 98.

Awaiting a Deliverer

Nevertheless, the broader literary context might signal some hope. The story of Saul is often compared to the period of Judges,[33] and one of the resonances that may be noted between the two narratives is a similarity between Saul's campaign against the Philistines in chs. 13 and 14, and Gideon's war against the Midianites in Judg 6–7. The two stories show a striking resemblance. Both Saul and Gideon blow the horn (שׁוֹפָר) to gather the people (Judg 6:34; 1 Sam 13:3), while the rest of the troops are at some point sent to their tents (Judg 7:8; 1 Sam 13:2). The Israelites on both occasions hide in caves (מְעָרָת is mentioned in Judg 6:2 and 1 Sam 13:6) and tremble (the verb חרד is employed in both cases) before the enemy (Judg 7:3; 1 Sam 13:7). Both the Midianites and the Philistines gathered to fight in extraordinary numbers, their armies being described as "numerous as the sand on the seashore" (Judg 7:12; 1 Sam 13:5).[34] Anticipating the context of ch. 14, one may also add that both of these dreadful situations appear to have allowed a sign from God, assuring the brave hero (Gideon/Jonathan) of God's favor (Judg 6:36–40; 1 Sam 14:8–10). In each case YHWH's intervention eventually threw the enemy into a chaos in which they turned their swords against each other (Judg 7:22; 1 Sam 14:20). Most importantly, the smallness of Gideon's army (three hundred soldiers) and that of Saul's (six hundred)—as compared with the overwhelming numbers of the enemy—recalls the saying of YHWH concerning the unforeseen importance of those chosen few who are allowed to fight: "lest Israel boast over me, saying, 'My hand has saved me'" (Judg 7:2).[35]

This comparison with Gideon[36] serves to heighten the expectation that Saul or Jonathan might act in a similar manner: to take advantage

---

33. For example, Miller observes the connection between the cutting up of the ox in 1 Sam 11 and the tragic fate of the concubine from Bethlehem in Judg 19. See J. Maxwell Miller, "Saul's Rise to Power: Some Observations Concerning I Sam 9:1–10:16; 10:26–11:15 and 13:2–14:46," *CBQ* 36 (1974): 157–74, 165–68. For more points of contact consult A. Graeme Auld, *I & II Samuel: A Commentary*, OTL (Louisville, KY: John Knox, 2011), 139–40.

34. Judg 7:12 speaks of the army's camels being "countless as the sand on the seashore" (כַּחוֹל שֶׁעַל־שְׂפַת־הַיָּם לָרֹב). In 1 Sam 13:5 it is the troops who are "as the sand on the seashore" (כַּחוֹל אֲשֶׁר עַל־שְׂפַת־הַיָּם לָרֹב).

35. Some commentators highlight this specific comparison between Gideon and Saul. See, for example, Bodner, *1 Samuel*, 133.

36. On a smaller scale, the contrast between Israel's meager army and the large Philistine army with their more advanced weaponry sounds much like the description of a Philistine giant named Goliath in 1 Sam 17 awaiting an Israelite ready to meet him on the battleground. In both contexts the Philistine threat had, in terms of size and equipment, a mythical flavor, and caused fear and trembling in the Israelite camp (1 Sam 13:6; 17:11). In both contexts somebody withstood the overwhelming force of the oppressor, invoking a power even higher than that of the Philistines. The comparison to David's battle with Goliath in 1 Sam 17 suggests that desperate situations require faith in YHWH

of the unfortunate imbalance between the Israelite army and that of the Philistines, calling upon YHWH to achieve God's victory for his people.[37]

Signs of Tension between Saul and Jonathan

The narrative depicts the beginnings of a possible tension between Saul and Jonathan. Although it was Jonathan who attacked the Philistine outpost, it was Saul who summoned Israel and was credited with this initial stage of victory. Jonathan is not introduced as Saul's son, and in his act of provocation against the Philistines in the land seems to be acting independently of his father. Furthermore, the disclosure that only Saul and his son carried weapons, and thus could best face the Philistine oppression, adds an interesting twist to the story and raises the expectation that in the next chapter one of these two Israelites may take matters into his hands.

Preparatory Chapter

Finally, when read without the intrusive passage in vv. 4b and 7b–15a, no rejection or suspicion with regard to Saul is apparent in the narrative. Saul might be unnecessarily passive in the opening provocation against the Philistines, but those elements do not darken his character in any substantial way. Jonathan could be blamed for his rash attack as well, and the reader is left guessing which of them will stand up for Israel and YHWH in the ensuing narrative. Read this way, the chapter simply prepares the reader for the continuation of the story in ch. 14.

---

as a prerequisite of any successful maneuver vis-à-vis an overwhelming force. For a study highlighting David's faith in YHWH as the decisive factor in his success against the Philistine giant, see Benjamin J. M. Johnson, "Did David Bring a Gun to a Knife Fight? Literary and Historical Considerations in Interpreting David's Victory over Goliath," *ExpTim* 124 (2013): 530–37.

37. Dragga's stimulating article draws upon the NRSV reading of 1 Sam 12:11, where Samuel recalls four judges that preceded Saul. Dragga compares their deeds with Saul's actions and finds Saul wanting. See Sam Dragga, "In the Shadow of the Judges: The Failure of Saul," *JSOT* 38 (1987): 39–46, esp. 40–41.

1 Samuel 14

Chapter 14, which—from a literary point of view—seems to present one unit,[1] consists of two parts. The narrative section (1 Sam 14:1–46) high-lights the rivalry between Saul and his son Jonathan, contrasting their differing attitudes towards the battle with the Philistines and towards the discerning and accomplishing of God's will. Verses 47–52 then close the chapter by presenting Saul's successes in terms of his military endeavors and family relationships.

The Battle with the Philistines
(1 Samuel 14:1–46)

The battle between the Philistines and the Israelites is portrayed as happen-ing in one day. Although some events—such as the men who had been hiding in the Ephraimite hill country joining Saul after hearing of his army defeating the enemy (1 Sam 14:22)—are difficult to imagine as taking place between the morning and evening of the same day (1 Sam 14:24), the various references to "this day"[2] frame the chapter and help the reader to view the varied happenings in the chapter as tightly interconnected. The multiple actions and subplots are presented in the concentrated form of one long day.

Setting the Scene: Jonathan against Saul (1 Samuel 14:1–5)

The first five verses of the chapter introduce the main characters and set the scene of the initial provocation.[3] Along with his armor-bearer, Jonathan contemplates an attack on the Philistine military presence in the land in an

---

1. Of course, the text may contain various sources, but they are in this case more difficult to identify. See, for example, Stoebe, *Samuelis*, 261–62; and Joseph Blenkinsopp, "Jonathan's Sacrilege, 1 Sm 14:1–46: A Study in Literary History," *CBQ* 26 (1964): 423–49, esp. 423. An argument against the chapter's literary unity can be found, for example, in Franz Schicklberger, "Jonatans Heldentat: Textlinguistische Beobachtungen zu 1 Sam 14:1–23a," *VT* 24 (1974): 324–33.

2. The expression "It happened one day" (וַיְהִי הַיּוֹם) in 1 Sam 14:1 opens the section and the sentence "for [Jonathan] worked with God this day" (כִּי־עִם־אֱלֹהִים עָשָׂה הַיּוֹם הַזֶּה) in 1 Sam 14:45 closes it. In addition to these two places, references to "this day" (יוֹם with or without a definite article) can also be found in the MT text of 1 Sam 14:18, 23, 24, 28, 30, 31, 33, 37, and 38.

3. Thus also, for example, Bar-Efrat, *Samuel*, 136.

act reminiscent of his earlier provocation in 1 Sam 13:3. The text emphasizes that Jonathan—who, in fact, is referenced here as Saul's son—did not
tell his father of his plan to attack the Philistine outpost (1 Sam 14:1), and
that no one else among the people know about it either (1 Sam 14:3). Saul
was staying near Gibeah with his remaining six hundred men who did
not flee in fear of the Philistine army (1 Sam 13:15b), and with Ahijah—
the priest, who carried an ephod. While the presence of the ephod with
its ability to invoke YHWH's will (by way of Urim and Thummim) carries
positive overtones and anticipates the determining of God's will in the
chapter (1 Sam 14:18–19, 36–42), the reference to Ahijah's uncle Ichabod—
the son of Phinehas, from Eli's rejected family—may raise more ambiguous
conjectures (1 Sam 14:3).[4]

After introducing the chapter's main characters, the narrative turns its
attention to the geographical setting of the episode: it occurs in a rocky
terrain with two prominent cliffs providing a passage for Jonathan's provocation (1 Sam 14:4). There may be some value in the attempt to reconstruct
their precise historical background in the Wadi Suweinit,[5] but a more
fruitful approach seems to be to try to locate the reference in the wider
literary context of the story. The names of the rocks—בוֹצֵץ ("the slippery
one") and סֶנֶּה ("the thorny one")—may, as Hertzberg remarks for example,[6]
further enhance the description of Jonathan's tricky ascent to the Philistine
camp.

The opening of the chapter thus both intensifies and prefigures the
contrast between Saul and Jonathan in terms of their approach to the
Philistine threat, and what means they have at their disposal. Jonathan is
ready to attack the Philistine outpost, while Saul stays on the outskirts of
Gibeah, apparently inactive. Whereas Jonathan has with him a young man
who carries his weapons (presumably a sword and a spear, as mentioned in
1 Sam 13:22), Saul has by his side Ahijah, the priest, who carries an ephod.[7]
These two comrades—and the instruments they carry—will have a determining effect on the action taken by Saul and Jonathan in the subsequent

---

4. The ambiguity of Ahijah's presence is highlighted, for example, by Firth, *Samuel*,
162; and Fokkelman, *Crossing*, 48–49. On the genealogy and the link with the Elides, see
also Matitiahu Tsevat, "Studies in the Book of Samuel I. Interpretation of 1 Sam. 2:27–36:
The Narrative of *Kareth*," *HUCA* 32 (1961): 191–216, esp. 209–14.

5. Note the attempt made in N. Wyatt, "Jonathan's Adventure and a Philological
Conundrum," *PEQ* 127 (1995): 62–69. Similarly also Driver, *Notes*, 106.

6. Hertzberg, *Samuel*, 112. The meaning of these two names, however, is difficult
to ascertain. Van Wijk-Bos, for example, translates the rocks "Twinkler" and "Thorn."
Johanna W. H. Van Wijk-Bos, *Reading Samuel: A Literary and Theological Commentary*
(Macon, GA: Smyth & Helwys, 2013), 80.

7. Fokkelman draws attention to the contrast between Saul's priest who carries an
ephod (נֹשֵׂא אֵפוֹד in 1 Sam 14:3) and the soldier accompanying Jonathan who carries his
armor (נֹשֵׂא כֵלָיו in 1 Sam 14:1). See Fokkelman, *Crossing*, 49.

narrative: Jonathan will act as a military leader, gaining the advantage over Israel's main enemy, whereas Saul will use various religious means to alter the course of the ensuing conflict.

Jonathan's Attack against the Philistines (1 Samuel 14:6–15)

Verses 6–15 describe the reasons for and the content of Jonathan's courageous action. Whereas Saul has six hundred soldiers and a man to inquire of YHWH at his disposal, Jonathan achieves success with only his armorbearer. Despite the large size of the Philistine army, their dominance in terms of weaponry, and the rocky terrain ahead,[8] Jonathan resolves to find help in YHWH. He says: "Come, let us cross over to the garrison of those uncircumcised. Perhaps YHWH will act for us; for nothing can hinder YHWH from saving by many or by few" (1 Sam 14:6). On the one hand, Jonathan's dialogue with his armor-bearer reveals the rationale for his action: God does not need a big army to win the battle. On the other hand, his statement shows that he is unafraid to take risks even when he is uncertain concerning God's possible involvement in his plan: "*Perhaps* YHWH will act for us" (1 Sam 14:6).[9] These words are spoken in a situation and manner reminiscent of David in his battle with Goliath. Reference to the "uncircumcised" enemy (17:26, 36) and the inferiority of both Israelite heroes link these two pivotal stories in 1 Samuel. As with David, Jonathan believes in YHWH's power to overcome the multitude of YHWH's enemy regardless of human incapacity.

In this endeavor Jonathan's armor-bearer is of the same mind as his master. He answers Jonathan's proposal with the following words: "Do all that is in your heart; go ahead,[10] I am with you according to your heart" (עֲשֵׂה כָּל־אֲשֶׁר בִּלְבָבֶךָ נְטֵה לָךְ הִנְנִי עִמְּךָ כִּלְבָבֶךָ, 1 Sam 14:7). The armor-bearer's

---

8. Notice that Jonathan and his armor-bearer need to use their hands to climb up the cliff where the Philistine's military unit resides (1 Sam 14:13). Hertzberg further stresses that attempting to scale this impassable territory must be "either madness or faith" (Hertzberg, *Samuel*, 112).

9. Brueggemann states: "Jonathan is careful not to presume upon the freedom of Yahweh" (Brueggemann, *Samuel*, 103). See also similar comments with respect to statements containing אוּלַי in the Old Testament in David J. Reimer, "An Overlooked Term in Old Testament Theology—Perhaps," in *Covenant as Context: Essays in Honour of E. W. Nicholson*, ed. A. D. H. Mayes and R. B. Salters (Oxford: Oxford Universty Press, 2003), 325–46.

10. The presence of לָךְ with the verb נטה is unusual. Driver draws attention to "Turn aside (נְטֵה לָךְ) to your right or to your left" in 2 Sam 2:21—another text within the books of Samuel that contains both words—where the phrase "preserves the usual force of *incline*" (Driver, *Notes*, 107). Probably for this reason the LXX, where "heart" is the subject governing the verb, translates 1 Sam 14:7: "Do all towards which your heart inclines" (ποίει πᾶν ὃ ἐὰν ἡ καρδία σου ἐκκλίνῃ). See, for example, Bernard Grillet et al., *Premier livre des Règnes*, BdA 9.1 (Paris: Cerf, 1997), 254. However, with the NIV and NJPS, for example, and against the NRSV and McCarter, *I Samuel*, 236, I retain the meaning of motion, a common one for verbal roots with נטה.

solidarity—"as your heart is, so is mine"[11]—is then exemplified when he climbs up after Jonathan and engages in the battle. His actions mirror his pledge and together they model the correct attitude of a faithful servant.[12]

Jonathan comes up with a sign that will enable him and his servant to discern whether God is with them and if he will deliver the Philistines into Israel's hand.[13] Jonathan's proposal seems to have some affinities with the sign devised by Abraham's unnamed servant in Gen 24:10–27, who wants to discern God's will concerning the finding of a suitable wife for his master's son, Isaac.[14] The servant wishes to find a woman who, in a response to his request for water, quenches not only his own thirst but also of his camels (Gen 24:14). The idea behind this sign seems to be that a woman who went beyond his specific request would show characteristics of a good future wife: she would notice the needs of those around her, and be caring and faithful (as watering camels clearly takes time).

The important question in Jonathan's case is what the underlying principle behind the sign might be. Jonathan spells it out this way: "If they say to us: 'Stay still until we come to you,' then we will stand in our place and we will not go up to them. But if they say: 'Come up to us,' we will go up for YHWH has given them into our hand. That will be a sign for us" (1 Sam 14:9–10). The inner logic of the sign seems to focus on the difference between passivity (emphasized by the imperative "Stand still!" [דֹּמּוּ] in 1 Sam 14:9) and activity (expressed by "Come up!" [עֲלוּ] in 1 Sam 14:10). If the Philistines ask them to come up to them (presumably because they are not afraid of two ill-equipped individuals climbing the steep terrain), Jonathan and his armor-bearer will take it as a signal from God that what this situation requires is activity and courage. Therefore, when the Philistine soldiers encouraged them to come up, they apparently took this as a sign from YHWH and entered the Philistine outpost. Jonathan struck them, presumably with a sword or spear, while his armor-bearer finished them off (1 Sam 14:13).[15]

---

11. This apt NRSV translation recalls the Greek rendering of 1 Sam 14:7: ὡς ἡ καρδία σοῦ καρδία μοῦ.

12. This text will have a bearing upon the interpretation of 1 Sam 13:14, where one learns about crucial characteristics of Saul's successor. He must be a "person according to [YHWH's] heart" (אִישׁ כִּלְבָבוֹ). See pp. 193–95.

13. Saul's desire to avenge *his* enemies (1 Sam 14:24) may be contrasted with Jonathan's words to his armor-bearer in his initial attack where he mentions that "YHWH has given [the Philistines] into the hands of *Israel*" (1 Sam 14:12). Similarly also Stephen B. Chapman, *1 Samuel as Christian Scripture: A Theological Commentary* (Grand Rapids: Eerdmans, 2016), 133.

14. Although the word "sign" (אוֹת) does not appear in that text, the context shows that the servant is seeking some sort of direction from YHWH in order to know how to act, in a manner similar to that of Jonathan.

15. Some authors see here God at work. Fokkelman remarks that the Philistines "falling" before Jonathan in 1 Sam 14:13 may be understood as an act of prostration,

The consequences of this initial attack by Jonathan and his armor-bearer are captured in vv. 14 and 15, which are connected by the phrase "and there was" (וַתְּהִי). Verse 14 describes the immediate result of Jonathan's brave action—significant in terms of this battle of two Israelites against a Philistine garrison, but minimal as compared to what follows in the narrative—when about twenty Philistine soldiers are killed within a limited area of the battlefield.[16]

Nevertheless, it is the larger consequences of this first strike that are devastating to the Philistines. Verse 15, which describes these consequences, revolves around the verbal root "tremble" (חרד), occurring here three times. There was trembling (חֲרָדָה) in the camp, in the field, and among the people; the garrison and the raiders trembled (חָרְדוּ) as well; and the earth quaked. The text adds in summary that the resulting outcome was "a panic of God" (חֶרְדַּת אֱלֹהִים),[17] which further stresses the disproportion between the direct and indirect effect of Jonathan's action. The reference to an earthquake and the phrase referring to a "panic of God" both suggest that Jonathan's action was accompanied by unusual phenomena that may be attributed to divine intervention.[18]

The section 1 Sam 14:6–15 thus reveals Jonathan's rationale for his courageous action and its outcome. He relies on YHWH, for whom the smallness and ill-equipped nature of Israel's army presents no problem. Accompanied by his faithful armor-bearer, Jonathan devises a sign that assures him of God's favor and as a result he attacks the Philistines. While Jonathan's attack was a blow to the Philistine camp, the panic created by God is what provided the key difference in the ensuing battle.

Saul's Battle with the Philistines (1 Samuel 14:16–23)

Since both Jonathan and Saul are the main characters of this chapter, the narrative naturally shifts its attention to Saul's camp in order to illuminate his actions near Gibeah. As soon as Saul's watchmen notice the unusual

---

which might echo Dagon's falling in front of the ark in 1 Sam 5:3–4; see Fokkelman, *Crossing*, 51, and, similarly, Van Wijk-Bos, *Samuel*, 81.

16. The limited area seems to be indicated by the unusual phrase: "about half a furrow long in an acre of land" (כְּבַחֲצִי מַעֲנָה צֶמֶד שָׂדֶה, 1 Sam 14:14 NRSV). Nevertheless, the combination of the prepositions כְּ and בְּ is unusual (see GKC §118s-w). The LXX has a different text here: "with darts and with sling stones and with pebbles of the plain" (ἐν βολίσι καὶ ἐν πετροβόλοις καὶ ἐν κόχλαξιν τοῦ πεδίου, 1 Sam 14:14 NETS). But the reference to weapons here seems to be out of place. It is possible that the Greek version is interpreting this difficult text with reference to 1 Sam 13:19–22, where one learns of the shortage of military weapons on the Israelite side (thus Grillet et al., *Premier livre des Règnes*, 255). G. R. Driver takes a clue from Peshitta and argues for seeing here an idiom likening this blow to the Philistines to an act of plowing a field. See G. R. Driver, "Old Problems Re-examined," *ZAW* 80 (1968): 174–83, esp. 174.

17. This rendering seems preferable (see the LXX's ἔκστασις παρὰ κυρίου) to the NRSV translation, which takes the noun אֱלֹהִים as an intensifier: "a very great panic."

18. Thus, for example, Tsumura, *Samuel*, 363–64; and Klein, *1 Samuel*, 137.

movements in the Philistine camp, Saul gives orders to count his troops in order to discover who is missing from among them. Saul thus learns that Jonathan and his armor-bearer have left the camp (1 Sam 14:16–17). At that point Saul commands Ahijah, the priest, to bring an ephod, apparently in order that he may ascertain God's will with regard to the battle.[19] However, the uproar[20] in the Philistine camp interferes with the acquiring of God's oracle, and Saul proceeds to the battle without divine assurance (14:18–19). Nevertheless, no additional help from above is needed, which Saul's men discover as soon as they join the battle, since in the Philistine camp every man's sword is turned against his neighbor. This sort of confusion further underscores the divine activity undertaken on behalf of Jonathan and Israel.[21] Moreover, the resulting disarray among the Philistines also indicates that superior weaponry does not necessarily constitute an advantage – especially in a state of chaos, where it may lead to "friendly fire."

Verses 21 and 22 then depict a reversal of the dire situation of ch. 13. First, those Hebrews[22] who until then had been on the Philistine side deserted them and joined Saul and Jonathan in their assault upon their

---

19. The ancient versions differ in terms of which object of divination Ahijah brought to Saul. According to the Hebrew text, this relic is the "ark of God" (אֲרוֹן הָאֱלֹהִים). The text then adds: "for the ark of God was with the sons of Israel on that day" (כִּי־הָיָה אֲרוֹן הָאֱלֹהִים בַּיּוֹם הַהוּא וּבְנֵי יִשְׂרָאֵל). The ark was normally in Kirjat-jearim but *on this day*, as the MT text stresses, it happened to be here near the battle line (see Tsumura, *Samuel*, 366). However, in the Greek text Ahijah is asked to bring an ephod (εφουδ), and the narrator supplies the following explanation: "because he carried the ephod those days before Israel" (ὅτι αὐτὸς ἦρεν τὸ εφουδ ἐν τῇ ἡμέρᾳ ἐκείνῃ ἐνώπιον Ισραηλ). It is possible that the reference to the ark exhibits an older version of the narrative that was systematically replaced with the reference to the ephod (Philip R. Davies, "Ark or Ephod in 1 Sam 14:18," *JTS* 26 [1975]: 82–87). An attractive solution that tries to do justice to both readings has been offered by Andreas Scherer, who argues that an ephod possibly meant two things: it stood for a priest's clothing and also for the box containing the Urim and Thummim. The simple reference to the "chest" (אֲרוֹן)—perhaps containing the lots for assessing the divine will— was thus confused with the name for the ark of God; see Andreas Georg Scherer, "Das Ephod im alten Israel," *UF* 35 (2003): 589–604). The textual issue is difficult to decide. I am inclined to follow the LXX, which presents us with yet another reference to divination using the priest's ephod in 1 Samuel (for David's use see 1 Sam 23:9; 30:7).

20. Brueggemann notes that the disarray is "typical of the strategy of 'holy war' in which the confusion itself is a mode of combat (cf. Judg 6:19–21)" (Brueggemann, *Samuel*, 103). Similarly Blenkinsopp, "Jonathan's Sacrilege," 427–31. A nuanced account of YHWH's involvement in Israel's battles (which have been traditionally labeled "holy wars") can be found in Stephen B. Chapman, "Martial Memory, Peaceable Vision: Divine War in the Old Testament," in *Holy War in the Bible: Christian Morality and an Old Testament Problem*, ed. Heath A. Thomas et al. (Downers Grove, IL: IVP Academic, 2013), 47–67.

21. The noise (הָמוֹן) in 1 Sam 14:16, 19 and the panic (מְהוּמָה) in v. 20 associate this story with the devastating effect that the ark had on the Philistines in chs. 4–6 (הָמוֹן occurs in 4:14, and מְהוּמָה in 5:9, 11). For this observation, see Auld, *Samuel*, 154.

22. The Greek text of 1 Sam 14:21 contains the description "the slaves" (οἱ δοῦλοι) instead of "the Hebrews" of the MT.

oppressors.[23] Second, all the Israelites who were hiding in various inaccessible places (1 Sam 13:7) also decided to pursue the enemy, after hearing that the Philistines were fleeing the battle. Verse 23 then concludes the whole section, summarizing the outcome of the military conflict. The narrator's statement that "YHWH saved Israel on that day" (14:23) spells out the cause of what had just happened on the battlefield. It was YHWH that ensured Israelite victory as the battle crossed to Beth-aven, that is, further west from Michmash.[24]

Saul's Oath and Sacrifice (1 Samuel 14:24–35)

After the narrator has given an account of the battle leading to Israel's decisive victory, the story suddenly pauses and zooms in on happenings within the Israelite army. What was seemingly a straightforward victory becomes more complicated.

The People's Distress and Saul's Oath (1 Samuel 14:24)

The opening verse of the section already signals that things have not gone quite so smoothly for Israel. Despite the victory that YHWH brought *"on that day"* (בַּיּוֹם הַהוּא, 1 Sam 14:23), the MT in the second part of v. 24 states: "But the men of Israel were distressed (נִגַּשׂ) *on that day* (בַּיּוֹם הַהוּא). And Saul put the people under an oath saying: 'Cursed be any man who eats food before it is evening and I have avenged myself on my enemies.' So none of the people tasted food" (14:24).

This verse sets the stage for much of what follows in the rest of ch. 14. The verb נגשׂ ("be pressed" in Niphal) connects this distressing situation here in the midst of victory with the state of fear experienced by the Israelites in 1 Sam 13:6, where, having seen the multitude of the Philistines, they hid in caves and holes in the earth. This naturally provokes the question: What has caused such distress on the very same day in which they had the upper hand in battle?

The answer may be contained in the same verse as the Hebrew text makes it clear that Saul has placed the people involved in the battle under an oath. Many standard English translations deliberately connect the people's distress with Saul's oath by using the causative conjunctions and/or the past perfect tense,[25] yet this link is not explicit in the text, as the

---

23. The second part of v. 21 is grammatically difficult. Following other ancient versions (the Greek, for example, reads: ἐπεστράφησαν καὶ αὐτοὶ εἶναι μετὰ Ισραηλ, "they also turned to be with Israel"), I have emended the Hebrew text from סָבִיב וְגַם־הֵמָּה to סָבְבוּ גַם־הֵמָּה. The following verse also includes the construction גַם־הֵמָּה. See Driver, *Notes*, 110–11; Bar-Efrat, *Samuel*, 203; and Klein, *1 Samuel*, 132.

24. 1 Sam 13:5 indicates that Beth-aven is west of Michmash.

25. NIV reads: "because Saul had bound the people under an oath." NJPS has: "For Saul had laid an oath upon the troops." NASB reads: "for Saul had put the people under oath." NRSV in the main body of the text follows the LXX and says: "Now Saul committed a very rash act on that day. He had laid an oath on the troops."

conjunction connecting the two parts of the verse is a simple וְ. Bodner is correct that Saul's oath, which he imposes on the people, could be viewed as subsequent to the distress which the Israelites had experienced, and not the other way around.[26] The troops could have been exhausted from the long day of fighting and Saul, by issuing the oath, wanted to assure YHWH's victory in an important battle. On the other hand, however, and in view of their success in battle against the Philistines, Saul's oath seems like a more viable option for what created the stressful situation among his warriors.[27] Nevertheless, the text remains ambiguous as to cause and effect in this case.

Jonathan Trespasses Saul's Oath (1 Samuel 14:25–30)

The curse was obeyed by everybody except for Jonathan, who did not hear about his father's oath until after he had eaten some honey from honeycombs found in the forest,[28] being informed of it then by one of his fellow soldiers (1 Sam 14:25–28). The text describes Jonathan's action almost in slow motion ("he put forth the end of his staff, which was in his hand, and dipped it in the honeycomb, and returned his hand to his mouth"), and focuses on the effect of his eating (14:27). His eyes light up, and this experience eventually induces him to interpret his father's command negatively.

In fact, we are not told of Saul's intention in ordering the people to refrain from food in the narrative itself, although one may conjecture that – in order to progress quickly in the battle—he did not want his soldiers to be

---

26. Bodner, *1 Samuel*, 138. Similarly also Gordon, *1 & 2 Samuel*, 138; and Hertzberg, *Samuel*, 114. However, one wonders how could Saul issue his oath in the midst of a battle and deliver it to his army. See Tsumura, *Samuel*, 369.

27. The Greek version diverges from the MT on this occasion, emphasizing additionally Saul's culpability: "And Saul committed a great act of ignorance on that day" (καὶ Σαουλ ἠγνόησεν ἄγνοιαν μεγάλην ἐν τῇ ἡμέρᾳ ἐκείνῃ, 1 Sam 14:24). While this is a possible reading, it seems to be an interpretative gloss stressing Saul's guilt, which is not as explicit in the narrative as the Greek text indicates (although Grillet et al. helpfully comment that both the MT and LXX proleptically summarize the content of what follows, unfavorable to Saul; see Grillet et al., *Premier livre des Règnes*, 258). For this reason, and together with, for example, Hertzberg, *Samuel*, 114–15; and Bar-Efrat, *Samuel*, 204, I prefer the MT over the Greek version (against McCarter, *I Samuel*, 245; and Klein, *1 Samuel*, 130, 132).

28. I follow here the MT text of the difficult v. 25: "And the whole country went into the forest, and there was honey on the ground" (וְכָל־הָאָרֶץ בָּאוּ בַיָּעַר וַיְהִי דְבַשׁ עַל־פְּנֵי הַשָּׂדֶה). See also Robert Alter, *The David Story: A Translation with Commentary of 1 and 2 Samuel* (New York: Norton, 1999), 80. The LXX differs from the MT here, saying: καὶ πᾶσα ἡ γῆ ἠρίστα καὶ ιααρ δρυμὸς ἦν μελισσῶνος κατὰ πρόσωπον τοῦ ἀγροῦ ("And all the land ate the midday meal. And Iaar was a wood with a beehive on the ground," 1 Sam 14:25 NETS). The word ιααρ (or ιααλ, as in the LXX[BL]) is simply a transliteration of the Hebrew יַעַר (see Grillet et al., *Premier livre des Règnes*, 259). It is possible that the Greek text follows here an earlier, but already corrupt stage in the development of the text (McCarter, *I Samuel*, 245).

distracted with food preparation and consumption.[29] The only interpretation that the reader is given is Jonathan's, and it has a powerful effect upon one's reading of the narrative. Jonathan thinks that:

> My father has troubled (עָכַר) the land. See how my eyes have brightened (אֹרוּ עֵינַי) because I tasted a little of this honey. How much more so if only the people had surely eaten[30] from the spoil of their enemies which they found; for now the slaughter among the Philistines has not been great. (1 Sam 14:29–30)

The verb עכר resonates with Achan's crime, which brought trouble on Israel (Josh 6:18; 7:25), and adds an additional black cloud over Saul's action. Furthermore, the wordplay between Saul's curse (ארר) and the lighting (אור) of Jonathan's eyes highlights the contrast between the action of the Israelite king and that of his son. Jonathan argues in opposition to Saul and reasons that his father has, through his oath, prevented a greater victory over the Philistines, despite the narrator's comments in vv. 23 and 31 that the battle spread beyond the original site and the Israelites achieved a victory over the Philistines on a large scale.[31] Jonathan, who was successful in his initial attack on the Philistine garrison, does not think that Saul's oath was wise military strategy. His words are confirmed by the condition of the people as described in the subsequent verses.

The People's Sin and Saul's Sacrifice (1 Samuel 14:31–35)

After Jonathan's critique of his father's decision to impose the oath, the narrator offers a comment in line with Jonathan's. The battle has moved to Aijalon, further west towards the Philistines,[32] and "the people were very faint" (וַיָּעַף הָעָם מְאֹד, 1 Sam 14:31). This expression has already occurred in v. 28 (וַיָּעַף הָעָם), but there it was likely pronounced by the soldier informing Jonathan of Saul's curse and expressing his own interpretation of it.[33] The

---

29. Of course, one may suggest other, often more negative, reasons for Saul's oath. Chapman, for example, proposes that "Saul did not want any of his men to start dividing up the spoil until he had first pick" (Chapman, *1 Samuel*, 133).

30. The form of Jonathan's speech (the infinitive absolute with the perfect verb), which emphasizes that the people should surely eat (אָכֹל אָכַל) in v. 30, forms a contrast to the words of the anonymous soldier who insists that Saul has surely sworn (הַשְׁבֵּעַ הִשְׁבִּיעַ) that they must not eat in v. 28.

31. Polzin highlights this fact and considers this to be contrary to Jonathan's interpretation (Polzin, *Samuel*, 136). But the point of Jonathan's speech seems to be that without Saul's oath the victory could have been greater, which does not devalue the enormity of Israel's success thus far.

32. Tsumura remarks that Aijalon is twenty miles west of Michmash (Tsumura, *Samuel*, 374). The Israelites thus pushed the Philistines far back towards their territory. The distance suggested sounds as excessive as the size of the Philistine army.

33. NRSV includes the words "and so the troops are faint" in the soldier's speech. Nevertheless, it is interesting that the phrases "they were faint" (v. 28) and "they were very faint" (v. 31) form an inclusio for Jonathan's speech and thus add credibility to his opinion.

weariness caused by this fast led to the breaking of the cultic prohibition against eating meat with the blood (עַל־הַדָּם)[34] in it, as the troops swooped down on the spoil (14:32–33).

Two problems seem to be involved here: the people eating the meat with the blood (עַל־הַדָּם), and their sacrificing the animals on the ground (אַרְצָה) rather than on the altar (1 Sam 14:32). The issue of the blood, however, seems to have prime importance as it is highlighted several times in this brief episode (1 Sam 14:32, 33, 34). The prohibition against eating meat with blood is mentioned several times in the Pentateuch (specifically in texts such as Gen 9:4; Lev 3:17; 7:26–27; 19:26; and Deut 12:15–16)[35] and is presupposed in the narrative. The blood was not to be consumed because blood carries life, which needs to be protected at all costs. The people were faint, and metaphorically without life; partaking of the blood thus could be seen as a natural way to have their life renewed.

When Saul learns of this incident, he warns the people of the sin they have committed and builds his first altar there,[36] on which he sacrifices the animals (1 Sam 14:33–35). Everything happening so far seems to have taken place on the same day (בַּיּוֹם הַהוּא in 14:31). For this reason, and given the proposed plan to pursue the Philistines at night (14:36), it is presumed that this incident occurred in the evening.[37]

Thus the "not-so-great" victory that Jonathan complained of is not the only negative effect of Saul's curse. The people were so faint that they trespassed YHWH's cultic injunction concerning food purity, and Saul had to avert their sin by erecting an altar and offering on it proper sacrifices to YHWH. One now wonders what consequences Jonathan's eating of the honey will have for the battle, and who will come to his aid. This is the theme of the next major section of 1 Sam 14.

Jonathan Prosecuted and Released (1 Samuel 14:36–46)

Saul's Second Inquiry of God (1 Samuel 14:36–37)

Once Saul has settled the matter of the breach of the cultic prohibition on blood, and the soldiers have been fed, he wants to move ahead and pursue the enemy by night so that the Israelites might plunder the

---

34. The preposition עַל is likely idiomatic and means "together with" (thus, for example, Driver, *Notes*, 115; Klein, *1 Samuel*, 139; and Bar-Efrat, *Samuel*, 206). While the preposition בְּ represents a usual way of expressing the meaning "with," עַל can function this way as well (see, e.g., *IBHS* 217; and against Hertzberg, *Samuel*, 115–16). In addition to this, the prohibition in Lev 19:26 ("You shall not eat anything with the blood") features עַל.

35. Deuteronomy 12:15–16 probably represents the closest foundational text for 1 Sam 14:32–34 in terms of its wording.

36. 1 Samuel 14:35b literally says: "that altar he began to build to YHWH" (אֹתוֹ הֵחֵל לִבְנוֹת מִזְבֵּחַ לַיהוָה). Tsumura comments that the sentence seems to emphasize that "this was Saul's first serious attempt to worship the Lord" (Tsumura, *Samuel*, 376).

37. See, for example, Gordon, *1 & 2 Samuel*, 140; and Hertzberg, *Samuel*, 115.

Philistines and not leave a single one of them alive. Although the Israelites agree, a priest—somewhat surprisingly—steps in and urges that they should first inquire of YHWH (1 Sam 14:36).[38] Saul thus asks YHWH whether he should go and pursue the Philistines but receives no answer (1 Sam 14:37). This is a perplexing turn of events, as the only possible answers to one's question, when the Urim and Thummin were used, were either "yes" or "no." Commentators, when they choose to comment on this issue, resort to speculations,[39] as there is no indication in the text how the understood use of the lots could yield no answer. Perhaps the most that one can reasonably point out in this regard, is that YHWH's silence in response to Saul's request is in line with his unsuccessful attempts later in the narrative to make God speak to him (most memorably in 1 Sam 28:6),[40] which may be contrasted with David's frequent intercommunication with the deity (e.g. 1 Sam 23:2, 4; 30:8).

Jonathan Chosen by Lot (1 Samuel 14:38–44)

Saul's conclusion is that there must be some reason for God's silence, and that reason is somebody's sin.[41] He quickly issues another oath: "For as long as YHWH, who saves Israel, lives, even if it is Jonathan, my son, he will surely die" (1 Sam 14:39). After this pronouncement it is not God[42] but rather the people[43] who respond with silence (both vv. 37 and 39 contain the verb ענה), thus prefiguring their support of Jonathan a few verses later. At this point, Saul devises (as did Jonathan) a sign to discern God's mind as to why YHWH has remained silent.[44] He puts all the people on one side and

---

38. The motives of the priest's request to turn to YHWH are not clear. Fokkelman reasons that "[t]he priest was not very attuned to his Lord, since otherwise he would have omitted this suggestion" (Fokkelman, *Crossing*, 71). One can only note that the priest's speech includes "here" (הֲלֹם) as a possible reference to the altar, which has been built there.

39. Bergen suggests that perhaps "three outcomes were possible in a consultation involving revelatory devices: yes, no, and neither (cf. also 28:6)." See Bergen, *1, 2 Samuel*, 160. Klein reasons that "he received no answer at all, which presumably was as good as a 'no'" (Klein, *1 Samuel*, 139). Smith cautiously remarks that "how the priest discovered Yahweh's refusal to answer we are not told" (Smith, *Samuel*, 121).

40. One may also note that God's silence in answering is predicted by Samuel in 1 Sam 8:18 as a result of the people's disobedience. This is noted by Long, *Reign*, 123–24, but criticized by Murphy, because Saul has yet to perform these monarchic offenses; see Francesca A. Murphy, *1 Samuel*, BTC (Grand Rapids: Baker, 2010), 130.

41. Miscall understands Saul's words in 1 Sam 14:38 to be "this sin" (הַחַטָּאת הַזֹּאת), and the reference to Jonathan found so readily on Saul's lips to be a sign that Saul has already suspected Jonathan to be somehow guilty on this occasion (Miscall, *1 Samuel*, 96).

42. Klein comments: "their silence echoed that of God" (Klein, *1 Samuel*, 139–40).

43. One may point out that there are several thematic doublets in this segment. Twice the people answer Saul: "Do as it seems good to you" (in response to the continuing battle [v. 36] and the lot [v. 40]). Twice we do not hear an answer (from God about pursuing the Philistines [v. 37] or from the people about the oath mentioning Jonathan explicitly [v. 39]).

44. Thus, for example, Polzin, *Samuel*, 133.

himself and Jonathan on the other side. When Saul and Jonathan are indicated by the Urim and Thummim, the same test is put forward to decide between them. Finally, Jonathan is indicated by lot and must expose what he has done. After he reports that he has tasted a bit of honey, Saul repeats the oath[45] (his second in the story), stressing that Jonathan has to die.[46]

Jonathan Released by the People (1 Samuel 14:45–46)

After Jonathan announces to his father that he is ready to die,[47] the people step in to save him from death. Their former silence with regard to Saul's reference to Jonathan in his second oath turns into outward disagreement here. They sharply oppose Saul, issue another vow, and argue that Jonathan has accomplished a great victory for Israel and worked with God to achieve it. Thus, the people rescue Jonathan and he does not perish (1 Sam 14:45). As a consequence of this revolt of the people Saul breaks off his pursuing the Philistines, giving them a chance to return to their homes (14:46).

---

45. 1 Sam 14:44 has almost the same wording as 14:39. The MT text of 1 Sam 14:44 does not contain a reference to the recipient of the curse (the text simply says: כֹּה־יַעֲשֶׂה אֱלֹהִים) as is common in such oath formulas (as, e.g., in 1 Sam 3:17: כֹּה־יַעֲשֶׂה־לְּךָ אֱלֹהִים), but is added in many English translations (e.g. NRSV, NIV), based on the LXX, Syr., or Vulg. Driver suggests that the phrase "to me" was not expressed but presupposed here, as well as in 1 Kgs 19:2 (Driver, *Notes*, 118). Ziegler, on the other hand, thinks that the absence of the recipient is intentional and views it as a weakness on Saul's part as "a deliberate indication of Saul's inability to assume personal responsibility in leadership"; see Yael Ziegler, "'So Shall God Do . . .': Variations of an Oath Formula and Its Literary Meaning," *JBL* 126 (2007): 59–81, esp. 70. Although one may read the absence of the recipient in the oath formula this way, I think that it largely depends on the overall characterization of Saul in the whole narrative and not the other way around.

46. The story is quite straightforward with the exception of vv. 41 and 42. In 1 Sam 14:41 the Hebrew text contains only these words of Saul: "And Saul said to YHWH, God of Israel: Give wholeness! (הָבָה תָמִים)." The speech could make some sense, but seems to finish too abruptly (perhaps due to homoioteleuton, when "a scribe's eyes skipped from 'Jonathan my son' to 'Jonathan his son' and left out everything in between" [Klein, *1 Samuel*, 132]). Therefore many English translations (e.g. NRSV, NIV, NJSP) follow the suggestions of the Greek text here, where one gains a better understanding of Saul's thinking and what the procedure might have looked like: "Why have you not answered your servant today? If this guilt is in me or in my son Jonathan, O LORD God of Israel, give Urim; but if this guilt is in your people Israel, give Thummim" (1 Sam 14:41 NRSV). This seems to be a reasonable solution, although the exact procedure of the lot-casting is not of fundamental importance to the main message of the passage. The Hebrew text of v. 42 is also brief: "And Saul said: 'Throw (the lot) between me and Jonathan, my son.' And Jonathan was taken." The Greek version adds the following words in the middle of the sentence concluding Saul's speech: "'whoever the Lord should indicate by lot, let him die.' And the people said to Saoul, 'This thing is not to be.' And Saoul prevailed over the people, and they cast the lot between him and Jonathan his son" (1 Sam 14:42 NETS). This verse, however, is completely understandable in the Hebrew and the addition from the Greek text is unnecessary, although its portrait of the growing tension between the people and Saul anticipates their disagreement in the next section.

47. However, notice the NIV translation: "And now must I die?"

Two significant questions arise here. First, how is it possible that Saul's oath, the breach of which seemed to be the cause of God's silence, could be thwarted by the people's objection?[48] The answer is not clear, although it is plausible to suggest that Jonathan was indeed guilty but not as guilty as if he had consciously overstepped God's command.[49] By unknowingly breaking Saul's own oath, Jonathan could be rescued by his fellow soldiers if he had acted with YHWH's help, which is precisely what the people argued.

Second, it is noteworthy that the people's reaction indirectly challenges Saul. If Jonathan worked with God on that day, with whom did Saul work? Or, to put it slightly differently, who has committed the greater offense? On the one hand, Saul's curse, which caused hunger among the troops, eventually led to the breaking of the cultic prohibition against eating meat with the blood. Jonathan, on the other hand, broke only Saul's command, and not YHWH's injunction. Similarly, Jonathan's tasting of the honey surely seems trivial when compared to the devouring of raw meat by the troops. One feels that Jonathan is the less guilty party in this controversy, yet the lot still points to him as the one who has caused God's silence regarding the question of whether to continue pursuing the Philistines. The story leaves this conundrum unanswered. In a manner similar to the partial victory over the Philistines, the narrative finishes with signs of incompleteness, leaving the reader to ponder the possible outcomes of this battle for both Jonathan and Saul. However, before the reader is given a closer look at Saul's other adventures, the present chapter closes with a report of Saul's successes.

Saul's Successes
(1 Samuel 14:47–52)

Chapter 14 finishes with three paragraphs devoted to the overall success of Saul's military career, some details of his family, and the ongoing conflict with the Philistines. After Saul had assumed the kingship over Israel, he fought with all its surrounding enemies (1 Sam 14:47). The list of conflicts includes the ongoing war with the Philistines (14:47, 52) and the defeat of the Amalekites (14:48), echoing the events of chs. 13 and 14, and prefiguring

---

48. This seems a legitimate question even though, as Ziegler points out, the breaking of an oath in the Old Testament is not uncommon (Ziegler, "God," 64–65, esp. 65). Similarly Paul Sanders, "So May God Do to Me!," *Bib* 85 (2004): 91–98, esp. 96.

49. According to Keil and Delitzsch, Jonathan unconsciously overstepped a human command, and he did so with God's empowerment. See Carl Fridrich Keil and Franz Delitzsch, *Biblical Commentary on the Books of Samuel*, trans. James Martin (Edinburgh: T&T Clark, 1880), 147. Similarly, Bergen supposes that even the word of a king was ultimately only "the word of a human being," which could have been overruled by the people who swore by "the life of Yahweh" (Bergen, *1, 2 Samuel*, 161).

the incident related in the following chapter. The account of Saul's family includes the list of Saul's three sons, with Jonathan positioned as the first-born, which might indicate a continuing dynasty for Saul through his oldest son, especially given the success he has just accomplished in the battle near Michmash (14:49). The text also names Saul's wife Ahinoam,[50] his two daughters, and Abner, the commander of Saul's army and his cousin (or an uncle) (14:50–51).[51] The last verse of the chapter reminds us that the war with the Philistines was not over and that Saul would continue to fight against them for the rest of his life, adding whatever strong or mighty man he could find to his army (14:52).[52]

The summary of Saul's kingship is not short on success. He delivered Israel from those who plundered it, was able to have a numerous family (which could suggest the possibility of a dynasty), and kept up the battle with the Philistines, Israel's prime enemy. Saul was acting as king, waging Israel's battles, fulfilling the people's expectations as expressed when they asked Samuel for king (1 Sam 8:20). The conclusion of ch. 14 paints a more successful portrait of Saul than what the reader gets from the rather ambivalent development of the skirmish at Michmash.[53] The ending of the present chapter seems to leave the reader with a positive impression of Saul. Despite some missteps in the battle with the Philistines, Saul remains to be YHWH's chosen king, whose sons, most notably Jonathan, may continue to cherish hopes for succeeding him as the Israelite monarch.

Summary

Chapter 14 continues the themes present in the preceding chapter, and thus some comment is called for on the topics that were introduced there – specifically on the unevenness of the conflict between the Israelites and the Philistines, and the tension between Saul and Jonathan.

---

50. The fact that Saul had only one wife portrays him in a more favorable light, at least in the eyes of contemporary Western readers, than one may get from the frequent references to David's extensive harem. Similarly also Van Wijk-Bos, *Samuel*, 83–84.

51. For the argument that Abner was Saul's uncle, see Tsumura, *Samuel*, 385. For a broader discussion, see McCarter, *I Samuel*, 256.

52. Saul's incessant military activity may stand in contrast to the periods of rest that David enjoyed in his career (2 Sam 7:1).

53. Of course, some features in 1 Sam 14:47–52 may be interpreted negatively. Saul may, for example, be viewed as incapable of achieving what he was chosen for, namely the subjugation of the Philistines (see, e.g., Firth, *Samuel*, 167). Moreover, the last clause of v. 47 (וּבְכֹל אֲשֶׁר־יִפְנֶה יַרְשִׁיעַ) may be translated as "wherever he turned, he acted wickedly," which would present much darker portrait of his military achievements (thus, for example, Hertzberg, *Samuel*, 119). Nevertheless, the verb רשע in its Hiphil form (see Deut 25:1) might carry the meaning "inflict punishment" (thus, for example, Alter, *David*, 85; see also the NIV translation). The Greek text turns this verb into a positive one: "Wherever he turned, he was victorious (ἐσῴζετο)," possibly because it read there יִוָּשֵׁעַ (thus Driver, *Notes*, 120).

YHWH's Victory over the Philistines

The first part of the narrative focuses on Israel's surprising victory over the Philistines. Although the Philistines were superior both in numbers and weaponry, they experienced a significant defeat because Jonathan trusted YHWH and found a reliable companion for his endeavor in his armor-bearer. Jonathan's unexpected ascent through rocky terrain delivered the first blow to the Philistine camp. Yet the confusion created by YHWH was the real source of the Philistine troubles as they turned their swords against each other in panic. Despite the fact that the Israelites did not issue a final and complete blow to the Philistine enemy, Jonathan's action brought a certain amount of unity to the disarrayed Israelites, as the "Hebrews" joined Saul's forces in the battle. Israel thus managed to liberate itself, at least temporarily, from Philistine dominance.

The narrative underscores that Jonathan's faith in YHWH and YHWH's intervention in the battle are the most important elements here, effectively changing the odds of the military conflict and achieving Israelite victory. Following upon my treatment of ch. 13, it may be highlighted here that Jonathan, accompanied by his soldier, becomes the awaited deliverer that Israel needed.

The Difference between Saul and Jonathan

The tension between father and son, prefigured in ch. 13, is given sharper contours in the present narrative. Here Saul and Jonathan are contrasted at several levels. Whereas Saul waits at Gibeah even though he has six hundred men at his disposal, Jonathan is not afraid to take action because he believes in YHWH and is accompanied by his faithful servant. Saul's passivity is more evident precisely because it is depicted against the backdrop of Jonathan's risky action.

Another fundamental difference between the two characters is that of Saul's piety and Jonathan's practicality. Saul is portrayed by the narrative as a religious man who twice consults the deity, who builds an altar and thus averts the people's transgression of the food law, and who seems to be intent on keeping to what YHWH desires. However, his appeals to the religious side of things are not altogether successful, and his directives deprive the people of energy in their pursuit of the enemy.[54] Jonathan, on the other hand, exemplifies faith in YHWH in practical action and shows a strategic mind capable of leading Israel in battle. He can assess well the situation at hand and take appropriate steps in order to accomplish what seems most profitable for Israel. In his attack upon the Philistine outpost, however, he becomes isolated from his father and king, and from his

---

54. Similarly Klein, *1 Samuel*, 137; Tsumura, *Samuel*, 366; and Brueggemann, *Samuel*, 106.

army as well, and unwittingly violates Saul's oath. Both men act with faith; yet their trust in YHWH has different shapes and brings different results.

One of the more suggestive appropriations of the tension between Saul and Jonathan is that of Oliver O'Donovan, found in his attempt to chart the contours of political theology based on interaction with the Bible and church history, where he distinguishes between the more traditional approach—characterized, among other things, by the invocation of YHWH and the use of various liturgical means (such as liturgy and prayer)—and the warrior-hero type of warfare, reflected chiefly by Jonathan and David.[55] Here, O'Donovan includes a comment on the narrative at hand, which demonstrates well, to his mind, this category of Israel's warfare:

> Curiously sandwiched between two episodes which criticize Saul for dis-regard of the cultic proprieties in warfare (confirming, from the opposite point of view, that there was a major controversy about the matter at that time) we find a lengthy narrative (1 Sam. 14) which sets Saul up as the representative of an immobile, priest-bound and altogether self-destructive approach to battle, contrasted with the heroic *élan* of his son, which is prepared to venture his life on the insecurity of a "perhaps" (1 Sam. 14:6). This bitter satire holds that the father was prepared to slay his victorious son for a breach of ritual; but the good sense of the people prevailed, which knew what "he wrought with Elohim that day" (14:45), a phrase eloquent of the new claim made for the warrior-hero, right down to its use of the more neutral term for God.[56]

Jonathan, in O'Donovan's construal, is a type of warrior-hero who is not bound to the sacral character of the war, as Saul is, but approaches the battle heroically, based on a mere "perhaps," and not after consulting traditional religious oracles.

It should be pointed out that O'Donovan's categories (in 1 Sam 14, for example) are not as fixed as he portrays them as being. He writes that "the sacred battle is paradoxically unexpected in its course and outcome; the forces of nature are involved in securing Yhwh's victory (Josh. 7:5–8)."[57] The paradoxical and unexpected nature of the battle is, however, exempli-fied in ch. 14 by Jonathan's attack. The earthquake and panic that followed upon this initial provocation exemplified YHWH's power and favor long before Saul joined the battle (1 Sam 14:15). Nevertheless, his scheme might have some heuristic value for my attempt to understand the difference between Jonathan and Saul based on their portrayal in ch. 14. While this

55. Oliver O'Donovan, *The Desire of the Nations: Rediscovering the Roots of Political Theology* (Cambridge: Cambridge University Press, 1996), 53–56.
56. O'Donovan, *Desire*, 55–56.
57. O'Donovan, *Desire*, 55.

difference does not need to stand for two distinct ways of *Israel's warfare*, it describes quite usefully how Jonathan and Saul differ in *their* approach to the battle. Jonathan's focus on the uncertainty of the battle, and the energy with which he enters it, contrasts with Saul's passivity and almost palpable strife for certainty in religious matters. Saul, who is accompanied by a priest, is connected more firmly to the religious system of which he is a participant. On the other hand, Jonathan is consistently mentioned with his armor-bearer and is portrayed as moving quickly ahead in the battle when he senses God's favor.[58] Jonathan seems to act with greater freedom than the overzealous Saul and thus accomplishes more.

Saul Remains Chosen King

Despite the ambiguous portrayal of some of Saul's actions in ch. 14, including his rushed oath that caused the transgression of Israel's cultic law and almost cost the life of his son, Saul remains God's favored king. When the lot is cast between Saul and Jonathan, Jonathan is revealed as the guilty party that stalled Israel's success in the battle. The deity thus continues to align with Saul and his decisions. When this facet is combined with the portrayal of Saul's successes in the concluding section of the chapter (1 Sam 14:47–52), then it appears that the overall status of Israel's first king remains unchanged. In spite of a number of missteps, Saul continues to receive God's favor and protection. When the narrative is read without the intrusive section in 1 Sam 13:7b–15a, Saul enters ch. 15 as the person chosen by YHWH.

---

58. Perhaps Brueggemann touches on something analogous when he says that "Saul is a burdened man whose faith is serious, even if misguided. Jonathan is a simpler person, more free in his faith" (Brueggemann, *Samuel*, 107). Similarly Murphy, *1 Samuel*, 132.

16

1 Samuel 15

The purpose of this part of my study is to present a close reading of a pivotal section in the story of Saul's rejection—ch. 15 of 1 Samuel. This chapter portrays a divinely sanctioned war against Amalek which Saul and his people waged but not in the manner prescribed by YHWH and his prophet, which in turn cost Saul his throne. When read without the intrusive section in 1 Sam 13:7b–15a, the present chapter contains the *only* account of Saul's rejection and thus provides a fundamental piece in the puzzle of Saul's fall in chs. 13–15.

Samuel's Charge
(1 Samuel 15:1–3)

Chapter 15 begins with Samuel's charge to Saul. No time frame is given by the narrator and the text quickly moves to the command itself, introducing the four major characters of the chapter.[1]

Samuel

Samuel presents himself as the one who was sent by YHWH to anoint Saul (1 Sam 15:1). By emphasizing the first person singular ("*me* YHWH sent," אֹתִי שָׁלַח יְהוָה), Samuel highlights his role in establishing Saul's kingship. Although it was Israel who asked for a king (8:5), and it was YHWH who selected Saul for this office (9:16), Samuel played a significant intermediary role in Saul's chosenness. Samuel's anointing, coupled with a sequence of extraordinary signs, launched Saul's leadership career (10:1–13) and served as a basis for his authority. Although this emphasis may be evaluated somewhat suspiciously, as the prophet's desire to keep the king under his thumb,[2] it may also suggest more neutrally that Samuel's position as Saul's kingmaker and tutor gives him a special right to a hearing from Saul.

---

1. I am following here the useful way of setting up the issue presented in Stephen Yonick, *Rejection of Saul as King of Israel according to 1 Sm 15: Stylistic Study in Theology* (Jerusalem: Franciscan, 1970), 16–41.

2. For example, Middleton questions Samuel's intentions here and asks: "Is [Samuel] reminding Saul who is really in control here, so that Saul will not even think of questioning his instructions (in YHWH's name) to execute holy war against the Amalekites (15:2–3)?" See J. Richard Middleton, "Samuel *Agonistes*: A Conflicted Prophet's Resistance to God and Contribution to the Failure of Israel's First King," in *Prophets, Prophecy, and Ancient Israelite Historiography*, ed. Mark J. Boda and Lissa M. Wray Beal (Winona Lake, IN: Eisenbrauns, 2013), 69–91, esp. 79.

Saul

Samuel's words also say something about Saul's role as king, which impacts the progression of the story. Not only is he indebted to Samuel as his king-maker (1 Sam 10:1), he is also made king over YHWH's people—a fact emphasized in Samuel's words. Saul is a ruler "over his [YHWH's] people (עַל־עַמּוֹ), over Israel (עַל־יִשְׂרָאֵל)" (15:1).[3] This, in turn, might indicate that Saul is not free to rule in any way he pleases but rather his kingship is subordinated to God's words and plans.[4] At the outset, his dependence on YHWH is highlighted in several ways.

YHWH

God is introduced in the story by his covenant name YHWH, but the actual charge to annihilate the Amalekites is prefaced with the formula: "thus says YHWH of hosts" (כֹּה אָמַר יְהוָה צְבָאוֹת, 1 Sam 15:2). This "standing formula with the prophets," as Smith characterizes it,[5] occurs in the books of Samuel in a military context (1 Sam 4:4; 17:45) and/or in connection with the ark of the covenant (1 Sam 4:4, 2 Sam 6:2, 18).[6] The combination of sacred and military overtones might provide a fitting framework in the present context as well, as the phrase prepares the setting for God's involvement in the upcoming military attack.[7]

Another observation relates to the way God's words are narrated. In the Hebrew text Samuel says: "and now listen to the voice of the words of YHWH" (וְעַתָּה שְׁמַע לְקוֹל דִּבְרֵי יְהוָה, 1 Sam 15:1).[8] This seems to be a peculiar way of constructing the phrase, since the command "listen to the words of YHWH" would seem sufficient.[9] The inclusion of "voice," however, may be important in terms of evoking resonances later in the chapter, when Samuel hears the voice of sheep among the Israelites (15:14), when

---

3. Some MT and LXX manuscripts omit "his people." Klein and McCarter follow the shorter version (Klein, *1 Samuel*, 144–45; McCarter, *I Samuel*, 258, 260).

4. Saul's election as king was closely connected with his task to lead Israel in battle (1 Sam 8:20; 10:1 [LXX]; 12:12).

5. Smith, *Samuel*, 131.

6. Even though some exceptions exist. Note, for example, Hannah's prayer in 1 Sam 1:11.

7. Klein suggests that the title "is especially appropriate for a holy war context" (Klein, *1 Samuel*, 148). Similarly Yonick, *Rejection*, 32.

8. Again, the manuscript support for the full MT reading is not unanimous. Some MT witnesses have only "to the words of YHWH" and LXX[B] has "to the voice of YHWH."

9. Tsumara comments that "this phrase is unusual in Hebrew and seems to be redundant" (Tsumura, *Samuel*, 389). The peculiar phrase occurs in several places in Deuteronomy, where it is used to indicate that YHWH overheard the sound of Israel's words spoken in private (Deut 1:34; 5:25), or to convey that the people heard the sound of YHWH's words (Deut 4:12). A similar emphasis can also be found in Dan 10:9. See also S. R. Driver, *A Critical and Exegetical Commentary on Deuteronomy*, ICC (Edinburgh: T&T Clark, 1902), 88; and Stoebe, *Samuelis*, 283.

he accuses Saul of disobeying YHWH's voice (15:22–23), and when Saul confesses that he yielded to the people's voice (15:24). Furthermore, the catchwords "voice" (קוֹל) and "listen/obey" (שָׁמַע) connect the instruction to destroy the Amalekites with the emphasis, prevalent in ch. 12, placed upon listening to God's voice as a prerequisite for a successful monarchy under God (esp. 1 Sam 12:14–15).[10] Israel and its leader should live in obedience to YHWH and his voice—a fundamental feature of Israel's life, exemplified most concisely in the book of Deuteronomy (e.g. Deut 13:5; 15:4–5; 26:17),[11] and seemingly finding its way also into the construal of Israel's kingship in 1 Sam 15.[12] This connection might then signify, in Saul's case, that the general requirement to obey God's voice finds its specific expression in the charge to devote Amalek to the ban.

Amalek

Verses 2 and 3 present the core of YHWH's message as communicated through Samuel. They spell out the specific rationale for the act of the annihilation (חרם) of Amalek, and prescribe the extent to which the task was to be fulfilled.[13]

Herem

For modern readers the practice of *herem* is probably one of the most difficult Old Testament concepts to comprehend. Although there is not adequate space here to explore it in detail, a few words about its nature and its place within 1 Sam 15 will help frame this idea for the discussion that follows.

---

10. Similarly also Firth, *Samuel*, 171–72. The catchword "voice" occurs six times in 1 Sam 15 and five times in 1 Sam 12.

11. Although 1 Sam 12 differs from other Samuel material that exemplifies Deuteronomistic features, I regard the chapter as continuing the main Deuteronomistic themes. For a defense of this view, see McCarter, *I Samuel*, 219–21; Klein, *1 Samuel*, 114; and Walter Dietrich, *Samuel*, BKAT 8/1 (Neukirchen-Vluyn: Neukirchener, 2005–10), esp. 529–30. For the contrary opinion, see Anthony F. Campbell and Mark A. O'Brien, *Unfolding the Deuteronomistic History: Origin, Upgrades, Present Text* (Minneapolis: Fortress, 2000), 246–47; and Auld, *Samuel*, 127.

12. The link between the story of Saul's rejection and the Shema is the subject of Ko's article: Ming Him Ko, "Fusion-Point Hermeneutics: A Theological Interpretation of Saul's Rejection in Light of the Shema as the Rule of Faith," *JTI* 7 (2013): 57–78. For a study stressing the Dtr influence on ch. 15, see Fabrizio Foresti, *The Rejection of Saul in the Perspective of the Deuteronomistic School: A Study of 1 Sm 15 and Related Texts*, ST 5 (Rome: Edizioni del Teresianum, 1984).

13. A good introductory article on Amalek is Gerald L. Mattingly, "Amalek," *ABD* 1:169–71. For a full-length recent monograph on the subject, see Hans Andreas Tanner, *Amalek: der Feind Israels und der Feind Jahwes: Eine Studie zu den Amalektexten im Alten Testament* (Zurich: TVZ, 2005). For a useful entry into various ways in which Amalek is understood within Jewish tradition, see Avi Sagi and Batya Stein, "The Punishment of Amalek in Jewish Tradition: Coping with the Moral Problem," *HTR* 87 (1994): 323–46.

Ḥerem is a religious concept,[14] in which the objects devoted to the ban – be they things, animals, or most horrifyingly, people—are irrevocably removed from the ordinary realm and given to the deity.[15] Whatever is devoted to *ḥerem* is thus contrasted with those items that can be kept, used, or redeemed. Also, it is useful to distinguish between the so-called war-חרם and priestly-חרם[16]—the former labels those items determined for destruction as something to be detested or abhorred (a classic example is Deut 7:25–26), whereas the latter labels them as something holy (see Lev 27:28–29)—although both forms are used to designate certain objects to be set apart for God. In 1 Sam 15 it is the "war-חרם" that we have in view.

The reason that this kind of *ḥerem* is so frightening is, I think, twofold, and relating to its scope and its origin. First, *ḥerem* encompasses the total destruction of the whole group of people, and thus in its extent demonstrates totality.[17] This totality is evident in Samuel's charge to Saul,[18] who is told that the Israelites are to "kill both men and women, child and infant, ox (שׁוֹר) and sheep (שֶׂה), camel (גָּמָל) and donkey (חֲמוֹר)" (1 Sam 15:3).[19] Israel is not to have compassion on anyone, and the spoils of the defeated army are not to be taken, as everything devoted to destruction belongs to God.[20]

Second, the ancient practice of *ḥerem* is often either sanctioned or even directly initiated by the deity.[21] In our case it is Samuel speaking on God's behalf who commands the destruction of the Amalekites, the institution of

---

14. The two most comprehensive monographs on the institution of *ḥerem* are: C. H. W. Brekelmans, *De herem in het Oude Testament* (Nijmegen: Centrale Drukkerij, 1959); Philip D. Stern, *The Biblical Ḥerem: A Window on Israel's Religious Experience*, BJS 211 (Atlanta, GA: Scholars Press, 1991).

15. For a good working definition, see Lohr, *Chosen*, 208.

16. The distinction between them is made, for example, by Stern, *Ḥerem*, 125–26; and Douglas S. Earl, *Reading Joshua as Christian Scripture*, JTI Sup 2 (Winona Lake, IN: Eisenbrauns, 2010), 96–97.

17. Nelson states: "The matter of totality was central to the *ḥerem* ideal." Richard D. Nelson, "*Ḥerem* and the Deuteronomic Social Conscience," in *Deuteronomy and Deuteronomic Literature: Festschrift for C. H. W. Brekelmans*, ed. Marc Vervenne and Johan Lust, BETL 133 (Louvain: Peeters, 1997), 39–54, esp. 47.

18. It may be noted that the command "devote to the ban" (הַחֲרַמְתֶּם) in the Hebrew text is in the plural, even though it is issued to an individual, Saul. It is conceivable to read this as the joint responsibility of both Saul and the people, although Saul, as the people's leader, seems to carry the greater part. See Caroline Nolan, "The Rejection of Israel's First King," *ITQ* 73 (2008): 355–68, esp. 362

19. The reference to animals, as Bodner remarks, has resonances with Judg 6:4–5, where the Amalekites plundered the Israelite territory. The Amalekites left no sheep (שֶׂה), ox (שׁוֹר), or donkey (חֲמוֹר) in Israel, and used camels (גָּמָל) in their raid (Bodner, *1 Samuel*, 150). A distant memory thus might be sharpened by certain more recent events.

20. Although this strict standard was not upheld in every case (see, e.g., Josh 8:1–2), the focus on total destruction is an important facet of *ḥerem* and signals that a partial fulfillment of YHWH's ban is not an option.

21. Even though in some situations the initiation comes from the people (e.g. Num 21:1–3). Similarly Stern, *Ḥerem*, 137.

ḥerem thus not only involving the destruction of a whole group of people, regardless of gender or age, but also originating with YHWH.

Ḥerem towards Amalek

The reason given for the punishment of Amalek[22] in 1 Sam 15:2–3 is their attack upon the Israelites as they came out of Egypt.[23] This tension between Israel and Amalek is referenced in several texts, namely Exod 17:8–16, Num 14:39–45, and especially Deut 25:17–19,[24] with which our text in 1 Samuel has several intertextual resonances.[25] For this reason it is worth quoting it at length:

> Remember (זְכוֹר) what Amalek did to you on the road when you came out of Egypt. How he met you on your way, and struck down all who lagged behind you when you were faint and weary, and he did not fear God. Therefore, when YHWH your God has given you rest from all your enemies around you, in the land that YHWH your God gives you as an inheritance to possess, you shall erase (תִּמְחֶה) the remembrance (זֵכֶר) of Amalek from under heaven. Do not forget. (Deut 25:17–19)

I will make several observations concerning this connection between 1 Sam 15 and these pentateuchal texts that might help to illuminate the framework of Samuel's instruction to devote Amalek to the ban.[26]

---

22. The biblical material consistently uses the name "Amalek" and never "the people of Amalek" or "the sons of Amalek." Benno Jacob reasons that this is no accident and the Torah refuses to provide a proper title for this people; see Benno Jacob, *The Second Book of the Bible: Exodus*, trans. Walter Jacob (Haboken, NJ: KTAV, 1992), 491. This gives some credence to an interpretative strategy that views Amalek symbolically. See Stephen B. Chapman, "Perpetual War: The Case of Amalek," in *The Bible and Spirituality: Exploratory Essays in Reading Scripture Spiritually*, ed. Gordon J. McConville et al. (Eugene, OR: Cascade, 2013), 1–19, esp. 9.

23. The MT reads "when he [Amalek] put against him [Israel] on the road (אֲשֶׁר־שָׂם לוֹ בַּדֶּרֶךְ)" (1 Sam 15:2). McCarter follows Deut 25:18 (אֲשֶׁר קָרְךָ בַּדֶּרֶךְ) with reference to the LXX of 1 Sam 15:2 (ὡς ἀπήντησεν αὐτῷ ἐν τῇ ὁδῷ) and reconfigures the text as saying "when he confronted them on the road" (McCarter, *I Samuel*, 260). However, the text seems comprehensible without this alteration. For a defense of the MT wording, see Driver, *Notes*, 122; or Tsumura, *Samuel*, 390.

24. Since the only reference to the original battle between Israel and Amalek can be found in Exod 17:8–16, Deut 25:17–19 is traditionally understood as a commentary on the same episode, accentuating different aspects of the conflict. Langner is rather isolated in arguing that the two texts refer to separate events; see Allan M. Langner, "Remembering Amalek Twice," *JBQ* 36 (2008): 251–53.

25. See Yonick, *Rejection*, 35–36, and Klein, *1 Samuel*, 148. Nevertheless, it should be highlighted that the pentateuchal texts never make reference to *ḥerem* when addressing the fate of the Amalekites. 1 Samuel 15 is alone in punishing Amalek with the ban. Thus Stern, *Ḥerem*, 166–69; and his earlier Philip D. Stern, "1 Samuel 15: Towards an Ancient View of the War-Herem," *UF* 21 (1990): 413–20. More recently also Chapman, *1 Samuel*, 137, n. 47. Despite this incongruence, I think, one needs to illuminate the connection that 1 Sam 15:2 makes with the event in the Pentateuch.

26. There is at least one other text that may have a bearing on the enmity between Israel and Amalek. In Num 14:39–45 the Israelites, despite Moses's warning, go to Canaan

First, several remarks can be made about the nature of Amalek's attack referenced in this text. The Amalekite aggression took place at a moment when Israel was faint and weary, and was targeted at those who were struggling to keep up with the main body of the Israelites (הַנֶּחֱשָׁלִים אַחֲרֶיךָ).[27] When this text is read together with the remark in Exod 17:8—"Amalek came and fought with Israel"—occurring in a context where Israel neither attempted to pass through Amalek's territory, nor were the Amalekites protecting their own land,[28] the deviousness of their aggression comes to the forefront. Their unprovoked attack upon the weakest of Israel seems unconventional even in the biblical depiction of ancient military combats.[29]

Furthermore, because Amalek assaulted the weakest of Israel, he is labeled in Deut 25:18 as one who "does not fear God." According to Moberly, the phrase "fear of God" in the Old Testament signifies "moral restraint out of respect for God, a moral restraint specifically that refuses to take advantage of a weaker party when it would be possible to do so with apparent impunity."[30] This fundamental respect for life the Amalekites, at least according to Deut 25:17–19, did not embody. Moberly's conclusion describes the logic of the ban well: "Its logic appears to be that the attack on defenseless people constitutes such a fundamental denial of God that those who do such things thereby deny their own humanity and so lay themselves open to a treatment not otherwise given to other human beings."[31] It was the malicious attack upon the most vulnerable of Israel that was behind Israel's animosity towards Amalek and YHWH's order of the ban in 1 Sam 15.[32] They respected neither human conventions nor God, and therefore became liable to be subjected to this horrifying ordeal.

---

and are attacked by the Amalekites and the Canaanites, who pursue them in battle as far as Hormah (Num 14:45). The last word of the chapter is חָרְמָה with the definite article attached to it. It likely stands for a place, but given our present discussion, it is worth noting that it comes from the verbal root חרם. Is it possible that Israel was pursued, among others by Amalek, almost to destruction? Thus, for example, Timothy R. Ashley, *The Book of Numbers*, NICOT 4 (Grand Rapids: Zondervan, 1993), 274.

27. The plural participle נֶחֱשָׁלִים comes from the root חשל and occurs only here in the Old Testament. *HALOT* 1:362 translates this expression "those who worn out, stragglers."

28. Thus, for example, Umberto Cassuto, *A Commentary on the Book of Exodus*, trans. Israel Abrahams (Jerusalem: Magnes, 1968), 204.

29. Similarly Chapman, "War," 15.

30. R. W. L. Moberly, *The Bible, Theology, and Faith: A Study of Abraham and Jesus* (Cambridge: Cambridge University Press, 2000), 92–94, esp. 92. Leviticus 19:14 serves as a good example of this principle.

31. Moberly, *Bible*, 93.

32. Jacob emphatically comments that "a true holy war could be waged only against those who broke the holy peace" (Jacob, *Exodus*, 490).

Second, it is not only the nature of the Amalekite attack on Israel that is particularly troubling, but also its timing. Amalek was the first enemy that fought against the Israelites on their way out of Egypt.[33] The importance of the crime is thus heightened because it occurred at a formative stage in Israel's history: during the exodus from Egypt and before Israel settled in Canaan.[34] In a certain sense, the journey from Egypt to Canaan differed from any other stage in Israel's history: the only time that *ḥerem* could be implemented was either during Israel's settlement in the land (Deut 7:1–6,) or because of what happened on their journey into the land (1 Sam 15:2–3). Intrinsic to the concept of Israel's election is the idea of a promised land (Deut 4:37–38), a place where the chosen people could form its own distinct identity, embodying YHWH's view of life. Israel's election thus does not function in an abstract vacuum, but is rooted in particular historical reality. Israel experienced God's favor through YHWH's deliverance from Egypt and their journey to the promised land.[35] In this regard, the attempt to block Israel's entry into the land could have interfered with something larger than Israel's earthly pilgrimage: it could be viewed as an attack on the dynamics of Israel's election as such.

Third, and following up on the previous point, the practice of *ḥerem* is closely linked with the notion of election (Deut 7:1–8).[36] Israel's commitment to YHWH is demonstrated, however incomprehensible it may sound to our modern ears, through its dedication to *ḥerem*. In this context, as Christa Schäfer-Lichtenberger says: "The execution or not execution

---

33. Hertzberg notes that the Amalekites are "the people . . . regarded by the tradition as *the* opponent, which first and most obviously sought to deny Israel entry into the Promised Land" (Hertzberg, *Samuel*, 124). Similarly also J. Gordon McConville, *Deuteronomy*, ApOTC (Leicester: Apollos, 2002), 372–73.

34. Notice that the Kenite act of compassion (חֶסֶד) towards the Israelites also occurred on the way out of Egypt (1 Sam 15:6). Interestingly, the examples of both Rahab (Josh 2:12, 14) and the Kenites (1 Sam 15:6) indicate that those who showed *ḥesed* towards the Israelites on their way to the promised land could escape the annihilation proscribed by *ḥerem*. For a thoughtful wrestling with the issue of *ḥerem* in Joshua, and the place of Rahab in the story, see Earl, *Joshua*, 124–27, 140–48.

35. McDonald stresses that the election of Israel in Deuteronomy is closely linked with the journey from Egypt to the promised land and the oath to the fathers. See Nathan MacDonald, *Deuteronomy and the Meaning of 'Monotheism'*, FAT 2/1 (Tübingen: Mohr Siebeck, 2003), 159.

36. See especially R. W. L. Moberly, "Toward an Interpretation of the Shema," in *Theological Exegesis: Essays in Honor of Brevard S. Childs*, ed. Christopher Seitz and Kathryn Greene-McCreight (Grand Rapids: Eerdmans, 1999), 124–44, esp. 133–37; or his more recent R. W. L. Moberly, "Election and the Transformation of *Ḥērem*," in *The Call of Abraham: Essays on the Election of Israel in Honor of Jon D. Levenson*, ed. Gary A. Anderson and Joel S. Kaminsky (Notre Dame, IN: University of Notre Dame Press, 2013), 78–79.

of *ḥerem* indicates Israel's obedience towards YHWH."[37] Seen from this perspective, Saul's mission is not insignificant. It has the potential to reveal something fundamental concerning his commitment to YHWH.[38]

Fourth, Israel should remember what Amalek did to them, and wipe out their remembrance once they establish themselves in the land and achieve peace from their enemies.[39] Presumably only then would they be strong enough to take on their most infamous foe. This task—expressed as YHWH's own responsibility in Exod 17:14—is then given to the Israelites to carry out in Deut 25:19.[40] The summary statement in 1 Sam 14:47–48 can then serve as a signal that Israel has reached the desired level of stability, preparing the way for Samuel's command.[41] The commission that Saul is now ordered to carry out, is not a reaction to some existing threat posed by one of Israel's neighbors, but is a matter of Israel's memory of a treacherous act which should be now brought to justice.[42]

In summary, Amalek is singled out as an object of destruction because of what they did to the most vulnerable of the weary Israelites during the formative stage of their journey to the promised land. Amalek's assault threatened Israel's very existence. Under Saul's reign, Israel appears to have reached the point of stability envisaged in Deut 25:19, and is called on to

---

37. Christa Schäfer-Lichtenberger, "Bedeutung und Funktion von *Ḥerem* in biblisch-hebräischen Texten," *BZ* 38 (1994): 270–75, esp. 272: "Vollzug oder Nicht-vollzug des *Ḥerem* ist Indikator für Israels Gehörsam gegenüber JHWH." She links this aspect of *ḥerem* especially with Josh 2–8, but in n. 10 also connects it with 1 Sam 15. Similarly Nathan MacDonald, who calls *ḥerem* "an expression of devoted love" (MacDonald, *Monotheism*, 108).

38. This way, the ban represents a kind of test for Saul. Similarly Earl, who says: "The extreme חרם serves as a rhetorical function to sharpen the test; how will one tested respond in the most demanding circumstances (limit-situations), i.e. amid genocide and riches?" (Earl, *Joshua*, 199, n. 4).

39. Although the verb מחה ("wipe off" or "erase") found both in Exod 17:14 and Deut 25:19—especially when seen in connection with term "obliteration" present, for example, in Num 5:23—may give credence to a symbolic interpretation, the way the verb is used in military contexts suggests that it is yet a different way to describe someone's destruction (see most notably Deut 9:14; 2 Kgs 14:27). I think Chapman, in his attempt to pave the way towards a peaceful vision of the Old Testament, steers too much in the direction of the metaphorical reading when he says that "the verb in this context probably does mean something like 'obliterate,' but still only indirectly and figuratively" (Chapman, "War," 10). For another attempt to read the texts featuring Amalek non-violently, consult Shalom Carmy, "The Origin of Nations and the Shadow of Violence: Theological Perspectives on Canaan and Amalek," *Tradition* 39 (2006): 163–99.

40. I regard this discrepancy between what YHWH would do and what Israel should do a typical characteristic of the mutuality of their relationship. Even though these differences may be explained by pointing to different textual sources, I see theological value in trying to understand them as saying something complementary about the relationship between God and his people.

41. Similarly also Jacob, *Exodus*, 490.

42. Nevertheless, note Samuel's reference to Agag's acts that Israel presumably still remembers in 1 Sam 15:33.

march towards its notorious enemy and to punish them. Furthermore, the ban, given its nature, has the capacity to demand Saul's obedience in the most challenging of circumstances and might thus function as a test of his loyalty to YHWH.

It is my contention that these observations may enhance our understanding of the troubling aspects of the command to annihilate the Amalekites in the present chapter. Nevertheless, I do not wish to deny that the concept continues to remain morally disturbing.

Saul's Implementation of the Ban against Amalek (1 Samuel 15:4–9)

The Battle (1 Samuel 15:4–7)

The description given of Israel's attack on the Amalekites does not reveal any disrespect on Saul's part toward YHWH's command. On the contrary, it paints a rather positive picture of Saul's obedience to Samuel's command and his ability to lead his people.

In response to Samuel's charge,[43] Saul summons the people at Telaim[44] and does a count to determine their numbers (1 Sam 15:4a).[45] A sizeable army of two hundred thousand people on foot, as well as ten thousand people of Judah, obeys his command and comes to fight with Amalek (15:4b).[46] The multitude of Saul's army in this instance stands in sharp contrast to the number of people prepared to fight against the Philistines in ch. 13, where at the highest moment of that military operation Saul had three thousand men at his disposal (13:2). Realistically, it is hard to believe that Israel could suddenly assemble such a large army,[47] but from

---

43. 1 Samuel 15:4 is linked with 1 Sam 15:1–3 by two catchwords: שמע and פקד. See also Yisca Zimran, "'The Lord Has Rejected You as King Over Israel': Saul's Deposal from the Throne," *JHebS* 14 (2014): art. 5, pp. 1–18, esp. 6, https://doi:10.5508/jhs.2014.v14.a5.

44. The area of Telaim (טְלָאִים) is often equated with the town of Telem (טֶלֶם), which was, according to Josh 15:24, located in the south of Judah. See Smith, *Samuel*, 133; Driver, *Notes*, 122; and McCarter, *1 Samuel*, 266. The Greek text contains "Gilgal" (Γάλγαλα), possibly in an attempt to harmonize with the meeting place between Saul and Samuel later in the chapter (1 Sam 15:12).

45. Auld draws attention to the fact that in the books of Samuel, Saul "is the noted tally-keeper," citing 1 Sam 11:8; 13:15; 14:17; 15:4; 20:6 as examples (Auld, *Samuel*, 167). One wonders if Saul's desire to know how many people are on his side stems from his inclination to be overly sure as to whether he has enough resources to engage in various conflicts.

46. The distinction between the men of Judah and the rest of the army hints at the possibility that even though Judah participated in the battles led by Israel's first king, it kept its uniqueness and distinction (see also 1 Sam 11:8). For the view that Israel was never fully incorporated into Saul's kingdom, see Klein, *1 Samuel*, 149. For a slightly different opinion, see Tsumura, *Samuel*, 393.

47. The LXX has even larger numbers, still mirroring, however, the unevenness between Judah and the rest of Israel: "four hundred thousand troops and from Judah thirty thousand troops."

the literary point of view the high numbers suggest that Saul's call was effective and provided him with resources that could accomplish the task he was charged with.[48]

Saul approaches his mission with carefulness. He lays wait in the valley, close to the city of Amalek,[49] and approaches the Kenites, urging them—by the sequence of three consecutive imperatives, "Go! Leave! Withdraw!"—to depart, so that they would not be destroyed together with the Amalekites (1 Sam 15:5–6). The reason given is again related to the Israelite journey out of Egypt, where the Kenites acted towards the Israelites with kindness (חֶסֶד) (Judg 1:16), which is implicitly contrasted with the disrespectful behavior of the Amalekites. Whereas the Amalekites will perish, the Kenites are spared for their kindness and Saul makes sure that they have a chance to escape, which they use. Saul thus brings out to the open what may be implicitly part of the biblical portrayal of ḥerem: one's ḥesed has a potential to deliver a person or a group of people from the ban.[50]

Verse 7 narrates that Saul smote Amalek in the area from Havilah to Shur, which is east of Egypt. The description is peculiar and creates interpretative problems.[51] If Shur is located near Egypt (see Gen 25:18), and Havilah may be found in West Arabia, then the battle traversed the enormous distance ranging from Arabia to Egypt, which seems improbable.[52] Perhaps one way

---

48. Klein wonders whether this large army could signal the lack of an excuse on Saul's part for failing to carry out YHWH's command (Klein, 1 Samuel, 149).

49. It is interesting that Amalek, otherwise portrayed as living south of Israel, in the wilderness of Negev (Num 13:29; see Mattingly, "Amalek," 170), is described here as inhabiting a city. For this reason, McCarter suspects the accuracy of this report (McCarter, I Samuel, 266). The LXX has here the plural, "cities," which, according to Budde, should be preferred; see Karl D. Budde, Die Bücher Samuel, KHC 8 (Tübingen: Mohr, 1902), 108. On the other hand, Edelman, who proposes that Saul, in fact, fought against the Amalekite enclave in the north sees in this singular reference a proof of her theory; see Diana Edelman, "Saul's Battle against Amaleq (1 Sam 15)," JSOT 35 (1986): 71–84, esp. 75–76. Nevertheless, perhaps the singularity of the location serves a literary strategy: Amalek is portrayed as contained in a specific place, which makes the Israelite raid possible.

50. See p. 157, n. 34 above.

51. Therefore scholars have suggested various emendations. McCarter substitutes the "wadi" for חֲוִילָה because Havilah is thought to be on the west edge of the Arabian Peninsula (W. W. Müller, "Havilah [place]," ABD 3:82) and thus too far from the site of the battle (McCarter, I Samuel, 261). However, as others have remarked, this suggestion has no textual basis, the Greek text not differing here from the MT. See Klein, 1 Samuel, 150; and Tsumura, Samuel, 394. Driver suggests reading "from Telaim" (Driver, Notes, 123) and Seebass reconfiguring the word as עֵילָם; see Horst Seebass, "Der Ort Elam in der südlichen Wüste und die Überlieferung von Gen 14," VT 15 (1965): 389–94.

52. It is also peculiar that Gen 25:18 contains the almost exact phrase "from Havilah to Shur, which is east of Egypt" (מֵחֲוִילָה עַד־שׁוּר אֲשֶׁר עַל־פְּנֵי מִצְרַיִם)—where it stands for the borders of the Ishmaelite territory—as found in 1 Sam 15:7 (מֵחֲוִילָה בּוֹאֲךָ שׁוּר אֲשֶׁר עַל־פְּנֵי מִצְרַיִם). Some scholars have therefore proposed a plausible solution for its presence in 1 Sam 15:7: the author of 1 Sam 15 borrowed the description from the book of Genesis. See Driver, Notes, 123; and McCarter, I Samuel, 261.

forward is to suggest that the final version of the text may continue what seems to be the intention in chs. 13 and 14 to portray the battle in gigantic proportions: it links a large area (v. 7) with large numbers (v. 4).[53] Given the biblical attestation that Shur formed one boundary of Amalekite territory (1 Sam 27:8), the text creates the impression that the vast army of Israel (numbering over two hundred thousand) subdued Amalek in every corner of its land.[54]

Saul is thus portrayed in these verses as obedient to YHWH and to his prophet, and as a skilful military leader of his people, implementing *ḥerem* with an ability suited to this tricky ancient practice. He was able to muster a large army and defeat the enemy over a large area, while giving those who had showed kindness to Israel a chance to escape. The positive portrayal of Saul in this section of ch. 15, however, changes quickly when one reads the report of the battle itself.

The Account of the Ban (1 Samuel 15:8–9)

Up to this point, Saul seems to have behaved in a way proportionate to God's command. The text now, however, reveals some of the troubling aspects of his campaign, as it relates that the Kenites were not the only people that Saul spared.

Verses 8 and 9 offer a somewhat different portrayal of the battle. Verse 8 says that Saul captured Agag, the king of Amalek, alive, while destroying the rest of the people with "the sword." Then, the next verse announces that "Saul and the people spared Agag and the best of the sheep and the cattle—the fat ones[55] and the young rams[56]—and all that was good" (1 Sam 15:9). While the text leaves unresolved for now who was responsible for what,[57] the logic of the campaign seems to be that the Israelite

---

53. Similarly Klein, *1 Samuel*, 150.

54. The connection between 1 Sam 15:7 and Gen 25:18 may be read as highlighting Amalek's double status. On the one hand, as Ishmael they are not part of God's chosen people. On the other hand, their existence is traced back to Israel's ancestors.

55. I am following McCarter here, who reconstructs the word הַמִּשְׁנִים ("double portions") as "fat ones" (הַשְּׁמֵנִים). Some MT manuscripts testify to this reading, together with the LXX (τῶν ἐδεσμάτων), and the occurrence of this word in Ezek 34:16 supports it. See McCarter, *I Samuel*, 262.

56. The MT here has הַכָּרִים, "the young rams"; the Greek text reads τῶν ἀμπελώνων, "vineyards," which likely took the Hebrew word to be the plural of כֶּרֶם, "vineyard." I take the *waw* before the "fat ones" as explicative, stressing which animals were best from the herd of sheep and cattle: those which were fat and young. See Tsumura, *Samuel*, 395.

57. Of course, the sentences "Saul took Agag" in v. 8 and "Saul and the people spared Agag and the best of the animals" in v. 9 may be viewed as contradictory. Seebass, for example, views them as one of the doublets present in the chapter, which eventually leads him to posit two different traditions merged in 1 Sam 15. See Horst Seebass, "1 Sam 15 als Schlüssel für das Verständnis der sogenannten königsfreundlichen Reihe 1 Sam 9:1–10:16, 11:1–15 und 13:2–14:52," *ZAW* 78 (1966): 148–79. Synchronically, I take the inclusion of the people as indicative that both Saul and the people were involved in the action. The specific contours of their actions will become clearer later.

army captured what was the most valuable—the Amalekite king and best of their animals—and devoted to *ḥerem* the people and those animals that were "despised[58] and worthless."[59] On the one hand, these acts contradict Samuel's command to devote everything to the ban—a fact highlighted by the repetition of the two verbs that featured earlier in 1 Sam 15:1–3: Saul and the people spared (חמל) Agag and the best animals, and devoted to the ban (חרם) only what was not valuable (15:9). On the other hand, however, these verses leave some important issues unclear. What was Saul's role versus that of the people in capturing rather than destroying the best of Amalek?[60] More importantly, *why* did they exclude the Amalekite king and the most prized animals from *ḥerem*? One may speculate that the soldiers wanted to gain some spoils from the battle—a move specifically forbidden in wars of *ḥerem*—but there may have been more noble motivations at play, as Saul's own defense later reveals. By leaving these significant questions unanswered, the narrative thus prompts the reader to follow the storyline further.

YHWH's Conversation with Samuel (1 Samuel 15:10–12)

The narrative suddenly shifts from the battle scene,[61] and announces the coming of God's word to Samuel, likely in a nocturnal vision (1 Sam 15:10). YHWH informs his prophet: "I have repented (נחמתי)[62] that I made Saul

---

58. As Driver reasons, the unintelligible נְמִבְזָה is likely a scribal error for נִבְזָה (Driver, *Notes*, 124). The word would then be the Niphal feminine singular participle from the root בזה denoting something that is "despised."

59. The Hebrew word נָמֵס, which the MT text has here, comes from the root מסס, meaning in its Niphal form something which melts away or becomes weak. This reading is possible, and has been adopted by the NIV and NJPS. However, the participle is masculine, not feminine as the preceding one, leading Driver to suggest that the word might be emended to נִמְאֶסֶת, from מאס, meaning "rejected" or "worthless" (Driver, *Notes*, 124–25). This reading has been adopted by many commentators (e.g. McCarter, *I Samuel*, 262; Klein, *1 Samuel*, 146; and Tsumura, *Samuel*, 393) and some English translations (e.g. NRSV, ESV). The Greek text containing ἐξουδενωμένον ("worthless" or "of no value") makes this interpretation preferable.

60. David reproaches the Amalekite who claimed that he killed Saul, that he did not fear to stretch out his hand and strike YHWH's anointed one (2 Sam 1:14). Regardless of whether this story is fictitious or not, Saul's death is interestingly intertwined with Amalek.

61. It might seem trivial, but I would note that the narrative does not dwell on what could apparently be a bloody description of the battle, but focuses instead on what is central to the concept of *ḥerem*—Israel's obedience or disobedience to YHWH's voice.

62. Some Greek manuscripts contain here a form of verb, παρακαλέω ("comfort"), perhaps to avoid suggesting that God changes his mind. Aejmelaeus sees in this one of the examples of intentional change from the Hebrew text. See Anneli Aejmelaeus, "A Kingdom at Stake: Reconstructing the Old Greek—Deconstructing the *Textus Receptus*," in *Scripture in Transition: Essays on Septuagint, Hebrew Bible, and Dead Sea Scrolls in Honour of Raija Sollamo*, ed. Anssi Voitila and Jutta Jokiranta, JSJSup 126 (Leiden: Brill, 2008), 353–66, esp. 354–57.

king for he turned away (שָׁב) from following me and did not establish my words (וְאֶת־דְּבָרַי לֹא הֵקִים)" (15:11). This announcement makes Samuel angry, and he cries out to YHWH all night. When he rises early next morning to meet Saul, he is told that Saul went to Carmel. There Saul erected a pillar for himself,[63] after which he went down to Gilgal (15:12).[64]

These two verses signal a tension between a recanting deity and an angry prophet on the one hand, and a victorious king on the other, which prepares the reader for the disparity between the views of Samuel and Saul in the next section. Saul is not in hiding or ashamed of what he has done. On the contrary, he sets up a pillar, possibly commemorating his victorious campaign, and is on the move toward Israel's sacred site. Samuel is about to encounter, not a man with any regrets, but a confident military leader.

Two observations seem crucial to our discussion. First, it seems noteworthy that before the reader hears more about Saul's responsibility and his possible motives for taking the best of the spoil from Amalek, one learns of YHWH's reaction. His message is brief: YHWH is sorry that he made Saul king. Among other things, in using the Hebrew words נחם and שׁוב, the speech introduces the topic of repentance, prevalent in the rest of the chapter (נחם is found in 1 Sam 15:29 [×2] and 35; שׁוב in 15:25, 26, 30 and 31).[65] Although a fuller treatment of this complex issue must await those parts of the narrative in which Samuel accuses Saul, some basic contours of the question can already be spelled out here. Because Saul turned (שׁוב) from following YHWH, YHWH repented (נחם) that he had made Saul king. Although the different choice of two words testifies to a general difference between God's change of mind and that of humans, YHWH's announcement also suggests that Saul's specific behavior played a significant part in

---

63. Literally, Saul put up a "hand" (יָד). The LXX also has χεῖρα. 2 Samuel 18:18 speaks of the monument (מַצֶּבֶת) that was erected to perpetuate Absalom's memory. Presumably, this pillar was erected to commemorate Saul's victory over the Amalekites. See Klein, *1 Samuel*, 151; and Tsumura, *Samuel*, 397.

64. The LXX[B] contains the following appendix, which takes Samuel as a subject: "And he turned around his chariot and went down to Gilgal to Saul. He was just offering a whole burnt offering to the Lord, the best of the spoils he brought from Amalek." The Greek text anticipates vv. 15 and 21, where Saul states that the reason for bringing the best of the animals was to sacrifice them at Gilgal, and suggests that the sacrifice has already started. For a discussion of this verse in the Greek, see Grillet et al., *Premier livre des Règnes*, 275–76; and Stephen Pisano, *Additions or Omissions in the Books of Samuel: The Significant Pluses and Minuses in the Massoretic, LXX and Qumran Texts*, OBO 57 (Freiburg: Vandenhoeck & Ruprecht, 1984), 204–7.

65. The difference can be observed, for example, in Jer 18:8. See the discussion of this issue in R. W. L. Moberly, "Does God Change?," in *Old Testament Theology: Reading the Hebrew Bible as Christian Scripture* (Grand Rapids: Baker Academic, 2013), 107–43, esp. 121; or R. W. L. Moberly, "God Is Not a Human that He Should Repent (Numbers 23:19 & 1 Samuel 15:29)," in *God in the Fray: A Tribute to Walter Brueggemann*, ed. Tod Linafelt and Timothy K. Beal (Minneapolis: Fortress, 1998), 112–23, esp. 115.

God's decision. YHWH is about to alter his plans, because Saul altered his: instead of obeying YHWH's words (1 Sam 15:1) he neglected them (1 Sam 15:11).

Second, it is also worth emphasizing that Samuel was angry and cried to YHWH all night (1 Sam 15:11). On the one hand, it may be attractive to speculate to whom this anger was directed—to YHWH or Saul?—and to propose various reasons for it.[66] In the end, however, we simply do not know, and it is probably best to regard this outburst of emotion, as Fokkelman does, as "an appeal to the reader's imagination and empathy."[67] The observation that Samuel mourns YHWH's denunciation of Saul seems to be a more profitable one. This makes most sense if this is the first time Samuel has heard of YHWH's repenting that he has made Saul monarch. When read without the intrusive segment of 1 Sam 13:7b–15a, ch. 15 presents *the only* rejection of Saul in chs. 13–15, in which case Samuel is understandably troubled by this change in God's favor. This little observation seems to strengthen the possibility of reading the narratives of Saul's rejection without that intrusive section.

Samuel's Conversation with Saul
(1 Samuel 15:13–26)

This long conversation between Samuel and Saul, containing the rejection of Saul by God, presents the climax of the whole chapter. Many of the catchwords and themes introduced so far appear here in a masterfully complex narrative, which, for the sake of clarity, can be divided into two smaller sections.

Accusation and Defense (1 Samuel 15:13–21)

The first section begins with Saul's blessing of Samuel and his announcement that he has indeed "established the word of YHWH" (הֲקִימֹתִי אֶת־דְּבַר יְהוָה, 1 Sam 15:13), directly contradicting what we have just heard from YHWH in v. 11. However, Samuel asks a question that plays on the terms "obey/listen" and "voice," and challenges the claim that Saul carried out God's command: "What is this voice (קוֹל) of sheep in my ears, and the voice (קוֹל) of cattle that I hear (שֹׁמֵעַ)?" (1 Sam 15:14). Samuel was already informed by YHWH that Saul has transgressed God's command, so the purpose of the question was likely not to learn what had happened—it

---

66. Tsumura suggests that Samuel shares YHWH's anger with Saul (Tsumura, *Samuel*, 396). Firth conjectures that since Samuel spends the whole night calling to YHWH, he is angry with him (Firth, *Samuel*, 174). If he is angry with God, why? Does he feel pity for Saul (thus Hertzberg, *Samuel*, 133) or for himself? Jobling points at the latter when he reasons that Samuel mourns the loss of a king he can control (Jobling, *Samuel*).

67. Fokkelman, *Crossing*, 92

was rather to elicit an acknowledgment of guilt from Saul.[68] Saul, however, points to the people as those responsible for the omission: "They have been brought from the Amalekites;[69] the people spared the best of the sheep and the cattle, in order to sacrifice them to YHWH, your God,[70] but the rest they have devoted to the ban" (1 Sam 15:15). The phrase "the best of the sheep and the cattle" is the same as in v. 9, but here Saul, contrary to the narrator's view of the battle, shifts responsibility to the people and offers an underlying reason for their action: they wanted to sacrifice them to YHWH.

Samuel is not persuaded. He interrupts Saul and proceeds to offer a fuller explanation of the king's fault. Saul is the head of Israel's tribes, not an insignificant Benjamite as he had thought,[71] and was sent on a specific mission. He was commanded to place the Amalekites—here described as "the sinners, the Amalekites" (1 Sam 15:18)[72] in terms going beyond the earlier portrayal in v. 2—under the ban. Samuel thus rhetorically tightens his case. Saul's actions as the Israelite monarch bear special responsibility, and his appointed task was directed toward those who are not innocent but sinners.

At last Samuel issues an explicit question pointing out the crucial difference between God's command and Saul's action: "Why did you disobey the voice of YHWH and swoop on the spoil and do what is evil in the eyes of YHWH?" (וְלָמָּה לֹא־שָׁמַעְתָּ בְּקוֹל יְהוָה וַתַּעַט אֶל־הַשָּׁלָל וַתַּעַשׂ הָרַע בְּעֵינֵי יְהוָה, 1 Sam 15:19). The use of the verb עיט and the noun שָׁלָל sets up

---

68. Samuel's question is not dissimilar to the questions posed by God to the first couple in Gen 3:9–13. In their answers, both the man and the woman also put forward someone else's misbehavior. For this connection see Firth, *Samuel*, 174; and Tsumura, *Samuel*, 398. Bartor examines these sorts of questions in Asnat Bartor, "The 'Juridical Dialogue': A Literary-Judicial Pattern," *VT* 53 (2003): 445–64.

69. I take the Hebrew הֱבִיאוּם ("they have brought") as the impersonal passive construction. See Tsumura, *Samuel*, 398. The Greek text of the 1 Sam 15:15 has ἤνεγκα, "I brought." McCarter follows the LXX reading in his reconstruction of the text (McCarter, *I Samuel*, 263). Nevertheless, the rest of the verse, even in the Greek, shifts responsibility to the people.

70. Several times in the narrative Saul uses the phrase "YHWH, your God" when speaking to Samuel (1 Sam 15:15, 21, 30). Does this reflect something about Samuel, as Middleton indicates, when he suggests that "Samuel has been so successful in positioning himself as YHWH's unique spokesman that Saul has been unable to develop any independent relationship with God?" See Middleton, "Samuel," 79. In any case, it seems to indicate a certain distance between Saul and YHWH. Consider Chapman, *1 Samuel*, 141.

71. Samuel here draws upon a similar statement issued by Saul himself when Samuel hinted at his special status within Israel in 1 Sam 9:21. See also Zimran, "Lord," 14—though I think it places too much weight on this phrase to see in it "the human prism through which Saul regards the kingship" (Zimran, "Lord," 18).

72. The LXX adds to the Hebrew text εἰς ἐμέ, "against me."

an intertextual echo with the situation in the previous chapter, where "the people swooped down on the [Philistine] spoil" (וַיַּעַט הָעָם אֶל־שָׁלָל) and began to eat meat with the blood (14:32).[73] Thus, from the narrative point of view, Saul might be viewed as being accused of a similar misdeed. What was earlier pronounced a "sin against YHWH" (14:33) is now called "evil in YHWH's eyes" (15:19). Nevertheless, if one takes with seriousness Saul's later claim that the best animals were captured in order to enable an appropriate sacrifice to YHWH, then one understands that Saul may have been confused when Samuel characterized his actions as swooping down upon the spoil.[74] In the previous chapter he built an altar and sacrificed, precisely in order to prevent sinful behavior. How can these two sacrifices have such different results? What is behind Saul's denial of Samuel's accusation could be either an insincere evasion or a sincere confusion. The significance of these interpretive options becomes evident even in the following verses, where Saul introduces something unmentioned thus far in the narrative. Saul protests: "I obeyed the voice of YHWH and went on the path which YHWH sent me" (15:20a). Then for the first time he distinguishes between his own responsibility and that of the people: "I have brought Agag, the king of Amalek, and the Amalekites I devoted to the ban. The people took from the spoil sheep and cattle, the best of what was devoted to the ban, to sacrifice it to YHWH, your God, at Gilgal" (15:20b–21).

Saul's response may be evaluated from different directions. First, Saul distances himself from the sparing of the animals, which was the action directly challenged by Samuel in v. 14. If we take Saul's words in v. 21 as a truthful account of what transpired in the war against Amalek, then the capturing of Agag was Saul's own idea, while the taking of the spoils was initiated by the soldiers.[75] However, it is noteworthy that Saul does acknowledge that what the people took was devoted to the ban. Saul's acquiescence towards the people's actions might stem from his experience in ch. 14, where the people, contrary to the casting of the lot and to his own declaration, saved Jonathan, while here they saved some of the spoil.

---

73. I acknowledge that this connection becomes plausible only when one reads the *Qere* of 1 Sam 14:32 (וַיַּעַט) and not the *Ketib* (וַיַּעַשׂ). In this I follow Driver, who thinks that the presence of the verb עיט is "evidently correct" here (Driver, *Notes*, 115, 126). However, this perhaps suggests a reading of 1 Sam 14:32 in the light of 1 Sam 15:19. This is a reason why Seebass thinks that the sentence in 1 Sam 15:19 rather belongs to ch. 14 (Seebass, "Schlüssel," 150).

74. Hawk sees the positive effect of Saul's sacrifice in ch. 14 as rescuing Israel from chaos and setting the stage for a new reconfiguration of Israel under David. See L. Daniel Hawk, "Saul's Altar," *CBQ* 72 (2010): 678–87.

75. This, in turn, can help to explain the mixed account of the battle as described in vv. 8–9.

On the other hand, however, one may ask why Saul did not oppose his soldiers when he was explicitly told by the prophet not to spare anything. If he knew that the people wanted to take the best animals, should he not, as Israel's king, resist the people's urges?

Second, Saul brings up the capturing of Agag, but offers no explanation for this curious omission from the ban. The reader is thus left guessing as to what the reasons are for this sparing of the Amalekite king.[76] On the one hand, Saul is not at all ashamed or sorrowful because of this act, prompting one to wonder whether Agag also was intended to be sacrificed before YHWH at Gilgal. On the other hand, if anybody was most responsible for the behavior of Amalek, it was presumably their king, and thus one would expect him to be the prime candidate for the implementation of the ban. It is curious that in the previous chapter Saul was ready to kill his own son, yet here he is not willing to kill the Amalekite king, the head of the "sinners, the Amalekites."

Third, Saul repeats his earlier argument that the animals were brought to Gilgal in order to be sacrificed there (1 Sam 15:15, 21), which prompts the question: Is not sacrifice itself, in fact, quite indistinguishable from *ḥerem*? At this point it might be helpful to introduce David Gunn's contribution to the problem of Saul's rejection,[77] which is perhaps most successful in defending Saul against Samuel's charges. Having looked at Saul's rejection in ch. 13 and finding the problems there to be based on Samuel's preference for a different interpretation of his charge,[78] Gunn turns to ch. 15 and focuses on the difference between חרם and זבח. In the end, he does not see any significant distinction between the two, because *ḥerem*, as he says, is "something akin to the notion of 'sacrifice.'"[79] This leads him to a strikingly more positive account of Saul's fault:

> Now we have a completely different view of what is going on: to be sure, Saul and the people had not "devoted to destruction" the best of the livestock *on the spot*, at the scene of the battle (or wherever), but that was because they had decided it would be more appropriate to "devote" it to Yahweh at his own sanctuary. Seen in this light, of course, the sparing of the *best* of the spoil makes excellent sense, for how could they bring what was despised and worthless back to Gilgal to sacrifice formally to their God?[80]

---

76. Klein illustrates well this ambiguous aspect of Agag's capture when he asks: "Was Saul ready to break the ban in order to complete some kind of deal with the Amalekites? Or did he wish to use Agag as a trophy of war (cf. 1 Sam 18:6–7)?" (Klein, *1 Samuel*, 150).

77. David M. Gunn, *The Fate of King Saul: An Interpretation of a Biblical Story*, JSOTSup 14 (Sheffield: JSOT Press, 1980).

78. Gunn, *Saul*, 39–40.

79. Gunn, *Saul*, 46.

80. Gunn, *Saul*, 47; italics his.

Gunn thus comes to a conclusion similar to the one he arrived at in the case of ch. 13.[81] It was Samuel who viewed *ḥerem* and sacrifice as mutually incompatible; for Saul there was no significant incongruity between them.[82] This does not mean that Saul is blameless but that his fault is a minor one, possibly realized only during the course of Samuel's interrogation. The nature of Saul's problem then, according to Gunn, was "a theological 'error', yes; an unwitting 'sin', perhaps; but a sin of devastating consequence, warranting God's rejection, surely not."[83]

Gunn's appraisal is a potent one as it reorients the traditional interpretation of Saul's fault, viewing him as culpable of an unconscious transgression at most. His proposal stands at the pinnacle of a range of other interpretive possibilities that view Saul as a devout, albeit mistaken, person who sincerely wanted to please his God. I have looked here at the various ways the story may be understood, partly because it is at this point that the narrative is most open to diverging interpretations, and also because in the very next verse Samuel turns the discussion in a specific direction. The narrative itself does not, interestingly, question Saul's honesty in suggesting that the animals were kept to be sacrificed— there is no hint, for example, that this is only a pretext for the motive of personal gain—but seems to take it seriously. As the story continues, the subject of sacrifice is approached in a famous poetical speech, offered by Samuel.[84]

Rejection and Confession (1 Samuel 15:22–26)

Samuel, in language resembling the prophetic critique of empty cultic practices,[85] issues this statement:

---

81. See Gunn, *Saul*, 56.

82. See Gunn, *Saul*, 50.

83. Gunn, *Saul*, 54. In the end, Gunn reasons that Saul's failure results from YHWH's reluctant stance toward kingship displayed in 1 Sam 8–12 (Gunn, *Saul*, 123–26). Similarly also L. Daniel Hawk, "Saul as Sacrifice: The Tragedy of Israel's First Monarch," *BRev* 12 (1996): 20–25, 56; or, with wider implications for Israel during the time of the divided kingdom, Bernard Gosse, "Du rejet de Yahvé par Israël au rejet d'Israël et de Juda par Yahvé dans les livres de Samuel et les livres des Rois," *ZAW* 112 (2000): 550–63.

84. Nevertheless, I wonder if God's instruction to Samuel in the next chapter (1 Sam 16:2), where he is instructed to pretend that he is going to offer a sacrifice when in reality his task is to anoint Saul's successor, does not present an implicit critique of Saul's claim that Israel is going to sacrifice the spoils at Gilgal (1 Sam 15:15, 21). I follow Gordon's lead in this, who remarks concerning ch. 16 that this instance of a deceiver being deceived falls more appropriately into the category of irony than ethics. It seems possible that Samuel is using the same pretext as that Saul did in ch. 15. See Robert P. Gordon, "Simplicity of the Highest Cunning: Narrative Art in the Old Testament," *SBET* 6 (1988): 69–80, esp. 79–80.

85. Thus also McCarter, *I Samuel*, 267, who cites Isa 66:2b–4 and Hos 6:6. Firth adds Amos 5:18–24 and Mic 6:8 (Firth, *Samuel*, 175).

Does YHWH delight in burnt offerings and sacrifices more than in obeying YHWH's voice (כִּשְׁמֹעַ בְּקוֹל)?
Behold, to obey is better than to sacrifice (שְׁמֹעַ מִזֶּבַח טוֹב) and to heed than the fat of rams.
For rebellion is as the sin of divination and stubbornness is as worthless idolatry.[86]
Because you have rejected the word of YHWH, he has rejected you as king. (1 Sam 15:22–23)

Samuel puts forward two comparisons in his speech. First, in contrast to Gunn's defense of Saul, he stresses obedience over sacrifice. According to Samuel's words, the matter of *ḥerem* is directly related to the sphere of obeying the voice of YHWH. Such uncompromising obedience has not been present in Saul's case, according to Samuel. He did not listen to (שמע) YHWH's voice, and no sacrifice is able to remedy this crucial omission.[87] Thus, if one views Samuel as a reliable interpreter of YHWH's purposes,[88] then no ritual can substitute for obedience, which is here closely tied to YHWH's command of *ḥerem*. Of course, one can still make a case, as Gunn does, that Saul is not guilty of sin in ch. 15, but the narrative takes the opposite turn here.[89] The ban, as I have suggested before, has the potential to test one's loyalty in the most demanding conditions. Saul is found to be lacking in this respect, and his (possibly honest) desire to sacrifice cannot alter his fate.

Second, Samuel likens rebellion to the act of divination, and stubbornness to worthless idolatry. The main thrust of this comparison seems to be that rebellion and stubbornness challenge the supreme position of

---

86. I take the words וְאָוֶן וּתְרָפִים (literally "wickedness and Teraphim") to be a hendiadys, meaning something like "worthless idolatry" or "evil idols." Similarly Klein, *1 Samuel*, 153. For another verse that links both words, see Zech 10:2: "Idols utter nonsense" (הַתְּרָפִים דִּבְּרוּ־אָוֶן).

87. The main difference between sacrifice and *ḥerem* seems to consist in the question of who designates what should be given to the deity. In the example of חרם it is usually God who decides what falls under this category (Num 21:2–3 is an exception). In situations of זבח it is the worshipper who selects, within certain parameters, what he deems suitable as a sacrifice to YHWH. Similarly Hertzberg, *Samuel*, 128; and Firth, *Samuel*, 175. Further, for a broader argument that the ban is distinct from sacrifice, see Nelson, "Herem," 47–48; and Earl, *Joshua*, 98–99. For seeing sacrificial overtones in *ḥerem*, consult Lohr, *Chosen*, 214; and Joel S. Kaminsky, *Corporate Responsibility in the Hebrew Bible*, JSOTSup 196 (Sheffield: Sheffield Academic, 1995), 80.

88. Samuel is introduced as a reliable interpreter of YHWH in 1 Sam 3:19–21, which underscores his prophetic role (see also Stoebe, *Samuelis*, 279–80). Nevertheless, Samuel's judgment is shown to be deficient in 1 Sam 16:7.

89. Nonetheless, Gunn's interpretation still has its attraction, as it derives its strength from a more miniscule issue on Saul's part in 1 Sam 13:7b–15a. For this reason, I will return to his exposition when I comment on the account of Saul's rejection in its canonical form.

YHWH as much as turning to idols or divination.[90] Paradoxically, Saul towards the end of his life consults a witch from Endor in order to inquire of YHWH (the verbal root "divine," קסם, occurs both in 1 Sam 15:23 and 28:8). Whereas in ch. 28 Saul will learn from Samuel of his ensuing death, here he learns only of the end of his royal career, as Samuel narrates God's decision already known to the reader from 15:11.[91] Because Saul has rejected God's command, God has rejected him as king over Israel (15:23). This second comparison thus builds upon the first, opening up a specific perspective on Saul's character. Instead of honoring YHWH, he challenges God's authority in deciding not to fulfill the ban in its entirety. Saul's authority over Israel is then rejected in return.

In response to this verdict, Saul confesses: "I have sinned and transgressed what came from YHWH's mouth and your words[92] for I feared the people and obeyed their voice" (חָטָאתִי כִּי־עָבַרְתִּי אֶת־פִּי־יְהוָה וְאֶת־דְּבָרֶיךָ כִּי יָרֵאתִי אֶת־הָעָם וָאֶשְׁמַע בְּקוֹלָם, 1 Sam 15:24). Saul, in straightforward terms, acknowledges that he has sinned (חָטָאתִי)[93] and transgressed what God and Samuel said, and recants what he had claimed earlier in his dialogue with Samuel when he insisted on his innocence (15:13, 20). The explanation given for Saul's misdeed is his fear of the people. When this is contrasted with ch. 12, where the fear of YHWH is laid down as a precondition for a successful monarchy under God (12:14–15), then one can feel the force of Saul's failure even stronger: the fear of YHWH was replaced with the fear of the people.[94]

Thus, if one reads the story with (rather than against) the grain, Saul appears guilty. Nevertheless, his penitent words sound like sincere contrition. Even if he does quickly add a request that seems a bit too self-oriented for one who has just recognized his guilt—"Please, forgive my

---

90. As Firth says: "such practices deny Yahweh's authority" (Firth, *Samuel*, 176). Divination is condemned in Deut 18:10 and 2 Kgs 17:17.

91. Foresti sees 1 Sam 15 and 28 functioning as a "diptych," in which Samuel solemnly announces in ch. 28 what was already decided in ch. 15 but suspended until later (Foresti, *Rejection*, 180).

92. It seems to me that Saul here acknowledges that Samuel and YHWH say the same. I do not take the *waw* dividing the two phrases as explicative, as indicated by Fokkelman, *Crossing*, 104. Rather, the text can be taken as Saul co-joining the authority of YHWH and Samuel, whom he had dissociated earlier in the narrative (1 Sam 15:15, 21).

93. Beyond the contours of ch. 15 Saul uses the same phrase "I have sinned" as an expression of his guilt when speaking with David (1 Sam 26:21). Within the corpus of Samuel's books, David speaks this way with Nathan (2 Sam 12:13) and with YHWH himself (2 Sam 24:10, 17).

94. Janzen stresses that Saul is unable to control Israel—something that he, as YHWH's vassal, is supposed to do in order to colonize the rebellious Israel. Therefore, Saul's military successes cannot remedy his failure in obedience in cultic matters. See David Janzen, *The Necessary King: A Postcolonial Reading of the Deuteronomistic Portrait of the Monarchy*, HBM 57 (Sheffield: Sheffield Phoenix, 2013), 144–51.

sin and return with me and I will bow down to YHWH" (1 Sam 15:25)[95]—
one can feel sympathy for this king whose fate hangs in the balance.
However, Samuel remains unmoved. Because YHWH has rejected Saul,
he will not return with Saul. The prophet remains on YHWH's side and
is not willing to join Saul despite his declaration of guilt. At least, so it
appears at first.

Torn Robe
(1 Samuel 15:27–31)

Samuel's refusal to accompany Saul to worship YHWH, however, takes
a different turn when Samuel attempts to leave and a piece of a cloak is
torn as a result. Samuel construes this tear as an additional sign of Saul's
rejection: God has torn from Saul his kingdom and has given it to his
neighbor, somebody who is better than Saul (1 Sam 15:28). Furthermore,
Samuel proceeds to issue a surprising statement stressing God's unwillingness to change his mind (1 Sam 15:29). Despite this emphasis on
God's immutability—which one might expect also to characterize God's
prophet—Samuel, after hearing yet another salvo of Saul's requests,[96]
returns with the rejected king to worship YHWH (1 Sam 15:30).

At least three issues regarding this brief paragraph should be considered.
First, what is the significance of the torn corner of the robe (and whose
robe was it)? Second, what might the reference to Saul's rejection and the
hint of his successor mean at this stage of my experimental reading? Third,
how can the declaration that Israel's God will not repent best be evaluated,
in light of the fact that a change of YHWH's mind constitutes a central
element of this chapter?

The Significance of the Torn Robe

The text is ambiguous in terms of whose robe was partially destroyed. It
literally says: "As Samuel turned to go away, he seized the hem (כְּנַף) of his
robe and it tore" (1 Sam 15:27).[97] Despite this ambiguity, the meaning that
fits best with the overall trajectory of the story is that which sees the cloak

---

95. Frisch notes the parallel between Saul's contrition here and that of Pharaoh
in Exod 10:17. See Amos Frisch, "'For I Feared the People, and I Yielded to Them'
(I Sam 15,24)—Is Saul's Guilt Attenuated or Intensified?," *ZAW* 108 (1996): 98–104, esp.
102–3. Frisch regards this comparison as justifying a negative evaluation of Saul's repentance.

96. For a synchronic comparison of Saul's two confessions of sin in the chapter, see
V. Philips Long, "Interpolation or Characterization: How Are We to Understand Saul's Two
Confessions?," *Presb* 19 (1993): 49–53.

97. The LXX, 4QSam[a], and Peshitta try to resolve the ambiguity by inserting the
subject "Saul" before the verb קרע, which could be vocalized either passively (וַיִּקָּרַע) or
actively (וַיִּקְרַע).

as belonging to Samuel.[98] As Samuel is about to leave, Saul, in a desperate attempt to prevent the prophet's departure,[99] seizes his garment, which accidentally results in something that appears to have a greater significance.[100] Although the text is silent about the explicit reason for the change in Samuel's position,[101] one may conclude at any rate that Saul's desperate gesture did the trick, as Samuel now accompanies the king to Gilgal.[102]

What is more significant, however, is that even this gesture Samuel turns into its opposite: a sign confirming Saul's rejection, prefiguring several other situations where Saul tries to stop David at all costs, but always loses more ground in return. Another act of cutting the hem (כָּנָף), this time of Saul's cloak by David, is likewise used in 24:5 (ET 24:4) to signify something similar. Regardless of the intentions of the human participants, on each occasion the torn cloak is associated with the transfer of the kingdom to David and is used in the narrative against Saul (15:28; 24:21 [ET 24:20]).[103]

---

98. See, for example, McCarter, *I Samuel*, 268; Klein, *1 Samuel*, 153; and Tsumura, *Samuel*, 406. For a thorough discussion of various possibilities with more tentative conclusions, see Annett Giercke-Ungermann, "Vom Griff nach dem Obergewand zum Entzug der Königsherrschaft: Überlegungen zu 1 Sam 15,27–29," *BZ* 55 (2011): 75–86.

99. I think this is the simplest solution. Scholars have suggested various proposals as to what the meaning of this gesture might be. Conrad surveys several Mari texts in an attempt to demonstrate that the grasping of Samuel's cloak could symbolize encroaching upon the prophet's authority. See Diethelm Conrad, "Samuel und die Mari-'Propheten': Bemerkungen zu 1 Sam 15:27," in *XVII Deutscher Orientalistentag*, ed. W. Voight, ZDMGSup 1 (Weisbaden: Franz Steiner, 1969), 273–80. Brauner, relying on the Old Aramaic and Akkadian equivalent of "seizing the hem" argues that the gesture presents a final act of Saul's supplication and submission. See Ronald A. Brauner, "'To Grasp the Hem' and 1 Samuel 15:27," *JANESCU* 6 (1974): 35–38. Similarly Paul A. Kruger, "The Symbolic Significance of the Hem (*kānāf*) in 1 Samuel 15:27," in *Text and Context*, ed. W. Claasen, JSOTSup 48 (Sheffield: Sheffield Academic, 1988), 105–116, esp. 111.

100. Both Stoebe and Viberg think that the torn robe was a mere accident; see Stoebe, *Samuelis*, 291; Åke Viberg, "Saul Exposed by Irony: A New Understanding of 1 Samuel 15:27 Based on Two Symbolic Acts," *SEÅ* 70 (2005): 301–8, esp. 306.

101. Tsumura says: "Perhaps it is out of his personal concern for Saul (v. 35), or perhaps out of concern for the national 'order' if it were known that the Lord no longer recognized Saul" (Tsumura, *Samuel*, 408).

102. I note here Alter's proposal when he thinks that Samuel in fact did not go with Saul. He says: "the expression 'turn back with,' as in verse 30, and 'turn back from' [literally, after] are antonyms, the latter meaning unambiguously 'to abandon.' Samuel is completing his rejection of Saul here by refusing to accompany him in the cult, shaming him by forcing him to offer the sacrifice without the officiating of the man of God" (Alter, *David*, 93). Alter's reading remains a possibility even though, in my judgment, it makes better sense to regard Samuel as accompanying Saul in worship.

103. Similarly Ora Horn Prouser, "Suited to the Throne: The Symbolic Use of Clothing in the David and Saul Narratives," *JSOT* 71 (1996): 27–37, esp. 29. Viberg sees in this usage a Deuteronomistic hand (Viberg, "Saul," 307). Both authors also cite 1 Kgs 11:30–39, where Ahijah's prophetic mantle is torn into twelve pieces to symbolize the division of Israel's kingdom and the transfer of kingship to non-Davidic hands (Prouser, "Throne," 29; Viberg, "Saul," 307).

Samuel's word is thus confirmed by a prophetic sign,[104] and Saul's fate is sealed.

YHWH's Rejection of Saul

Samuel's confirmation of Saul's rejection is declared this way: "YHWH has torn the kingdom of Israel from you today, and has given it to your neighbor who is better than you" (קָרַע יְהוָה אֶת־מַמְלְכוּת יִשְׂרָאֵל מֵעָלֶיךָ הַיּוֹם וּנְתָנָהּ לְרֵעֲךָ הַטּוֹב מִמֶּךָּ, 1 Sam 15:28). This pronouncement contains several noteworthy features. First, it may be contrasted with the depiction of Saul when he first appeared on the scene. The text portraying his handsome appearance literally says: "and there was no man among the sons of Israel better than him" (וְאֵין אִישׁ מִבְּנֵי יִשְׂרָאֵל טוֹב מִמֶּנּוּ, 1 Sam 9:2). Here, however, the reader is told that the kingdom has been given to somebody *better* than Saul,[105] which might indicate that the excellence of Saul's successor will consist in something other than his physical quality.[106] Second, the new king will be Saul's neighbor (רֵעַ). This is a broad term, the meaning of which (when not used in a reciprocal sense) ranges from "friend" or "neighbor" to "member of the same clan."[107] Nevertheless, when seen through the requirements for Israel's kingship as spelled out in Deut 17:14–15, then its most likely meaning in this context is "fellow Israelite."[108] The traditional conditions for Israel's kingship thus seem to be reaffirmed in Samuel's words—the concrete meaning of which, however, must await the story's development.[109] For now the range of possibilities is wide open. Third, the rejection concerns Saul personally. This was already the case in 1 Sam 15:26, before the incident with the torn mantle, where one reads: "You have rejected the word of YHWH, and YHWH has rejected you [singular] (וַיִּמְאָסְךָ) from being king over Israel." The same emphasis is repeated here: "YHWH has torn the

---

104. Thus Giuseppe Bettenzoli, "Samuel und das Problem des Königtums: Die Tradition von Gilgal," *BZ* 30 (1986): 222–36, esp. 231–32.

105. Johannes Klein reasons: "Das Gegenüber von 9,2 und 15,28 muss demnach so gedeutet werden, dass ausgesagt wird, dass es zum Zeitpunkt der Wahl Sauls keinen Besseren ab.... In der Zwischenzeit ist jedoch eine Entwicklung eingetreten. Zur Zeit, wo 15,28 ausgesprochen wird, ist Saul nicht mehr der Beste." Johannes Klein, *David versus Saul: Ein Beitrag zum Erzählsystem der Samuelbücher*, BWA(N)T 158 (Stuttgart: Kohlhammer, 2002), 56.

106. As 1 Sam 16:6–7 indicates directly: the new king should have surpassing inward qualities.

107. See D. Kallermann, "רֵעַ," *TDOT* 13:522–32, esp. 525–26.

108. Deut 17:14–15, which uses not the noun "neighbor"(רֵעַ) but rather "brother"(אָח), stresses that the future king must be an Israelite. Nevertheless, elsewhere in Deuteronomy—where it is emphasized that certain privileges are to be bestowed upon a fellow Israelite and not a foreigner—both terms are used interchangeably (see, e.g., Deut 15:2–3).

109. I think it noteworthy that when the witch of Endor brought up Samuel's spirit, he reaffirmed his earlier pronouncement, but only this time does he name Saul's successor: "YHWH has torn the kingdom from your hand and given it to your neighbor, David" (1 Sam 28:17).

kingdom of Israel from you [singular] (מֵעָלֶיךָ) today" (1 Sam 15:28). The one rejected is Saul himself, which indicates that none of the characters introduced in the story so far is excluded from being Saul's successor. This opens up a path, explored later in my study, to a different understanding of the account of Saul's rejection than has often been proposed. Fourth, Samuel's interpretation of the torn robe makes reference to the specific time when this rejection and transfer of God's favor has taken place. It has happened "today" (הַיּוֹם). This temporal designation gives the impression that this is the day of Saul's demise, and that no prior decision had been made in this regard. It is only after Saul's incomplete implementation of *ḥerem* in the battle against Amalek that YHWH has rejected him as king over Israel. The canonical reading usually overshadows this feature of the story, but it comes to the fore when the narrative is read without the section 1 Sam 13:7b–15a. Verse 28, once these few observations have been made, thus plays a significant role in my experimental reading of Saul's failure, a role which I will build upon in my overall evaluation of Saul's rejection.

Divine Repentance

One perhaps can see—if the story's frame of reference is accepted—how it is that Saul was guilty of not implementing *ḥerem* upon the Amalekites, but how can we understand God's refusal to reinstate Saul after he has confessed his guilt? Why is God not willing, so to speak, to repent of his repentance? As Exum aptly puts it: "The question is not why Saul is rejected. That we know, regardless of whether we consider the rejection justified by Saul's actions. The question is why there is no forgiveness."[110] This leads us to a problematic issue of God's repentance.

One of the difficulties of ch. 15 is that Samuel's talk of God's unwillingness to repent is delivered in the midst of a narrative dealing primarily with YHWH's repentance over having made Saul king. Verse 11 states YHWH's displeasure with Saul's campaign against Amalek: "I have repented (נִחַמְתִּי) that I made Saul king, for he turned away (שָׁב) from following me." Similarly, the conclusion of the whole chapter affirms this decision: "YHWH repented (נִחָם) that he made Saul king over Israel" (15:35). These statements stand in apparent contradiction to Samuel's pronouncement of God's non-repentance in 15:29: "Moreover, the Everlasting One of Israel[111] does not deceive or repent, for he is not a human being that he should repent." How can one best interpret this puzzle?

110. J. Cheryl Exum, *Tragedy and Biblical Narrative: Arrows of the Almighty* (Cambridge: Cambridge University Press, 1992), 40, cited in Van Wijk-Bos, *Samuel*, 84.

111. The meaning of the epithet נֵצַח יִשְׂרָאֵל is difficult to ascertain. A standard translation is "Glory of Israel" (NRSV, NIV, NJPS). I opt for the meaning "Everlasting One of Israel," which stresses the duration involved in the noun נֵצַח, and which fits the tenor of the saying focused on the constancy of God. Similarly McCarter, *I Samuel*, 260; Bodner, *1 Samuel*, 161; and Middleton, "Samuel," 84–85.

It should be noted at the outset that the idea of God's repentance represents something of a theological axiom within the Old Testament,[112] and this needs to be emphasized despite some uneasy tension with the classically formulated notion of divine immutability.[113] As Moberly summarizes his extensive probing of this issue, "God in some way takes into account how people respond such that it makes a difference in what He will do."[114] Both 1 Sam 15:29 and its sibling Num 23:19, where one can read the principal statements concerning God's repentance, need to be seen within this framework. They contradict (or complement) the axiom concerning the divine responsiveness to people's actions. In what way can the assertion of divine immutability fit within the larger canvas of God's relationship with Israel and the world?

Of course, one option to account for this apparent discrepancy is to posit various sources beneath, or redactions of, the text.[115] This, of course, is a plausible scenario, but it still leaves unanswered the question of how one might read the text in its received form.[116] A second option is to highlight one voice in the story and suppress another. In this case, given the ample indications in the Old Testament of God's responsiveness, one could question Samuel's insistence on God's unwillingness to change his mind and suggest that the prophet spoke out of anger and resentment and that his words here do not have a normative function.[117] A third option— directly opposed to that just presented—lies in the supposition that both God's repentance and his non-repentance say something essential about the divine character. God is *both* responsive to human affairs *and* free in his decisions.[118] The fourth option then focuses on the specific case of Saul's rejection. The statement concerning God's change of mind does not

---

112. Genesis 6–9, Exod 32, and Jonah 3 provide prime examples of this phenomenon. An ability to repent is listed among God's attributes in Jonah 4:2 and Joel 2:13.

113. See, for example, Raney's essay devoted to setting up the contrast between God's immutability and the Old Testament portrayal of the deity: Donald C. Raney, II, "Does YHWH *Naham*? A Question of Openness," *SBLSP* 42 (2003): 105–15.

114. Moberly, "Change," 120. Moberly explores the topic of divine repentance especially in this work and also in his earlier study, "Human," 112–23.

115. Thus, for example, McCarter, *I Samuel*, 268. Similarly Foresti, *Rejection*, 28–29.

116. It should be recorded that McCarter is well aware of this (McCarter, *I Samuel*, 268).

117. In this regard, one should note especially Middleton's careful analysis of Samuel's not-so-positive traits throughout 1 Sam 1–15, which allows him to suggest that the prophet's insistence on Saul's rejection stems from Samuel's inflexible understanding of the divine nature (God should not be influenced by humans) and his indignation regarding the monarchy in general and the choice of Saul as king in particular (Middleton, *Samuel*, 69–91, esp. 81–85). Similarly also Yairah Amit, "'The Glory of Israel Does Not Deceive or Change His Mind': On the Reliability of Narrator and Speakers in Biblical Narrative," *Proof* 12 (1992): 201–12, esp. 205.

118. Hertzberg suggests that God's repentance means that the deity is not bound by his own decree (Hertzberg, *Samuel*, 126).

formulate a general principle of God's character. Rather, Saul's rejection is the specific matter of which YHWH will not repent.[119]

The irrevocability of Saul's rejection is the main subject of Moberly's study, which puts forward two main ideas regarding 1 Sam 15:29 and its sibling text, Num 23:19. First, Moberly notes how these two statements define God's non-repentance vis-à-vis human repentance. In a fashion akin to apophatic theology they demonstrate what YHWH is not: he does not lie or speak falsely, and in changing his mind he is not like a human being.[120] This observation—supported by the occurrence of differing terms for divine (נחם) and human repentance (שׁוב)—sets an important parameter for future investigation as it explains that God repents on a different level from that of human beings: "It is not mutuality and responsiveness in relationship, but insincerity and faithlessness that are specified for denial."[121] Second, both texts concern election: Num 23:19 occurs in the midst of Balaam's forced attempt to curse Israel (Num 22–24),[122] while 1 Sam 15 is concerned with the divine choice of David, hinted in v. 28. Moberly concludes:

> Whether or not Samuel is to be imagined as in some way knowing the identity of the neighbor before the visit to Jesse, the knowledge that David is the divinely chosen successor to Saul is presupposed by the narrator of 1 Samuel 15, who tells the story thus. It is this oncoming event—that God will give the kingship of Israel to David—that sets the context of verse 29 and explains why verse 29 is formulated as a general principle about God, that "God does not repent."[123]

YHWH's unwillingness to repent of Saul's rejection thus stems from his commitment to David.[124] As Moberly notes, this solution does not, in fact, explain the conundrum on a rational level, but points to the inexplicable

---

119. According to Gordon, it is the rejection of Saul that is irrevocable (Gordon, *1 & 2 Samuel*, 146).

120. Moberly, "Change," 131–32.

121. Moberly, "Change," 132

122. See the discussion in Moberly, "Change," 132–34.

123. Moberly, "Change," 134–38, esp. 137

124. Fretheim similarly sees David's election as a reason for the insertion of v. 29. He further suggests that the reason God placed the election of David on a different footing is because he learned something from his experiment with Saul. Consult Terence E. Fretheim, "Divine Foreknowledge, Divine Constancy, and the Rejection of Saul's Kingship," *CBQ* 47 (1985): 595–602, esp. 599. Similarly also Middleton, Samuel, 88–89. The idea of an experiment is reminiscent of Sonnet's proposal, which suggests that the Hebrew root נחם occurs at crucial junctions in the Old Testament signifying a "false start" with respect to a covenant between the deity and humankind in general or Israel in particular. See Jean-Pierre Sonnet, "God's Repentance and 'False Starts' in Biblical History (Genesis 6–9; Exodus 32–34; 1 Samuel 15 and 2 Samuel 7)," in *Congress Volume Ljubljana 2007*, ed. André Lemaire, VTSup 133 (Leiden: Brill, 2010), 469–94.

nature of the divine love with which he clings to those whom he chooses; and David remains in the biblical account more favored than his predecessor. [125]

Moberly's proposal is relevant to my study, as it explores the nature of chosenness. God's decision to remain loyal to Israel in general and to David in particular is visible in other places in the Old Testament (e.g. Ps 110:4), [126] and within the Samuel narrative it appropriately reflects God's faithfulness to David despite his obvious shortcomings—even though, of course, God's selection of David does not occur until ch. 16 and thus (especially when one reads the narrative without 1 Sam 13:7b–15a) the identity of Saul's successor is not yet evident. I will try to supplement Moberly's proposal by revisiting his argument concerning the difference between the Hebrew verbs נחם and שׁוב. The specific nature of this difference may also be found, in my opinion, in the section 1 Sam 15:24–31, even though the word שׁוב is not used here as something indicating repentance, but speaks rather of Samuel's proposed or actual "re-turning." First, Saul urges the prophet: "Return with me (שׁוּב עִמִּי) so that I may bow down to YHWH" (1 Sam 15:25). Samuel refuses this request and says: "I will not return with you" (לֹא אָשׁוּב עִמָּךְ, 1 Sam 15:26), and proceeds to stress God's decision to reject the one who rejected God's words. This, however, changes after Saul tears off the corner of Samuel's robe. Saul continues his pleading with the prophet in the course of which he again issues the same imperative: "Return with me!" (שׁוּב עִמִּי, 1 Sam 15:30). "And Samuel turned back (וַיָּשָׁב) after Saul and Saul bowed down to YHWH" (1 Sam 15:31). This cluster of occurrences of the root שׁוב surrounds the emphatic declaration that YHWH will not repent (נחם) concerning Saul's rejection (1 Sam 15:29). Specifically, Samuel's first decision not to accompany Saul to worship YHWH, and his later repentance thereof, may be contrasted with YHWH's initial choice of Saul and his repentance of making him king. YHWH's נחם is not Samuel's שׁוב, as the former seems to indicate something more stable, durable, and sincere. Samuel finally goes with Saul but, as his insistence on God's rejection of Israel's king suggests, he remains convinced of Saul's denunciation. While his outward action seem to express a certain loyalty to Saul, inwardly he is persuaded of his rejection. In a similar way, Saul first turns from his decision to follow God's direction (at least according to YHWH's evaluation in 1 Sam 15:11), and then is sorry about his merely partial fulfillment of *herem*. Yet, as his words reveal, the sincerity of his confession is tempered by his quick

---

125. Moberly, "Change," 138.

126. Psalm 110:4 expresses God's commitment to David in this way: "YHWH has sworn and will not repent: you are a priest forever, in the order of Melchizedek." Moberly uses this verse as a springboard for arguing that this specific kind of oath concerns the election of Israel and David (see Moberly, "Human," 116).

request to be honored by Samuel before the elders of Israel (1 Sam 15:30). One may thus question the genuineness of his "repentance." Both of the main human agents in the chapter thus exemplify what human repentance means: it is less reliable, less stable, and more shallow. In contrast, YHWH's repentance is deeper and more firm.

Furthermore, Samuel's emphasis on God's unwillingness to repent concerning Saul's rejection and David's election in 1 Sam 15:29 is needed in terms of the narrative flow. In its absence one might perhaps take Samuel's return with Saul to Gilgal as proof of YHWH's forgiveness of Saul. Since Samuel is YHWH's prophet, one could take his actions as being in line with the divine mind. Verse 29 thus effectively distances YHWH's actions from Samuel's accompaniment of Saul. Without this, one might be less certain about David's election in the next chapter.

The preceding evaluation attempts to reconfigure Moberly's argument regarding God's repentance in 1 Sam 15. Since YHWH's unwavering commitment to David still lies in the future, the narrative may be read as another example in which the fickleness of human characters differs from YHWH's more stable and enduring change that nevertheless takes human actions seriously.

Completion
(1 Samuel 15:32–35)

The chapter finishes with two concluding sections. First, Samuel turns his attention to Agag, who seems to hope that his life will be spared (1 Sam 15:32–33).[127] The prophet, however, thinks otherwise and, after first giving a reason for Agag's punishment—as Agag's sword left women childless, so now Samuel's sword will make Agag's mother childless—completes what Saul left unfinished and kills the foreign leader.[128] The introduction

---

127. There is a textual and an interpretive problem in v. 32 regarding the adverbial expression (מַעֲדַנֹּת) indicating how Agag approaches the prophet. Klein follows the LXX τρέμων, "trembling," possibly derived from the Hebrew root מעד, "stumble" (Klein, *1 Samuel*, 146; similarly also Driver, *Notes*, 129; and Smith, *Samuel*, 142). On the other hand, some versions indicate that Agag could be approaching Samuel more optimistically, likely taking the word as עדן, "bliss" (Aq., Sym., Tg.Jon.). Thus Bar Efrat suggests that Agag's approach was cheerful (Bar-Efrat, *Samuel*, 223). Finally, McCarter, with one eye on the only other occurrence of מַעֲדַנֹּת in the Old Testament in Job 38:31, translates the phrase "in fetters" or "in bands" (the word can be derived from ענד, "bind"). See McCarter, *I Samuel*, 264. If Agag approached Samuel hesitantly, than one can read his inner monologue as "Surely this is the bitterness of death" (NRSV). If he went to the prophet cheerfully, then one translates the latter part of the verse: "Surely the bitterness of death is past" (NIV). For a good overview of the options, which concludes that the current text is a conflation of two different versions, see Shemaryahu Talmon, "1 Sam 15:32b. A Case of Conflated Readings," *VT* 11 (1961): 456–57.

128. This may be viewed as an "implicit criticism of Saul." Thus Fokkelman, *Crossing*, 109. See also Hertzberg, *Samuel*, 129; and Polzin, *Samuel*, 142–45, esp. 144.

of retaliation comes as a surprise at this point, because—in the logic of ch. 15—Amalek was not subjected to *ḥerem* because he had recently fought with Israel but because he was their ancient foe. Within the immediate literary context, Samuel's words may perhaps be viewed as an attempt to bring closer to the present the appeal to the Amalekites' atrocities of an earlier time: the death sentence upon Agag might be linked with ch. 14 and its reference to Amalek who is counted among Israel's current enemies (14:48).[129] Nevertheless, the explicit reference to a payback for something that Agag has personally done seems unexpected in the context of ch. 15.

Furthermore, the manner, in which Samuel kills Agag (the text says that Samuel "hewed (וַיְשַׁסֵּף) Agag in pieces" [NRSV])[130] and the location of this act, which is specifically identified as "before YHWH in Gilgal" (1 Sam 15:33), raise the question again as to whether *ḥerem* is not closely connected with sacrifice. Although this possibility cannot be rejected, one must bear in mind that Samuel killed Agag in the place to which Saul brought him. The Amalekite king was in Gilgal, which was Israel's special religious location. There Saul bowed down to YHWH and there Samuel completed *ḥerem* by executing the Amalekite leader. The manner of Agag's death has ritual overtones, but its precise meaning is not certain.[131]

The second element present at the end of ch. 15 is a focus on the strained relationship between the prophet and Saul (1 Sam 15:34–35). Despite the likely proximity of Ramah to Gibeah,[132] the narrator points out that Samuel never saw Saul again, grieved over Saul, and YHWH repented that he had made Saul king.[133] The assertion that there was no future meeting between the king and his prophet is, in fact, in direct contradiction to the events of 1 Sam 19:22–24, where Saul lay naked before Samuel, prophesying. Regardless of how the tension between the two passages may be resolved,[134] the chapter finishes on a sad note. The relationship between Samuel and Saul is broken and the reason for this is YHWH's repentance over Saul.

---

129. Note also the peculiar reference to Agag in Num 24:7.

130. The meaning of the Piel imperfect וַיְשַׁסֵּף is uncertain. Both Peshitta and Targum point to the meaning "cut to pieces" (*HALOT* 2:1609) The Greek text has ἔσφαξεν, "slaughtered," which is retained in the Greek text of the Old Testament for ritual sacrifice (see, e.g., Lev 4:24, 29, 33).

131. McCarter suggests that it might perhaps point to a "punishment for covenant violation" (McCarter, *I Samuel*, 269), which may fit with the description of the Amalekites in 1 Sam 14:48 as those who plundered Israel.

132. Tsumura says it is less than ten miles (Tsumura, *Samuel*, 411). See also Arnold, "Gibeah," 2:1007–9.

133. Thus NRSV. NJPS suggests that the conjunction may be taken causatively: "But Samuel grieved over Saul, because the Lord regretted that He made Saul king."

134. For example, Bodner says that "since Saul is barely clothed and madly prophesying in that scene, I assume it does not really count as a 'meeting' in the normal sense" (Bodner, *1 Samuel*, 164).

It should be noted that Samuel's mourning seems to be connected with YHWH's repentance of his former decision to make Saul king over Israel. Samuel's emotional distress concerning God's rejection of Saul thus brackets the long dialogue between the prophet and the king (1 Sam 15:11, 35), and serves as yet another marker that ch. 15 makes good sense when read without the section 1 Sam 13:7b–15a. *This* is the occasion on which Saul is rejected, and this rejection causes Samuel to mourn over the king whom he appointed.

Summary

Before closing up my experimental reading of chs. 13–15 with a summary of the main findings concerning the notion of Saul's rejection when the narrative is read without 1 Sam 13:7b–15a, I will make a few comments related to 1 Sam 15 itself and its connection with the preceding chapters.

Learning Wrong Lessons

When one reads chs. 13–15 together, it can be seen how Saul's behavior in ch. 15 might be influenced by his experiences in 1 Sam 13–14. In the first battle, Saul appears perhaps somewhat passive as a leader—especially as compared with the more energetic Jonathan—but devout and religious in his attempt to secure God's favor. In the second, particularly concerning the practice of *ḥerem*, Saul is more relaxed or even "creative" in trying to find various ways to circumvent God's command to annihilate the Amalekites.

This difference could possibly be explained by the suggestion that Saul has learned the wrong lessons from the battle portrayed in 1 Sam 13:1–14:46. Presumably, he spared Agag because he had witnessed the sparing of Jonathan by the people (1 Sam 14:45). On that occasion the lot pointed to Jonathan as the guilty party, yet when the people acted to save him, YHWH did not protest. Since God did not interfere then, why would he do so now? The two acts, however, are not alike. As the people argued, Jonathan brought Israel victory that day, and played the most essential role in the battle against the Philistines, whereas Agag was perhaps the person most responsible for the Amalekite atrocities (1 Sam 15:33). Gordon notes this contrast when he says: "But perhaps the most paradoxical feature of all, when chs 14 and 15 are read together, is that the man who was prepared to see his own son die because of his rash imposition of an oath was willing to spare Agag the king of the Amalekites."[135] As did the people in ch. 14, Saul let somebody escape the death sentence, but this time it was not a person who fought the battle on YHWH's side, but one who was a leader of YHWH's enemies.

---

135. Gordon, *I & II Samuel*, 58.

Furthermore, something analogous may be observed in Saul's handling of the spoil. In ch. 14 it is Jonathan who disapproves of his father's oath to abstain from any food in Israel's pursuit of the Philistines. He points out how a little honey energized him, and laments: "How much better if this day the people had eaten freely of the spoil of their enemies which they have found; for now the slaughter among the Philistines has not been great" (1 Sam 14:30). It could be this earlier piece of Jonathan's advice that is behind Saul's willingness to let the people take freely from the spoil of the Amalekites (15:21). Nevertheless, while Jonathan's complaint makes sense in the course of an exhausting battle lasting the whole day (14:31), the situation is quite different in ch. 15. The description of the campaign against Amalek does not mention any fatigue on Israel's part. On the contrary, the large size of the Israelite army, and the briefness with which the actual battle is reported, create an impression that the attack was swift and sudden. Moreover, the animals are taken to be sacrificed at Gilgal, suggesting that there was no pressing need on the part of the Israelites to satisfy their hunger.

It should also be underscored that ch. 15 presents a strikingly different overall picture of battle. In ch. 14, everything was initiated by the characters in the story: Jonathan's attack, Saul's oath and sacrifice, the people's redemption of Jonathan. In ch. 15, the main course of events is, so to say, top down: Samuel announces that God orders the destruction of the Amalekites, leaving almost no space for human inventiveness. Saul is told what he should do and warned to obey YHWH's voice. He has a good-size army to accomplish the task and, from the narrative point of view, Amalek is concentrated in a well-defined space. His duty thus appears manageable, yet Saul does not accomplish it. This is significantly different from desperate conditions described in 1 Sam 13:1–14:46, where a much smaller group of Israelites without a suitable weaponry faced a much larger enemy, and where a creative and bold action was needed to achieve Israel's victory. Here the success of Saul, and thus of Israel, consisted in something different: in obeying God's will. The two battles are fundamentally different, and require different attitudes on the part of Israel and particularly Saul—who may have learned something from the earlier battle with the Philistines but misjudged the different demands which the new situation required.

Saul Rejected because of His Disobedience

The major issue in ch. 15 revolves around the concept of obedience and its concrete requirement here, *ḥerem*. The ban seems to be particularly suited to drawing out one's loyalty to the deity in a situation that is most demanding. Saul is urged to listen to YHWH's command concerning the Amalekites, and to follow it through with punctuality. Despite the possibility that some of Saul's defense of his actions may have been well meant, he is rejected by Samuel because he has failed to carry out *ḥerem* with completeness.

The requirement to obey YHWH receives additional stress when viewed in connection with ch. 12, where Samuel lays out the prerequisites for kingship under YHWH. In that chapter a picture of a successful monarchy is presented in which both king and people follow YHWH and fear him (1 Sam 12:14–15). Chapter 15 then introduces a situation where Saul fails to listen to YHWH and obeys the voice of the people instead. He fears the people rather than YHWH (15:24), which could be understood as an example of the kind of failure that might provoke YHWH to turn his hand against Israel and its king (12:15). Saul has not fulfilled this basic requirement and is consequently rejected as king.

Nevertheless, even if Saul's failure is made somewhat comprehensible by attending closely to the flow of ch. 15 and to its wider context, one still may ask if Saul deserves such harsh punishment, especially when he confesses his sin and seeks forgiveness. Even if one sees Saul as insincere and shallow in his remorse, the firmness of God's sudden verdict lingers over the story. Saul seems to be abandoned too quickly by the deity, especially given David's later misdeeds (most famously that depicted in 2 Sam 11).

Various Ways to Read the Narrative

The strong contrast between YHWH's attitude here towards Saul and that exhibited later to David, coupled with the ambiguities inherent in the multifaceted narrative of ch. 15, are what is behind the various attempts to read this story with suspicion. David Gunn's assessment of Saul's rejection is perhaps the most potent of these,[136] and aptly makes use both of the ambiguities in the text and the comparison with David in moving towards a more positive appraisal of Saul. This way of approaching the narrative, I believe, acquires even greater potency when one reads chs. 13–15 in its canonical form. However, before I embark on this task, I need to summarize my observations concerning the reading of these chapters without 1 Sam 13:7b–15a.

---

136. Gunn, *Saul*, 33–56, 115–31. Consider also Middleton, "Samuel," 69–91; Tamás Czövek, *Three Seasons of Charismatic Leadership: A Literary-critical and Theological Interpretation of the Narrative of Saul, David and Solomon* (Oxford: Paternoster, 2006), esp. 41–99; or Marti J. Steussy, *Samuel and His God* (Columbia, SC: University of South Carolina Press, 2010).

17

1 Samuel:
Evaluation of the Experimental
Reading

Having charted some of my observations resulting from a close reading of chs. 13–15, I will present here my evaluation of these chapters when they are read without the intrusive segment in 1 Sam 13:7b–15a. I will summarize my findings from the preceding discussion, and argue that this experimental reading yields a somewhat different interpretation both of Saul's rejection and the identity of his successor.

The Only Rejection of Saul

When one reads ch. 15 without having previously read 1 Sam 13:7b–15a, it becomes clear that Saul's failure is unprecedented in the narrative and comes as a surprise. First, it should be noted that Samuel reacts with anger when he learns of God's decision to depose Saul of kingship, crying to YHWH all night (15:11). One cannot be sure about the precise content of Samuel's cry, yet the emotional reaction displayed by Samuel suggests that God's sentence concerning Saul is something new to him. Second, Samuel's spoken interpretation of the torn robe makes reference to the specific time when this rejection and the transfer of God's favor takes place. Samuel says: "YHWH has torn the kingdom of Israel from you today (הַיּוֹם)" (15:28). This gives the impression that this is the day of Saul's demise, and that no prior decision was made in this regard. Third, the conclusion of the whole story is stated thus: "Samuel mourned over Saul. And YHWH repented that he made Saul king over Israel" (15:35). Not only Samuel but also God is portrayed here as trying to come to terms with Saul's rejection, which makes most sense if this is the *only* occasion in the whole narrative on which Saul is rejected.

There are clues in the text, then, that may justify a reading of the narrative without the awkward segment in 1 Sam 13:7b–15a. Saul is rejected by YHWH only after his war with Amalek. The battle against the Philistines in chs. 13–14 may present some features in the portrayal of Saul that remain ambivalent, but he still continues to be God's favored king. It is only in ch. 15 that the deity rejects him as king over Israel.

The Rejection Concerns Saul Personally

YHWH's rejection of Saul in ch. 15 concerns Saul personally. This is emphasized several times in the chapter. First, YHWH repents that he has made
Saul king (1 Sam 15:11). This announcement, made to Samuel, contains
no indication whatever that YHWH's decision concerns anybody else in
Saul's immediate family. Second, Samuel's speech to the perplexed king
stresses the singularity of God's rejection. 1 Samuel 15:26 states: "You have
rejected the word of YHWH, and YHWH has rejected you [singular] (וַיִּמְאָסְךָ)
from being king over Israel." Similarly, when Samuel uses the incident with
the torn robe to press further his argument, he says: "YHWH has torn the
kingdom of Israel from you [singular] (מֵעָלֶיךָ) today" (15:28). Saul's personal
failure brought his own demise. Nobody else in Israel is even mentioned by
name in ch. 15, and thus Saul's rejection opens up a wide range of possible
candidates to become his successor in leading Israel as a nation.

The Neighbor Better than Saul

Samuel's announcement concerning the end of Saul's reign contains
a piece of information about Saul's replacement, who is designated as
a "neighbor who is better than [Saul]" (1 Sam 15:28). But who is this
mysterious person? Based on the preceding narrative, with the reference
to Saul's unfortunate sacrifice at Gilgal left out, it could very well be Saul's
son Jonathan, who does not feature in the narrative of 1 Sam 15 and who
has proved to be in a certain sense better qualified than his father to lead
Israel in its battle.[1] It is true that the term "neighbor" (רֵעַ) in 1 Sam 15:28
is not the most natural term to use of one's son, given that it denotes a
more distant relationship—but this argument assumes that Samuel knew
who the new king would be. As we can see in Samuel's mistaken guess in
Bethlehem (1 Sam 16:7), however, he did not know the identity of Saul's
successor. As I have pointed out before,[2] the term רֵעַ, especially when
seen through the lens of the Deuteronomistic legislation about kingship,[3]
most likely means "a fellow Israelite." It is a general term that must be
filled with a more precise meaning as the story develops. This notion
is confirmed when one compares Samuel's oracle to Saul with Nathan's

---

1. When Dietrich comments on Saul's two rejections, he also sees Jonathan as the
most obvious candidate for Israel's kingship—until one encounters David later in ch. 16:
"In beiden Fällen konfrontiert der Prophet den König mit der Aussicht, dass das Königtum
einem anderen übergeben werde. Saul weiß nicht—und auch wir Lesenden wissen nicht—,
wer das sein könnte. Die nächstliegende Antwort ist: Jonatan, der sich gegen die Philistier
so glänzend hervortut. In 1 Sam 16 werden wir erfahren, wer es ist: David" (Dietrich,
Samuel, 6).

2. See p. 173.

3. Deuteronomy 17:14–15 stresses that the future king must be an Israelite.

prophecy delivered to David after he commits adultery with Bathsheba. After Nathan artfully exposes the depth of David's fall, he adds these words to signal that the future will bring a disastrous reversal of David's actions: "I am going to raise up evil against you from your house; I will take your wives before your eyes, and give them to your neighbor (רֵעַ), and he shall lay with your wives in the sight of this very sun" (2 Sam 12:11). This prophetic pronouncement is then fulfilled when David's son Absalom sleeps with his father's concubines on the roof of a palace, and thus in the sight of all Israel, in 2 Sam 16:22. Therefore, if we stay within the contours of the narrative as presented up to this point, Jonathan is at least a plausible answer to the riddle of 1 Sam 15:28, especially when the refusal in ch. 15 concerns Saul as an individual. Saul failed to carry out *ḥerem* with complete obedience, which cost him the kingship. It is plausible to suggest that his throne will be occupied by someone who has already demonstrated faith and courage in battle.[4] This person could be his son.

Conclusion concerning the Experiment

In our experimental version of the text, Saul is rejected by the deity only in ch. 15, and this makes good sense within the narrative. Samuel learns that YHWH repents that he had made Saul king only after the battle with Amalek. Both Samuel and YHWH struggle with Saul's failure. Saul's rejection simply took place *on that day*.

Saul's earlier actions in the battle with the Philistines showed that in some sense he lacked the daring qualities of his son, but neither the story of the lot, nor Saul's successes in battle and in life, prepare the reader for his bitter ordeal in ch. 15. Once Saul is rejected, however, Jonathan's abilities are seen in a new light. When one reads the narrative without 1 Sam 13:7b–15a, and reaches the point where Samuel speaks about a fellow Israelite who is better than Saul, Jonathan becomes a plausible person to fulfill this role.

This interpretation, however, changes dramatically when the story is read in its canonical form and Saul is already rejected by the deity before his battle with the Philistines. In order to understand better how this segment modifies one's reading of the narrative, I will focus first on the interpretation of the segment 1 Sam 13:7b–15a itself and then put forward my evaluation of Saul's portrayal as it appears in the canonical text.

---

4. Jonathan is not the only one who has a good record in this regard. David will emphasize the same qualities when he is questioned by Saul before his battle with Goliath (1 Sam 17:34–37).

18

1 Samuel 13:7b–15a

The purpose of this section of my study is to attend to the exegetical and interpretative difficulties contained in 1 Sam 13:7b–15a, being the passage describing Samuel's rejection of Saul.[1] It is a key segment in my discussion of Saul's demise and for this reason deserves close attention.

Saul Waiting and Acting
(1 Samuel 13:7b–9)

The beginning of the passage returns to the gathering of the Israelite troops at Gilgal in v. 4. Reacting to the multitude of the Philistines progressing against Israel, many of the Israelites hid or ran away across the Jordan (1 Sam 13:6–7a). Saul, however, was still at Gilgal. The soldiers who remained loyal to their king were in a state of dismay, being portrayed as those who "trembled behind him" (חָרְדוּ אַחֲרָיו, 1 Sam 13:7b).[2] While in the present segment the verb underscores the gravity of the Israelite condition, in connection with ch. 14—where the verb "tremble" (חרד) describes the state of panic in the Philistine camp after Jonathan's attack on their garrison (1 Sam 14:15)—it might suggest that Jonathan's provocation reversed the fortune in the war between the two armies: the Israelites tremble now, but it will be the Philistines who will shudder when the real battle begins.

Saul and his army found themselves in a dire situation that grew worse as time progressed. The text suddenly reveals that Saul is supposed to wait for Samuel: "He waited seven days,[3] the time appointed[4] by

---

1. The word "Gilgal"—also left out in my experimental reading—does not significantly affect the general tenor of the passage and thus will not be included in the present discussion.

2. The Greek text has here the verb ὁ λαὸς ἐξέστη, "the people were amazed." The description of the state of the Israelites thus shifts a little. In the Greek text, the people are "confounded" (thus NETS) or "startled," whereas the MT conveys the sense of fear and despair. The Greek verb ἐξίστημι is typically used by the LXX where the MT has חרד in 1 Samuel (e.g. 1 Sam 4:13; 14:15; 16:4; 21:2; 28:5).

3. The verb יחל ("wait") in the beginning of v. 8 is written in Niphal as וַיִּיחֶל (similarly Gen 8:12). The *Qere* suggests the Hiphil form וַיּוֹחֶל, attested in 1 Sam 10:8 and 1 Sam 18:14. There is, however, no apparent difference in meaning between the two forms.

4. The noun used here is מוֹעֵד, which generally means either an appointed "time" or "meeting" (*HALOT* 1:557–58). In connection with seven days, it likely defines a specific period determined by the prophet (besides the references mentioned above, see also 1 Sam 9:24 and 20:35). The LXX translates it here and in v. 11 with μαρτύριον, meaning

Samuel,[5] but Samuel did not come to Gilgal, and the people began to scatter from him" (1 Sam 13:8). Saul waits the whole week—the time span determined by Samuel—but the prophet does not arrive at the appointed meeting.[6] This difficult posture of inactivity while facing the danger of the Philistines further thinned Israel's already decimated army, as more troops kept abandoning Saul. At this point it is Samuel, not Saul, who failed in his task.[7] Saul, and Israel with him, seem to be in danger, which calls for some sort of action.

Saul's action of choice is sacrifice. The king gives orders to bring him the burnt offering and peace offerings, and he proceeds to offer the burnt offering (1 Sam 13:9). The reference to the burnt offering (עֹלָה) and peace offering (שֶׁלֶם), as well as the reference to waiting (יחל) for the period of seven days (שִׁבְעַת יָמִים) at Gilgal, provides a connection with Samuel's instruction in 10:8. According to this verse, these offerings were supposed to be brought by Samuel himself: "And you shall go down before me to Gilgal; and I will go down to you to offer burnt offerings and sacrifice peace offerings. Seven days you shall wait until I come to you and will declare to you what to do" (10:8). Based on these parallels, one may reason that Saul's effort to wait for Samuel in 13:8–9 goes back to 10:8. For example, Philip Long defends this literary link when he reasons that Samuel's encouragement to act in 10:7 ("do whatever your hand finds to do") in the vicinity of the Philistine garrison at Gibeah (10:5) is eventually fulfilled by Jonathan when he attacks the Philistines' army at the same place (13:3).[8] According to Long, this act of provocation sets Samuel's command into motion and it is at this point—after the initial attack against the Philistines—that Saul needs to wait for the prophet to perform religious rituals and receive further instructions before the actual war breaks out.[9]

"testimony." This choice, influenced possibly by the expression "tent of meeting" (אֹהֶל מוֹעֵד in Hebrew; ἡ σκηνή τοῦ μαρτυρίου in Greek), is in congruence with two other translations of מוֹעֵד in 1 Samuel (9:24 and 20:35). See Grillet et al., *Premier livre des Règnes*, 242–43.

5. The Hebrew text contains אֲשֶׁר שְׁמוּאֵל ("that Samuel"). The verb seems to have dropped out. Driver suggests שָׂם ("put, appoint"), which I follow (Driver, *Notes*, 100). Another possibility is to take the Greek text into consideration (ὡς εἶπεν Σαμουηλ) and to propose אָמַר (Budde, *Samuel*, 87).

6. At least this seems to be the prima facie meaning. However, for some commentators it is unclear whether "we have simply reached the seventh day, or whether the seventh day has elapsed" (e.g. Firth, *Samuel*, 154). While this possibility remains open, the wording of v. 8 seems to justify Israel's king as he did what he was asked to do. Thus, I agree with Fokkelman, who notes: "Saul is keeping to both the spirit and the letter of the agreement" (Fokkelman, *Crossing*, 36).

7. Polzin characterizes Samuel negatively, as somebody who continually lacks the proper insight into God's plan. In his view, YHWH's choice of David is primarily a correction of Samuel, not of Saul (Polzin, *Samuel*, 130–31, esp. 131).

8. Long, *Reign*, 51–66.

9. Long, *Reign*, 60–65.

As I have indicated earlier,[10] the two texts are separated by a narratival and chronological gap. It seems improbable that the instruction to wait for Samuel—issued several chapters earlier during Saul's youth—would still be in effect some ten or twenty years later. The narratival and temporal gap may suggest that the passage 1 Sam 13:7b–15a is the work of a later editor who inserted it into the text in an attempt to tie Saul's involvement in the battle against the Philistines with the failure to annihilate the Amalekites in ch. 15.[11] Nevertheless, when one wants to read the narrative synchronic-ally, the connecting points between 1 Sam 10:8 and 13:8 indicate that the link still seems the most plausible literary explanation of Saul's problem in the present passage.[12]

Samuel's Arrival
(1 Samuel 13:10–12)

Ironically, Samuel arrives as soon as Saul finishes presenting the burnt offering, and Saul goes out to meet him and bless him (1 Sam 13:10). Saul's innocent approach towards Samuel is reminiscent of his welcome of the prophet in 1 Sam 15:13. This echo naturally evokes the events of ch. 15 where the topic of sacrifice also plays a prominent role and Saul fails in his obedience to Samuel's charge (1 Sam 15:3). If one is aware of this connec-tion, Saul's optimistic gesture towards the prophet may be viewed with suspicion. Nevertheless, within the section itself, Saul seems to be justified to greet the prophet with confidence. He was facing an army overwhelm-ingly larger and better equipped than his own, his men were deserting him, and he waited for the allotted amount of time prescribed by Samuel.

When Samuel arrives, he asks only a brief question: "What have you done?" (1 Sam 13:11a). Saul, in turn, offers a lengthy rationalization of his deed, which consists of three points: I saw that the people were scat-tering, you did not come at the appointed time,[13] and the Philistines gathered at Michmash (1 Sam 13:11b). Saul's answer is consistent with the narrator's description of the events in the preceding verses.[14] Saul

---

10. See pp. 122–23.

11. See Wellhausen, *Prolegomena*, 258. Notice also slightly different proposals in Smith, *Samuel*, 93–94; and McCarter, *I Samuel*, 20, 228.

12. It seems more probable than, for example, Tsumura's theory, wherein he suggests that "waiting for seven days" might be a religious custom characteristic of ancient Israel, possibly connected with the cultic site of Gilgal. According to him, "people could 'wait on God at Gilgal for seven days' on many occasions" (Tsumura, *Samuel*, 340–41, esp. 341).

13. I do not think that Saul needs to be viewed negatively here. Klein, for example, suggests this when he considers the emphatic "you" (אַתָּה) an attempt to shift the blame onto Samuel and the people (Klein, *1 Samuel*, 126).

14. See the comparison between vv. 5, 8, and 11 provided by Polzin, *Samuel*, 129. Murphy comments that "Saul gives three perfectly understandable reasons for flouting Samuel's instruction" (Murphy, *1 Samuel*, 110).

does not seem to bluff or deceive, but candidly explains to the prophet what has been taking place at Gilgal. Verse 12, however, supplements what the reader already knows with the additional insight into Saul's motivation for sacrificing the burnt offering.[15] He says: "Now the Philistines will come down upon me at Gilgal and I have not entreated the face of YHWH. So I forced myself and offered the burnt offering" (1 Sam 13:12). In my opinion, this important verse adds at least three additional pieces of information that are important for our understanding of Saul's view of the situation at Gilgal.

First, Saul is afraid of the imminent attack from the Philistines' camp. Although the assault will not happen immediately, as one knows from the rest of 1 Sam 13—where the two armies faced each other and the Philistines used their dominance to plunder the Israelite land—Saul still has good reasons to worry about the Philistine threat. Saul's men are scattering in fear, and the king has to do something to prepare for the ensuing conflict.

Second, Saul exposes his rationale for offering the sacrifices when he says: "and I have not entreated the face of YHWH" (וּפְנֵי יְהוָה לֹא חִלִּיתִי). The phrase "to entreat the face of YHWH" usually conveys the meaning of beseeching God's favor.[16] Although the idiom might be used in situations when one wants to manipulate God,[17] in many examples it describes a request in which the petitioner implores YHWH's help in a time of trouble, and the phrase is evaluated by the surrounding literary context positively.[18] In Saul's situation, it is an understandable religious strategy to achieve success in a battle where the odds are clearly against Israel.[19]

---

15. Verse 12 seems to narrate Saul's inner thoughts: "I said" (וָאֹמַר).

16. The verb חלה in its Piel form means "make weak" or "soften" (see *HALOT* 1:317). Perhaps for this reason, Klein suggests that Saul wanted to "put God in a gentle mood" (Klein, *1 Samuel*, 126). The connection with gaining God's favor can be seen in Ps 119:58 and Mal 1:9.

17. Firth views Saul as trying to manipulate YHWH based on the use of the phrase in texts such as 1 Kgs 13:6, where he translates it "mollify" (Firth, *Samuel*, 155). In Firth's view, the story of the ark in 1 Sam 4 already showed that such an approach is unacceptable. He summarizes: "The tragedy of Saul's action is that he offered the sacrifice to mollify Yahweh, when it was his willingness to wait in the face of the Philistine threat that would have demonstrated his commitment to Yahweh's way" (Firth, *Samuel*, 157). However, Jeroboam's request to the anonymous man of God to entreat for his withered hand in 1 Kgs 13:6 does not need to bear negative overtones. Rather, it can describe a well-motivated effort to change God's verdict. See, for example, Keith Bodner, *Jeroboam's Royal Drama* (Oxford: Oxford University Press, 2013), 106. It seems to me that it is Firth's overall negative assessment of Saul that leads him to view even this detail suspiciously.

18. Besides the verses quoted above, note Exod 32:11; 2 Kgs 13:4; 2 Chr 33:12; Jer 26:19; and Zech 8:21, 22.

19. As Gordon puts it: "Saul's concern that he had not entreated Yahweh's favour could be pious or prudential; no king liked going into battle without first seeking favourable omens" (Gordon, *1 & 2 Samuel*, 134).

Third, Saul's act of sacrifice is prefaced with the verb אפק in Hithpael (אֶתְאַפַּק), which often has the reflexive meaning: "control oneself." This understanding is evident in the story of Joseph in Genesis where it depicts his ability or inability to control himself (Gen 43:31; 45:1). In 1 Sam 13:12, however, Saul does not refrain from doing something, but does the exact opposite: he compels himself to act, just as the NRSV translates at this point: "so I *forced* myself, and offered the burnt offering." This seems like a plausible conjecture even though it would be the only occurrence of this meaning in the Old Testament.[20] In Saul's own words, the difficult situation in which Saul found himself forced him to do something that he was not naturally inclined to try: to offer an imploring sacrifice to the deity.

As the leader of the Israelite army, Saul was in an unenviable position. His men began to desert him when he continued to wait for the arrival of the prophet. Despite apparently enduring the whole specified period of seven days, Samuel failed to appear. Saul thus decided to act. He forced himself to step into the cultic sphere and offered the burnt offering. Although it is possible that some of his acts may be viewed suspiciously, his words mirror the description of the situation offered by the narrator, and his inner motivations seem equally reasonable. None of this, however, has a positive impact on the prophet.

Samuel's Rejection of Saul
(1 Samuel 13:13–14)

Samuel harshly accuses Saul and announces the discontinuation of Saul's dynasty with decisive force:

> And Samuel said to Saul: "You have done foolishly. You have not[21] kept the commandment of YHWH, your God, that he commanded you. YHWH would have established your kingdom over Israel forever, but now your kingdom will not continue. YHWH has sought a man for himself according to his heart and YHWH has commanded him to be a ruler over his people, for you have not kept that which YHWH commanded you." (1 Sam 13:13–14)

This is a crucial piece of the whole segment and therefore requires close consideration. First, Samuel reproves Saul that he has acted foolishly (נִסְכָּלְתָּ),[22] and announces, somewhat surprisingly, that by this deed Saul has

---

20. *HALOT* 1:80 suggests that this opaque meaning of the same verb might be rendered "pluck up courage" or "venture."

21. Some scholars suggest to emend the opening לֹא ("not") to לֻא/לֹא ("if"), which better fits the apodosis כִּי. See McCarter, *I Samuel*, 226; Smith, *Samuel*, 99; and Budde, *Samuel*, 87. However, Samuel's pronouncement is understandable without this change.

22. The Hebrew verbal root סכל often describes actions that show the lack of the appropriate knowledge of God and/or the inability to discern what is right and beneficial for the given situation. See 1 Sam 26:21; 2 Sam 24:10; Eccl 7:17; Jer 4:22; 5:21. Here it may refer either to Saul's sacrifice or to the lost chance to establish his dynasty in Israel.

forfeited his opportunity to establish his house in Israel's monarchy. If Saul had acted rightly, YHWH would have established his kingdom over Israel. Under these circumstances, however, Saul's kingship will not continue. Viewed from a certain angle, this statement should perhaps raise suspicion. It may be that the announcement of an enduring dynasty would have been more comprehensible if Saul had established his kingdom, thereby proving to be the right person for the task—perhaps after he won the battle with the Philistines and secured his kingdom from the enemies (1 Sam 14:47–52). In fact, this is what happens in the case of his successor David, to whom YHWH offers an eternal house after David settled in his own house and rested from all his enemies (2 Sam 7:1). However, the pronouncement concerning the discontinuation of Saul's house comes early—literally a few verses after the introduction into his reign (1 Sam 13:1).

Furthermore, it is striking that the promise of a lasting dynasty is referenced only after it is practically nullified. Brueggemann exposes this aspect of Samuel's oracle when he highlights that "the promise was never announced until this moment of rejection, which is too late."[23] Brueggemann thus aptly points out that Saul has learned of the promise only *a posteriori*, when it could not become a motivational force for his behavior. The fact that Saul did not know that he had a chance to have his sons sitting on Israel's throne in perpetuity seems to weaken somewhat the actuality of God's promise.

Despite these two points, Samuel's words imply that Saul and his sons could establish an enduring dynasty in Israel. This is the promise famously given to David: "I will raise your offspring after you, who will come from your body, and I will establish his kingdom. He shall build a house for my name, and I will establish the throne of his kingdom forever (עַד־עוֹלָם)" (2 Sam 7:12–13).[24] At least in terms of potentiality, the same promise was in store for Saul. Despite the difference between YHWH's disposition toward David and that toward Saul (notably spelled out in 2 Sam 7:15),[25] Samuel seems to indicate that Saul has been offered the same promise that will consequently be offered to David.[26]

---

23. Brueggemann, *Samuel*, 100–101, esp. 100.

24. Both 1 Sam 13:13–14 and 2 Sam 7:12 use the cluster of verbs קוּם and כּוּן.

25. However, the unconditional promise given to David is presented with conditions when reiterated to Solomon (1 Kgs 2:4; 8:25; 9:4–9). Notice also the tension between the everlasting oath given to David and the reality of God's rejection of this covenant as expressed by the psalmist in Ps 89:20–53 (ET 89:19–52). The issue remains a vexing problem. Nevertheless, one should remember that the idea of the unconditional covenant with David represents a root of biblical messianism.

26. Brueggemann also stresses this startling aspect after he considers various critical readings of Samuel's words: "On any of these readings of v. 13b the implications are staggering. Samuel's late, conditional promise from Yahweh suggests that the Bible might not have turned out to be a pro-David book but could have been a Saulide document" (Brueggemann, *Samuel*, 101). For the renewed emphasis on the possibility of Saul's dynasty,

Second, the reference to the perpetuity of Saul's kingdom brings into focus his descendants. Saul's disobedience, as evaluated by the prophet, causes the cessation of his dynasty. This is made clear in the insistence on Saul's kingdom, which, suddenly, cannot be established forever (עַד־עוֹלָם) and will not continue (1 Sam 13:13–14a). The phrase עַד־עוֹלָם expresses stability and/or perpetuity, and, as the link with 2 Sam 7:13 shows, it is closely connected with the ability to establish one's dynasty. Nevertheless, the emphasis on endurance and stability does not mean that God's decision cannot be altered. The Saulides, as well as the Elides (1 Sam 2:30), are examples from within 1 Samuel that suggest that the misbehavior of the main representatives of both families caused God to revoke his promise.[27] Saul's house will not continue in Israel because his sons will not be allowed to reign for perpetuity. As McCarter succinctly summarizes: "It is not Saul's reign that is at stake. It is his dynasty."[28]

Third, the part of Samuel's statement that seems to focus on the present and personal consequences of Saul's apparent failure—"YHWH has sought a man for himself according to his heart and YHWH commanded him to be a ruler over his people" (1 Sam 13:14b)—also needs to be viewed in the light of the previous observation. On the one hand, Saul's rejection simultaneously introduces another person's election. YHWH will appoint a leader (נָגִיד)[29] over Israel who will substitute Saul.[30] On the other hand, David remains an outcast and fugitive until Saul dies alongside his sons in battle (1 Sam 31:6), even though David was anointed by Samuel long before this event (1 Sam 16:13). Only after their tragic deaths is David publicly anointed in Hebron (2 Sam 2:4). Furthermore, as Kaminsky points out in his article focusing on the irrevocable nature of Israel's election, Saul remains God's chosen throughout this tumultuous

---

see also Michael Avioz, "Could Saul Rule Forever? A New Look at 1 Samuel 13:13–14," *JHebS* 5 (2005): art. 16, pp. 1–9, https://10.5508/jhs.2005.v5.a16.

27. Tsevat looks closely at some of the dynastic promises made עַד־עוֹלָם and remarks: "The Hebrew words for 'everlasting' or 'steadfast' and related notions do not by and in themselves connote infinitude and absoluteness." See Matitiahu Tsevat, "Studies in the Book of Samuel III. The Steadfast House: What Was David Promised in II Sam. 7:11b–16?," *HUCA* 34 (1963): 71–82, esp. 76.

28. McCarter, *I Samuel*, 229.

29. The difference between נָגִיד and מֶלֶךְ is not clear. With regard to נָגִיד, McCarter suggests that, apart from some exceptions, "the term regularly refers to the king-designate" (McCarter, *I Samuel*, 179). This seems like a reasonable suggestion, but note also Murray's opinion that argues that נָגִיד acts like a vassal of the divine monarch. See Donald F. Murray, *Divine Prerogative and Royal Pretension: Pragmatics, Poetics and Polemics in a Narrative Sequence about David (2 Samuel 5.17–7.29)*, JSOTSup 264 (Sheffield: Sheffield Academic, 1998), 281–301, esp. 299.

30. The reference to נָגִיד connects 1 Sam 13:14 with 1 Sam 10:1 and the moment of Saul's anointing, as it is pointed out, for example, by Otto Kaiser, "Der historische und der biblische König Saul. (Teil II)," *ZAW* 123 (2011): 1–14, esp. 10.

period.[31] David is clearly favored by YHWH—as it is demonstrated through the presence of YHWH's spirit with David (1 Sam 16:13) and the attacks of the evil spirit from the same deity on Saul (1 Sam 16:14)—yet Saul does not lose his special place as Israel's king. At least in David's eyes, Saul is still God's anointed even after his rejection in 1 Sam 13–15 (1 Sam 24:7 [ET 24:6]; 2 Sam 1:14, 16).[32] Saul's rejection takes effect only after his death, and only thereafter does David ascend to Israel's throne instead of one of Saul's sons.

Fourth, at this point in the narrative the reader can only speculate who will be God's next choice: the one portrayed here as a man according to YHWH's heart (כִּלְבָבוֹ). Nevertheless, the present segment effectively narrows down—both in terms of his characteristics and his origin—the pool from which the future candidate for Israel's throne will be chosen. On the one hand, the person who is designated כִּלְבָבוֹ seems to be in need of possessing a certain disposition of the heart. This traditional understanding has been recently challenged by McCarter, who argues that the phrase does not say anything about David's heart but rather is related to God's choice and desire:

> This [phrase] has nothing to do with any great fondness of Yahweh's for David or any special quality of David, to whom it patently refers. Rather it emphasizes the free divine selection of the heir to the throne, as the alternative to the endurance of Saul's kingship over Israel forever.[33]

According to McCarter, the above-mentioned phrase does not indicate anything regarding David's inner quality—which makes him a fitting candidate for Israel's throne—but is instead a reference to God's sovereign choice. God will select a person of his own choosing. McCarter's position has proved to be quite influential,[34] no doubt due to its focus on David's moral lapses, which contradict David's seemingly higher

---

31. Joel S. Kaminsky, "Can Election be Forfeited?," in *The Call of Abraham: Essays on the Election of Israel in Honor of Jon D. Levenson*, ed. Gary A. Anderson and Joel S. Kaminsky (Notre Dame, IN: University of Notre Dame Press, 2013), 44–66, esp. 51–54.

32. Kaminsky views Eli's and Saul's fate similarly and concludes: "Perhaps what we have here is simply a recognition that in ancient Israel, short of death, a king once anointed could not be unanointed or step down" (Kaminsky, "Election," 53).

33. McCarter, *I Samuel*, 229. McCarter references 1 Sam 14:7; Ps 20:5 [ET 20:4]; and Jer 3:15 to support his argument. I would contest 1 Sam 14:7 because I see here a correspondence between the hearts of Jonathan and his armor-bearer ("I am with you according to your heart" [הִנְנִי עִמְּךָ כִּלְבָבֶךָ], that is, "as your heart is, so is mine" [NRSV]), but would add 2 Sam 7:21 in McCarter's support: "Because of your word and according to your heart (וּכְלִבְּךָ) you made all this greatness and to make it known to your servant."

34. Consider: John Goldingay, *Old Testament Theology*. Vol. 1, *Israel's Gospel* (Downers Grove: InterVarsity Press, 2003), 557; Steven L. McKenzie, "Saul in the Deuteronomistic History," in *Saul in Story and Tradition*, ed. Carl S. Ehrlich and Marsha C. White, FAT 47 (Tübingen: Mohr Siebeck, 2006), 62; and Bodner, *1 Samuel*, 170.

moral convictions vis-à-vis Saul.[35] Although this reading has its validity, there are good reasons, in my opinion, to see the future candidate for the Israelite throne as also displaying characteristics that are in line with God's heart.[36] Saul's successor is depicted in 1 Sam 15:28 as someone "better than [Saul]." Furthermore, YHWH's refusal of Eliab, who is portrayed as a person of high stature (resembling Saul),[37] indicates that David's true quality is hidden from normal human perception (1 Sam 16:7).[38] Later biblical tradition describes David's heart as being "wholly with YHWH" in contrast to Solomon, whose heart "was not wholly with YHWH, his God, as was the heart of David, his father (כִּלְבַב דָּוִיד אָבִיו)" (1 Kgs 11:4).[39] Finally, the rejection of the priestly line of the Elides, in a way analogous to Saul's rejection, announces that God will raise up "a faithful priest who will do according to what is in my heart (בִּלְבָבִי) and my soul (וּבְנַפְשִׁי)" (1 Sam 2:35). There seems to be similar inner logic between the two rejections that might indicate that God will seek a person whose heart will be better prepared for the task at hand. The new king, hinted at in 1 Sam 13:14, thus seems to possess inner qualities that will distinguish him from Saul.[40]

Yet the inner characteristics are not the only way in which the text narrows down the group of Saul's potential successors. When my experimental reading of 1 Sam 13–15 is contrasted with the canonical version

---

35. See, for example, Tony W. Cartledge, *1 & 2 Samuel*, SHBC 8 (Macon, GA: Smyth & Helwys, 2001), 174–75.

36. In many ways, in what follows, I am indebted to Johnson's article on this subject. See Benjamin J. M. Johnson, "The Heart of YHWH's Chosen One in 1 Samuel," *JBL* 131 (2012): 455–67.

37. Eliab may be viewed as Saul's stand-in. Saul's extraordinary stature is mentioned in 1 Sam 9:2; 10:23. See Lyle M. Eslinger, "'A Change of Heart': 1 Samuel 16," in *Ascribe to the Lord: Biblical and Other Studies in Memory of Peter C. Craigie*, ed. Lyle M. Eslinger and Glen Taylor, JSOTSup 67 (Sheffield: JSOT Press, 1988), 341–61, esp. 346–47. Bodner, on the other hand, sees Eliab as a corrective figure for Samuel here, or later for David: Keith Bodner, "Eliab and the Deuteronomist," *JSOT* 28 (2003): 55–71.

38. Nevertheless, David's inner quality does not mean that he cannot be of handsome appearance. On the contrary, his beauty is mentioned in 1 Sam 16:12. As Moberly states: "Samuel has to learn that if attractive appearance does not determine God's choice, neither does it preclude it" (Moberly, *Bible*, 107, n. 53).

39. 1 Kings 15:3 similarly compares David and Abijam. Notice also the occurrence of the phrase in Jer 3:15 and the New Testament appropriation of the tradition concerning David's heart where he is portrayed as the one who did what God wanted him to do (Acts 13:22).

40. Although this does not need to mean that he will be morally superior to Saul. Judah is also perhaps less noble than Reuben, yet he is a more practical man, ready to use the opportunity when the time is ripe. I am inclined to agree with Bosworth's brief study of David's portrayal that states that "a critical reading of the Books of Samuel suggests that Yhwh has purposes independent of ethics." See David A. Bosworth, "Evaluating King David: Old Problems and Recent Scholarship," *CBQ* 68 (2006): 191–210, esp. 210.

of the text, one may better see how the present segment stresses that the next leader will not be from Saul's own family. The future king will not be his son Jonathan, who features prominently in the subsequent narrative concerning the battle with the Philistines and is a person of courage and faith—demonstrating perhaps the inner disposition required for the king that should lead Israel in battles. It is only after the war with Amalek in 1 Sam 15 that the reader meets David—the man whose heart is somehow better equipped to face the challenges of being a leader under YHWH (1 Sam 16:7)—yet David's shadow lingers over the present passage despite him not being named here. Jonathan has been disqualified even before he can demonstrate his exemplary qualities because YHWH has rejected his father's house.

Fifth, Samuel says: "You have not kept the commandment of YHWH, your God, which he commanded you" (לֹא שָׁמַרְתָּ אֶת־מִצְוַת יְהוָה אֱלֹהֶיךָ אֲשֶׁר צִוָּךְ, 1 Sam 13:13). Samuel's speech is carefully built around the topic of a commandment,[41] which brings to the forefront the issue of obedience; however, one needs to ask which commandment Saul has overstepped, and the vagueness of Samuel's charge is part of the problem.[42] As I have pointed out, in the present form of the canonical text, it likely has something to do with Samuel's instruction in 1 Sam 10:8.

In general, two possible explanations may be offered for Saul's failure, and these are based on 10:8. First, Saul's sacrifice could be seen as encroaching upon Samuel's authority, since 10:8 attributed the right to offer sacrifices to Samuel.[43] This is possible, but one should remember that David offers both burnt and peace offerings (2 Sam 6:17–18)[44]—an act that apparently did not offend the deity—and, also, Saul builds an altar and offers sacrifices to avert consequences of Israel's sin in the next chapter (1 Sam 14:34–35).[45] The second possibility is that Saul did not wait long enough. Perhaps, as David Gunn suggests, the main point of Samuel's charge was not to wait for seven days, but to wait *until Samuel arrives* ("seven days you will wait until I come to you," 1 Sam 10:8).[46] Possibly Saul's impatience, as well his offering the burnt sacrifice in place of the prophet, explain Samuel's issue with Saul. However, it should be

41. The verb צוה occurs three times in these two verses and the noun מִצְוָה once.

42. Ko tries to illuminate this commandment by viewing it in connection with the Shema (Ko, "Hermeneutics," 57–78).

43. Klein cautiously hints at this explanation (Klein, *1 Samuel*, 127).

44. A peculiar version of Saul's fault is presented by Popović, who suggests that Saul's problem consisted in offering peace offerings that were intended to be used only in the aftermath of the battle, not as preparation for it (Popović, "Fault," 167–68).

45. Berges points out the textual link with Samuel's sacrifice in 1 Sam 7:9, after which YHWH accomplished an unexpected victory over the Philistines, and suggests that whereas Samuel sacrificed peacefully, Saul did so in haste (Berges, *Verwerfung*, 52–53).

46. Gunn, *Saul*, 39.

stressed that 1 Sam 10:8 offers only Samuel's command, not YHWH's,[47] and even if the word of the prophet is so interwoven with the word of God that they cannot be effectively distinguished, one wonders if Saul's actions require such a harsh treatment.

Nevertheless, the topic of disobedience in connection with sacrifice, which seemed incomprehensible in the context of ch. 13, makes more sense when ch. 15 enters the picture. When seen in this light, sacrifice underscores, rather than alleviates, Saul's disobedience. Verses 13–14 of the present chapter thus may be read as an interpretative gloss preparing the reader to attune to the complexities of another ritual sacrifice at the same cultic shrine at Gilgal. It is obedience, not sacrifice, that YHWH desires (1 Sam 15:22).[48]

The key portion of Samuel's oracle in vv. 13–14 raises several important issues pertinent to the interpretation of the canonical text. Saul had a chance to establish his dynasty in Israel for perpetuity. However, due to his disobedience—the contours of which are not altogether clear in the immediate literary context—he has lost this possibility on the day of his first sacrifice at Gilgal. Although it is Saul who is found wanting by the prophet, the rejection issued here pertains primarily to his sons. The new leader will not only demonstrate different internal qualities from those of Saul, but, more importantly, will not be Saulide. Finally, the command that Saul allegedly oversteps links the present segment with ch. 15. In this view, Saul demonstrates disobedience to YHWH's instruction (by offering sacrifice) in both instances.

Samuel's Departure
(1 Samuel 13:15a)

The narrative gives Saul no space to respond. His active role was concluded at v. 12, and his opinion regarding the deed at hand is overshadowed by Samuel and his authoritative pronouncement. It is Samuel who is in charge here, and once he finishes his critique of Saul, the section mentions only Samuel's departure. The Hebrew text of 1 Sam 13:15a says: "And Samuel got up and went up from Gilgal to Gibeah of Benjamin." This conclusion of the episode is somewhat surprising, since the tense dialogue between Samuel and Saul would more naturally lead to a parting of ways between the prophet and king. This way, however, Samuel ends up in a city that

---

47. Exum remarks: "[Samuel's] accusation, 'You have not kept the commandment of Yhwh,' sheds no light on precisely what Saul had done wrong, especially since the narrative records no instructions from Yhwh, but only from Samuel (10:8)" (Exum, *Tragedy*, 27–28). Similarly Middleton, who states: "I can find no rational explanation for Saul's supposed disobedience in ch. 13, beyond Samuel's resentment (Middleton, *Samuel*, 77).

48. Similarly also Kaiser, "König II," 10–11.

is associated with Saul (see 1 Sam 11:4), and to which Saul and his army in fact relocate in v. 16.[49] Interestingly, the Greek text contains a longer version of the story, which mentions only Samuel's departure from Gilgal and, more in line with the continuation of the narrative, moves Saul to Gibeah: "And Samuel got up and departed from Gilgal on his way and the remnant of the people went up behind Saul to meet the people of war. When they came from Gilgal to Gibeah of Benjamin, Saul counted the people."[50] This reading seems to present a better transition to the next passage,[51] but the consequences of this interpretative choice are minimal. Even though the Greek text suggests that the prophet and the king likely parted in their respective destinations (in a way reminiscent of 1 Sam 15:34), the main point of both 1 Sam 13:7b–15a and ch. 15 is Saul's rejection, which, however, does not lead to the imminent cessation of his reign. Samuel leaves and Saul still needs to deal with the Philistine danger. Both rejections in chs. 13 and 15 thus announce God's decision to nullify his promise to Saul while simultaneously leaving him in office.

Summary

The intrusive segment 1 Sam 13:7b–15a significantly changes one's reading of Saul's rejection. Saul is in a desperate situation. Despite being in grave danger from the Philistines and waiting for the prophet (for the time appointed by him), Saul is rejected by Samuel when he appears at Gilgal. Saul's activity may possibly contain some weaknesses, but nothing prepares the reader for Samuel's severe refusal of the king. The link between 1 Sam 10:8 and 13:8 may suggest some underlying reasons for the line that Saul has crossed, but Samuel's vague accusation focusing on the overstepping of YHWH's command seems to set the issue in a different frame of reference. It is in connection with ch. 15 that "the commandment of YHWH" is most intelligible. Therefore, my next step will consist in reading the section 1 Sam 13:7b–15a in connection with the rest of the narrative describing Saul's fall from God's favor, and in offering a canonical interpretation of the story vis-à-vis my experimental reading.

---

49. I rely on my previous discussion where I have suggested that Gibeah and Geba likely refer to the same location (p. 127, n. 11).

50. Driver attempts to reconstruct the possible Hebrew *Vorlage* behind the Greek text and suggests that since the phrase "from Gilgal" occurs twice in the sentence, the text in between could have been left out due to haplography (Driver, *Notes*, 101–2).

51. Pisano states that "the LXX constitutes an excellent narrative bridge, designed to smooth over a contradiction in the text caused by the insertion of the story of Saul's sacrifice" (see Pisano, *Additions*, 182). The Greek text is preferred also by McCarter, *I Samuel*, 227; Klein, *1 Samuel*, 122; and Gordon, *1 & 2 Samuel*, 134. The Hebrew version is favored by Fokkelman, *Crossing*, 43; Polzin, *Samuel*, 131, and Tsumura, *Samuel*, 349.

19

1 Samuel: Evaluation of the Canonical Reading

The segment 1 Sam 13:7b–15a considerably changes one's reading of Saul's rejection. The following are the most important ways in which this portion alters one's interpretation of 1 Sam 13–15.

Saul's Negative Evaluation

When the story is prefaced with events depicted in 1 Sam 13:7b–15a, Saul is portrayed more negatively in the narrative than in the experimental version of chs. 13–15. This affects the way in which one reads the story in several ways. First, one may read the conflict with the Philistines differently. On the one hand, Saul's positive assessment (which was visible, for example, when he prevented a further sacrilege by erecting an altar and by sacrificing animals on it [1 Sam 14:33–35]) could be overshadowed by the prophet's negative reaction to Saul's apparent misuse of sacrifice in chs. 13 and 15. Similarly, Saul's military successes, which receive attention in 1 Sam 14:47–52, may be underappreciated in light of Saul's hesitant tactic towards the Philistines in chs. 13 and 14, or may be otherwise read almost as a conclusion of Saul's career.[1]

On the other hand, since Samuel has rejected Saul's dynasty, Jonathan is not a viable option for Israel's kingship despite his positive appraisal in chs. 13–14. Consequently, his courageous faith is seen as merely anticipating something about a certain type of person whom YHWH favors; this is possibly a prefigurement of the one who will eventually become Saul's successor and who will, in the same way as Jonathan, fight Israel's battles in Saul's place.[2] Therefore, Jonathan may help the reader to come to terms with David's succession of Saul.[3]

---

1. Stoebe suggests this reading in Stoebe, *Samuelis*, 278.

2. As I have pointed out earlier, the contrast with the largeness of the Philistine army with their more advanced weaponry in ch. 13 evokes the description of a Philistine giant named Goliath in 1 Sam 17 awaiting an Israelite ready to meet him on the battleground (p. 132, n. 36).

3. For a thoughtful engagement with this issue see David Jobling, *The Sense of Biblical Narrative*, 2nd ed., 2 vols., JSOTSup 7 (Sheffield: JSOT Press, 1986), 1:12–30.

Furthermore, one may see a similar reconfiguration of the material in ch. 15. As with the positive remarks about Saul in chs. 13–14, the markers of immediacy in chs. 15 may also be downplayed when read in the canonical version of the text. The reference to *this day* (1 Sam 15:28) may be read metaphorically, indicating the urgency of this new situation, or as yet another step in the downward spiral of Saul's fall. In portraying Samuel's emotional reaction (1 Sam 15:11, 35), the narrative here may be viewed as allowing space for the narrator's perspective on the prophet's feelings—a perspective perhaps not fitting the matter-of-fact report in ch. 13. Samuel's anger and mourning may also be symptoms of coming to terms with the finality of Saul's rejection. In short, when one reads ch. 15 with the knowledge of Samuel's rejection of Saul, one is predisposed to view Saul negatively. This opens the way for a closer consideration of the topic of obedience to YHWH's command, which is central for both 1 Sam 13:7b–15a and ch. 15.

To Obey Is Better than Sacrifice

The connection between disobedience and sacrifice that is evident in 1 Sam 13:7b–15a may become an interpretative lens through which one may gain greater clarity concerning the events of ch. 15, where the reasons for ignoring the ban in favor of sacrificing the Amalekite animals may be interpreted as pious. Saul himself connects the decision to capture Agag and the best of the Amalekite animals alive with obedience to YHWH (1 Sam 15:20–21). Furthermore, as I have tried to argue, Saul's ambiguous actions in ch. 15 could have resulted from the happenings in ch. 14, where sparing someone from the divine verdict did not lead to any severe circumstances. When one approaches the narrative from this angle, then it is plausible to view Saul as a mistaken, albeit devout, leader who tries his best to learn from his actions and please God.

Much changes, however, when the narrative is read in dialogue with Saul's first sacrifice in 1 Sam 13:7b–15a, where the offering of the burnt sacrifice is labeled as an act of disobedience towards YHWH (1 Sam 13:13). Although the precise content of this command is not explicit, the prophet's resolute denouncement hangs over the narrative that follows. Saul has already failed in his obedience to YHWH's command, and therefore it is not surprising that he is lax in obeying the deity again. The place (Gilgal) and the occasion (sacrifice) are the same. It is not hard to imagine that the problem (disobedience) may also be the same in both cases. Saul's problem in ch. 13, when seen through the lens of ch. 15, may be seen as befitting Samuel's exclamation: "To obey is better than sacrifice" (1 Sam 15:22).[4]

---

4. Hertzberg touches on something similar when he says: "It is [the compiler's] purpose to show that Saul's kingship was perverted right from the beginning; the first king

The section 1 Sam 13:7b–15a creates a shadow under which one reads the remainder of Saul's story—with an eye on Saul's fault.

David's Shadow

The biggest shift takes place, however, in understanding Saul's rejection and assessing the possible identity of his successor. It is by no means peculiar that, in the canonical rendering of the narrative, Saul is rejected twice. It is this tension between the two rejections that creates an interpretative conundrum akin to the tension between the portrayal of Judah and Joseph in the Genesis material. One way to do justice to the existence of this double rejection in the narrative is to interpret the first instance in ch. 13 as a rejection of Saul's dynasty and to see the second occurrence in ch. 15 as a refusal of Saul as a person. This position is expressed, for example, by David Firth when he introduces his interpretation of ch. 15:

> The second stage of Saul's rejection is reached. Ch. 13 saw the loss of dynastic status, but Saul remained as king. Although ch. 14 showed some successes, it was still critical of his leadership, especially compared with Jonathan. Just as Saul moved towards the throne through three key stages (anointing, acclamation, battle victory), his removal takes three stages (loss of dynasty, announcement of loss of rule, and death).[5]

Firth connects the beginning of Saul's reign with its end. As the narrative portrays Saul ascending to Israel's throne in three stages (10:1; 10:20–24; 11:25), his removal is also portrayed as happening three times; in each case Saul is assisted by Samuel. In 13:7b–15a, Saul loses the possibility to establish his dynasty in Israel. Chapter 15 then narrates the loss of his rule. Finally, when Saul encounters his prophet the last time, he hears of his own impending death (28:18–19).

This interpretation has much to commend it, since the rejection of Saul in ch. 15 concerns Saul personally. However, its weakness lies in the observation that Saul retains his chosenness until his death.[6] Saul's rule may be rejected in ch. 15, and yet he reigns over Israel until he dies at the battle on Mount Gilboa.

Another possibility is to see the two rejections as occurring in stages. Hertzberg, for example, uses the analogy in which he portrays the first rejection as a bolt of lightning from the storm that was about to come.[7] Alternatively, the first rejection opens up the tension between Samuel/

---

trod a path with which the Lord was not pleased. This theological verdict is made on the strength of the Gilgal episode and is put before the period of Saul's reign like a clef on a music stave" (Hertzberg, *Samuel*, 106).

    5. Firth, *Samuel*, 171.

    6. As highlighted by Kaminsky, "Election," 52–53

    7. Hertzberg, *Samuel*, 124.

YHWH and Saul, and the second spells out the problem in detail. Again, this is a reasonable solution for a difficult problem—one that takes seriously the greater weight that the second rejection receives in the canonical text. Nevertheless, this kind of approach does not develop the difference between the rejection of Saul's house in 1 Sam 13:7b–15a and that of Saul himself in ch. 15.

Regardless of how we adjudicate the seeming conundrum within the present arrangement of the texts, the most important message seems to be that the identity of the new king—the neighbor better than Saul—must exist beyond the text we have read so far. Jonathan is disqualified, and one therefore needs to read further to learn about the person who will better fit God's image for Israel's leader.

On Reading the Narrative of Saul's Rejection

I hope that my thought experiment has helped to uncover something of the depth of the text at hand and has offered a fresh perspective regarding its interpretation. By way of conclusion, I would like to suggest ways in which this segment of 1 Sam 13:7b–15a makes a difference in the overall treatment of the story, focusing on the moral objections connected to Saul's rejection.

The segment in 1 Sam 13:7b–15a aggravates moral difficulties which one has with YHWH's rejection of Saul. Prefacing the story with the rejection of Saul thus allows for a more critical assessment of YHWH—or of his prophet—in the narrative of Saul's fall. When one learns so early into Saul's story about Samuel's unclear, albeit forceful, accusation, it is easier to suggest that either God or Samuel were for some reason against Saul from the start.[8] The canonical ordering of the material makes this interpretation an understandable reading strategy.

Nevertheless, a different approach opens up when one notices how the first rejection clears the way for the election of David later in the narrative. Jonathan will not become Saul's successor, nor can Saul hold on to his throne. It is David—who is hinted at in the narrative even before he appears on the scene—who will be a man according to God's heart. Also, looking back from this later point of view, the possible insertion in 1 Sam 13:7b–15a makes sense. Saul's choice of sacrifice is not the outworking of his devotion to YHWH, but instead it is due to his disloyalty.

This might, in turn, suggest that one fruitful way to read the canonical text of 1 Samuel, which may alleviate some of the problems associated with Saul's rejection, is to read it backwards (in a manner of speaking). Some clues in the text can be appreciated and more fully comprehended

---

8. See the studies mentioned on p. 182, n. 136.

only when they are read with the knowledge of the story's end. Stephen Chapman argues for something analogous when commenting on the relationship between 1 and 2 Samuel. He suggests that

> the style of the Samuel narrative typically involves spare storytelling without much explicit editorial intervention. Yet as the story continues, additional details and episodes play a retrospective role, compelling the reader to revisit earlier portions of the narrative and to pose new questions. This peculiar art of the storytelling leads readers to construct provisional reading strategies (or interpretations), which are then either sustained or rejected, confirmed or disconfirmed by the subsequent narrative. . . . Thus considerable skill is required for a sensitive reading of any particular passage in 1 Samuel because in a real sense one cannot interpret a single passage adequately without having a provisional understanding of the entire book.[9]

What Chapman proposes for reading 1 Samuel, and for interpreting both books attributed to Samuel together, I have applied when approaching the story of Saul's reign in 1 Sam 13–15. One can make fuller sense of the story's plot when the conventional straightforward reading is supplied with an understanding of how the storyline finishes. It is perhaps not beneficial to pit these approaches against each other. It is interesting that Gunn's work, for example, draws its strength precisely from the straightforward reading of the narrative. When one considers Saul as not guilty in ch. 13—for which the ambiguity of Samuel's command certainly allows—one is more inclined to view Saul as correspondingly honest, albeit confused, in ch. 15.[10] Something similar can be observed when one reads the story backwards. Saul's disobedience at Gilgal, which also involves sacrifice, informs one's reading of the peculiar episode in 1 Sam 13:7b–15a. The resulting *second narrative*[11] then adds a slightly different perspective to the linear interpretation of the text. A theologically robust reading that is attentive to the convoluted nature of the biblical text thus benefits from both approaches. One ought, first, to follow the story as it develops, and then reread the narrative with the guidance of the story's denouement.

9. Chapman, *1 Samuel*, 64–65.

10. See Gunn, *Saul*, 56.

11. For grounding of this approach, see David C. Steinmetz, "Uncovering a Second Narrative: Detective Fiction and the Construction of Historical Method," in *The Art of Reading Scripture*, ed. Ellen F. Davis and Richard B. Hays (Grand Rapids: Eerdmans, 2003), 54–65.

20

Conclusion

In the hope that this study will contribute to the current discussion of election in the Old Testament, I have focused on two Old Testament narratives: Joseph's story in Gen 37–50 and the tale of Saul's reign in 1 Sam 13–15. I have observed that both narratives contain certain passages—Gen 38 and 49 in the Joseph story and 1 Sam 13:7b–15a in the Saul narratives—that seem intrusive in their literary context. I acknowledge that certainly there are other smaller passages, both within and outside of these texts, that may have been under the influence of later editorial work. Additionally, it is also possible that some material may have dropped out, and this possibility could also be examined (the transition between 1 Sam 10 and 11 comes to mind). Nevertheless, it seems to me that the awkwardness of these larger segments within these narratives, which more obviously relate to the notion of chosenness, justifies my decision to examine their impact upon the final form of the text. The bulk of the study has consisted of a thought experiment. I have read these two narratives first without and then with these intrusive segments, in order to see what difference their placement and message might make to the picture of election presented.

This concluding chapter of my book will attempt to bring together and expound upon the most important findings from my thought experiments concerning the material in Genesis and 1 Samuel. However, before I proceed further, I want to issue a few words of caution. First, there undoubtedly are differences between the two experiments, the most significant probably being the difference in the length and focus of the two texts under investigation. Whereas Gen 37–50 comprises the whole story of Joseph and his brothers, in which one can find the full scope of interplay between the chosen Joseph and his unfavored brother Judah, 1 Sam 13–15 consists of only one, albeit important, portion of the Saul narratives, in which David is never explicitly mentioned. Nevertheless, as I have argued, David's future appearance is alluded to in the canonical version of 1 Sam 13–15. Furthermore, a treatment of the full range of Saul's stories (not to mention David's) would go far beyond the scope of the present study, since the textual complexities of chs. 13–15 are so extensive that their adequate treatment has required a space more or less equivalent to that devoted to the study of the longer Joseph cycle. For these reasons, I narrowed down my second thought experiment to the exposition of 1 Sam 13–15.

My second remark attempting to nuance the argument concerns the way in which my analysis contributes to formulating an interpretation of the final version of the biblical text. Due to the experimental nature of my approach, my conclusions necessarily carry hypothetical overtones. There is no direct evidence that the narratives underwent the redactional process presupposed in this study, and both narratives can, of course, be read in a number of different ways. Nevertheless, I hope that my two thought experiments may contribute something valuable towards the understanding of the canonical version of these multifaceted texts and the notion of election in the Old Testament more generally. As noted in the introductory chapter, in this study I have had two overarching goals: one theological and the other hermeneutical. To a summary of these I now turn.

Hermeneutical Concern

Reading Backwards

The bulk of this study has consisted in two thought experiments in which I read the materials of Genesis and 1 Samuel first without and then with the intrusive segments of Gen 38 and 49, and 1 Sam 13:7b–15a. These segments – both of which, interestingly, deal with unfavored characters, Judah and Saul—are often regarded as later insertions into the text. In this work I have tried to illustrate the usefulness of these historical-critical observations and to use them for a theologically robust reading of the narrative, as they become clues to the depth of the biblical material involved. In particular, as these segments appear to have been written with a knowledge of Judah's and David's future election, stemming from traditions that appeared later than those captured in the stories themselves, they may be seen as suggesting that one fruitful way of reading these complex stories is to read them, so to speak, backwards. More specifically, a reading that is attuned to the compositional depth of these narratives will combine a linear approach with a complementary method that rereads the narratives with an eye on their future denouement. Such a robust interpretation will not be simplistic – that is, reading the crucial stories of Israel's religious and political life as developing only from beginning to end—nor will it overwhelm the earlier stories with their later progress. A theologically rich approach will benefit from a dialogue between both linear and backwards readings that mirrors the development of the texts themselves.

If my conclusions are along the right lines, then these thought experiments may say something significant about the nature of biblical interpretation as such. Both the Joseph cycle and the Saul narratives seem to be retold with awareness that later developments did not reflect what seemed to be indicated in the way the story line was originally narrated. Ephraim is not, after all, the tribe out of which Israel's beloved monarch comes, and Jonathan did not become king after his father's rejection.

On the contrary, it is the tribe of Judah and a young man from Bethlehem named David that become God's choices for leading Israel. These cases of future elections were so fundamental to the identity of God's people that the Joseph cycle and the Saul narratives were rewritten so as to hint at the ultimate choice of Judah and David as understood in the later tradition.[1] These two narratives are thus witnesses to the composers of the biblical material not being afraid to modify earlier texts so as to guide the reader towards the culmination of those elements crucial to Israel's self-understanding: elements associated with the idea of chosenness.

On Reading the Old Testament

Two further observations come to mind concerning the way biblical texts are construed. Regarding the first, R. W. L. Moberly has already argued something similar concerning the relationship between Genesis and Mosaic Yahwism. In his book *The Old Testament of the Old Testament*, he suggests that the tension between the disclosure of God's covenant name YHWH to Moses in Exod 3:14 (and 6:3) and the frequent occurrence of this name in the earlier stories of the book of Genesis (for example, in Gen 4:26) might be explained as a deliberate modification of the Genesis material from the position of Mosaic Yahwism so that the God of the patriarchs would be seen as the same deity as the one that was later revealed to Moses.[2] Thus, concern as to the identity of God in the Pentateuch gave rise to the attempt to retell the preceding tradition in order to guide the reader towards understanding more easily that the God who met Moses in the desert and later delivered the Israelites out of Egypt is the same God that had chosen their forebears. In a similar way, the Genesis and 1 Samuel narratives contain segments that serve as pointers to the choice of Judah

---

1. Although my study has been driven predominantly by theological and hermeneutical concerns, it may also have some implications for socio-historical issues. If my thought experiments reveal something intrinsic to the composition of Old Testament narratives, it may then be suggested that the editors responsible for these putative insertions wished to highlight the choice of Judah and David, in narratives that originally centered on the important figures from the north (Joseph and Saul). While this hypothesis may be at odds with some more prevalent compositional theories (e.g. the documentary hypothesis and the Deuteronomistic History), it has some notable resonances with certain recent attempts to reconstruct the prehistory of the Old Testament. For example, both Daniel Fleming and Jacob Wright—each with a different approach and varying emphases – argue that the canonical text of the Old Testament is dominantly Judah's book, which incorporates earlier Israelite traditions and makes them their own. See Daniel Fleming, *The Legacy of Israel in Judah's Bible: History, Politics, and the Reinscribing of Tradition* (New York: Cambridge University Press, 2012); and Jacob L Wright, *David, King of Israel, and Caleb in Biblical Memory* (New York: Cambridge University Press, 2014). In general terms this is in agreement with my own findings. The socio-historical implications of my thought experiment may thus provide a fruitful ground for future study.

2. Moberly, *Old Testament*, esp. 78.

and David as disclosed in later narratives. The choice of a house and an individual different from those initially highlighted in these stories serves to orient the reader towards the identity of Israel's most enduring royal dynasty.

Second, something analogous has been traditionally proposed for the Christian appropriation of the first portion of their sacred Scripture, namely the Old Testament.[3] Of course, Christian tradition does not attempt to edit the Old Testament text. Nevertheless, the mode of the Christian approach to this group of texts is not dissimilar. What is recognized as God's election of Christ—who is understood to be the Davidic king (e.g. Matt 1:1; Rom 1:3; 2 Tim 2:8; Rev 3:7) from the tribe of Judah (e.g. Matt 1:2–3; Heb 7:14; Rev 5:5)—is so crucial for Christian self-understanding that it is used as an interpretative lens to guide one's reading of the Old Testament. A theologically fruitful Christian interpretation, then, reads the first portion of the Christian Scripture both forward and backward, and from the ensuing dialogue construes a theology sensitive both to New and Old Testaments. It seems to me that it is not without interest both to Christian and Jewish tradition that such an approach is already exemplified in the Old Testament itself, and—at least in the Joseph cycle and 1 Sam 13–15—is focused on the concept of election.

Theological Concern

Election and Kingship

The detailed analysis of the two biblical narratives under consideration required sufficient space in order to be convincing. This strategy has necessarily pushed the topic of election to the margins throughout the bulk of the book. Nevertheless, the notion of chosenness not only provided a significant impetus for my study but remained, I believe, a strong undercurrent throughout the analysis itself. Now it is time for this idea to resurface and receive fuller shape.

It should be emphasized that when one compares the experimental and canonical readings, one must be careful not to oversimplify the issue. The alternate versions of the two narratives under consideration do not simply shift their key characters from negative to positive (in Judah's case) or from positive to negative (in Saul's case). These narratives are much more nuanced and complex than that. Nevertheless, as I argued in the previous chapter, the canonical version of 1 Sam 13–15 effectively darkens Saul's portrayal, while the experimental version of the same story presents Saul in a better light. Similarly, the canonical text of the Joseph story presents Judah in a more positive light than does the experimental version. However, as I argue, if the notion of chosenness in these texts concerns

---

3. Moberly similarly discusses the relationship between the New and Old Testament in Moberly, *Old Testament*, 125–30.

kingship, then the difference between the two versions of each story is more significant. When Gen 37–50 is read without chs. 38 and 49, Joseph is portrayed as favored by his father and the deity, and remains a chosen son throughout. Furthermore, the hints of kingship present in the narrative seem to suggest that the future king will come from his seed, specifically from his younger and more favored son Ephraim. But when the recounting of Joseph's adventures in Egypt is preceded by that of Judah's sojourn in Canaan (where the latter gained two sons through a similarly peculiar twist of chosenness), and when Judah is portrayed in ch. 49 as the subject of his brothers' obeisance, one may conclude—in line with many later Old Testament narratives—that the future monarch will come through the tribe of Judah and the house of Perez. In a similar way, when one reads 1 Sam 13–15 without Saul's first rejection, his son Jonathan may be seen as the natural candidate to be Saul's successor. Only when the narrative is read with Saul's rejection in 1 Sam 13:7b–15a does one understand that God's rejection concerns not only Saul but Saul's dynasty, thus compelling the reader to look for the future king beyond the contours of this segment. In conclusion, the notion of chosenness in these narratives focuses on kingship, and the loss of this kind of favor with the inability to establish one's royal dynasty in Israel.

The Fate of the Unfavored

My primary goal has been to illuminate the fate of those who are not favored by God. In the Joseph story, it is Judah who rises from a less fortunate position to a place where he receives a blessing promising the future obeisance of his brothers. Saul undergoes the opposite trajectory. He is selected both by the people and by God, but is eventually rejected as king over Israel. I offer two final points with regard to these developments.

First, the sequences of these stories within the Genesis and 1 Samuel narratives seem to indicate that the notion of election is not something static and unchangeable. On the one hand, although Joseph's own life bears no marks that he has lost his special status, in the future tradition the tribe that gives Israel its favorite king is that of Judah. Thus Judah in a certain sense passes over Ephraim's privileged position as the tribe out of which Israel's kings will come. This turn of events is even more pronounced in the case of Saul, who is rejected by YHWH, and the kingdom, after a long period of waiting and many plots and battles, is given to David. On the other hand, these claims still need to be nuanced. Joseph is not characterized as ever having lost God's favor in the way that Saul did. He is the main character of the tale of Gen 37–50 and his children play an important part in future Israel. Even Saul seems to have retained his special position up to the point of his final denouncement by Samuel shortly before his death. The loss of God's favor is evident only in the lives of Joseph's and Saul's children. The change of status with regard to the kingship thus pertains only to the history of the tribe or house. It is Joseph's tribe and Saul's house that eventually lose their chosen place to their more famous counterparts.

This leads me to my second point. The choosing of Joseph to a lesser degree, and that of Saul to a greater degree, as a leader, in each case is overshadowed in the narrative by those who are later seen as forming the monarchic dynasty in Israel: Judah and David. In the canonical version of Gen 37–50, Joseph's leadership in Egypt and Jacob's special blessing on Ephraim, mirroring God's preference for the younger sibling, are prefaced by Judah's little tale announcing the special birth of Perez, the forefather of King David. Similarly, before one hears of the elaborate blessing given to Joseph in Gen 49, the reader already knows that the brothers will eventually bow down before Judah. The story of Saul's demise in the canonical version exemplifies this feature as well. Saul is rejected shortly into the battle with the Philistines and the prophetic denouncement targets Saul's dynasty, making obscure reference to a man according to God's heart who will occupy Israel's throne after Saul.[4] These segments effectively diminish Joseph's future importance, and darken Saul's portrayal. Yet, Joseph and Saul recede into the background only because space at a critical juncture in each story is given to a more fortunate neighbor. One may even say that their less fortunate position is merely relative.[5] On the one hand, this confirms that God deals with the world primarily through his chosen. Those who are unchosen derive their status from their relationship with the elect, and remain in the elect's shadow. On the other hand, however, this may give some hope for those who are concerned with the fate of the unfavored ones. Perhaps their relative status vis-à-vis those who are chosen is not the last word concerning their destiny.[6] Perhaps there is more to the fate of the unfavored than simply that which is made clear in the biblical narratives, where they remain eclipsed by their chosen neighbors.

---

4. This editorial strategy is analogous to the one explored in Milstein, *Master Scribe.*

5. Could not something of this sort also be applicable to the relationship between the chosen Israel and the unchosen nations? Their portrayal is often underdeveloped and, despite some indications that they have a certain relationship with God, they live their life in the shadow of the chosen people. For the suggestion that Judaism has traditionally been more hospitable to the non-elect than Christianity, see Kaminsky, *Jacob,* 172–77.

6. Saul's story seems to be a case in point. One must read beyond 1 Sam 13–15 to learn of Saul's end. Samuel's third announcement of Saul's rejection in 1 Sam 28 seals his fate. Perhaps unwilling to dissociate his life from his role as Israel's king, he dies prematurely in battle against his enduring foe, the Philistines.

Bibliography

Ackerman, James S. "Joseph, Judah, and Jacob." Pages 85–113 in *Literary Interpretations of Biblical Narratives*. Edited by Kenneth R. R. Gros Louis and James S. Ackerman. Nashville: Abingdon, 1982.

Aejmelaeus, Anneli. "A Kingdom at Stake: Reconstructing the Old Greek—Deconstructing the *Textus Receptus*." Pages 353–66 in *Scripture in Transition: Essays on Septuagint, Hebrew Bible, and Dead Sea Scrolls in Honour of Raija Sollamo*. Edited by Anssi Voitila and Jutta Jokiranta. JSJSup 126. Leiden: Brill, 2008.

Albright, W. F. *Excavations and Results at Tell El-Fûl (Gibeah of Saul)*. AASOR 4. New Haven: ASOR, 1924.

Alt, Albrecht. "God of the Fathers." Pages 3–86 in *Essays on Old Testament Religion*. Translated by R. A. Wilson. Garden City, NY: Doubleday, 1968.

Alter, Robert. *The Art of Biblical Narrative*. New York: Basic Books, 1981.

———. *The David Story: A Translation with Commentary of 1 and 2 Samuel*. New York: Norton, 1999.

———. *Genesis: Translation and Commentary*. New York: Norton, 1996.

Amit, Yairah. "'The Glory of Israel Does Not Deceive or Change His Mind': On the Reliability of Narrator and Speakers in Biblical Narrative." *Proof* 12 (1992): 201–12.

Anderson, Bradford A. *Brotherhood and Inheritance: A Canonical Reading of the Esau and Edom Traditions*. LHBOTS 556. New York: T&T Clark, 2011.

Anderson, Gary A. *Christian Doctrine and the Old Testament: Theology in the Service of Biblical Exegesis*. Grand Rapids: Baker Academic, 2017.

Andrew, M. E. "Moving from Death to Life: Verbs of Motion in the Story of Judah and Tamar in Gen 38." *ZAW* 105 (1993): 262–69.

Arnold, Bill T. *Genesis*. NCBC. New York: Cambridge University Press, 2009.

Arnold, Patrick M. "Gibeah." *ABD* 2:1007–9.

Ashley, Timothy R. *The Book of Numbers*. NICOT 4. Grand Rapids: Zondervan, 1993.

Astour, Michael C. "Tamar the Hierodule: An Essay in the Method of Vestigial Motifs." *JBL* 85 (1966): 185–96.

Auld, A. Graeme. *I & II Samuel: A Commentary*. OTL. Louisville, KY: John Knox, 2011.

———. "Tamar between David, Judah and Joseph." *SEÅ* 65 (2000): 93–106.

Avioz, Michael. "Could Saul Rule Forever? A New Look at 1 Samuel 13:13–14." *JHebs* 5 (2005): art. 16, pp. 1–9. https://doi:10.5508/jhs.2005.v5.a16.

Bar-Efrat, Shimon. *Das erste Buch Samuel: Ein narratologisch-philologischer Kommentar*. Translated by Yvonne Szedlák and Walter Dietrich. BWA(N)T 176. Bern: Kohlhammer, 2007.

Barth, Karl. *Church Dogmatics*. Edited by G. W. Bromiley and T. F. Torrance. 4 vols. Edinburgh: T&T Clark, 1957–75.

Bartor, Asnat. "The 'Juridical Dialogue': A Literary-Judicial Pattern." *VT* 53 (2003): 445–64.

Becking, Bob. "'They Hated Him Even More': Literary Technique in Genesis 37:1–11." *BN* 60 (1991): 40–47.

Bergen, Robert D. *1, 2 Samuel*. NAC 7. Nashville, TN: Broadman & Holman, 1996.

Berges, Ulrich. *Die Verwerfung Sauls: Eine thematische Untersuchung*. FB 61. Würzburg: Echter, 1989.

Bergman, Jan, H. Haag, and Helmer Ringgren. "בֵּן." *TDOT* 2:145–59.

Berlin, Adele. *Poetics and Interpretation of Biblical Narrative*. BLS 9. Sheffield: Almond Press, 1983.

Berlyn, P. J. "His Brother's Keeper." *JBQ* 26 (1998): 73–83.

Berman, Joshua. "Identity Politics and the Burial of Jacob (Genesis 50:1–14)." *CBQ* 68 (2006): 11–31.

———. "*Mishneh bereshit*: The Form and Content of Genesis 48." *Tradition* 25 (1990): 28–41.

Bettenzoli, Giuseppe. "Samuel und das Problem des Königtums: Die Tradition von Gilgal." *BZ* 30 (1986): 222–36.

Bird, Phyllis A. "The Harlot as Heroine: Narrative Art and Social Presupposition in Three Old Testament Texts." *Semeia* (1989): 119–39.

Blachman, Esther. *The Transformation of Tamar (Genesis 38) in the History of Jewish Interpretation*. CBET 71. Leuven: Peeters, 2013.

Blenkinsopp, Joseph. *David Remembered: Kingship and National Identity in Ancient Israel*. Grand Rapids: Eerdmans, 2013.

———. "Jonathan's Sacrilege, 1 Sm 14:1–46: A Study in Literary History." *CBQ* 26 (1964): 423–49.

———. "Theme and Motif in the Succession History (2 Sam. xi 2ff) and the Yahwist Corpus." Pages 44–57 in *Volume du congrès, Genève, 1965*. VTSup 15. Leiden: Brill, 1965.

Bodner, Keith. *1 Samuel: Narrative Commentary*. HBM 19. Sheffield: Sheffield Phoenix, 2008.

———. "Eliab and the Deuteronomist." *JSOT* 28 (2003): 55–71.

———. *Jeroboam's Royal Drama*. Oxford: Oxford University Press, 2013.

Boecker, Hans-Jochen. *Die Josefsgeschichte (Genesis/1. Mose 37–50): Mit einem Anhang über die Geschichte der Tamar (38, 1–30) und die Stammessprüche (49, 1–28)*. Neukirchen-Vluyn: Neukirchener, 2003.

———. "Überlegungen zur 'Geschichte Tamars' (Gen 38)." Pages 49–68 in *"Ihr Völker alle, klatscht in die Hände!": Festschrift für Erhard S. Gerstenberger zum 65. Geburtstag*. Edited by Rainer Kessler, Kerstin Ulrich, and Gary S. Schwantes. EZ 3. Münster: LIT, 1997.

Borgman, Paul. *Genesis: The Story We Haven't Heard*. Downers Grove, IL: InterVarsity Press, 2001.

Bosworth, David A. "Evaluating King David: Old Problems and Recent Scholarship." *CBQ* 68 (2006): 191–210.

———. *The Story within a Story in Biblical Hebrew Narrative*. CBQMS 45. Washington, DC: Catholic Biblical Association of America, 2008.

———. "Weeping in Recognition Scenes in Genesis and *Odyssey*." *CBQ* 77 (2015): 619–39.

Brauner, Ronald A. "'To Grasp the Hem' and 1 Samuel 15:27." *JANESCU* 6 (1974): 35–38.

Brekelmans, C. H. W. *De herem in het Oude Testament*. Nijmegen: Centrale Drukkerij, 1959.

Brueggemann, Walter. *First and Second Samuel*. IBC. Louisville, KY: John Knox, 1990.

———. *Genesis*. IBC. Louisville, KY: Westminster John Knox, 1982.

Budde, Karl D. *Die Bücher Samuel*. KHC 8. Tübingen: Mohr, 1902.

Calvin, John. *Commentary on Genesis*. Translated by John King. 2 vols. Grand Rapids: Baker, 1996.

Campbell, Anthony F. and Mark A. O'Brien. *Unfolding the Deuteronomistic History: Origin, Upgrades, Present Text*. Minneapolis: Fortress, 2000.

Caquot, André. "Ben Porat (Genèse 49:22)." *Sem* 30 (1980): 43–56.

———. "La parole sur Juda dans le testament lyrique de Jacob (Gen 49:8–12)." *Sem* 26 (1976): 5–32.

Carmichael, Calum M. "Some Sayings in Genesis 49." *JBL* 88 (1969): 435–44.

Carmy, Shalom. "The Origin of Nations and the Shadow of Violence: Theological Perspectives on Canaan and Amalek." *Tradition* 39 (2006): 163–99.

Carr, David M. *Reading the Fractures of Genesis: Historical and Literary Approaches*. Louisville, KY: Westminster John Knox, 1996.

Cartledge, Tony W. *1 & 2 Samuel*. SHBC 8. Macon, GA: Smyth & Helwys, 2001.

Cassuto, Umberto. *Biblical and Oriental Studies*. Vol. 1. Jerusalem: Magnes, 1973.

———. *A Commentary on the Book of Exodus*. Translated by Israel Abrahams. Jerusalem: Magnes, 1968.

Chapman, Stephen B. *1 Samuel as Christian Scripture: A Theological Commentary*. Grand Rapids: Eerdmans, 2016.

———. "Martial Memory, Peaceable Vision: Divine War in the Old Testament." Pages 47–67 in *Holy War in the Bible: Christian Morality and an Old Testament Problem*. Edited by Heath A. Thomas, Jeremy Evans, and Paul Copan. Downers Grove, IL: IVP Academic, 2013.

———. "Perpetual War: The Case of Amalek." Pages 1–19 in *The Bible and Spirituality: Exploratory Essays in Reading Scripture Spiritually*. Edited by Gordon J. McConville, Andrew T. Lincoln, and Lloyd K. Pieterson. Eugene, OR: Cascade, 2013.

Childs, Brevard S. *Introduction to the Old Testament as Scripture*. Philadelphia: Fortress, 1979.

———. *The New Testament as Canon: An Introduction*. London: SCM, 1984.

Christensen, Duane L. "Anticipatory Paronomasia in Jonah 3:7–8 and Genesis 37:2." *RB* 90 (1983): 261–63.

Clifford, Richard J. "Genesis 37–50: Joseph Story or Jacob Story?" Pages 213–29 in *The Book of Genesis: Composition, Reception, and Interpretation*. Edited by Craig A. Evans, Joel N. Lohr, and David L. Petersen. VTSup 152. Leiden: Brill, 2012.

Clines, David J. A., ed. *Dictionary of Classical Hebrew*. 9 vols. Sheffield: Sheffield Phoenix Press, 1993–14.

Coats, George W. *From Canaan to Egypt: Structural and Theological Context for the Joseph Story*. CBQMS 4. Washington, DC: Catholic Biblical Association of America, 1976.

———. "Widow's Rights: A Crux in the Structure of Genesis 38." *CBQ* 34 (1972): 461–66.

Cohen, Jeffrey M. "Joseph under Suspicion." *JBQ* 29 (2001): 186–89.

Conrad, Diethelm. "Samuel und die Mari-'Propheten': Bemerkungen zu 1 Sam 15:27." Pages 273–80 in *XVII Deutscher Orientalistentag*. Edited by W. Voight. ZDMGSup 1. Weisbaden: Franz Steiner, 1969.

Coppens, J. "La bénédiction de Jacob: Son cadre historique à la lumiére des paralléles ougaritiques." Pages 97–115 in *Volume du Congrès: Strasbourg 1956*. Edited by G. W. Anderson. VTSup 4. Leiden: Brill, 1957.

Cott, Jeremy. "The Biblical Problem of Election." *JES* 21 (1984): 199–228.

Curtis, A. H. W. "Some Observation on 'Bull' Terminology in the Ugaritic Texts and the Old Testament." Pages 17–31 in *In Quest of the Past: Studies on Israelite Religion, Literature, and Prophetism*. Edited by A. S. van der Woude. Leiden: Brill, 1990.

Czövek, Tamás. *Three Seasons of Charismatic Leadership: A Literary-critical and Theological Interpretation of the Narrative of Saul, David and Solomon*. Oxford: Paternoster, 2006.

Davies, Philip R. "Ark or Ephod in 1 Sam 14:18." *JTS* 26 (1975): 82–87.

Demsky, Aaron. "Dark Wine from Judah." *IEJ* 22 (1972): 233–34.

Dietrich, Walter. *Die Josephserzählung als Novelle und Geschichtsschreibung: Zugleich ein Beitrag zur Pentateuchfrage*. BThSt 14. Neukirchen-Vluyn: Neukirchener, 1989.

———. *Samuel*. BKAT 8/1. Neukirchen-Vluyn: Neukirchener, 2005–10.

———. *Samuel*. BKAT 8/2. Neukirchen-Vluyn: Neukirchener, 2011–12.

Döhling, Jan-Dirk. "Die Herrschaft erträumen, die Träume beherrschen: Herrschaft, Traum und Wirklichkeit in den Josefsträumen (Gen 37,5–11) und der Israel-Josefsgeschichte." *BZ* 50 (2006): 1–30.

Donner, Herbert. *Die literarische Gestalt der alttestamentlichen Josephsgeschichte*. SHAW 2. Heidelberg: Carl Winter, 1976.

Dov Lerner, Berel. "Joseph the Unrighteous." *Judaism* 38 (1989): 278–81.

Dragga, Sam. "In the Shadow of the Judges: The Failure of Saul." *JSOT* 38 (1987): 39–46.

Driver, Godfrey Rolles. "Some Hebrew Roots and their Meanings." *JTS* 23 (1921): 69–73.

———. "Old Problems Re-examined." *ZAW* 80 (1968): 174–83.

Driver, S. R. *The Book of Genesis with Introduction and Notes*. 10th ed. London: Methuen, 1916.

———. *A Critical and Exegetical Commentary on Deuteronomy*. ICC. Edinburgh: T&T Clark, 1902.

———. *Notes on the Hebrew Text and the Topography of the Books of Samuel*. 2nd ed. Oxford: Clarendon, 1913.

Earl, Douglas S. *Reading Joshua as Christian Scripture*. JTI Sup 2. Winona Lake, IN: Eisenbrauns, 2010.

———. *Reading Old Testament Narrative as Christian Scripture*. JTISup 17. Winona Lake, IN: Eisenbrauns, 2017.

Ebach, Jürgen. *Genesis 37–50*. HThKAT 3. Freiburg: Herder, 2007.

Edelman, Diana. "Saul's Battle against Amaleq (1 Sam 15)." *JSOT* 35 (1986): 71–84.

Ehrlich, Arnold B. *Randglossen zur Hebräischen Bibel: Textkritisches, Sprachliches and Sachliches*. Vol. 1, *Genesis und Exodus*. Leipzig: Hinrichs, 1908.

Eissfeldt, Otto. "Silo und Jerusalem." Pages 138–47 in *Volume du Congrès: Strasbourg 1956*. Edited by G. W. Anderson. VTSup 4. Leiden: Brill, 1957.

Emerton, John A. "Examination of a Recent Structuralist Interpretation of Genesis 38." *VT* 26 (1976): 79–98.

———. "Judah and Tamar." *VT* 29 (1979): 403–15.

———. "Some Difficult Words in Genesis 49." Pages 81–93 in *Words and Meanings: Essays Presented to David Winston Thomas*. Edited by Peter R. Ackroyd and Barnabas Lindars. Cambridge: Cambridge University Press, 1968.

———. "Some Problems in Genesis 38." *VT* 25 (1975): 338–61.

Eslinger, Lyle M. "'A Change of Heart': 1 Samuel 16." Pages 341–61 in *Ascribe to the Lord: Biblical and Other Studies in Memory of Peter C. Craigie*. Edited by Lyle M. Eslinger and Glen Taylor. JSOTSup 67. Sheffield: JSOT Press, 1988.

———. *Kingship of God in Crisis: A Close Reading of 1 Samuel 1–12*. Edited by David M. Gunn. Sheffield: Almond Press, 1985.

Exum, Cheryl J. *Tragedy and Biblical Narrative: Arrows of the Almighty*. Cambridge: Cambridge University Press, 1992.

Fabry, Heinz-Jozef and Helmer Ringgren. "מרד." *TDOT* 9:15–19.

Fieger, Michael and Sigrid Hodel-Hoenes. *Der Einzug in Ägypten: Ein Beitrag zur alttestamentliche Josefsgeschichte*. Das Alte Testament im Dialog 1. Bern: Peter Lang, 2007.

Firth, David G. *1 & 2 Samuel*. ApOTC 8. Grand Rapids: InterVarsity Press, 2009.

Fleming, Daniel. *The Legacy of Israel in Judah's Bible: History, Politics, and the Reinscribing of Tradition*. New York: Cambridge University Press, 2012.

Fokkelman, Jan P. "Genesis 37 and 38 at the Interface of Structural Analysis and Hermeneutics." Pages 152–87 in *Literary Structure and Rhetorical Strategies in the Hebrew Bible*. Edited by L. J. Regt, Jan de Waard, and Jan P. Fokkelman. Assen: Van Gorcum, 1996.

———. *Narrative Art and Poetry in the Books of Samuel*. Vol. 2, *The Crossing Fates*. Assen: Van Gorcum, 1986.

Foresti, Fabrizio. *The Rejection of Saul in the Perspective of the Deuteronomistic School: A Study of 1 Sm 15 and Related Texts*. ST 5. Rome: Edizioni del Teresianum, 1984.

Freedman, David N. "Divine Names and Titles in Early Hebrew Poetry." Pages 77–130 in *Pottery, Poetry, and Prophecy: Studies in Early Hebrew Poetry*. Winona Lake, IN: Eerdmans, 1980.

Freedman, David N., J. R. Lundbom, and H.-J. Fabry. "חָנַן." *TDOT* 5:22–36.

Freedman, R. David. "'Put Your Hand under My Thigh'—Patriarchal Oath." *BAR* 2 (1976): 3–4, 42.

Fretheim, Terence E. "Divine Foreknowledge, Divine Constancy, and the Rejection of Saul's Kingship." *CBQ* 47 (1985): 595–602.

Frisch, Amos. "'For I Feared the People, and I Yielded to Them' (I Sam 15,24)—Is Saul's Guilt Attenuated or Intensified?" *ZAW* 108 (1996): 98–104.

Fritsch, Charles T. "'God Was with Him': A Theological Study of the Joseph Narrative." *Int* 9 (1955): 21–34.

Frolov, Serge. "Judah Comes to Shiloh: Genesis 49:10bα, One More Time." *JBL* 131 (2012): 417–22.

Fung, Yiu-Wing. *Victim and Victimizer: Joseph's Interpretation of His Destiny.* JSOTSup 308. Sheffield: Sheffield Academic, 2000.

Geoghegan, Jeffrey C. "Israelite Sheepshearing and David's Rise to Power." *Bib* 87 (2006): 55–63.

Gevirtz, Stanley. "Of Patriarchs and Puns: Joseph at the Fountain, Jacob at the Ford." *HUCA* 46 (1975): 33–54.

Giercke-Ungermann, Annett. "Vom Griff nach dem Obergewand zum Entzug der Königsherrschaft: Überlegungen zu 1 Sam 15,27–29." *BZ* 55 (2011): 75–86.

Goldin, Judah. "Youngest Son or Where does Genesis 38 Belong?" *JBL* 96 (1977): 27–44.

Goldingay, John. *Old Testament Theology: Israel's Gospel.* Vol. 1. Downers Grove: InterVarsity Press, 2003.

Golka, Friedemann W. "Genesis 37–50: Joseph Story or Israel–Joseph Story?" *CurBR* 2 (2004): 153–77.

Good, Edwin M. "'Blessing' on Judah, Gen 49:8–12." *JBL* 82 (1963): 427–32.

Gordon, Robert P. *1 & 2 Samuel: A Commentary.* Exeter: Paternoster, 1986.

———. *I & II Samuel.* Grand Rapids: Regency Reference Library, 1986.

———. "Simplicity of the Highest Cunning: Narrative Art in the Old Testament." *SBET* 6 (1988): 69–80.

———. "Who Made the Kingmaker?: Reflections on Samuel and the Institution of Monarchy." Pages 255–69 in *Faith, Tradition, and History: Old Testament Historiography in Its Near Eastern Context.* Edited by A. R. Millard, James K. Hoffmeier, and David W. Baker. Winona Lake, IN: Eisenbrauns, 1994.

Görg, Manfred. "Der gefärbte Rock Josefs." *BN* 102 (2000): 9–13.

Gosse, Bernard. "Du rejet de Yahvé par Israël au rejet d'Israël et de Juda par Yahvé dans les livres de Samuel et les livres des Rois." *ZAW* 112 (2000): 550–63.

Gottwald, Norman K. *The Tribes of Yahweh.* Sheffield: Sheffield Academic, 1999.

Granado Bellido, Carmelo. "Simbolismo del vestido: Interpretación patrística de Gen 49:11." *EstEcl* 59 (1984): 313–57.

Green, Barbara. *How Are the Mighty Fallen? A Dialogical Study of King Saul in 1 Samuel.* JSOTSup 365. Sheffield: Sheffield Academic, 2003.

———. *What Profit for Us?: Remembering the Story of Joseph.* Lanham, MD: University Press of America, 1996.

Greenspahn, Frederick E. *When Brothers Dwell Together: The Preeminence of Younger Siblings in the Hebrew Bible.* New York: Oxford University Press, 1994.

Greenstein, Edward L. "An Equivocal Reading of the Sale of Joseph." Pages 114–25 in *Literary Interpretations of Biblical Narratives.* Edited by Kenneth R. R. Gros Louis and James S. Ackerman. Nashville: Abingdon, 1982.

———. "The Formation of the Biblical Narrative Corpus." *AJSRev* 15 (1990): 151–78.

Grillet, Bernard, Michel Lestienne, Jean Massonnet, and Anita Méasson. *Premier livre des Règnes.* BdA 9.1. Paris: Cerf, 1997.

Gunkel, Hermann. *Genesis*. Translated by Mark E. Biddle. MLBS. Macon, GA: Mercer University Press, 1997.

Gunn, David M. *The Fate of King Saul: An Interpretation of a Biblical Story*. JSOTSup 14. Sheffield: JSOT Press, 1980.

Gunneweg, Antonius H. J. "Über den Sitz im Leben der sog. Stammessprüche (Gen 49, Dtn 33, Jdc 5)." *ZAW* 76 (1964): 245–55.

Guyette, Fred. "Joseph's Emotional Development." *JBQ* 32 (2004): 181–88.

Haarmann, Volker. *JHWH-Verehrer der Völke: die Hinwendung von Nichtisraeliten zum Gott Israels in alttestamentlichen Überlieferungen*. ATANT 91. Zurich: TVZ, 2008.

Hamilton, Victor P. *The Book of Genesis: Chapters 18–50*. NICOT 2. Grand Rapids: Eerdmans, 1995.

Harl, Marguerite. *La Genèse*. BdA 1. Paris: Cerf, 1986.

Harris, J. S. Randolph. "Genesis 44:18–34." *Int* 52 (1998): 178–81.

Hawk, L. Daniel. "Saul as Sacrifice: The Tragedy of Israel's First Monarch." *BRev* 12 (1996): 20–25, 56.

———. "Saul's Altar." *CBQ* 72 (2010): 678–87.

Heard, Christopher R. *Dynamics of Diselection: Ambiguity in Genesis 12–36 and Ethnic Boundaries in Post-exilic Judah*. SemeiaSt 39. Atlanta: SBL, 2001.

Hecke, Pierre van. "Shepherds and Linguists: A Cognitive-Linguistic Approach to the Metaphor 'God is Shepherd' in Gen 48,15 and Context." Pages 479–93 in *Studies in the Book of Genesis: Literature, Redaction and History*. Edited by André Wénin. BETL 155. Leuven: Peeters, 2001.

Heffelfinger, Katie M. "From Bane to Blessing: The Food *Leitmotif* in Genesis 37–50." *JSOT* 40 (2016): 297–320.

Hensel, Benedikt. *Die Vertauschung des Erstgeburtssegens in der Genesis: Eine Analyse der narrativ-theologischen Grundstruktur des ersten Buches der Tora*. BZAW 423. Berlin: de Gruyter, 2011.

Hertzberg, Hans Wilhelm. *I & II Samuel: A Commentary*. Translated by John Bowden. OTL. London: SCM, 1964.

Ho, Craig Y. S. "The Stories of the Family Troubles of Judah and David: A Study of Their Literary Links." *VT* 49 (1999): 514–31.

Honeyman, A. M. "Matthew V.18 and the Validity of the Law." *NTS* 1 (1954): 141–42.

Hoop, Raymond de. *Genesis 49 in Its Literary and Historical Context*. OtSt 29. Leiden: Brill, 1999.

———. "Genesis 49 Revisited: The Poetic Structure of Jacob's Testament and the Ancient Versions." Pages 1–32 in *Unit Delimitation in Biblical Hebrew and Northwest Semitic Literature*. Edited by Marjo Korpel and Josef Oesch. Pericope 4. Assen: Van Gorcum, 2003.

———. "'Then Israel Bowed Himself...' (Genesis 47.31)." *JSOT* 28 (2004): 467–80.

Huddleston, Jonathan. *Eschatology in Genesis*. FAT 57. Tübingen: Mohr Siebeck, 2012.

Huddlestun, John R. "Unveiling the Versions: The Tactics of Tamar in Genesis 38:15." *JHebs* 3 (2001): art. 7, pp. 1–18. https://doi:10.5508/jhs.2001.v3.a7.

Humphreys, W. Lee. *Joseph and his Family: A Literary Study*. Columbia: University of South Carolina Press, 1988.

Jacob, Benno. *Der erste Buch der Torah Genesis.* Berlin: Schocken, 1934.
———. *The Second Book of the Bible: Exodus.* Translated by Walter Jacob. Haboken, NJ: KTAV, 1992.
Jacobs, Mignon R. "The Conceptual Dynamics of Good and Evil in the Joseph Story: An Exegetical and Hermeneutical Inquiry." *JSOT* 27 (2003): 309–38.
Janzen, David. *The Necessary King: A Postcolonial Reading of the Deuteronomistic Portrait of the Monarchy.* HBM 57. Sheffield: Sheffield Phoenix, 2013.
Jericke, Detlef. *Die Ortsangaben im Buch Genesis: Ein historisch-topographischer und literarisch-topographischer Kommentar.* FRLANT 248. Göttingen: Vandenhoeck & Ruprecht, 2013.
Jobling, David. *1 Samuel.* Berit Olam. Collegeville, MN: Liturgical Press, 1998.
———. *The Sense of Biblical Narrative.* 2nd ed. Vol. 1. JSOTSup 7. Sheffield: JSOT Press, 1986.
Johnson, Benjamin J. M. "Did David Bring a Gun to a Knife Fight? Literary and Historical Considerations in Interpreting David's Victory over Goliath." *ExpTim* 124 (2013): 530–37.
———. "The Heart of YHWH's Chosen One in 1 Samuel." *JBL* 131 (2012): 455–67.
Kaiser, Otto. "Der historische und der biblische König Saul. (Teil II)." *ZAW* 123 (2011): 1–14.
Kallermann, D. "רֵעַ." *TDOT* 13:522–32.
Kaminsky, Joel S. "Can Election be Forfeited?" Pages 44–66 in *The Call of Abraham: Essays on the Election of Israel in Honor of Jon D. Levenson.* Edited by Gary A. Anderson and Joel S. Kaminsky. Notre Dame, IN: University of Notre Dame Press, 2013.
———. *Corporate Responsibility in the Hebrew Bible.* JSOTSup 196. Sheffield: Sheffield Academic, 1995.
———. *Yet I Loved Jacob: Reclaiming the Biblical Concept of Election.* Nashville: Abingdon, 2007.
Kapelrud, Arvid S. "Genesis xlix 12." *VT* 4 (1954): 426–28.
Kass, Leon R. *The Beginning of Wisdom: Reading Genesis.* Chicago: University of Chicago Press, 2003.
Kebekus, Norbert. *Die Joseferzählung: Literarkritische und redaktionsgeschichtliche Untersuchungen zu Genesis 37–50.* Internationale Hochschulschriften. Münster, New York: Waxmann, 1990.
Keil, Carl Fridrich and Franz Delitzsch. *Biblical Commentary on the Books of Samuel.* Translated by James Martin. Edinburgh: T&T Clark, 1880.
Kellermann, D. "צעד." *TDOT* 12:421–24.
Kim, Dohyung. "Genesis 37–50: The Story of Jacob and His Sons in Light of the Primary Narrative (Genesis–2 Kings)." *ExpTim* 123 (2012): 486–93.
Kim, Hyun Chul Paul. "Reading the Joseph Story (Genesis 37–50) as a Diaspora Narrative." *CBQ* 75 (2013): 219–38.
Klausner, Joseph. *Messianic Idea in Israel: From Its Beginning to the Completion of the Mishnah* Translated by W. F. Stinespring. New York: Macmillan, 1955.
Klein, Johannes. *David versus Saul: Ein Beitrag zum Erzählsystem der Samuelbücher.* BWA(N)T 158. Stuttgart: Kohlhammer, 2002.
Klein, Ralph W. *1 Samuel.* WBC 10. Dallas: Word, 1983.

Ko, Ming Him. "Fusion-Point Hermeneutics: A Theological Interpretation of Saul's Rejection in Light of the Shema as the Rule of Faith." *JTI* 7 (2013): 57–78.

Köckert, Matthias. "Mighty One of Jacob." Pages 573–75 in *Dictionary of Deities and Demons in the Bible*. Edited by Karel Van der Toorn, Bob Becking, and Pieter W. Van der Horts. Leiden: Brill, 1999.

Koepf-Taylor, Laurel W. *Give Me Children or I Shall Die: Children and Communal Survival in Biblical Literature*. Minneapolis: Fortress, 2013.

Korpel, Marjo C. A. *A Rift in the Clouds: Ugaritic and Hebrew Descriptions of the Divine*. UBL 8. Münster: Ugarit, 1990.

Kreuzer, Siegfried. "'War Saul auch unter den Philistern?' Die Anfänge des Königtums in Israel." *ZAW* 113 (2001): 56–73.

Kruger, Paul A. "The Symbolic Significance of the Hem (*kānāf*) in 1 Samuel 15:27." Pages 105–16 in *Text and Context*. Edited by W. Claasen. JSOTSup 48. Sheffield: Sheffield Academic, 1988.

Kruschwitz, Jonathan. "The Type-scene Connection betwen Genesis 38 and the Joseph Story." *JSOT* 36 (2012): 383–410.

Kugel, James L. *The Bible As It Was*. Cambridge, MA: Harvard University Press, 1997.

Kutler, Laurence A. "A 'Strong' Case for Hebrew *Mar*." *UF* 16 (1984): 111–18.

Lambe, Anthony J. "Judah's Development: The Pattern of Departure-Transition-Return." *JSOT* 83 (1999): 53–68.

Lanckau, Jörg. *Der Herr der Träume: Eine Studie zur Funktion des Traumes in der Josefsgeschichte der Hebräischen Bibel*. ATANT 85. Zurich: TVZ, 2006.

Langner, Allan M. "Remembering Amalek Twice." *JBQ* 36 (2008): 251–53.

Leuchter, Mark. "Genesis 38 in Social and Historical Perspective." *JBL* 132 (2013): 209–27.

———. "Jeroboam the Ephratite." *JBL* 125 (2006): 51–72.

Levenson, Jon D. *The Death and Resurrection of the Beloved Son: The Transformation of Child Sacrifice in Judaism and Christianity*. New Haven: Yale University Press, 1995.

Levin, Yigal. "Joseph, Judah and the 'Benjamin Conundrum'." *ZAW* 116 (2004): 223–41.

Lindblom, Johannes. "The Political Background of the Shilo Oracle." Pages 78–87 in *Congress Volume Copenhagen*. Edited by G. W. Anderson. VTSup 1. Leiden: Brill, 1953.

Lohr, Joel N. *Chosen and Unchosen: Conceptions of Election in the Pentateuch and Jewish–Christian Interpretation*. Siphrut 2. Winona Lake, IN: Eisenbrauns, 2009.

Long, V. Philips. "Interpolation or Characterization: How Are We to Understand Saul's Two Confessions?" *Presb* 19 (1993): 49–53.

———. *The Reign and Rejection of King Saul: A Case for Literary and Theological Coherence*. SBLDS 118. Atlanta, GA: Scholars Press, 1989.

Longacre, Robert E. *Joseph: A Story of Divine Providence; A Text Theoretical and Textlinguistic Analysis of Genesis 37 and 39–48*. Winona Lake, IN: Eisenbrauns, 1989.

Lowenthal, Eric I. *The Joseph Narrative in Genesis*. New York: Ktav, 1973.

Lüdemann, Gerd. *The Unholy in Holy Scripture: The Dark Side of the Bible.* Translated by John Bowden. London: SCM, 1997.

Lux, Rüdiger. *Josef: der Auserwählte unter seinen Brüdern.* BG 1. Leipzig: Evangelische Verlagsanstalt, 2001.

Macchi, Jean-Daniel. *Israël et ses tribus selon Genèse 49.* OBO 171. Göttingen: Vandenhoeck & Ruprecht, 1999.

MacDonald, Nathan. *Deuteronomy and the Meaning of 'Monotheism'.* FAT 2/1. Tübingen: Mohr Siebeck, 2003.

———. "Did God Choose the Patriarchs? Reading for Election in the Book of Genesis." Pages 245–66 in *Genesis and Christian Theology.* Edited by Nathan MacDonald, Mark W. Elliott, and Grant Macaskill. Grand Rapids: Eerdmans, 2012.

Malul, Meir. "More on *pachad yitschāq* (Genesis 31:42, 53) and the Oath by the Thigh." *VT* 35 (1985): 192–200.

Marx, Alfred. "'Jusqu'à ce que vienne Shiloh': Pour une interprétation messianique de Genèse 49,8–12." Pages 95–111 in *Ce Dieu qui vient: Études sur l'Ancien et le Nouveau Testament offertes au professeur Bernard Renaud à l'occasion de son soixante-cinquième anniversaire.* Edited by Raymond Kuntzmann. LD 159. Paris: Cerf, 1995.

Matthews, Kenneth A. *Genesis 11:27–50:26.* NAC 1B. Nashville: Broadman & Holman, 2005.

Matthews, Victor H. "The Anthropology of Clothing in the Joseph Narrative." *JSOT* 65 (1995): 25–36.

Mattingly, Gerald L. "Amalek." *ABD* 1:169–71.

McCarter, Kyle P. Jr. *I Samuel: A New Translation with Introduction, Notes, and Commentary.* AB 8. Garden City, NY: Doubleday, 1980.

McConville, J. Gordon. *Deuteronomy.* ApOTC. Leicester: Apollos, 2002.

McKenzie, Brian A. "Jacob's Blessing on Pharaoh: An Interpretation of Gen 46:31–47:26." *WTJ* 45 (1983): 386–99.

McKenzie, Steven L. "Saul in the Deuteronomistic History." Pages 59–70 in *Saul in Story and Tradition.* Edited by Carl S. Ehrlich and Marsha C. White. FAT 47. Tübingen: Mohr Siebeck, 2006.

McKeown, James. *Genesis.* THOTC 1. Grand Rapids: Eerdmans, 2008.

Menn, Esther Marie. *Judah and Tamar (Genesis 38) in Ancient Jewish Exegesis: Studies in Literary Form and Hermeneutics.* JSJSup 51. Leiden: Brill, 1997.

Merwe, B. J. van der. "Joseph as Successor of Jacob." Pages 221–32 in *Studia Biblica et Semitica: Theodoro Christiano Vriezen qui Munere Professoris Theologiae per XXV Annos Functus est, ab Amicis, Collegis, Discipulis Dedicata.* Edited by W. C. van Unnik and A. S. van der Woude. Wageningen: H. Veenman & Zonen, 1966.

Middleton, J. Richard. "Samuel *Agonistes*: A Conflicted Prophet's Resistance to God and Contribution to the Failure of Israel's First King." Pages 69–91 in *Prophets, Prophecy, and Ancient Israelite Historiography.* Edited by Mark J. Boda and Lissa M. Wray Beal. Winona Lake, IN: Eisenbrauns, 2013.

Miller, J. Maxwell. "Geba/Gibeah of Benjamin." *VT* 25 (1975): 145–66.

———. "Saul's Rise to Power: Some Observations Concerning I Sam 9:1–10:16; 10:26–11:15 and 13:2–14:46." *CBQ* 36 (1974): 157–74.

Millgram, Hillel I. *The Joseph Paradox: A Radical Reading of Genesis 37–50.* Jefferson, NC: McFarland, 2012.

Milstein, Sara J. *Tracking the Master Scribe: Revision through Introduction in Biblical and Mesopotamian Literature.* New York: Oxford University Press, 2016.

Miscall, Peter D. *1 Samuel: A Literary Reading.* Bloomington, IN: Indiana University Press, 1986.

———. "The Jacob and Joseph Stories as Analogies." *JSOT* 6 (1978): 28–40.

Mitchell, David C. "Messiah ben Joseph: A Sacrifice of Atonement for Israel." *RRJ* 10 (2007): 77–94.

Moberly, R. W. L. *The Bible, Theology, and Faith: A Study of Abraham and Jesus.* Cambridge: Cambridge University Press, 2000.

———. "By Stone and Sling: 1 Samuel 17:50 and the Problem of Misreading David's Victory over Goliath." Pages 329–42 in *On Stone and Scroll: Essays in Honour of Graham Ivor Davies.* Edited by James K. Aitken, Katharine J. Dell, and Brian A. Mastin. Boston: de Gruyter, 2011.

———. "Does God Change?" Pages 107–43 in *Old Testament Theology: Reading the Hebrew Bible as Christian Scripture.* Grand Rapids: Baker Academic, 2013.

———. "Election and the Transformation of Ḥērem." Pages 67–89 in *The Call of Abraham: Essays on the Election of Israel in Honor of Jon D. Levenson.* Edited by Gary A. Anderson and Joel S. Kaminsky. Notre Dame, IN: University of Notre Dame Press, 2013.

———. "Exemplars of Faith in Hebrews 11: Abel." Pages 353–63 in *The Epistle to the Hebrews and Christian Theology.* Edited by Richard Bauckham, Daniel R. Driver, Trevor Hart, and Nathan MacDonald. Grand Rapids: Eerdmans, 2009.

———. "God Is Not a Human that He Should Repent (Numbers 23:19 & 1 Samuel 15:29)." Pages 112–23 in *God in the Fray: A Tribute to Walter Brueggemann.* Edited by Tod Linafelt and Timothy K. Beal. Minneapolis: Fortress, 1998.

———. "Is Monotheism Bad for You? Some Reflections on God, the Bible, and Life in the Light of Regina Schwartz's *The Curse of Cain.*" Pages 94–112 in *The God of Israel.* Edited by Robert P. Gordon. UCOP 64. Cambridge: Cambridge University Press, 2007.

———. *The Old Testament of the Old Testament: Patriarchal Narratives and Mosiac Yahwism.* OBT. Minneapolis: Fortress, 1992.

———. "On Interpreting the Mind of God: The Theological Significance of the Flood Narrative (Genesis 6–9)." Pages 44–66 in *The Word Leaps the Gap: Essays on Scripture and Theology in Honor of Richard B. Hays.* Edited by Ross J. Wagner, Kavin C. Rowe, and Katherine A. Grieb. Grand Rapids: Eerdmans, 2008.

———. *The Theology of the Book of Genesis.* Cambridge: Cambridge University Press, 2009.

———. "Toward an Interpretation of the Shema." Pages 124–44 in *Theological Exegesis: Essays in Honor of Brevard S. Childs.* Edited by Christopher Seitz and Kathryn Greene-McCreight. Grand Rapids: Eerdmans, 1999.

Morag, Shelomo. "רענן כאזרה ומתערה (Psalms xxxvii:35)." *Tarbiz* 41 (1971): 1–23 (in Hebrew).

Moran, William L. "Gen 49,10 and Its Use in Ez 21,32." *Bib* 39 (1958): 405–25.

Müller, W. W. "Havilah (place)." *ABD* 3:82.

Murphy, Francesca A. *1 Samuel*. BTC. Grand Rapids: Baker, 2010.

Murray, Donald F. *Divine Prerogative and Royal Pretension: Pragmatics, Poetics and Polemics in a Narrative Sequence about David (2 Samuel 5.17–7.29)*. JSOTSup 264. Sheffield: Sheffield Academic, 1998.

Nachmanides. *Commentary on the Torah: Genesis*. Translated by C. Chavel. New York: Shilo, 1999.

Naumann, Thomas. "Der Vater in der biblischen Joseferzählung: Möglichkeiten einer Charaktermodellierung in biblischen Erzählungen." *TZ* 61 (2005): 44–64.

Nelson, Richard D. "*Ḥerem* and the Deuteronomic Social Conscience." Pages 39–54 in *Deuteronomy and Deuteronomic Literature: Festschrift for C. H. W. Brekelmans*. Edited by Marc Vervenne and Johan Lust. BETL 133. Louvain: Peeters, 1997.

Noble, John T. *A Place for Hagar's Son: Ishmael as a Case Study in the Priestly Tradition*. Minneapolis: Fortress, 2016.

Noble, Paul R. "Esau, Tamar, and Joseph: Criteria for Identifying Inner-biblical Allusions." *VT* 52 (2002): 219–52.

Nocquet, Dany. "L'Égypte, une autre terre de salut? Une lecture de Gn 45, 1–46, 7." *ETR* 84 (2009): 461–80.

Nolan, Caroline. "The Rejection of Israel's First King." *ITQ* 73 (2008): 355–68.

Nordheim, Eckhard von. *Die Lehre der Alten II: Das Testament als Literaturgattung im Alten Testament und im Alten Vorderen Orient*. ALGHJ 18. Leiden: Brill, 1985.

Noth, Martin. *The Deuteronomistic History*. 2nd ed. JSOTSup 15. Sheffield: Sheffield Academic, 1981.

Nötscher, Friedrich. "Gen 49,10: שׁילה = akk. *šēlu*." *ZAW* 47 (1929): 323–25.

O'Brien, Mark A. "The Contribution of Judah's Speech, Genesis 44:18–34, to the Characterization of Joseph." *CBQ* 59 (1997): 429–47.

O'Donovan, Oliver. *The Desire of the Nations: Rediscovering the Roots of Political Theology*. Cambridge: Cambridge University Press, 1996.

Patrick, Dale. "Election (Old Testament)." *ABD* 2:434–41.

Pehlke, Helmuth. "An Exegetical and Theological Study of Genesis 49:1–28." Ph.D. diss., Dallas Theological Seminary, 1985.

Pirson, Ron. *The Lord of the Dreams: A Semantic and Literary Analysis of Genesis 37–50*. JSOTSup 355. London: Sheffield Academic, 2002.

Pisano, Stephen. *Additions or Omissions in the Books of Samuel: The Significant Pluses and Minuses in the Massoretic, LXX and Qumran Texts*. OBO 57. Freiburg: Vandenhoeck & Ruprecht, 1984.

Polzin, Robert. *Samuel and the Deuteronomist: A Literary Study of the Deuteronomic History, Part 2: 1 Samuel*. San Francisco: Harper & Row, 1989.

Popović, A. "Saul's Fault in 1 Sam 13,7b–15a." *Anton* 68 (1993): 153–70.

Posnanski, Adolf. *Shiloh: Ein Beitrag zur Geschichte der Messiaslehre*. Leipzig: Ginrichs, 1904.

Preuss, Horst Dietrich. "הוה." *TDOT* 4:248–56.

Prouser, Ora Horn. "Suited to the Throne: The Symbolic Use of Clothing in the David and Saul Narratives." *JSOT* 71 (1996): 27–37.

Provan, Iain W. *Discovering Genesis: Content, Interpretation, Reception*. Grand Rapids: Eerdmans, 2015.

Rad, Gerhard von. *Genesis: A Commentary*. Translated by John H. Marks. Rev. ed. OTL. Philadelphia: Westminster John Knox, 1972.

———. "The Joseph Narrative and Ancient Wisdom." Pages 75–88 in *From Genesis to Chronicles: Explorations in Old Testament Theology*. Edited by K. C. Hanson. Translated by E. W. Trueman Dicken. Minneapolis, MN: Fortress, 2005.

———. "The Story of Joseph." Pages 19–35 in *God at Work in Israel*. Translated by John H. Marks. Nashville, TN: Abingdon, 1980.

Raney, Donald C., II. "Does YHWH *Naḥam*? A Question of Openness." *SBLSP* 42 (2003): 105–15.

Redford, Donald B. *A Study of the Biblical Story of Joseph: Genesis 37–50*. VTSup 20. Leiden: Brill, 1970.

Reimer, David J. "An Overlooked Term in Old Testament Theology—Perhaps." Pages 325–46 in *Covenant as Context: Essays in Honour of E. W. Nicholson*. Edited by A. D. H. Mayes and R. B. Salters. Oxford: Oxford Universty Press, 2003.

Reindl, J. "יצב/נצב." *TDOT* 9:519–29.

Rendsburg, Gary A. "David and His Circle in Genesis 38." *VT* 36 (1986): 438–46.

———. "Janus Parallelism in Gen 49:26." *JBL* 99 (1980): 291–93.

Reno, R. R. *Genesis*. BTC. Grand Rapids: Brazos, 2010.

Revell, E. J. "Midian and Ishmael in Genesis 37: Synonyms in the Joseph Story." Pages 70–91 in *The World of the Aramaeans I: Biblical Studies in Honour of Paul-Eugène Dion*. Edited by P. M. Michèle Davian, John W. Wevers, and Michael Weigl. JSOTSup 324. Sheffield: Sheffield Academic, 2001.

Rindge, Matthew S. "Jewish Identity under Foreign Rule: Daniel 2 as a Reconfiguration of Genesis 41." *JBL* 129 (2010): 85–104.

Rösel, Martin. "Die Interpretation von Genesis 49 in der Septuaginta." *BN* 79 (1955): 54–70.

Rosenbaum, M. and A. M. Silbermann, eds. *The Pentateuch with the Commentary of Rashi: Genesis*. Jerusalem: Silbermann, 1972.

Ruppert, Lothar. *Die Josephserzählung der Genesis: Ein Beitrag zur Theologie der Pentateuchquellen*. SANT 11. München: Kösel, 1965.

Sabottka, Liudger. "Noch einmal Gen 49:10." *Bib* 51 (1970): 225–29.

Sacks, Jonathan. N*ot in God's Name: Confronting Religious Violence*. New York: Schocken, 2015.

Sæbø, Magne. "Divine Names and Epithets in Genesis 49:24b–25a: Some Methodological and Tradition-historical Remarks." Pages 115–32 in *History and Traditions of Early Israel: Studies Presented to Eduard Nielsen*. Edited by André Lamaire and Benedikt Otzen. VTSup 50. Leiden: Brill, 1993.

Sagi, Avi and Batya Stein. "The Punishment of Amalek in Jewish Tradition: Coping with the Moral Problem." *HTR* 87 (1994): 323–46.

Salo, Vello. "Joseph, Sohn der Färse." *BZ* 12 (1968): 94–95.

Sanders, Paul. "So May God Do to Me!" *Bib* 85 (2004): 91–98.

Sanmartín, J. "Problemas de textologia en las 'Bendiciones' de Moises (Dt 33) y de Jacob (Gn 49)." Pages 75–96 in *El misterio de la palabra: Homenaje a*

Luis Alonso Schökel. Edited by Vicente Collado and Eduardo Zurro. Madrid: Ediciones Cristiandad, 1983.

Sarna, Nahum M. *Genesis: The Traditional Hebrew Text with the New JPS Translation*. JPSTC 1. New York: Jewish Publication Society of America, 1989.

Schäfer-Lichtenberger, Christa. "Bedeutung und Funktion von Ḥerem in biblisch-hebräischen Texten." *BZ* 38 (1994): 270–75.

Scherer, Andreas Georg. "Das Ephod im alten Israel." *UF* 35 (2003): 589–604.

Schicklberger, Franz. "Jonatans Heldentat: Textlinguistische Beobachtungen zu 1 Sam 14:1–23a." *VT* 24 (1974): 324–33.

Schimmel, Sol. "Joseph and His Brothers: A Paradigm for Repentance." *Judaism* 37 (1988): 60–65.

Schley, Donald. G. *Shiloh: A Biblical City in Tradition and History*. JSOTSup 63. Sheffield: JSOT Press, 1989.

Schlimm, Matthew R. *From Fratricide to Forgiveness: The Language and Ethics of Anger in Genesis*. Siphrut 7. Winona Lake, IN: Eisenbrauns, 2011.

Schmid, Konrad. "Die Josephsgeschichte im Pentateuch." Pages 83–118 in *Abschied vom Jahwisten: Die Komposition des Hexateuch in der jüngsten Diskussion*. Edited by Jan Christian Gertz, Konrad Schmid, and Markus Witte. BZAW 315. Berlin: de Gruyter, 2002.

Schmidt, Ludwig. *Literarische Studien zur Josephgeschichte*. BZAW 167. Berlin: de Gruyter, 1986.

———. *Menschlicher Erfolg und Jahwes Initiative: Studien zu Tradition, Interpretation und Historie in Überlieferungen von Gideon, Saul und David*. WMANT 38. Neukirchen-Vluyn: Neukirchener, 1970.

Schöpflin, Karin. "Jakob segnet seinen Sohn: Genesis 49,1–28 im Kontext von Josefs- und Vätergeschichte." *ZAW* 115 (2003): 501–23.

Schwartz, Regina M. *The Curse of Cain: The Violent Legacy of Monotheism*. Chicago: University of Chicago Press, 1998.

Seebass, Horst. "1 Sam 15 als Schlüssel für das Verständnis der sogenannten königsfreundlichen Reihe 1 Sam 9:1–10:16, 11:1–15 und 13:2–14:52." *ZAW* 78 (1966): 148–79.

———. *Geschichtliche Zeit und Theonome Tradition in der Joseph-Erzählung*. Gütersloh: Gütersloher Verlagshaus, 1978.

———. "The Joseph Story, Genesis 48 and the Canonical Process." *JSOT* 35 (1986): 29–43.

———. "Der Ort Elam in der südlichen Wüste und die Überlieferung von Gen 14." *VT* 15 (1965): 389–94.

———. "Die Stämmesprüche Gen 49:3–27." *ZAW* 96 (1984): 333–50.

Seitz, Christopher R. "Canonical Approach." Pages 100–102 in *Dictionary for Theological Interpretation of the Bible*. Edited by Kevin J. Vanhoozer, Craig G. Bartholomew, Daniel J. Treier, and N. T. Wright. Grand Rapids: Baker, 2005.

Sherman, Miriam. "Do Not Interpretations Belong to God? A Narrative Assessment of Genesis 40 as it Elucidates the Persona of Joseph." Pages 37–49 in *Milk and Honey: Essays on Ancient Israel and the Bible in Appreciation of the Judaic Studies Program at the University of California, San Diego*. Edited by Sarah Malena and David Miano. Winona Lake, IN: Eisenbrauns, 2007.

Short, J. Randall. *The Surprising Election and Confirmation of King David*. HTS 63. Cambridge, MA: Harvard University Press, 2010.

Sigmon, Brian O. "Shadowing Jacob's Journey: Gen 47:13–26 as a Sideshadow." *BibInt* 19 (2011): 454–69.

Ska, Jean Louis. "L'ironie de Tamar (Gen 38)." *ZAW* 100 (1988): 261–63.

———. "Judah, Joseph, and the Reader (Gen 42:6–9 and 44:18–34)." Pages 27–39 in *Das Alte Testament—Ein Geschichtsbuch?* Edited by Erhard Blum, William Johnstone, and Christoph Markschies. Münster: LIT, 2005.

Skinner, John. *A Critical and Exegetical Commentary on Genesis.* 2nd ed. ICC. Edinburgh: T&T Clark, 1930.

Smith, Henry P. *A Critical and Exegetical Commentary on the Books of Samuel.* ICC. Edinburgh: T&T Clark, 1899.

Smyth, Kevin. "The Prophecy Concerning Juda: Gen. 49:8–12." *CBQ* 7 (1945): 290–305.

Sommer, Benjamin D. *The Bodies of God and the World of Ancient Israel.* Cambridge: Cambridge University Press, 2009.

Sonnet, Jean-Pierre. "God's Repentance and 'False Starts' in Biblical History (Genesis 6–9; Exodus 32–34; 1 Samuel 15 and 2 Samuel 7)." Pages 469–94 in *Congress Volume Ljubljana 2007.* Edited by André Lemaire. VTSup 133. Leiden: Brill, 2010.

Sparks, Kent. "Genesis 49 and the Tribal List Tradition in Ancient Israel." *ZAW* 115 (2003): 327–47.

Speiser, Ephraim V. *Genesis.* AB 1. New York: Doubleday, 1964.

Spina, Frank Anthony. *The Faith of the Outsider: Exclusion and Inclusion in the Biblical Story.* Grand Rapids: Eerdmans, 2005.

Spurrell, G. J. *Notes on the Hebrew Text of the Book of Genesis: With Two Appendices.* Oxford: Clarendon, 1896.

Staalduine-Sulman, Eveline von. *The Targum of Samuel.* SAIS 1. Leiden: Brill, 2002.

Stark, Christine. *"Kultprostitution" im Alten Testament? Die Qedeschen der Hebräischen Bibel und das Motif der Hurerei.* OBO 221. Fribourg: Academic Press, 2006.

Steiner, Richard C. "Poetic Forms in the Masoretic Vocalization and Three Difficult Phrases in Jacob's Blessing: *yeter śĕʾēt* (Gen 49:3), *yĕṣûʿî ʿālāh* (49:4), *yābōʾ šîlōh* (49:10)." *JBL* 129 (2010): 209–35.

Steinmetz, David C. "Uncovering a Second Narrative: Detective Fiction and the Construction of Historical Method." Pages 54–65 in *The Art of Reading Scripture.* Edited by Ellen F. Davis and Richard B. Hays. Grand Rapids: Eerdmans, 2003.

Stern, Philip D. "1 Samuel 15: Towards an Ancient View of the War-Herem." *UF* 21 (1990): 413–20.

———. *The Biblical Ḥerem: A Window on Israel's Religious Experience.* BJS 211. Atlanta, GA: Scholars Press, 1991.

Sternberg, Meir. *The Poetics of Biblical Narrative: Ideological Literature and the Drama of Reading.* Bloomington: Indiana University Press, 1985.

Steussy, Marti J. *Samuel and His God.* Edited by James L. Crenshaw. Columbia, SC: University of South Carolina Press, 2010.

Stoebe, Hans Joachim. *Das erste Buch Samuelis.* KAT 8/1. Gütersloh: Gütersloh Verlagshaus, 1973.

Strawn, Brent A. *What Is Stronger than a Lion? Leonine Image and Metaphor in the Hebrew Bible and the Ancient Near East.* OBO 212. Gottingen: Vandenhoeck & Ruprecht, 2005.

Stuart, Douglas. *Old Testament Exegesis: A Handbook for Students and Pastors.* 3rd ed. Louisville, KY: Westminster John Knox, 2001.

Sweeney, Marvin A. "Samuel's Institutional Identity in the Deuteronomistic History." Pages 165–74 in *Construals of Prophecy in the Former & Later Prophets & Other Texts.* Edited by Lester L. Grabbe and Martti Nissinen. ANEM 4. Atlanta: SBL, 2011.

Swenson-Méndez, Kristin M. "The Relationship of Judah and Joseph in Genesis 49." Ph.D. diss., Boston University, 2001.

Swenson, Kristin M. "Crowned with Blessings: The Riches of Double-meaning in Gen 49,26b." *ZAW* 120 (2008): 422–25.

Sykora, Josef. "The Mission that Transforms: A Development of Joseph's Character in Genesis 37–50." *CTR* 4 (2015): 11–18.

Syrén, Roger. *The Forsaken First-born: A Study of a Recurrent Motif in the Patriarchal Narratives.* JSOTSup 133. Sheffield: Sheffield Academic, 1993.

Talmon, Shemaryahu. "1 Sam 15:32b. A Case of Conflated Readings." *VT* 11 (1961): 456–57.

Tanner, Hans Andreas. *Amalek: der Feind Israels und der Feind Jahwes: Eine Studie zu den Amalektexten im Alten Testament.* Zurich: TVZ, 2005.

Torrey, Charles C. "The Messiah Son of Ephraim." *JBL* 66 (1947): 253–77.

Treves, Marco. "Shiloh (Genesis 49:10)." *JBL* 85 (1966): 353–56.

Tsevat, Matitiahu. "Studies in the Book of Samuel I. Interpretation of 1 Sam. 2:27–36: The Narrative of *Kareth*." *HUCA* 32 (1961): 191–216.

———. "Studies in the Book of Samuel III. The Steadfast House: What Was David Promised in II Sam. 7:11b–16?" *HUCA* 34 (1963): 71–82.

Tsumura, David T. *The First Book of Samuel.* NICOT. Grand Rapids: Eerdmans, 2007.

Van Wijk-Bos, Johanna W. H. *Reading Samuel: A Literary and Theological Commentary.* Macon, GA: Smyth & Helwys, 2013.

Vawter, Bruce. "Canaanite Background of Genesis 49." *CBQ* 17 (1955): 1–18.

———. *On Genesis: A New Reading.* New York: Doubleday, 1977.

Viands, Jamie. *I Will Surely Multiply Your Offspring: An Old Testament Theology of the Blessing of Progeny with Special Attention to the Later Prophets.* Eugene, OR: Wipf & Stock, 2013.

Viberg, Åke. "Saul Exposed by Irony: A New Understanding of 1 Samuel 15:27 Based on Two Symbolic Acts." *SEÅ* 70 (2005): 301–8.

Waltke, Bruce K. *Genesis: A Commentary.* Grand Rapids: Zondervan, 2001.

Weeks, Stuart. *Early Israelite Wisdom.* Oxford: Clarendon, 1994.

Weimar, Peter. *Die doppelte Thamar: Thomas Mann's Novelle als Kommentar der Thamarerzählung des Genesisbuchs.* BthSt 99. Neukirchen-Vluyn: Neukirchener, 2008.

———. "Gen 47, 13–26—ein irritierender Abschnitt im Rahmen der Josefsgeschichte." Pages 125–38 in *Auf dem Weg zur Endgestalt von Genesis bis II Regum: Festschrift Hans-Christoph Schmitt zum 65. Geburtstag.* Edited by Ulrike Schorn and Martin Beck. BZAW 370. Berlin: De Gruyter, 2006.

Weisberg, Dvora E. "The Widow of Our Discontent." *JSOT* 28 (2004): 403–29.

Wellhausen, Julius. *Die Composition des Hexateuchs und der historischen Bücher des Alten Testaments*. Berlin: Georg Reimer, 1899.

———. *Prolegomena to the History of Ancient Israel with a Reprint of the Article "Israel" from the Encyclopaedia Britannica*. Translated by Sutherland J. Black and Allan Menzies. Edinburgh: A. & C. Black, 1885.

Wenham, Gordon J. *Genesis 16–50*. WBC 2. Waco, TX: Word, 1994.

Wénin, André. *Joseph ou l'invention de la fraternité: Lecture narrative et anthropologique de Genèse 37–50*. Le livre et le rouleau 21. Brussels: Lessius, 2005.

Westermann, Claus. *Genesis 37–50: A Commentary*. Translated by John J. Scullion. CC. Minneapolis: Augsburg, 1986.

———. *Joseph: Eleven Bible Studies on Genesis*. Translated by Omar Kaste. Minneapolis: Fortress, 1996.

Wevers, John W. *Notes on the Greek Text of Genesis*. SBLSCS 35. Atlanta: Scholars Press, 1993.

White, Hugh C. "The Joseph Story: A Narrative Which 'Consumes' Its Content." *Semeia* 31 (1985): 49–69.

———. "'Where Do You Come From?' Genesis 37, 39–45, 50." Pages 232–75 in *Narration and Discourse in the Book of Genesis*. Edited by Hugh C. White. New York: Cambridge University Press, 1991.

Wilcox, Pete. *Living the Dream—Joseph for Today: A Dramatic Exposition of Genesis 37–50*. London: Paternoster, 2007.

Wildavsky, Aaron. "Survival Must Not Be Gained through Sin: The Moral of the Joseph Stories Prefigured through Judah and Tamar." *JSOT* 62 (1994): 37–48.

Williams, Stephen N. *The Election of Grace: A Riddle without Resolution?* Grand Rapids: Eerdmans, 2015.

Willis, John T. "The Expression *be' acharith hayyamin* in the Old Testament." *ResQ* 22 (1979): 54–71.

Wilson, Lindsay. *Joseph, Wise and Otherwise: The Intersection of Wisdom and the Covenant in Genesis 37–50*. PBM. Carlisle: Paternoster, 2004.

Wolde, E. J. van. "Texts in Dialogue with Texts: Intertextuality in the Ruth and Tamar Narratives." *BibInt* 5 (1997): 1–28.

Wright, Jacob L. *David, King of Israel, and Caleb in Biblical Memory*. New York: Cambridge University Press, 2014.

Wyatt, N. "Jonathan's Adventure and a Philological Conundrum." *PEQ* 127 (1995): 62–69.

Yonick, Stephen. *Rejection of Saul as King of Israel according to 1 Sm 15: Stylistic Study in Theology*. Jerusalem: Franciscan, 1970.

Ziegler, Yael. "'So Shall God Do...': Variations of an Oath Formula and Its Literary Meaning." *JBL* 126 (2007): 59–81.

Zimmerli, Walther. *Ezekiel 1: A Commentary on the Book of the Prophet Ezekiel, Chapters 1–24*. Translated by Ronald E. Clements. Hermeneia. Philadelphia: Fortress, 1979.

Zimran, Yisca. "'The Lord Has Rejected You as King Over Israel': Saul's Deposal from the Throne." *JHebS* 14 (2014): art. 5, pp. 1–18. https://doi:10.5508/jhs.2014.v14.a5.

Zobel, Hans-Jürgen. *Stammesspruch und Geschichte: Die Angaben der Stammessprüche von Gen.49, Dtn 33 und Jdc 5 über die politischen und kultischen Zustände im damaligen "Israel"*. BZAW 95. Berlin: Töpelmann, 1965.
Zucker, David. "Seize the Moment." *JBQ* 37 (2009): 197–99.

Index of Authors

Index of References